Bandwidth

How Mathematics, Physics,
and Chemistry Constrain Society

Foreword by Susan Avery

Bandwidth

How Mathematics, Physics, and Chemistry Constrain Society

Alexander Scheeline

University of Illinois at Urbana-Champaign, USA

World Scientific

NEW JERSEY • LONDON • SINGAPORE • BEIJING • SHANGHAI • HONG KONG • TAIPEI • CHENNAI • TOKYO

Published by

World Scientific Publishing Co. Pte. Ltd.
5 Toh Tuck Link, Singapore 596224
USA office: 27 Warren Street, Suite 401-402, Hackensack, NJ 07601
UK office: 57 Shelton Street, Covent Garden, London WC2H 9HE

Library of Congress Cataloging-in-Publication Data
Names: Scheeline, Alexander, author.
Title: Bandwidth : how mathematics, physics, and chemistry constrain society / Alexander Scheeline.
Description: Hackensack, NJ : World Scientific, [2023] | Includes bibliographical references and index.
Identifiers: LCCN 2022031927 | ISBN 9789811237874 (hardcover) | ISBN 9789811238543 (paperback) | ISBN 9789811237881 (ebook) | ISBN 9789811237898 (ebook other)
Subjects: LCSH: Science--Social aspects. | Mathematics--Social aspects.
Classification: LCC Q175.5 .S27 2023 | DDC 303.48/3--dc23/eng20230328
LC record available at https://lccn.loc.gov/2022031927

British Library Cataloguing-in-Publication Data
A catalogue record for this book is available from the British Library.

For any available supplementary material, please visit
https://www.worldscientific.com/worldscibooks/10.1142/12304#t=suppl

Desk Editor: Shaun Tan Yi Jie

Typeset by Stallion Press
Email: enquiries@stallionpress.com

Dedicated

To the memory of Dwight Nicholson,
Professor of Physics, University of Iowa
who introduced me to Lyapunov exponents, universality,
period doubling bifurcations, and chaos

Murdered November 1, 1991

An event that forced me to reconsider what I previously
was certain was true

Foreword

This new book by Professor Alexander Scheeline provides a fresh approach to the discussion of the power and limitations of science in addressing society's challenges. He illustrates how science, technology, engineering, and mathematics (STEM) can describe and guide society, but that knowledge is interpreted by the varied cultural and linguistic constraints that humans have accepted – our "potential well biases" in the words of Prof. Scheeline. It is this bias in concert with the information bandwidth that individuals have accepted that determine what information we access, how we interpret that information, and how we act upon that information. Prof. Scheeline uses examples complete with the mathematics of the measurements, to show how measurement, potential wells, and bandwidth limitations inform our understanding of the world. He also provides a discussion of the limitations of his approach.

From my own perspective as an atmospheric scientist, I appreciate this different approach as it helps to explain the challenges we face in addressing large global problems such as climate change and biodiversity loss. Our planet is an interacting system of the ocean-atmosphere-land and its biodiversity. Each of these components is measurable and can be addressed by science with the complete set of physical, biological, and chemical measurements that can be incorporated in models of our integrated Earth system. However, the greater challenge is the societal responses to addressing the impact we have on our planet which are framed by human, cultural, religious, and policy perspectives. In *Bandwidth,* Scheeline describes this connectivity through the use of system mathematics. He strives for rigor and clarity in representing these interacting systems and challenges the reader to think differently.

This would be an appropriate textbook for university-level courses in the sciences (including physical, biological, and social sciences) and engineering that engage and support interdisciplinary thinking and different approaches. The book will speak most clearly to those with at least a rudimentary understanding of math and statistics, but is illuminating to a broader audience as well. As I prepared this Foreword, I found myself challenged and I kept going back to read select sections of the book. In that sense, it is not only a potential textbook, but one that becomes a reference book – it stimulates one to constantly re-read and in the re-reading gain additional perspective.

Susan Avery
Boulder, CO
January 2023

Preface and Acknowledgements

Many scientists have tried to bridge the difference in worldview between science and other approaches to thinking (business, economics, religion), and many people who are not scientists have tried to make sense of how scientists think. This book is one more try, but with a twist: I am not avoiding mathematics. I am using mathematical descriptions of scientific and engineering phenomena to describe people, society, and alternative views of everyday experience. In an effort to streamline writing this book and to spare the reader, I am limiting literature citations to those I feel are most salient rather than attempting to be comprehensive. It will be interesting to see how critics and other readers respond. Citations can show where the logic comes from, but it's not authority that decides what is valid in mathematics, it's proof. Equations are a compact notation to express meaning.

Some years ago, I thought Raima M. Larter had already written this book, or at least a book covering much of the same ground. Alas, when she finished it, she didn't publish it. When I asked her in the summer of 2018 if she ever would, she said no, and that I should write my own treatise. When I was negotiating with World Scientific Publishing Co. about writing *Bandwidth*, I mentioned Raima's unpublished work. They asked her to finish and publish it (Larter, 2021), so you can now read both of them! A single contact led to a bifurcation.

Raima and I had a joint National Science Foundation grant in the late 1990s to study oscillating biochemical reactions. Her emphasis was theoretical (but she and her research group also did experiments), while my emphasis was on experiments (but I and my research group also did theoretical calculations). Both of us were part of the chaos and nonlinear dynamics communities within physical and analytical chemistry that blossomed after Ed Lorenz's paper on chaos in atmospheric chemistry appeared in 1963 (Lorenz, 1963) and Richard Noyes brought news of Belousov and Zhabotinskii's work on oscillating reactions to the U.S. in 1968, having heard of it from Hans Degn at a conference in Prague (Winfree, 1984). Art Winfree connected the oscillating reaction work to *The Geometry of Biological Time* (Winfree, 2001), and groups in Denmark and Japan worked on chaos in biochemical networks (Scheeline *et al.*, 1997). Eventually, the connection between nonlinear systems and sociology dawned on a number of people, including Albert-László Barabási, Yaneer Bar Yam, my late, lamented colleague Alfred Hubler, and many others.

Earlier, as communications networks grew, Bell Laboratories hosted brilliant scientists and engineers who worked out the limits of such networks. These include Harry Nyquist, Claude E. Shannon, and the inventors of the transistor, John Bardeen, William Shockley, and Walter Brattain. Shockley proved to be an embarrassment to many (go look him up!), while the others provided a rigorous mathematical and material basis for modern analog and digital electronics. At first glance, their work seems to be far removed from public policy. By the time you have read this book, I hope you will see the policy implications of their work.

Writing has a way of reminding authors of how little they know and how many people influenced what they are trying to say. Among the people who have contributed ideas and perspectives to what I present are: William Berkson, John Boyd, Stanley R. Crouch, Gerald Edelman, Sam Harris, Gary M. Hieftje, Norman Hills, Gary Horlick, Linda Kaufman, David H. Levy, Howard V. Malmstadt, Morton Meyers, Brian J. Mork, Charles J. Patton, Michael Shermer, Robert G. Spira, Raymond S. Vogel, John P. Walters, the nearly 100 students and post-doctoral fellows who were members of my research groups at the University of Iowa and University of Illinois at Urbana-Champaign, and the members of the University of Illinois Department of Chemistry and University of Illinois Center for Complex Systems Research. At some level, probably everyone I ever met contributed something, but who has the bandwidth to list (or read) all those thousands of names?

In recent years, pronouns have become problematic. I try to avoid gender-related pronouns, since most of what I talk about applies to all humans (and maybe insightful porpoises). While "they" works for third person plural, the formerly accepted "s/he" is now deprecated. I reserve second person "you" to mean specifically you, the reader. Voice also matters. Passive voice is stodgy. In the first draft manuscript, I often said, "one may do this or that." Neutral? Yes. Stuffy? The reviewers thought so. "A person can ..." allows for either the reader or an unnamed third party to operate in the specified fashion. All of this stems from one of the conflicts in science. We (that is, scientists and others who share my biases) like to think that what we learn through science is independent of whomever figures something out. Yet, science is embedded in language and culture, and many quantum phenomena link aspects of reality that are distant in space and time. Are there aspects of science that transcend humans attaching language, and thus explanation, to the phenomena? I maintain the answer is yes. Yet, one of the central messages of this book is that what is important and how it is perceived is strongly influenced by context. In trying to pull the observer out of the observation, there is inevitably verbal awkwardness.

Commonly, a book begins with a chapter summarizing the content, then presents the content in detail, and finally ends with a chapter reprising the content. I have taken a different and, to some reviewers, confusing approach. Instead of going into detail about why I use equations, why the book is titled as it is, and what order the discussion will follow, I just plunge in, and it will be several chapters before you realize what all the pieces are and how they fit together. I am sharing with you how I perceive people learn, especially outside of formal classes. Someone starts down a road, aggregates ideas and insights, and then, eventually, a clear picture emerges from the fog. Declaring the direction at the start may guide the reader, but it hides the random walks and misdirections that frequently characterize scientific thinking and (I hope) progress. Declaring the path up front also creates a potential well (Chapter 10) that unnecessarily constrains the reader. Nevertheless, for those insistent on the usual structure, I provide a Chapter Zero. I hope you'll skip it on first reading!

A note to the reader: Every author has some ego tied up in their work. I hope as many copies of this book sell as the number of times my wife, Alice Berkson, has said, "not everybody thinks like you." Of course, she's right. But there ARE people who think like me. So as you read this tome, remember that some readers will be thinking, "ah, finally someone who gets me," while others will be shaking their heads, agreeing with Alice, and wondering what strange wiring my brain has. My hope is that by the time you finish this book, you'll understand why there are so many ways to perceive, interact with, and influence reality, and that even ways that seem absurd or incomprehensible in one context may be appropriate and useful in another.

In addition to Alice, I thank Ross Bettinger, Ewa Kirkor, Peter Strizhak, and Theo Mowdood for early readings of the manuscript and their many helpful suggestions. I also thank David H. Levy, comet hunter extraordinaire, who has been part of my scientific life for 56 years and who gave me license to write in first person singular. Anywhere you find a sentence containing "I", rewrite it in passive voice to see how this book would have read absent his influence. You, too, will thank him.

I thank polymath Susan Avery for her Foreword. Her impact on atmospheric science, science management, and policy have been huge. I have no idea how she has the bandwidth to do it all and still fly all across the world, while taking in at least her fair share of opera.

Several figures were expertly drawn by Dorothy Loudermilk, for which I thank her. My editor at World Scientific, Shaun Tan Yi Jie, has been most helpful and patient through the birthing of this book, for which I thank him.

To report errata or ask questions of the author, go to www.bandwidththebook.com.

Alexander Scheeline
Champaign, IL
Started July 5, 2018
Version of November 12, 2022

About the Author

Dr. Alexander Scheeline is Professor Emeritus of Chemistry at University of Illinois at Urbana-Champaign, USA. He is an elected Fellow and Honorary Member of the Society for Applied Spectroscopy, as well as Founder and President of SpectroClick Inc., a firm developing hand-held spectrometers, and Founder and Vice-President of Anchor Science LLC, a materials development partnership. He has published over 130 articles in international peer-reviewed journals, and is known for his work in optical spectrometry, instrument design, sensors, ultrasonically levitated drops, oxidative stress, chemical kinetics, oscillatory chemical reactions, and the dynamics of non-linear systems. His numerous awards include the Distinguished Service Award, Special Publications Award and (twice) W. F. Meggers Award (Society for Applied Spectroscopy), Distinguished Service Award and Innovation Award (Federation of Analytical Chemistry and Spectroscopy Societies), AE50 Award (American Society of Agricultural and Biological Engineers), and the ACS Newsmaker Award (American Chemical Society). He holds a BS in Chemistry from Michigan State University and a PhD in Chemistry from the University of Wisconsin-Madison, USA.

Contents

List of Variables

Symbol	Meanings	Units
A	Age, absorbance, amplitude, acceleration	Years, unitless, unitless, meter second^{-2}
$\mathbf{a}$	Acceleration vector	Meter second^{-2} (in each direction)
a	Activity, human societal growth parameter	Molar, dimensionless
a_X	Debye–Hückel size parameter	Angstrom or nanometer
$\mathbf{B}$	Magnetic field	Gauss or Tesla
b	Path length for absorbance, intercept, rootworm in-migration rate	Meter, varies, population density per unit time
C	Character, concentration, correlation, covariance, corn population, comprehension	Unitless, molar, unitless, unitless, dimensionless plant density, none
C_A	Total concentration of all ionization states of a weak acid A summed over all ionization levels	Molar

(Continued)

(*Continued*)

Symbol	Meanings	Units
C_i	Concentration of *i*th species	Molar
c	Speed of light, offset in corn population	Meter second^{-1}, dimensionless plant density
c_m	Complex Fourier term for harmonic *m*	
D	Decision, diffusion coefficient, demand, distance	Unitless, meter^2 second^{-1}, none, meter
d	Derivative, depth, distance, dimension	Unitless, meter, meter, unitless
E	Electric field, energy	Volt/meter, Joule
E^*	Energy of excited state	Joule
$\mathbf{E}$	Electric field vector	Volt/meter (in each direction)
e	Base of natural logarithms 2.71828182846…	Unitless
	Also charge (analogous to *q*)	Coulomb
F	Fluorescence signal, formal system, friendship	Ampere or Coulomb, none, unitless
F'	Fluorescence relative to maximum available signal	Unitless
$\mathbf{F}$	Force vector	Newton (in each direction)
f	Function, frequency	Varies, second^{-1} (Hertz)
G	Gravitational constant, Gibbs free energy	Meter^3 kilogram^{-1} second^{-2}, Joule or calories
g	Function	Varies
H	Hamiltonian (sum of kinetic and potential energy)	Joule
H	Human population, enthalpy	Dimensionless population density, Joule or calories
$\mathbf{H}$	Magnetic induction	Gauss (or Tesla) Ampere^2 Newton^{-1}

(*Continued*)

Symbol	Meanings	Units
h	height	Meter
I	Intensity, current, information	Watt m^{-2} $sterad^{-1}$, ampere, none
I_0	Reference intensity	Watt m^{-2} $sterad^{-1}$
I_{dark}	Dark current, dark intensity	Ampere, Watt m^{-2} $sterad^{-1}$
I_{fluor_bkrnd}	Fluorescence background intensity	Watt m^{-2} $sterad^{-1}$
I_{fluor_sample}	Sample fluorescence intensity	Watt m^{-2} $sterad^{-1}$
I_{stray}	Stray light intensity	Watt m^{-2} $sterad^{-1}$
i	$\sqrt{-1}$, time-varying current, number series index	None, Ampere, none
J	Judgment, emissivity	Unitless, Watt $meter^{-3}$
$\mathbf{J}$	Current density (vector)	Ampere $meter^{-2}$ (in each direction)
j	$\sqrt{-1}$ if i means current	
K	Absolute temperature	Kelvin
K_a	Ionization constant	
K_{eq}	Equilibrium constant	Varies
k	Reaction rate constant, number series index, spatial frequency	$Second^{-1}$, none, $meter^{-1}$
k_B	Boltzmann's constant	1.3806×10^{-23} Joule $Kelvin^{-1}$
L	Lagrangian (kinetic energy minus potential energy)	Joule
L	Length, language, labor	Meter, none, none
l	Scale length	Meter
M	Measurement	Unitless
m	Slope, mass, integer index	Varies, kilogram, none
N	Number of points	None

(*Continued*)

(Continued)

Symbol	Meanings	Units
n	Refractive index	Unitless
O	Optimism	Unitless
P	Preference, probability, amount of product, population	Unitless, unitless, moles or moles liter^{-1}, unitless
P_{max}	Maximum possible amount of product	Moles or moles liter^{-1}
P^*	Population of excited state	Unitless
pH	$-\log_{10}$(hydrogen ion activity)	Unitless
pK	$-\log_{10}$(K)	
p	Critical exponent, preference	Unitless, unitless
$\mathbf{p}$	Momentum vector	Kilogram meter second^{-2} (in each direction)
q	Electric charge	Coulomb
R	Resistance, regulation, remainder, count rate, amount of reactant, reflectance, rootworm population	Ohm, none, none, second^{-1}, molar, unitless, dimensionless population density
R_0	Initial amount of reactant, initial amount of material	Molar, moles or number of molecules
r	Correlation coefficient	Unitless
$\hat{r}$	Unit vector in direction of **r**	
$\mathbf{r}$	Position vector in 3 dimensions	Meter, meter, meter
$\mathbf{r}'$	Position vector in 3 dimensions distinct from **r**	Meter, meter, meter
S	Scale factor, signal, entropy, supply, speed	Situationally dependent, situationally dependent, Calories Kelvin^{-1} or Joule Kelvin^{-1}, unitless, meter second^{-1}

(*Continued*)

Symbol	Meanings	Units
s	Slope in second linear variable	Varies
T	Temperature, total time	Kelvin or degree, second
T_C	Phase transition or critical temperature	Kelvin
t	Time (with various subscripts to identify particular circumstances)	Second
U	Energy	Joule
W	World state	Markov function
w	Weighting factor	Unitless
V	Variance, electric potential, potential energy, volume, velocity	Varies, Volt, Joule, meter^3 or liter, meter second^{-1}
$\mathbf{v}$ $\mathbf{v}_0$	Velocity vector Initial velocity vector	Meter second^{-1} (in each direction)
V_{ep}	Volume at equivalence point	Liter or milliliter
x	Generic variable, position in horizontal direction	Varies, meter
x_{fp}	Fixed point, i.e., value for x that iterates to itself	
y	Generic variable, position in vertical direction	Varies, meter
Z	Integer charge	None
z	Generic variable, position in third dimension	Varies, meter
$\hbar$	Planck constant/2π	Kilogram meter^2 second^{-1}
δ	Small difference	
ε	Molar absorptivity, error, mathematical interval, dielectric constant, permittivity of free space	Liter mole^{-1} centimeter $^{-1}$, varies, none, unitless, meter^{-3} kilogram^{-1} second^4 ampere^2 = meter^4 kilogram^{-1} second^2 Coulomb^2

(*Continued*)

(*Continued*)

Symbol	Meanings	Units
λ	Wavelength, nonlinear parameter; Lyapunov exponent	Meter (though more commonly nanometer or Angstrom), none
μ	Ionic strength	Molar
μ_0	Permeability of free space	Newton ampere^{-2}
v ν	Frequency	Second^{-1} (Hertz)
$\bar{\nu}$	Wavenumber	Centimeter^{-1}
ϕ	Phase shift	Radian or degree
φ	Angle (typically perpendicular to θ)	Radian or degree
$\hat{\varphi}$	Unit vector in direction of φ	
π	3.14159…	
ρ	Density, charge density	Kilogram meter^{-3}, Coulomb meter^{-3}
σ	Standard deviation, scattering or absorption cross-section	Varies, meter^2
σ_V	Noise voltage	Volt
τ	Time distinct from t, detector pulse width	Second
θ	Angle	Radian or degree
$\hat{\theta}$	Unit vector in direction of θ	
ξ	Correlation length	Meter
ω	Angular frequency ($2\pi\nu$ or $2\pi f$), root of $A + B\omega + C\omega^2 + D\omega^3 = 0$	Radian second^{-1}, none
ω_0	A specific ω	
χ	Selectivity factor	Unitless
$\int$	Integral	
Σ	Sum	
Π	Product	

(*Continued*)

Symbol	Meanings	Units
Δ	Difference or incremental range	
∇	Three-dimensional differentiation	
∂	Partial derivative	

0

Spoiler Alert

The standard sequence for books is: introduce readers to the key concepts, deliver the promised content, then summarize, recapitulating the key concepts. This gives the reader the illusion that the author is fully in command, knew from the start what he or she would say, wrote the book from front to back, and that the book supports a thesis. That's not how I wrote *Bandwidth*. I'd like to invite you to share the journey, since understanding how my thinking evolved is a part of what I want to communicate.

My basic assumptions are that measurement is the stimulus upon which understanding is built, but each of us can only make a limited number of measurements in a lifetime. If you want to experience where these assumptions lead as an emerging story, now's a good time to skip to Chapter 1. When you're all done, if you want to see if what you learned is what I intended, come back and finish this chapter. If you want to follow the standard route through this book, then continue reading here.

I stand most of the what-is-science-and-how-did-we-get-here genre of popular science books on their head. I presume quantum mechanics, statistical mechanics, relativity, information theory, chemical analysis, and related fields adequately describe the tangible world. Instead of starting with Francis Bacon and Galileo, I start by describing how decisions get made from measurements.

Whenever possible, I use equations to express my ideas, since mathematics provides a compact language to explain relationships.

How does one measurement relate to another? Through correlation, the topic of Chapter 2. There's also a discussion of the difference between correlation and causation. Here you see a thought quirk that is quite helpful in designing chemical instrumentation (my profession, my passion, and a thread connecting many of the ideas in the book), but that sometimes can make topical transitions a bit head-snapping. I do not treat topics linearly; I treat them as an idea tree.

While one idea follows from another, the presentation meanders, connecting central ideas to related ideas. The goal is to form a network of concepts, not a linear sequence. Just as an artist considers color, shape, support surface texture, and proportion all at once, so a scientific understanding of a problem or situation requires that multiple concepts be used simultaneously. I connect the various levels of detail and approach in Chapter 16, yet the discussion in that late chapter infuses the approach throughout the book.

As a chemist, my instincts are to always include details and mechanisms in addition to declarative statements. Saying "the sky is blue" may match your experience, but both "sky" and "blue" are subjective terms. Discussing such an idea leads to exposition on looking through the atmosphere, Rayleigh scattering, spectral dispersion, and how we distinguish colors.

Consistent with my approach of starting with the results of 19th- and 20th-century ideas rather than with how those ideas came to be, Chapters 3 and 4 discuss noise and signals. Every textbook I've ever seen starts with signals and presents noise as interfering with signals. I see the particulate structure of matter as inherently noisy, and describe signals as arising out of noise. Is it forward thinking to present these topics in reverse?

Lest the reader think that measurement presents some single, unalterable, determinate Truth, Chapter 5 brings uncertainty into the discussion. Uncertainty doesn't just come from noise. It also comes from complexity and the finite amount of time available for a measurement. Measurements can't be made at an infinite rate nor over periods greater than the time since an experiment was started. Extrapolation beyond what we reliably measure is dangerous. This chapter formalizes understanding of the limitations. Chapter 6 further refines the consequences of uncertainty by looking at what happens when we select some finite number of data points, as is commonly done with digital equipment. Analog equipment as was used from the earliest days of electronic measurement has similar constraints, but analog measurements are becoming so uncommon that I don't emphasize the difficulties they encounter.

Chapter 7 is the heart of the matter – how much information can anyone obtain, given that they have to perceive information before acting on it? When I started the book, I thought this would be the central chapter and, indeed, it is critically important. But seeing all of the connecting ideas, including looking at early 21st-century societies and how they function, I was forced to the conclusion that Chapter 7, while discouraging, is overly optimistic. Chapter 10, describing how people get trapped in wells of limited information, turned out to be central. *Science itself is one of many possible potential wells* – one way to perceive the universe. Each subspecialty (biology, physics, chemistry) and sub-subspecialty (analytical chemistry, physical chemistry, ...) resides within its disciplinary potential well.

While I, as a scientist, think a scientific approach to understanding existence beats any other approach I've encountered, Chapter 10 leaves room for other approaches. In my world, I don't act on what I can't measure. In a spiritual world, one highly values notions that cannot be measured. The two approaches don't speak the same language, have the same values, evaluate the same dilemmas, or necessarily share the same interests. Is it any wonder that attempts to see their shared values and insights often fail? Yet, as the subtitle of this book indicates, no matter how much one's spiritual perspective may differ from what science understands, there are certain core insights from science that constrain how society can function. Gravity can be resented, but it can't be ignored.

Bridging from bandwidth to potential wells, Chapters 8 and 9 include two concepts central to measurement science: detection limits and dynamic range. What's the least amount of something one can sense? What range of measurements can we make? Humanity's measurement range has exploded since 1600. Before instrumentation, time spanned from 0.1 s to a few thousand years. Now it covers at least 39 orders of magnitude, from the lifetime of a muon (10^{-23} s) to the apparent age of the universe (13 billion years). Other measurables, including chemical amounts or concentrations, cover many orders of magnitude. Yet, no one instrument spans this entire range. We don't use telescopes to look at bacteria, nor microscopes to look at stars. Detection limits and dynamic range force measurement scientists to have some sense of modesty. We understand we face boundaries, and we drop into one of those Chapter 10 potential wells or silos.

Chapters 11 through 13 look at complexity – what happens when multiple phenomena interact. Chapter 14 is a bit of a breather. By this point, I've discussed so much about measurement and the complexity of the world that we need to consider categories of measurement. Classification is renamed triage. An answer that comes out as a number is quantification. An answer that is expressed verbally is a qualitative result. However, classification, qualification, and quantification are more intimately related than may be initially apparent, so I explain the connections.

It is easy to think of rigorous subjects that do not appear in this book. Chapter 15 deals with how much we can understand in an internally consistent way using only a finite amount of information (and we recall from Chapter 7 that we always have only a limited amount of information). No matter how many more topics I might have added, no matter how lengthy this book became, there would still be inconsistencies in our understanding of life, the environment, and everything else. One of the beauties of science is that, in limited ways, it can sense its own finitude.

Finally, following the development through the first 15 chapters, I address religion, politics, business and the economy. I conclude by discussing research, critiquing some of the ideas that formed my personal potential well half a century ago in the hopes that current readers can learn from the critique and experience different perceptual limitations from mine. You will doubtlessly find different misperceptions half a century in the future. There's no shame in being the first person tripped up by an invisible pothole. There should be shame in being the 27th, as that means 26 people before you didn't fix the pothole, blockade it, or mark it as a problem. I wish the reader sufficient insight and inventiveness that they build their own potential well, with novel assets, and that they thus improve humanity's lot.

The appendices provide a little enrichment and insight. Appendix I shows how to assemble a photometer using a laser pointer and other materials commonly found around many homes. In playing with the components, I figured out how to make a measurement that eluded me for over 45 years. Appendix II takes interpersonal relationships and re-envisions them in the language of nonlinear systems. This may help clarify what is meant by iterated maps on the interval (Chapters 5 and 11) and suggest personal situations can be thought of using physics, chemistry, and engineering paradigms. Finally, Appendix III gives an overview of calculus so that someone who hasn't previously encountered the subject can learn the vocabulary used throughout the book. I have one data point as to the utility of this appendix. My grandson, then age 14 and having not previously encountered the subject, found it comprehensible. As you will soon learn, no single measurement allows much knowledge of anything, and thus it is with the utility of this appendix!

In summary, scientific language can frame a worldview. Much of human behavior has analogies in the inanimate world readily described by equations, but the complexity of society means our behavior has passed through a phase boundary into which no plausible rate of information transmission can unify our viewpoints. Further, because of the potential wells or silos in which we inevitably operate, we will always exist in an inconsistent society. Force or violence cannot make us uniform, so an enlightened existence means leaving room for people in all the other potential wells, some of which we see (and often judge wanting) but many of which we don't have a way to know are there. Please join me in my well; there are enough equations for all of us.

1

Measurement

How do we know anything? We have to sense[1] it. Some of what we sense is abstract: love, bias, happiness. Other perceptions are tangible: hardness, fluidity, temperature. Not every living thing thinks in a way with which humans can communicate. Ever had a conversation with an amoeba? Its language skills are lacking, but it does respond to chemicals. However, every living thing interacts with its environment. That is, life does not ignore the rest of the universe; it responds to what it senses. When one part of the universe responds to something that was initiated at another point in space-time, we call the moment of interacting with that other point in space-time *measurement*. The time to which we respond is always prior to the moment of measurement. The place at which we respond is typically separated from where the measured event occurs.

Sometimes measurements are qualitative, other times quantitative (but see Chapter 14). The tension in the air just before a thunderstorm is sensed qualitatively; the outcome of the measurement isn't numerical. Distance, measured with a ruler, is measured

[1]Sense? Perceive? Transduce? Interact? Whole books could replace this single word. As explained in the box on p. 7, I mean this as: one part of the universe is perturbed by another.

My explanation of measurement assumes that quantum mechanics and relativity are accepted as two of the bases for understanding existence. While learning science, I was exposed to the sequence: pre-historic people, Greeks, Romans, Arabs for algebra, Renaissance, Galileo, Newton, the great 19th-century mathematicians and Western European physicists and natural philosophers, Planck, Einstein, Bohr, and then modernity. In this chapter, I start by assuming Einstein got General Relativity right, and Heisenberg, Bohr, Feynman, and their contemporaries got Quantum Mechanics right, so let's start there. It's no different from starting a history curriculum with the rise of China and India or pre-1492 Western Hemisphere societies. There's so much information that there is no start, there is no end, so just dive in!

quantitatively; a number results. One of many scientific activities is to attempt to make measurements quantitative. Putting numbers on measurements or attributing numbers to sensed quantities is fraught both with possibility and complications. For much of human history, light seemed to move so fast that it was considered to be instantaneously everywhere once it shone. From the time of Galileo to the mid-20th century, making precise measurements of the speed of light consumed many a scientist's career. Nowadays, the speed of light is a defined quantity, a ruler if you will. The speed of light is a fundamental reference, since that speed, as far as two centuries of experiments have determined, in the absence of solids, liquids, gases, plasmas, or any other matter with which to interact, appears to be the same to everyone. That speed is defined to be 299,792,458 meters per second. "What's a meter? What's a second? What's division? What do those numbers mean?" Clearly, this fundamental constant, the very basis for defining quantitative measurement in our time, is a social convention. The speed itself is not a convention; in whatever way any culture measures the speed of light in vacuum, so far as humans can tell, that speed is the same. But numbers, units, and measurement are all items devised by humans. If you aren't the human who devised these, then someone has to teach you what the symbols (2,4,5,7,8,9, place value, commas, meters, seconds, division) mean before you can even start to wrap your head around "what everyone knows." Is it any wonder that some fraction of the species finds science and engineering foreign? In fact, science is a set of languages as surely as Greek, Russian, and English are languages. Trying to speak the language without growing up in the culture that gives rise to the language is difficult.

Among the languages used by science is mathematics, as equations can be precise and compact in expressing relationships. How can we translate this chapter's first paragraph into math? We express the ideas as symbols.

$$M(\mathbf{r},t)=f\left(\int_{-\infty}^{t}\int_{\mathbf{r}'\neq\mathbf{r}} g(\mathbf{r},t)\,drdt\right) \tag{1.1}$$

(If you aren't familiar with the notations of calculus, see Appendix 3 for a quick tutorial.) The symbols f and g denote functions, mathematical tools that take some information as input and generate a well-defined output. Equation (1.1) can be read as "a measurement M at a position $\mathbf{r}$ and time t is a function f of the integrals over all prior time and all points in space other than $\mathbf{r}$ of the behavior of the universe at all those time and space points as acted upon by a function g." Colloquially, what we measure here and now depends on what went on elsewhere previously. So why bother with an equation? If we can figure out what the functions f and g do, we often can understand why the measurement M came out as it did. We may be able to predict future measurements or see connections among past measurements. In other words, we can understand the past and extrapolate to the future. Some readers may feel, "I don't need an equation to do that." In some instances, you are correct. But in other cases, you aren't. Further, sometimes the world surprises us. How do we know if we should be surprised by something? Only if we know what to expect can we decide that some occurrence is unexpected. To the ancients, the southward trek of the sun from June to December was frightening. What if the sun drifted so far south that it never came back? The world would go dark and we'd freeze to death! To sun worshipers, there was a correlation between praying and convincing the sun god to return the glowing orb to the north each year. After Copernicus figured out that the earth orbited the sun, it became obvious that the seasons are due to the tilt of the earth's axis with respect to the earth's orbit about the sun and that the sun will come back north every year whether or not there are humans, whether or not there are sun worshipers. An equation and a geometric picture of the solar system effectively ended sun worship as a plausible religion. Or not. What if you believe in Ra and have no regard for orbital mechanics? We'll get to that. Let me give you a hint of my viewpoint: I'm a scientist, and science, mathematics, and engineering make sense to me. But not everyone is a scientist, and science doesn't make sense to everyone. Throughout this book, I will be discussing science while attempting to leave room for people who distrust science and modernity as much as I like an ordered, technological world.

Every interaction between one object and another involves measurement. Some amount of energy is liberated or consumed in making the measurement. Drop a rock in a puddle, and gravitational energy is turned into kinetic energy of the rock, then into motion of the water, and finally into heat as the energy is dissipated into the environment. The way we humans know the sun is up or down is from the presence, or absence, of heat and light flowing from the orb in the sky to our skin, eyes, or instruments. Plants respond to the solar presence by synthesizing oxygen and sugar; rocks respond by heating up. I have only described these measurements imprecisely. If the sun comes up in Alaska on December 21, the extent of heating or photosynthesis will be a lot less than if it rises over Argentina on the same day (the beginning of summer in the southern hemisphere). While we measure at every moment, we cannot describe those measurements well just with words. We need to add numbers and relationships. If the relationships are described in words, they are models of what is going on. Add in equations, and we have quantitative models.

1.1 Words and Equations

It is no accident that when we meet people, we "take their measure." Who are they? From what we see, what do we surmise about them? From what we hear, what more can we learn? As we interact more, do we confirm our initial impressions or do we change our initial evaluations? Rev. Martin Luther King Jr.'s famous epigram, "I hope my children will not be judged by the color of their skin but by the depth of their character" is a recommendation that an instantaneous, superficial observation be overridden by a less obvious, but more relevant, measurement only possible at a later time. Perhaps we could say, in concise mathematical notation:

$$\begin{aligned} J &= f(C(d)) \\ J &\neq g(S(\lambda)) \end{aligned} \tag{1.2}$$

where J is judgment of an individual, f and g are functions, d is depth, C is character, S is the properties of skin, and λ is wavelength. King's statement is eloquent, but equation (1.2) is concise (Figure 1.1). Further, it suggests that King's statement is incomplete. If a team is picking a basketball player, important parameters

Figure 1.1. Rev. Dr. Martin Luther King, Jr. at the Lincoln Memorial, August 1963, reimagined mathematically. Reproduced with permission from the Associated Press.

are missing. Shooting accuracy, height, and perhaps jumping ability might also be considered. I assure the reader that my incompetence at shooting precludes my selection for any basketball team, independent of the variables in equation (1.2). Basketball judgment might be better expressed as

$$J = M(C(d), A, h) \tag{1.3}$$

where A is accuracy and h is height. Some might argue about the relative importance of the variables. Still others, thinking of the relative importance of role modeling and winning championships, might wonder about whether $C(d)$ should be the first consideration. While physics describes the trajectory of a basketball (Figure 1.2), many variables of the players, the arena, the fans, and the social context influence what trajectory the basketball follows at any moment.

In any event, the variables in equation (1.3) pose a problem. Measuring height is simple because there is a reference for length. While that standard has evolved from the cubit in antiquity to the

Figure 1.2. Basketball as physics. Parabolic arc superimposed to highlight ballistics. The purpose of offense is to set the ball's trajectory so it terminates in the net, while the defense seeks to disrupt the trajectory. J in equations (1.3) – (1.5) is a proxy for the ability to generate or disrupt such trajectories.

wavelength of atomic emission from a cesium atom today, everyone can agree on height as an objectively measurable quantity. Shooting accuracy is more difficult; people have good days and bad days, they respond differently to various defenses, and so instead of being a single number, it is a number with great uncertainties. But how can character be measured? Would any two people measure it the same way? Even when we agree that it matters, what is the standard unit?

The astute reader will notice that equations (1.2) and (1.3) are missing a variable that appears in equation (1.1): time. To continue with the basketball analogy, Michael Jordan was not as able a player when he was 2 years old as he was in his 20s, and any Washington Wizards fan can lament that he wasn't as good in 2003 as he was in 1998. So perhaps we should write

$$J(t) = M(C(d(t)), A(t), h(t)) \tag{1.4}$$

Mr. Jordan reached his full height before he joined the National Basketball Association, so while equation (1.4) is correct, showing height as being time-dependent is probably a distraction. Height matters, but the minor changes in height of young to middle-aged adults are irrelevant to one's evaluation of a professional athlete. The other time dependencies are clearly justifiable. Let's try again:

$$J(t) = M(C(d(t)), A(t), h) \tag{1.5}$$

We could keep doing this and eventually find a model for selecting basketball players. Someone else beat us to the punch, starting with baseball. Billy Beane's *Moneyball* talks about the use of statistics to build optimized teams. As we will see later, discrete statistics are a good way to deal with measured data when there are a countable number of measurements. Continuous variables often work better when we have portions of the world moving smoothly through space and time.

It's easy to see the act of measurement when stepping on a scale or measuring height. It's a bit harder when navigating the world as a whole. When do we measure the speed of a car coming down the street — when it's far away? When it passes us? Both? How precisely can we measure that speed? If we paint two stripes on the street at positions d and d_0 and measure how many seconds it takes for the car to pass between those lines, we could say

$$v = \frac{d - d_0}{t - t_0} \tag{1.6}$$

where velocity (what we hope to learn) = distance (that we've measured between the stripes) divided by time interval (that we measure as the car cruises along). Do we measure when the front wheels cross the lines? When the rear wheels cross? What happens if the car stops halfway between the lines so the driver can ask for directions from the neighbors? If we use a watch and our eyes, we can measure the travel time to within 1 second, or maybe some fraction of a second. If, however, we assemble some electronic gizmo, we might be able to measure with a resolution of one millisecond. Or we could ask the driver what the speedometer read as they were coming down the street. Answering even a seemingly simple question turns out to be fairly complicated.

1.2 Decisions, Decisions

Yet everything we know is based on measurement. Sometimes it's measurements we make ourselves. Sometimes it's what others make. Sometimes we trust prior generations to have made them. What if there are errors? What if what we think was measured and what was actually measured were different? Later chapters will talk about some of the limitations of measurements. I have yet to meet a person who doesn't regard at least some measurements with skepticism. Yet, somehow, we make decisions based on the sum of all our measurements (either made by us directly or as reported to us by others). Can we write that down as an equation?

Based on equation (1.1),

$$D = P\left(\sum_i M_i(\mathbf{r},t)\right) = P\left(\sum_i f_i\left(\int_{-\infty}^{t} \int_{\mathbf{r}'\neq\mathbf{r}} g(\mathbf{r},t)\,dr\,dt\right)\right) \tag{1.7}$$

That is, the decision D is arrived at by processing a large number of measurements M_i using function P. We enumerate those measurements as one for $i = 0$, one for $i = 1$, and so on up to some maximum. That maximum is less than infinity. Every decision is based on a finite amount of information, and there is always information from times and places that are not considered.

Information can assume many forms. Read this sentence. You did? Good. In following the instruction of that three-word sentence, you carried out a complicated set of measurements. If you are using your eyes to look at a computer screen or printed page, light left the surface on which the sentence appeared, was focused onto your retina, causing various proteins to rearrange, exciting your optic nerve, which led to pattern detection in your brain, which led to concept formation and probably a double-take that the instruction in the sentence told you to do what you had already done. If you are sight-impaired, perhaps the printed word was converted to a time-dependent waveform, which was converted to sound (pressure waves in the air), which impinged on your eardrum, connecting to the fluid in your cochlea via middle ear bones, the pressure waves were converted to nerve impulses, and then the information rejoined the path used by sighted people for pattern recognition. If your native language is not English, additional language conversion had to happen somewhere between my typing and your understanding what I wrote.

Every time information takes a new form, the conversion from one form to another is called *transduction*. Electricity to light in an LED or fluorescent fixture? Transduction. Pattern imposition by having the printed page have different reflectivity at different positions? Transduction. Light to nerve impulse? Transduction. And so on. Every time there is transduction, there is a possibility of error. If there's glare off the screen or page, you might miss something. Perhaps the easiest way to see this is to photocopy a document, and then photocopy the photocopy, and so on. Each photocopying requires light to be generated, reflected from the master, observed by a photosensor, processed by a computer, and written onto a piece of paper. After iterating through a few copies, the crispness

Figure 1.3. Youngsters playing "Telephone".

in the original document will be replaced by fuzzy gray. Eventually, except for large areas with solid colors, all the detail is lost. In the party game "Telephone" (Figure 1.3), even if the players play it straight, carefully trying to repeat what each heard from the previous player, what comes back to the initial player is unlikely to be what they originally said. Of course, in the game, the addition of errors is frequently intentional, but in many measurements, the errors are unintentional. Information degrades every time it is relayed from one place to another, from one time to another, or transduced.

One way of saying that people agree about something is to say that they make the same decision (for whom to vote, what flavor of ice cream to choose, what time to get up in the morning). In other words, for two people (number them 1 and 2),

$$D_1 = D_2 \tag{1.8}$$

If two people make the same decision, do they do it for the same reason? Not necessarily. We can write that down with help from equations (1.7) and (1.8).

If $D_1 = D_2$, then

$$P\left(\sum_i f_i\left(\int_{-\infty}^{t}\int_{\mathbf{r}'\neq\mathbf{r}} g(\mathbf{r},t)\,dr\,dt\right)\right)_1 = P\left(\sum_i f_i\left(\int_{-\infty}^{t}\int_{\mathbf{r}'\neq\mathbf{r}} g(\mathbf{r},t)\,dr\,dt\right)\right)_2 \quad (1.9)$$

It does not follow that the f or g functions are the same, only that the consequence of processing those functions ends up at the same place. Drivers of two cars approaching an intersection may both decide to go straight through, but one of them has a green light, the other a red light, and the decision to be at mid-intersection at the same moment can be quite messy. In general, when people agree on something, it does not follow that their agreement is due to the use of common measurements and logic.

Do you always order the same flavor of ice cream? When possible, I order my all-time favorite, University of Wisconsin Babcock Hall mint chocolate chip. But I'm rarely in Madison, Wisconsin, so I often order something else. In this case

$$D_1(t_1,\mathbf{r}_1) \neq D_1(t_2, \mathbf{r}_2) \quad (1.10)$$

Since we know that at some place and some time, $D_1(t_x,r_x)$ has only a single value (I decide to have a particular cone at that place and time), the fact that I choose different cones at other places and times means that the sums and integrals in equation (1.7), while being formally correct, may not give a clear or accurate prediction of the future. Too many new times and positions influence an individual to be certain of what they'll decide. Conclusion: measurement is a necessary, but not sufficient, basis for understanding what is happening. Even if we could record every measurement, we would rapidly be overwhelmed with data, and we'd have to suppress some of the information we garnered in order to do anything other than drown in it.

How much information can we bring to bear on a decision? How do we avoid being overwhelmed by measurements? How many measurements can people actually make, either consciously or unconsciously? And when we can't make or process

Information is defined at https://www.merriam-webster.com/dictionary/information (April 17, 2022) in four different ways with several sub-definitions. As used here, I am employing definition 1, subheadings b through d:

"b: the attribute inherent in and communicated by one of two or more alternative sequences or arrangements of something (such as nucleotides in DNA or binary digits in a computer program) that produce specific effects

c(1): a signal or character (as in a communication system or computer) representing data

c(2): something (such as a message, experimental data, or a picture) which justifies change in a construct (such as a plan or theory) that represents physical or mental experience or another construct

d: a quantitative measure of the content of information, specifically a numerical quantity that measures the uncertainty in the outcome of an experiment to be performed"

enough measurements to make wise decisions, how do we proceed? The next few chapters address this dilemma. But first I need to say a bit more about scientific measurement. Up to this point, measurement has been about the seeing-hearing-smelling-tasting-balancing-touching interactions of living creatures with the world. Birds can sense magnetic fields. All living things detect chemical substances and respond to some of them. Transduction and response occur for every piece of matter all the time. What organisms add is a systemic response, not just a passive response. For example, heating water can get it to boil; the molecules in the liquid can gain enough energy to escape the liquid and diffuse through the surrounding gas or vacuum. But it takes an organism to detect that the water is getting hot and to either ignore that, turn off the heat source, or yell "ouch" when they get scalded.

> Declarative information is information that can be reported symbolically in words, numbers, pictures, or other abstractions. Tacit information is information for which there is not, at least yet, a symbolic representation. The existence of the planet Uranus was tacit information until 1781. Light from it had been reaching the earth for billions of years, but humans only gave it a name when William Herschel spotted it.

But scientific measurement, carried out either by people or by instruments designed by people, adds a number of features, among them selectivity, specificity, calibration, standardization, and validation. Based on some anticipated correlation (Chapter 2) between some measurement result and some question someone wishes to ask in order to improve a decision, they may use the accumulated wisdom of humanity (equation (1.7)) to intentionally augment declarative information. Given a (perhaps astute) preconceived notion of what is to be measured, the inquirer chooses a series of activities (seeing, smelling, building miles-long particle accelerators and using them for a decade or two) that they anticipate will select for the desired information. If the activities tightly focus on the desired information, they are selective; if they aren't flim-flammed by undesired interactions, they are specific. If the signal processing is done in units that are widely accepted (meter, volt, second), the instrument is said to be calibrated. If the results have been compared to those for a previously characterized specimen and the answers come out the same, the measurement is standardized. (A thermometer without numbers on it transduces information, but not in a particularly useful form. If it's a digital thermometer based on a thermistor, and if the output is reported in microamperes, the thermometer is standardized in electrical terms, but it still isn't useful. Only when that current is reported in degrees and at the freezing point of water it outputs 0° Celsius or 32° Fahrenheit is it thermometrically standardized). But how do we know that a thermometer that reads 0 today will read 0 correctly at any other time when it should? Figuring out how to ensure that the reading isn't a fluke and that it can reliably report that of which it is asked is validation.

1.3 Validation: Carbon Dioxide

I am not going to try to teach an entire course in chemical and instrumental analysis in this chapter. But I am going to give an example of how vague measurement evolves into validated measurements. By the 19th century, enough was understood about how heat flows between media at different temperatures that it was feasible to ask, "is the temperature of the earth due solely to heating from the sun and radiative emission back into space?" Note that without understanding that the earth orbits the sun, the earth spins on its axis, and outside the atmosphere while there are small numbers of particles mostly it's a substance-less vacuum, the question doesn't even come up. The question is a consequence of the answer to many prior questions. Culture is the consequence of groups of people choosing to emphasize particular answers to selected questions (although I doubt an anthropologist would say it that way). In any event, it became clear that something or several somethings were keeping the earth warmer than just the energy balance between earth and sun. The discovery of radioactivity helped explain the imbalance; radioactive substances in the interior of the earth heat the planet to some degree. But that still couldn't account for everything. With the development of instruments that could sense colors outside of human perception (ultraviolet and infrared wavelengths), it became clear that the atmosphere is not clear — the substances that make it up are opaque at some wavelengths and thus trap energy, keeping the planet from freezing over or drying out. Oxygen, nitrogen, argon, water, carbon dioxide, and everything else in the atmosphere absorb some colors of light. Given the wavelengths at which the earth emits light (mostly in the infrared part of the spectrum), water and carbon dioxide are primarily responsible for trapping heat. (I suspect you see where this is going. Stay with me.)

If you web-surf to https://www.esrl.noaa.gov/gmd/ccgg/trends/data.html, you can download the data taken on Mauna Loa that records the amount of CO_2 in the atmosphere monthly since 1958. I show that data (just quoting, no additional interpretation) in Figure 1.5A. It looks like the concentration has increased from

315 parts per million by volume (ppmv) to 415 ppmv. Do you believe it? No, I don't mean "do you believe that humans have caused this increase," a controversy that has roiled politics for decades. I mean "do you believe that the CO_2 concentration has increased?" Do you trust the measurement and its interpretation? Is the measurement valid?

To answer that question, you need to know how the measurement was made and how the instrument was standardized. CO_2 absorbs certain wavelengths of infrared light, and it shouldn't surprise you that the extent of light diminution by CO_2 is called absorbance. "What's that?" If you double the amount of CO_2, you cut in half the amount of light that can pass through an air column of fixed length[2]. You can see this yourself. Get some of your favorite colored beverage (Kool-Aid, Crystal Lite, Jim Beam, Coor's Light, ...). First, shine a flashlight into the bottom of the glass and get an impression of how bright the light is. Pour a few inches of beverage into a glass and again shine the flashlight into the bottom. You'll see less light getting through (if it's red Kool Aid, the amount of green and blue light will diminish; if it's brown as are the alcoholic beverages, all colors will be diminished). Pour in an additional few inches of beverage. The amount of light will again decrease. You've just demonstrated the Beer-Lambert Law (and earned the right to a few sips):

$$A(\lambda) = \varepsilon(\lambda)bC \tag{1.11}$$

where A is absorbance, epsilon (ε) is a scale factor that varies with color or wavelength lambda (λ), b is the distance the light travels through the liquid (how deep was the beverage?), and C is the concentration of whatever is absorbing light (the coloring agents in the beverages or CO_2 in the atmosphere). Probably you realized that your eye can tell that the amount of light goes down as the beverage gets deeper, but trying to measure a number using the naked eye is unreliable. There are electronic means to measure light

[2]Almost. Recent work by Mayerhöfer, Popp, and co-workers has discussed important details and nonlinearities. Their work is referenced in Appendix 1.

intensity. In fact, we call the amount of light that is seen in the absence of an absorbing substance the "reference intensity" or I_0, and the amount of light that makes it through when the absorber is present the "sample intensity", I. It turns out

$$A(\lambda) = -\log_{10} \frac{I(\lambda)}{I_0(\lambda)} \tag{1.12}$$

For more details, see Appendix 1, which shows how to make a spectrometer using a laser pointer as drawn in Figure 1.4. You should never look directly into a laser — even weak ones can easily blind you. Actually, you shouldn't look straight into a bright flashlight either, but many, including the author, have done so with non-fatal results.

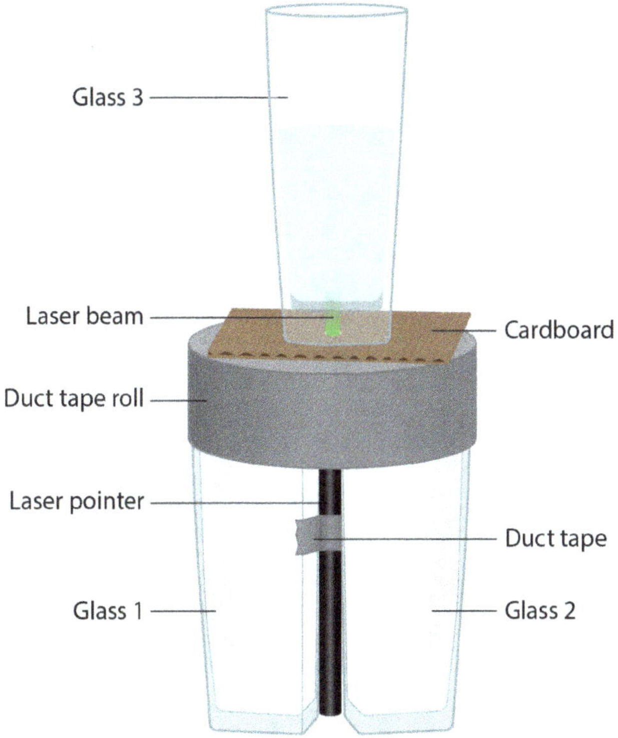

Figure 1.4. Drinking glass colorimeter.

So now we have connected concentration, path length, molecular structure (that's what ε does for us), and the measurement of light intensity. If we know ε, we can find C if we know b. If we know C we can find ε. For the CO_2 measurement, we can find ε only if we have some sample of known concentration. Finding ε is what constitutes calibration (FINALLY I get to the point. What took so long? Too much vocabulary!). The way atmospheric CO_2 concentration is measured is to take the ratio of absorbance of the atmosphere over a fixed path length b and compare that to a known concentration of CO_2 at the same temperature and pressure in a calibrated mixture:

$$\frac{A_{atmosphere}}{A_{standard}} = \frac{C_{atmosphere}}{C_{standard}} \tag{1.13}$$

We've left out a lot of niggling details, but that's mainly what's going on. But there's a huge problem lurking in equation (1.13). You saw for yourself that A can be observed. But to get a valid answer, we need to be able to trust $C_{standard}$. Where does that come from, and how can we trust it? In Figure 1.5B, I show that if there is a

A)

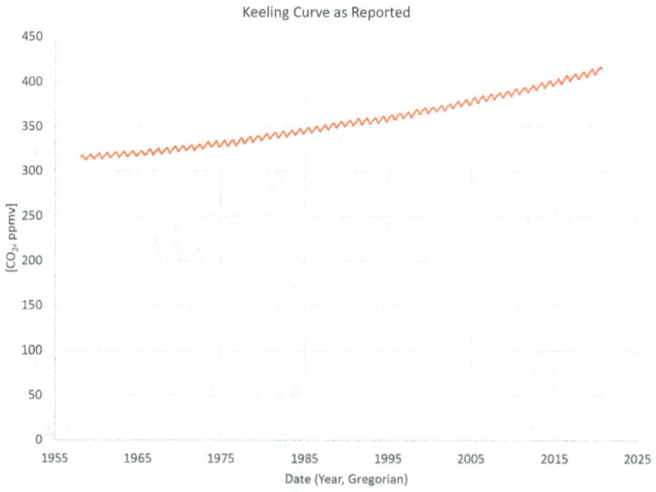

Figure 1.5. The Keeling Curve and the role of stable standards. A) Data reported by NOAA. B) Interpretation of data assuming stable standards. C) Interpretation of data if standards drift 5%/decade (compounded).

B)

C)

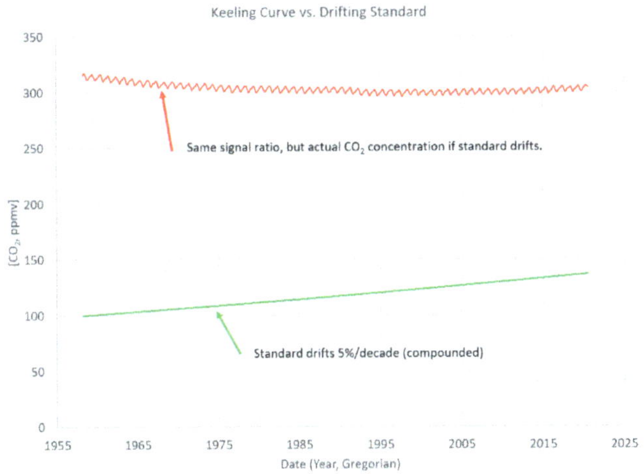

Figure 1.5. (*Continued*)

standard with $[CO_2] = 100$ ppmv and that concentration is the same year after year, then the ratio in equation (1.13) will vary from 3.15 to 4.15 over the period from 1958 to 2020. But what if the standard concentration drifts? I took a wild guess and said, "what if the concentration of the standard increases by 5% per decade, so that when the folks in Hawaii observe the standard, they think the concentration is 100 ppmv, but it was actually 105 ppmv in 1968, 110 ppmv in 1978, and so on?" The ratio on the left side of equation (1.13) is observed — that didn't change, but if the denominator on the right side changed, look at how atmospheric CO_2 concentration would truly have changed in Figure 1.5C. There's no significant change at all! The validity of the carbon dioxide increase assertion rests on the validity of the concentration standard! The future of humanity, or at least its politics and economics, rests on whether the standards are constant!

Fortunately, there are skilled people who are well aware of this problem. CO_2 gas standards are referenced to standards prepared by the United States Department of Commerce, National Institute of Standards and Technology in Gaithersburg, MD. They've been making such standards since long before anyone worried about the long-term trend of CO_2 in the atmosphere. How do they do it? They pump all the gas out of a container — and prove to their satisfaction that the container really is empty. They then introduce some CO_2 into the container, bringing the total weight to a target value (and also measuring how close the weight is to that desired). They add additional, weighed amounts of other atmospheric gases into the container. Thus, unless the calibration of the balance they use drifts between weighings, the concentration of CO_2 in synthetic air will be accurate. Of course, they monitor the balance to make sure it isn't drifting. Voila! The standard is reliable, so the reference concentration is reliable, and to the best of our knowledge Figures 1.5A and 1.5B represent reality, not Figure 1.5C.

There are many additional issues in making accurate measurements, but the logic shown above of devising a measurement, looking hard for problems in measuring, and then devising methods to ensure that the problems are inconsequential, is how scientific measurements are best made. Notice, however, that each scientific measurement contains within it innumerable measurements in the sense of equation (1.1). It has frequently been observed that you can't manage what you can't measure. The question we address in this book is: how many measurements can be brought to bear on

Precision vs. Accuracy

A measurement is precise if it gives close to the same answer every time it's made. If I measure the distance from Chicago to New York and get 11,111 km, 11,112 km, 11,110 km, the precision of the measurement is ±1 kilometer.

A measurement is accurate if it gives a value that accords with humanity's best understanding of what is correct. Google tells me it is 790.1 miles from Chicago to New York via I-90 and I-80. That's 1,274 km. Clearly, the precise number in the preceding paragraph is wildly inaccurate – it's too big by almost a factor of 10. However, if repeated measurements gave 1,200 km, 1,300 km, 1,400 km, the measurement would only be inaccurate by 26 km (less than one standard deviation), but less precise (±100 km) than the earlier measurement.

any given problem, and what are the consequences of the answer being "fewer than infinity"?

In summary,

- Decisions are based on processed information.
- There are always uncertainties in the quantities being observed or measured.
- There are always uncertainties in the measurement process.
- There is always information that has not been collected due to assumptions, made by investigators, that specific influences on an observed process are not relevant to the data collection effort and thus may be ignored without undue error being introduced into the measurement process.
- There may be errors introduced into the measurement of a process that result from ignorance of factors relevant to the process, i.e., unknown unknowns, which are not included in the definition of the process's operation.

- There is always information that has not been measured due to distance, time, or lack of a means to convert information from its native state to that which humans (or their agents, computers) can process.
- All decisions thus have a non-negligible chance of being suboptimal, particularly in light of measurements from additional times and positions that become accessible after the fact.

2

Correlation vs. Causation

The sun rose in the east and I got out of bed. Since I live a stereotypical life, I get up in the morning and sleep at night, a luxury that many life safety personnel, delivery people, pilots, and bakers do not have. Thus, sunrise and my awakening are correlated in time. My bed and I are correlated in space (until I leave it behind). Did I influence the sun's rise? No. I did not cause the sun to rise, nor, actually, did the sun cause me to arise (I like to sleep late on weekends). Correlation means that two events occur at about the same time or place in an observable and repetitive manner. However, that may be pure coincidence, or have negligible relationship between one event and another. Causation means that one item or activity initiates another activity or modifies a behavior. Heating causes the hard, rigid structure of ice to undergo the phase change known as melting, as water transitions from solid to liquid form. Cooling causes the opposite phase change, as water freezes. Let's deal with correlation before we discuss causation.

Correlation has two related, but not identical, definitions. The correlation of two functions is the integral of their product:

$$C(f,g,\mathbf{r},t)=\iint_{V}\int_{t_1}^{t_2} f(\mathbf{r},t)g(\mathbf{r},t)d\mathbf{r}\,dt \tag{2.1}$$

We integrate over all of space and over a relevant range of time. Often, the first step in evaluating the integral is to determine what small volume is relevant and to assume the functions have a value of zero everywhere else. Throughout this book, the important arguments about whether quantum phenomena pervade the universe, so that assigning $C(f,g,\infty,t) = 0$ is debatable, will be ignored.

Using equation (2.1) as it stands gives values for C that vary from $-\infty$ to $+\infty$. There's nothing wrong with that, but it makes using the equation awkward. Commonly, a first cousin of each of the functions is more convenient — a normalized function, one where the original functions f and g are multiplied by a craftily chosen constant, f_{norm} and g_{norm} respectively.

$$\begin{aligned} 1 &= f_{norm}\iint_{V}\int_{t_1}^{t_2} f^2(\mathbf{r},t)d\mathbf{r}\,dt \\ 1 &= g_{norm}\iint_{V}\int_{t_1}^{t_2} g^2(\mathbf{r},t)d\mathbf{r}\,dt \end{aligned} \tag{2.2}$$

Astonishingly,

$$\left(f_{norm}g_{norm}\right)^{1/2}\iint_{V}\int_{t_1}^{t_2} f(\mathbf{r},t)g(\mathbf{r},t)d\mathbf{r}\,dt \tag{2.3}$$

can still have values between $-\infty$ to $+\infty$! That is, the product of two functions, each of which has finite area, can blow up. Dealing with such behavior when the real world does not diverge is the province of Renormalization Group Theory, the basis for much of particle physics, explanations of phase changes (melting, boiling, freezing), and quantum field theory. We briefly present it in Chapter 12. One of the luxuries of writing this book in the 21st century is that anyone interested in digging deeply into the Renormalization Group can look it up; its details are not needed for the main thrust of this book. Kent Wilson's 1971 articles in *Physical Review* are useful for those who want the details (Wilson, 1971a,

How can equation (2.3) give an infinite result if both f and g give finite integrals? Here's an example that bothered physicists from Newton's time until the 1950s because it meant that the self-interaction energy of charged particles was infinite:[1]

$$f(t)=1/t^{1/2} \quad t_2=-t_1 \quad f \text{ independent of } \mathbf{r}$$
$$g(t)=1/t^{3/2} \quad t_2=-t_1 \quad g \text{ independent of } \mathbf{r}$$
$$\iint_V \int_{t_1}^{t_2} f^2(\mathbf{r},t)d\mathbf{r}\,dt=\int_{-t_1}^{t_1}\frac{dt}{t}=0$$
$$\iint_V \int_{t_1}^{t_2} g^2(\mathbf{r},t)d\mathbf{r}\,dt=\int_{-t_1}^{t_1}\frac{dt}{t^3}=0$$
$$\iint_V \int_{t_1}^{t_2} f(\mathbf{r},t)g(\mathbf{r},t)d\mathbf{r}\,dt=\int_{-t_1}^{t_1}\frac{dt}{t^2}=2\int_0^{t_1}\frac{dt}{t^2}=-2t^{-1}\Big|_0^{t_1}=\infty$$

1971b, 1983). So from here on, we'll assume that the examples we care about from equation (2.3) are finite. In fact,

$$-1\le f_{norm}g_{norm}\iint_V \int_{t_1}^{t_2} f(\mathbf{r},t)g(\mathbf{r},t)d\mathbf{r}\,dt\le 1 \tag{2.4}$$

The correlation of a function with itself is autocorrelation, while the correlation of one function with another is cross-correlation.

What happens if we cross-correlate a function with a time-shifted version of itself? I.e.,

$$\iint_V \int_{t_1}^{t_2} f(\mathbf{r},t)f(\mathbf{r},t+\tau)d\mathbf{r}\,dt \tag{2.5}$$

If f is extended in time or space and varies periodically, then every time τ changes by one period of the function, the value of the integral repeats. Thus, sine and cosine functions, correlated with time-shifted versions of themselves, behave periodically. If f is non-zero only over a small region, then the correlation of a function with

[1] f and g in fact cannot be normalized because their integrals are 0. Adding $e^{-|t|}$ to each would make the functions normalizable, not change the basic argument, but require more algebra that might obscure the important point about divergence.

A)

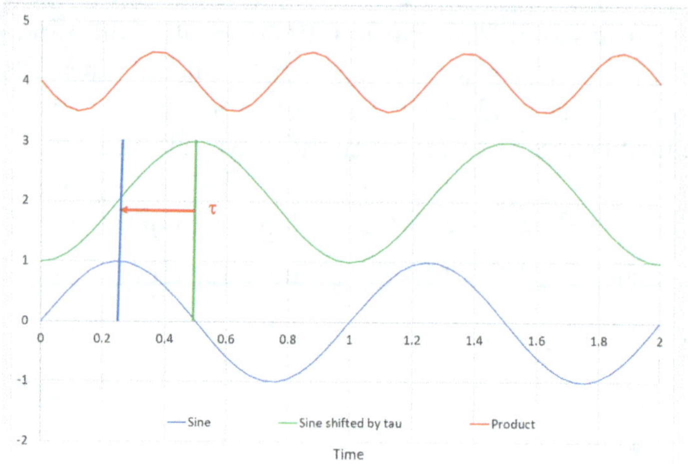

B)

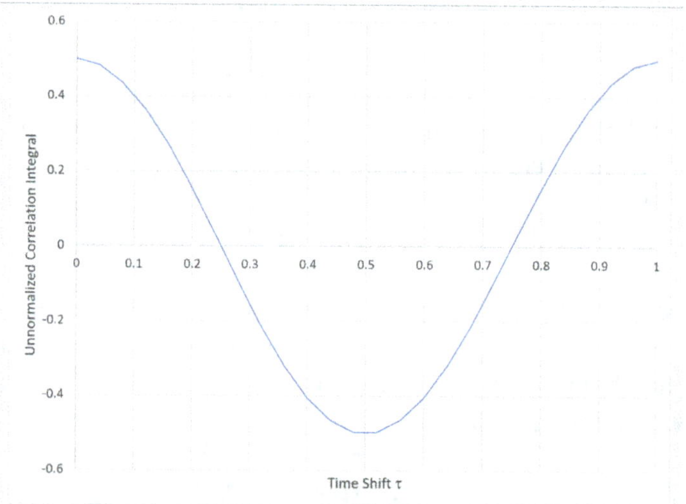

Figure 2.1. Sine wave phase shifts. Inset A shows $\sin(2\pi t)$ in blue and $\sin(2\pi(t-0.25))$ in green. This quarter wavelength shift corresponds to $\tau = -0.25$; the red arrow shows that the green waveform is delayed by a quarter of the sine wave period. The product of the blue and green curves, the argument of the correlation integral, is shown in red. Inset B shows the value of the correlation integral over a single cycle of the reference sine wave when τ varies from 0 to 1. A shift of either 0 or 1 is equivalent to autocorrelation. A shift of 0.5 shows anti-correlation, i.e., the two functions are the same in magnitude but have opposite sign at every time. For shifts of 0.25 or 0.75, the functions are 90° out of phase and the integral is zero. For situations where the correlation integral is 0, the functions are said to be orthogonal.

its time- or space-shifted self has a single peak (or, if you work on some pathological situations, a few peaks). Figure 2.1A shows $\sin(2\pi t)$, the same function time delayed by an amount τ, and the product of those two functions which is the argument of the integral in equation (2.5). Figure 2.1B shows, for $0 \le \tau \le 1$, the value of the convolution integral in equation (2.5), $(\cos(2\pi\tau))/2$. Where is the integral largest? When τ is 0, i.e., for the autocorrelation function. When the integral in equation (2.5) is maximally negative, the two waves are anticorrelated. Figure 2.2 shows cross-correlation of a triangle function with itself. Note that in the latter case, the peak of the cross-correlation occurs when the shift τ is 0. The inset shows various shifts of the triangle pulse from the reference centered at 0.5, and the range of overlap where the integral in equation (2.5) is non-zero.

While the examples in Figures 2.1 and 2.2 can be computed using only integrals that are taught in Calculus 1, more

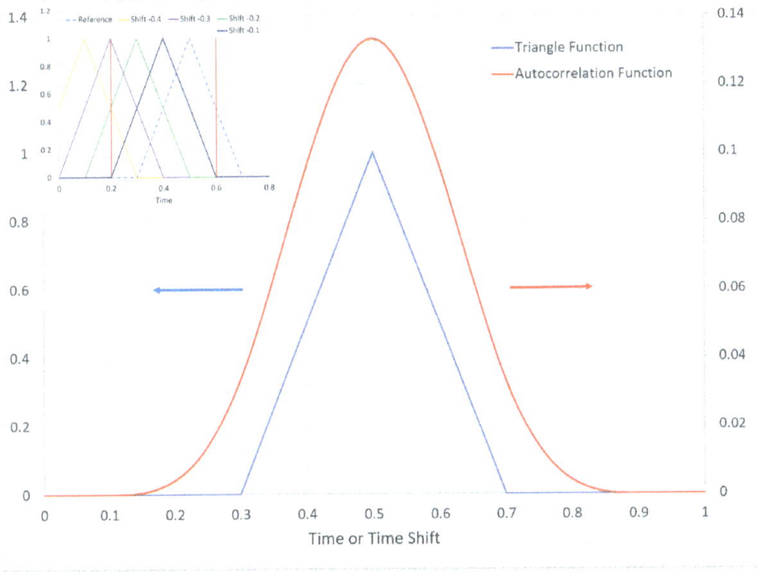

Figure 2.2. Autocorrelation of a triangle function. The function is shown as a solid blue line in the main figure and as the dashed line in the inset. The red line shows the value of the (unnormalized) correlation integral for various values of τ. The inset shows the position of the triangle function for several τ values. For $\tau = -0.1$, the inset shows the waveform as a black line, and the two red lines show the range of τ for which the argument in equation (2.5) is non-zero for this τ.

complicated functions may not be so easily evaluated. In some cases, symbolic mathematics programs can provide formulas. You can surf to https://alpha.wolfram.com and type the integral in, or use *Mathematica* on a Raspberry Pi and see the calculus problem turned into an algebraic expression. However, generally it is so inefficient to do the integral for a particular value of τ in equation (2.5), change τ, integrate again (and so on) that it's fortunate there's a fast and easy way to do convolution integrals for arbitrary functions using Fourier transforms. We defer discussion of the Fourier transform to Chapter 6. Meanwhile, the Wikipedia article on convolution integrals can show you the details if you wish.

2.1 Causality and Correlation

Why go into all this discussion of correlation? Our experience is that time moves from past to future. There are all sorts of arguments about why this is so, and an aside on energy, entropy, and parity might explore some of the theories. But for our purposes, it's enough to observe: all common experience is that time is unidirectional. (There are actually a handful of time reversal asymmetry experiments in particle physics, but those occur at such short times and high energies as to be irrelevant to everyday life.) So for one event to be caused by another, the correlation integral needs to exhibit two properties: 1) The correlation integral needs to be non-zero. 2) The correlation interval must peak after the putative cause has occurred, i.e., for $\tau > 0$. If I get up before the sun rises, it is at least conceivable that I caused the sun to rise; if I get up afterwards, I couldn't have caused what came before.

But that leads to two lines of protest. "You got up because you wanted to see the sunrise, so you anticipated the event, and so there's a connection between the two events." Yes, the events are correlated, but they are independent. If I didn't realize what time I expected the sun to rise, I'd have no way to know when to set my alarm clock. So the sun didn't cause me to rise. Rather, the prediction, based on all human experience, that the sun would rise, led me to set my alarm. *Correlation does not imply causation.*

Secondly, there's a metaphysical argument: If I hadn't gotten up, maybe the sun wouldn't have risen. But since I get up every

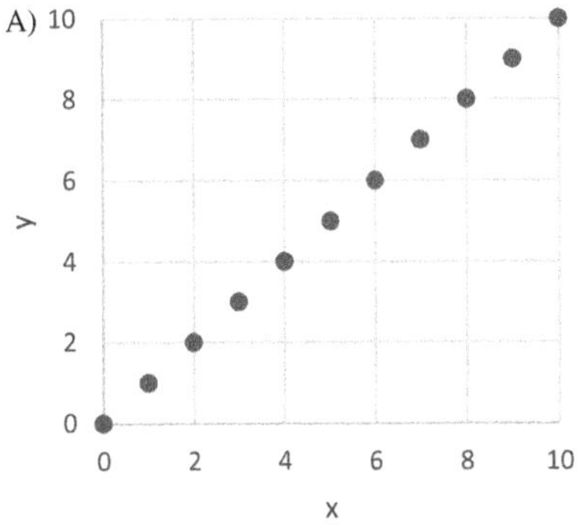

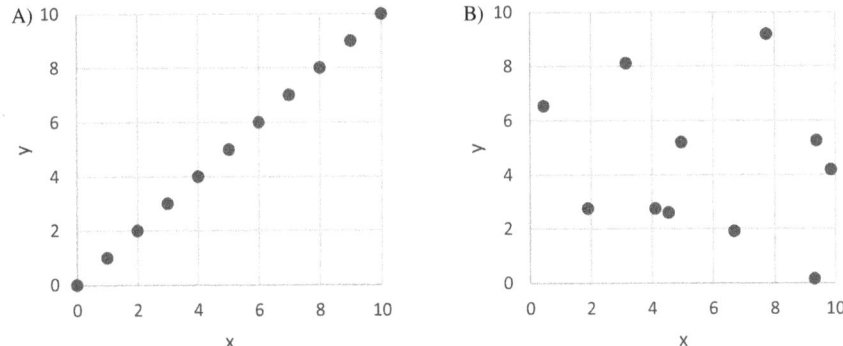

Figure 2.3. Two synthetic data sets.

day, there's no way to disprove (until I'm dead) that sunrise depends on my arising.

Ignoring arrogance, narcissism, and such, the easiest counter to the second argument is that reports of the sun rising have been handed down between generations since long before I came into the world. Therefore, there is a statistical argument that the sun's behavior is independent of my existence and thus, while events are correlated, the non-zero value of one of the functions in the correlation integral is unrelated to causation of the observed effect. This is the first place we encounter empirical realism. We can dream up all sorts of wild ideas about how the world works. However, if an overwhelming empirical record suggests that a mundane explanation works, we accept the simple explanation until and unless that explanation leads to an erroneous prediction. As Friar William of Ockham opined in the 14th century, *"Numquam ponenda est pluralitas sine necessitate"* — complex explanations ought not be sought when simple ones are sufficient.

But this poses another problem. If correlation cannot demonstrate causation, how do we demonstrate whether one event causes another, the second event causes the first, they were both caused by a third event, or they all just happen randomly to occur in juxtaposition to one another but really have no linkage to each other? We have already seen that the correlation integral has to be non-zero or we know the events are uncorrelated. As the mathematicians would say, correlation is a necessary but not sufficient condition to demonstrate causation.

Which brings us to the second meaning of correlation, a statistical definition. Take a look at Figure 2.3, insets A and B. In each inset, is there a relationship between the variables x and y?

It's pretty obvious that in inset A, $x = y$. In inset B, there is no obvious relationship between x and y. As an author, I of course created both data sets in a way where I could control where the points went, and inset B was my best attempt at plotting 11 random data points. See the box to learn how those points were generated. In inset A, the x and y values are highly correlated; in inset B, I hope they are not. But just because I intended no correlation of the numbers in inset B, did I succeed? Let's apply the common linear regression algorithm to both insets and see.

On October 18, 2020, I started an *Excel* spreadsheet and used the RAND() function to generate 1,000 random numbers. I then copied and pasted the values of those numbers into an adjacent column. Thus, the 1,000 numbers, nominally uniform between 0 and 1, are recorded so I can reuse them any time. That means those numbers are no longer random! But the column with RAND() is still present, so the values in that column continue to be pseudorandom. The data in Figure 2.3, Inset B, are the first 10 of the frozen pseudorandom numbers for the x values, and the next 10 as the pseudorandom y values. For all 1,000 values, the mean displayed as 0.502695 and the standard deviation displayed as 0.286951. Good statistical practice is to not report more significant figures than are justified by the data, so in fact the distribution has a mean of 0.5 ± 0.3. We will revisit significant digits in Chapter 3.

For inset A, no surprise, $x = y$ with better than 15 digits precision and the correlation coefficient (an indication of how well a straight line describes the data, a formula for which is in equation (2.17)) is 1.0000… . For inset B, the fitted equation is $y = 5.307 - 0.157\,x$, with a correlation coefficient of −0.0743. In other words, there's a slight indication that a line sloping down describes the data. Now we see, for the first time in this book, how statistics can be abused by those with ulterior motives. Suppose you have a vested interest in y decreasing as x increases. Maybe you are selling a dietary supplement, and you claim these data represent the performance of your supplement. x is supplement dose, y is weight above some desired level, and if y goes to 0, you've helped your customer lose weight. "The slope of the line is negative! While there's scatter in the data, take my super supplement and you'll lose weight!" To which I say, "nonsense," and you say, "but the slope of the regression line is negative." So I go back to my spreadsheet and look up the uncertainty (standard error) of the slope. It's 0.2825, meaning there is a 67% probability that the slope is somewhere between −0.157 − 0.2825 and −0.157 + 0.2825. The slope might be positive, i.e., your supplement has some likelihood (based on the data) of leading to people gaining weight! Darrell Huff's classic send-up, *How to Lie with Statistics* (Huff & Geis, 1993), discusses how misapplied or exaggerated statistical interpretation can be used for illicit manipulation. However, if you want to have some integrity, only claim that there is a trend when the uncertainty in a value is small compared to the number itself. Inset A is data falling on a straight line. Inset B is not. But there is nothing to prevent anyone from stuffing the data from inset B into a formula and getting out statistical nonsense.

Correlation, in a statistical sense, requires that the model we use for the data and the values we observe for data correspond closely. How closely depends on what question is asked. If we are trying to navigate a spacecraft to a remote planet, its clock's rate may need to be known to 1 part in 10^9 or better (the clock is off by 1 second in 31 years). If we're timing a track meet, the watches monitoring the 100-yard dash only need to be accurate to 1 part in 10,000 since a race takes about 10 s, the race time is measured in milliseconds, and so there are only 10,000 ticks to the clock monitoring the runners. And birthdays? A calendar is often good enough, 1 part in 366 (for someone born in a Gregorian leap year).

Now let's use all 1,000 of those pseudorandom numbers, scaled and offset so they uniformly range from 0 to 1. In Inset A of Figure 2.4, I simply plot them (offset by 2.5) in order with 0.1 time unit between them. In Inset B, I add the random numbers

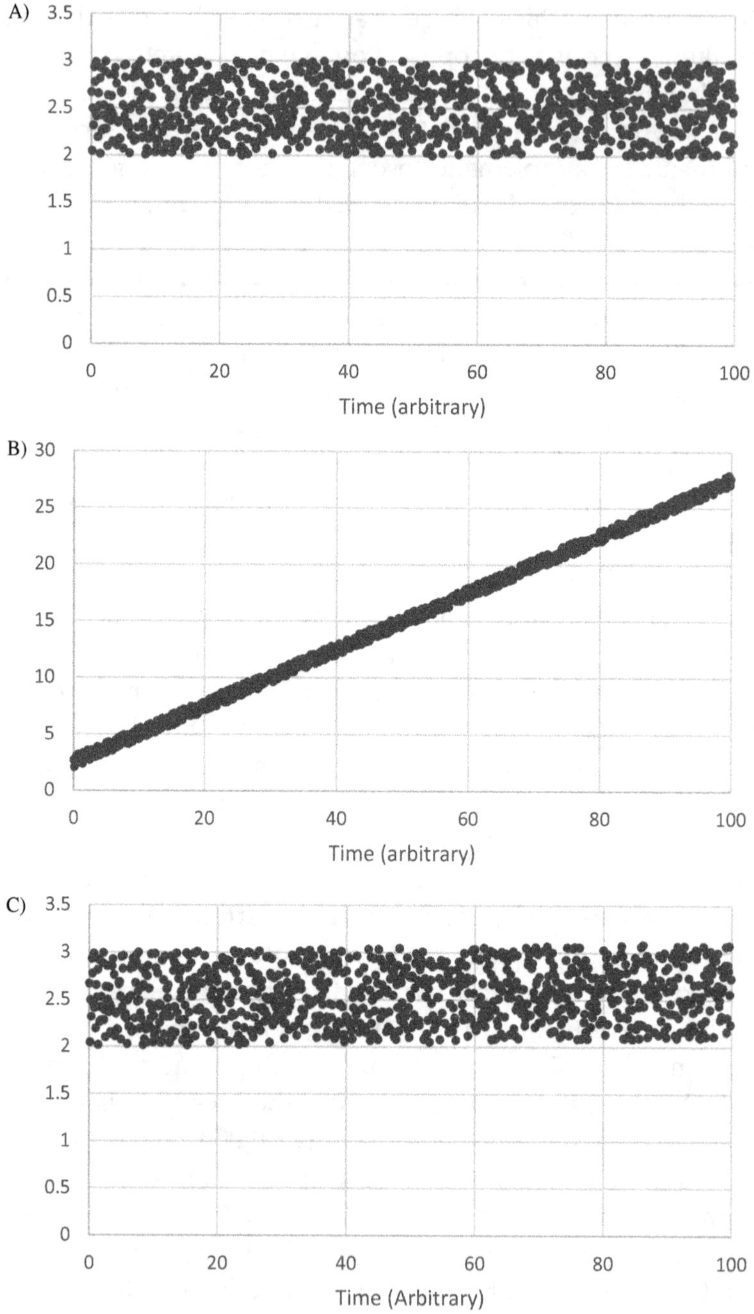

Figure 2.4. Pseudorandom numbers added to: A) 2. B) $2 + 0.25\ t$. C) See text for explanation.

to $y = 2 + 0.25\,t$. But what about Inset C? Is there a trend, or is the plot the same as Inset A?

If you look very closely, you may see that at the right end of Inset C, the scattered points rise slightly. Because you know that the same pseudorandom numbers are used in all three plots, you likely concluded that there is a little bit of an upslope in this inset. But if you didn't have that foreknowledge, would you have reached the same conclusion? How confident would you be that you were right? In fact, the slope here is 0.001, chosen to be just discernable but statistically insignificant. Using linear regression (which we'll discuss starting with equation (2.6)), the slope is 0.0012 ± 0.0003. The slope is distinguishable from zero, but a slope only ¼ as great would be indistinguishable.

Now we know that correlation must show that a subsequent event occurs after a causative event and the statistical basis for saying so has to be sufficiently strong that the sequence of events isn't a random fluke. That means we have to compare prediction to observation many times over. How do we know the sun will come up tomorrow morning? Until we look, we can't be sure, but written records going back thousands of years lead us to extrapolate that sunrise is likely. Egyptians, among others, left records that they saw the sun rise 5,000 years ago. That's at least 1,825,000 sunrises (ignoring leap year!) that have occurred without fail. It doesn't take a song from a musical to extrapolate "the sun will come out tomorrow". We have even more measurements to support the prediction of more sunrises. Every person has experienced sunrise; astronauts in low earth orbit get a sunrise every 1.5 hours. We see sunrise on planets and moons. And we have equations that explain and predict all these motions. Basically, short of an earth-shattering collision, nuclear war, or the end of the universe, sunrise is a safe bet. Someone living in 1400 would have said the same thing (without having the statistical tools to express their conclusion quite as precisely).

Most phenomena that are interesting, or worthy of comment, are not as reliable as the sunrise. The uncertainties are larger, and the number of plausible explanations is also larger. As already noted, the reason the ancient Egyptians would give for sunrise would differ significantly from our own, and those who, despite all evidence, proclaim that the earth is flat, would give yet other explanations.

My colleague Mark Ginsberg pointed out a correlation that, in retrospect, is risible, but, at the time he observed it, deceived a number of graduate students. Some atomic nuclei have quadrupole moments such that the spinning nucleus interacts with the electric fields in solids to give a nuclear quadrupole resonance (NQR) spectrum, detectable by pulsing a radio frequency field onto the solid, then listening to the nuclei rebroadcast the radiowaves as a "spin echo." Among the nitrogen-containing compounds with a distinctive NQR spectrum is TNT. Given its crystal structure, there are 12 resonances when the compound is cooled to 77 K, ranging from 767.7 kHz to 895.4 kHz. Because energy loss and dephasing are slow in solids, the resonances have a width of about 2.5 kHz. The result is that the spectrum is a series of spikes, right in the middle of the AM radio band. Inside a Faraday cage, a conducting box to exclude external electromagnetic fields, it wouldn't be a problem, but without such a cage, Mark reports, the apparatus did a better job of detecting WCBS from New York (880 kHz), WLS from Chicago (890 kHz), and WHAS from Louisville, KY (840 kHz) than TNT (Cardona *et al.*, 2015; Marino *et al.*, 1977)! "Listening to the radio is a blast!"

2.2 Extrapolation Is Dangerous

What's the correlation between your favorite source's weather forecast and what actually happens? Have you ever gone back and checked how accurate the forecast was? What about predictions of the economy — how good are they? As I write this, we are socially distancing during the great COVID-19 pandemic of 2020. Forecasts made in mid-2019 about the economy are looking quite foolish. On the other hand, predictions made in mid-2018 about mid-2019 weren't too bad. Correlation between prediction and actual events is highest when all the influences on the outcome are known. That is why it's fairly easy to predict where a spacecraft is going and hard to predict the economy, health, or politics. Once a spacecraft is launched, it's influenced by gravity, the solar wind, its own thermal radiation, and stellar light (most prominently, the sun). All of these values are known to high precision; there's not much that can go wrong. But when there are many interacting forces, some of them in turn influenced by third parties, it's a lot stickier. If in 1930, someone had predicted the state of Europe's economy in 1945, how accurate would they have been?

Nonetheless, people are always making predictions. For those predictions to be accurate, there must be correlation between the parameters being measured and the events they seek to predict. The outcomes must be due to causes that can be measured prior to the predicted event, and the outcomes also must be caused (triggered, initiated, guided) by the measured inputs. What distinguishes a scientific approach from others in making predictions is that, if the predictions fail, the question is immediately, "Why? What inputs did we mismeasure or misconstrue? What correlations did we fail to take into account? Do the parameters we used relate to actual causation?" We will deal later with situations or ways of thinking where such critical analysis is not employed. Sciences focus on those aspects of the world where we can make models with identified inputs and propose correlations between inputs and outputs. Science can be successful when outputs are caused exclusively by inputs we can measure or by inputs whose magnitudes are so small or so constant that we can omit them from our model.

In reality, it's even harder than that. In Isaac Newton's world, cause led to effect, which became the cause for the next effect, and so on. It was a linear, sequential world. Humans live in a complex, nonlinear world, in which the same input parameters can give different outcomes, and where different input parameters can give the same outcomes. In the language we used in Chapter 1, different measurements can lead to the same D in equation 1.7. That means that when people are involved, the correlation between inputs and outputs is imperfect.

Suppose you encourage someone to try something new. For some people, that increases the likelihood they'll try it, while for others it decreases the likelihood. We measure the inputs, as we described in Chapter 1, bring the inputs to bear, and the correlation for one person under a set of conditions might be +0.8 and for another person under similar conditions –0.8. At that point, psychologists and social scientists are reduced to measuring statistical averages rather than precise cause and effect. This often leads to a situation related to Figure 2.3B.

What happens when we look for correlations using only a small number of data? Let's look at the situation in Figure 2.4A, where we saw that the expected equation for a line through the data, $y = 2.5$, was closely matched by a regression line $y = 2.494 + 0.000165t$. The uncertainty in the slope is ±0.0003, twice as large as the slope, so the slope is indistinguishable from zero. And, of course, looking at Figure 2.4A, it certainly looks, subjectively, like there's no slope. But what happens if we use fewer data points? Do we still get a statistically zero slope? Table 2.1 presents two sets of slopes based on 10 subsets each of the data. For the examples using 100 points each, the points are the first 100, second 100, and so on, of the 1,000 data points plotted in Figure 2.4A. For the examples using 10 points each, the data between points 601 and 700 are broken up into groups of 10 points each.

What do we see? There's a lot of variation in the fitted slopes, but the magnitudes of the slopes increase as the number of points

Table 2.1. Regression on subsets.

Subset Number	Regression Slope, 100 points	Regression Slope, 10 points
1	–0.00041	0.018971
2	0.001546	–0.02125
3	–0.00039	0.016001
4	–0.00113	–0.03551
5	0.001025	0.038844
6	0.000396	–0.04185
7	0.000957	–0.03181
8	–0.00023	–0.0291
9	–0.00094	–0.04466
10	0.000592	0.018102

considered decrease because of the variability of the data. That is, the extent of non-zero correlation appears larger the smaller the sample we use. And this is the source of much societal pain. Someone comes up with a new drug or a new device and tests it on a few patients or in a few situations. It looks like the innovation is working! There's a response in the direction that was hoped! Then more experiments are done, and the effect appears to be smaller. Finally, after many trials, the response is negligible. The tendency of fluctuations to average out over large numbers of trials is a consequence of the Central Limit Theorem of statistics. It is the graveyard of weakly correlated behaviors. It is also the source of tremendous political friction. "Inventor discovers miracle cure!" Except after many tests, it turns out that the inventor didn't discover anything with a response greater than the uncertainty in the measurements. Alas, for the needy or desperate, the first news article, based on only a few tests, raises false hopes, and when more rigorous, extensive trials fail to confirm the miracle, it is tempting to blame conspiracies, greedy kingpins, and other nefarious actors.

But as we have demonstrated, for small numbers of tests, the magnitude of correlations is typically larger than for large numbers of tests. Only when the number of tests is huge and the correlations are still present, can we trust that there's something real occurring. Even then, while causation implies that correlation happened, correlation does not necessarily imply causation. Causation requires temporal sequence from cause to effect, and high statistical probability over many measurements that specific correlated events occur in the order: cause first, then effect. Large effects are easier to measure than small effects, partially because measurement errors and the behavior of observed systems fluctuate from average values.

The next chapter delves into fluctuations. As hinted at in the current chapter, here is the punch line before we even start: the fluctuations, where the equations and experiments aren't perfectly correlated, are probably more important than the mean, predicted values, but American culture (and quite a few others) focus mainly on mean values, not fluctuations.

Now, finally: how to obtain the slope and intercept of a set of data best modeled as a straight line. Notice: if the data are not well modeled as linear, there's nothing to stop you from using these equations — inappropriately. A common abuse of equations is to mindlessly apply them even when they shouldn't be applied. We've already noted one way to such abuse occurs: using too few data and ignoring the uncertainty in fitting parameters.

2.3 Least Squares Linear Regression

If data fall along a Euclidean line, the model for what is happening is:

$$y = b + mx \tag{2.6}$$

where y is the value of the function at some position x, m is the slope of the line and b is the intercept, i.e., $y(0)$. Common practice is to use x as the independent variable if position or some general variable is the driver for the problem. If time is the independent variable, then $y = b + mt$, and just substitute t below anywhere I show x. Additionally, stay tuned for other linear equations, where there are more than two parameters. A linear equation is one where the unknown parameters multiply independent variables. The case of nonlinear equations, where the parameters are not separate from the independent variables (say, q is a parameter and the equation being modeled is $y = A \sin qt$), requires more elaborate methods.

Let's start with the simplest situation. Assume we know x so precisely that we can ignore any measurement errors in each of those x values. All the errors are in measurements of y. Make some number of measurements N, and number the measurements as y_1, y_2, y_3, ... y_N. Each has an error or uncertainty, ε_1, ε_2, ..., ε_N. For some particular measurement k in the list,

$$y_k = b + mx_k + \varepsilon_k \tag{2.7}$$

Add up all N experiments:

$$\begin{aligned}\sum_{k=1}^{N} y_k &= \sum_{k=1}^{N} b + \sum_{k=1}^{N} m x_k + \sum_{k=1}^{N} \varepsilon_k \\ \sum_{k=1}^{N} y_k &= Nb + m \sum_{k=1}^{N} x_k + 0\end{aligned} \tag{2.8}$$

Σ means "add everything up". Since the errors are presumed to be random, the sum of the errors should be 0. Rigorously, the sum of the random errors is only zero if an infinite number of measurements are available, but we approximate the sum as zero regardless of N. With all those measurements, we should be able to manipulate the sums to solve for m and b. But at this point, we only have one equation and two unknowns. As with so much in mathematics, to get an answer we intelligently and honestly cheat. Multiply both sides of equation (2.7) by x_k, and add all the terms up.

$$\begin{aligned}\sum_{k=1}^{N} x_k y_k &= \sum_{k=1}^{N} b x_k + \sum_{k=1}^{N} m x_k^2 + \sum_{k=1}^{N} \varepsilon_k x_k \\ \sum_{k=1}^{N} x_k y_k &= b \sum_{k=1}^{N} x_k + m \sum_{k=1}^{N} x_k^2 + 0\end{aligned} \tag{2.9}$$

Recall that all the x's and y's are just numbers we know, so anything inside the summation signs are numbers we have in hand.

$$\begin{aligned}\sum_{k=1}^{N} y_k &= Nb \quad + m \sum_{k=1}^{N} x_k \\ \sum_{k=1}^{N} x_k y_k &= b \sum_{k=1}^{N} x_k + m \sum_{k=1}^{N} x_k^2\end{aligned} \tag{2.10}$$

We can solve for the parameters b and m:

$$b = \frac{\sum_{k=1}^{N} y_k \left(\sum_{k=1}^{N} x_k\right)^2 - \sum_{k=1}^{N} x_k \sum_{k=1}^{N} x_k y_k}{N\sum_{k=1}^{N} x_k^2 - \left(\sum_{k=1}^{N} x_k\right)^2}$$
$$m = \frac{N\sum_{k=1}^{N} x_k y_k - \sum_{k=1}^{N} x_k \sum_{k=1}^{N} y_k}{N\sum_{k=1}^{N} x_k^2 - \left(\sum_{k=1}^{N} x_k\right)^2} \tag{2.11}$$

I hope that these formulas lead to a whole avalanche of questions. What if the model has more than two parameters? Are there any simplifications of these equations? What if the uncertainty in x isn't small? What if the model isn't linear? What if there is correlation between the error and the value of y? Let's give some brief answers to some of these questions.

If the model has more than two parameters, just solve more simultaneous equations:

$$y = b + mx + sz \tag{2.12}$$

has z as an additional independent variable. Now the solution is:

$$\begin{aligned}
\sum_{k=1}^{N} y_k &= Nb + m\sum_{k=1}^{N} x_k + s\sum_{k=1}^{N} z_k \\
\sum_{k=1}^{N} x_k y_k &= b\sum_{k=1}^{N} x_k + m\sum_{k=1}^{N} x_k^2 + s\sum_{k=1}^{N} x_k z_k \\
\sum_{k=1}^{N} z_k y_k &= b\sum_{k=1}^{N} z_k + m\sum_{k=1}^{N} x_k z_k + s\sum_{k=1}^{N} z_k^2
\end{aligned} \tag{2.13}$$

We now have three equations and three unknowns. The same logic can be used for more parameters, though as we will see, the more parameters there are, the more sensitive the fitting process is to errors. Further, a lot more points are needed to reliably determine those parameters. A particularly common situation is where $z = x^2$. Equation (2.13) then becomes

$$\begin{aligned}
\sum_{k=1}^{N} y_k &= Nb + m\sum_{k=1}^{N} x_k + s\sum_{k=1}^{N} x_k^2 \\
\sum_{k=1}^{N} x_k y_k &= b\sum_{k=1}^{N} x_k + m\sum_{k=1}^{N} x_k^2 + s\sum_{k=1}^{N} x_k^3 \\
\sum_{k=1}^{N} x_k^2 y_k &= b\sum_{k=1}^{N} x_k^2 + m\sum_{k=1}^{N} x_k^3 + s\sum_{k=1}^{N} x_k^4
\end{aligned} \tag{2.14}$$

It is particularly easy to see how we can fit coefficients of polynomial curves $y = b + mx + sx^2 + ax^3 + px^4 + \ldots$ using this arrangement (with, again, the caveat that very high-order polynomials present problems). The formulas for finding the coefficients can be compactly written if we use determinates. Restating equation (2.11),

$$b = \frac{\begin{vmatrix} \sum_{k=1}^{N} y_k & \sum_{k=1}^{N} x_k \\ \sum_{k=1}^{N} x_k y_k & \sum_{k=1}^{N} x_k^2 \end{vmatrix}}{\begin{vmatrix} N & \sum_{k=1}^{N} x_k \\ \sum_{k=1}^{N} x_k & \sum_{k=1}^{N} x_k^2 \end{vmatrix}} \qquad m = \frac{\begin{vmatrix} N & \sum_{k=1}^{N} y_k \\ \sum_{k=1}^{N} x_k & \sum_{k=1}^{N} x_k y_k \end{vmatrix}}{\begin{vmatrix} N & \sum_{k=1}^{N} x_k \\ \sum_{k=1}^{N} x_k & \sum_{k=1}^{N} x_k^2 \end{vmatrix}} \tag{2.15}$$

Once the pattern is stated, building up to bigger systems is comparatively easy:

$$b=\frac{\begin{vmatrix}\sum_{k=1}^{N} y_k & \sum_{k=1}^{N} x_k & \sum_{k=1}^{N} x_k^2\\ \sum_{k=1}^{N} x_k y_k & \sum_{k=1}^{N} x_k^2 & \sum_{k=1}^{N} x_k^3\\ \sum_{k=1}^{N} x_k^2 y_k & \sum_{k=1}^{N} x_k^3 & \sum_{k=1}^{N} x_k^4\end{vmatrix}}{\begin{vmatrix}N & \sum_{k=1}^{N} x_k & \sum_{k=1}^{N} x_k^2\\ \sum_{k=1}^{N} x_k & \sum_{k=1}^{N} x_k^2 & \sum_{k=1}^{N} x_k^3\\ \sum_{k=1}^{N} x_k^2 & \sum_{k=1}^{N} x_k^3 & \sum_{k=1}^{N} x_k^4\end{vmatrix}} \quad m=\frac{\begin{vmatrix}N & \sum_{k=1}^{N} y_k & \sum_{k=1}^{N} x_k^2\\ \sum_{k=1}^{N} x_k & \sum_{k=1}^{N} x_k y_k & \sum_{k=1}^{N} x_k^3\\ \sum_{k=1}^{N} x_k^2 & \sum_{k=1}^{N} x_k^2 y_k & \sum_{k=1}^{N} x_k^4\end{vmatrix}}{\begin{vmatrix}N & \sum_{k=1}^{N} x_k & \sum_{k=1}^{N} x_k^2\\ \sum_{k=1}^{N} x_k & \sum_{k=1}^{N} x_k^2 & \sum_{k=1}^{N} x_k^3\\ \sum_{k=1}^{N} x_k^2 & \sum_{k=1}^{N} x_k^3 & \sum_{k=1}^{N} x_k^4\end{vmatrix}}$$

$$s=\frac{\begin{vmatrix}N & \sum_{k=1}^{N} x_k & \sum_{k=1}^{N} y_k\\ \sum_{k=1}^{N} x_k & \sum_{k=1}^{N} x_k^2 & \sum_{k=1}^{N} x_k y_k\\ \sum_{k=1}^{N} x_k^2 & \sum_{k=1}^{N} x_k^3 & \sum_{k=1}^{N} x_k^2 y_k\end{vmatrix}}{\begin{vmatrix}N & \sum_{k=1}^{N} x_k & \sum_{k=1}^{N} x_k^2\\ \sum_{k=1}^{N} x_k & \sum_{k=1}^{N} x_k^2 & \sum_{k=1}^{N} x_k^3\\ \sum_{k=1}^{N} x_k^2 & \sum_{k=1}^{N} x_k^3 & \sum_{k=1}^{N} x_k^4\end{vmatrix}} \tag{2.16}$$

Once the parameters are known, it's wise to wonder whether the model equation reflects reality. For example, if we fit $y = x^2$ to a linear equation using x,y pairs (0,0), (1,1), (2,4), and (3,9), the result is $y = 3x - 1$. Figure 2.5 confirms our intuition that the fit is poor and a straight line is not an accurate approximation to a parabola. Only if the values of y are highly uncertain (as we will discuss in the next chapter) might we think a linear model is sensible.

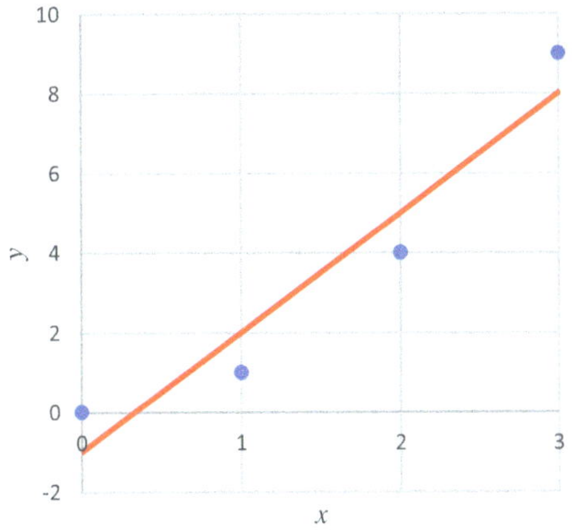

Figure 2.5. Fitting four points on a parabola using a linear model. Red line is linear regression; blue points are precise points on $y = x^2$.

2.4 Correlation Coefficient

Isn't there a better way than just looking at pictures and making judgments to describe how well a model fits data? Indeed there is, and it's the correlation coefficient. Let's not hide from the obvious: we now have two types of correlation in one chapter, several types of coefficients, and the main way to distinguish a coefficient in an equation from a correlation coefficient (that we'll define in a moment) from a correlation integral is to be looking at the equations and identifying the context. This sort of communication does not lend itself to off-hand discussion, and feeds on people's math phobias. But there are only so many words, and many more contexts (a hint at what we discuss in Chapter 7). Let's write down how to compute a number that tells us, in some non-arbitrary way, how well a model fits data. The Pearson Correlation Coefficient:

$$r = \frac{N\sum_{k=1}^{N} x_k y_k - \sum_{k=1}^{N} x_k \sum_{k=1}^{N} y_k}{\sqrt{\left(N\sum_{k=1}^{N} x_k^2 - \left(\sum_{k=1}^{N} x_k\right)^2\right)\left(N\sum_{k=1}^{N} y_k^2 - \left(\sum_{k=1}^{N} y_k\right)^2\right)}} \tag{2.17}$$

r is always between −1 (anti-correlated) and +1 (correlated). The sign matters mainly to inform whether the variable x causes an increase or decrease in y. Thus, if x is age and y is height, typically r will be positive for humans in the age range $0 \le x \le 20$ and negative for $50 \le x \le 120$. If we only care if variables are correlated, and not whether they are positively or negatively related, we can report r^2, which of course ranges between 0 and 1.

Some people are content with expressions like equation (2.17) that spell out how to do a calculation but are not particularly intuitive. We can rewrite it in a way that can have problems dealing with large numbers of data points but that may be conceptually clearer. In Chapter 3, we write down expressions, similar to ones we've already written, to compute the average value of variables. Symbolically, the average of all the x values is $\overline{x}$, and the average of all the y values is $\overline{y}$. We can then write down the variance of x and y, and also the covariance. Variance describes how inconstant an individual variable is (if your average weight during the year is 140 lbs, a small variance might be that it stays within 2 or 3 lbs of 140 all the time, while a large variance would be if you alternated between crash diets and gorging so your weight ran from 108 lbs to 200 lbs over the course of a year). Covariance looks at how related the fluctuations in one variable are with another, and that's closely related to r in equation (2.17). Specifically, with V for variance and C for covariance,

$$V_x = \sigma_x^2 = \frac{\sum_{k=1}^{N} (x_k - \overline{x})^2}{N} \qquad V_y = \sigma_y^2 = \frac{\sum_{k=1}^{N} (y_k - \overline{y})^2}{N}$$

$$C_{xy} = \frac{\sum_{k=1}^{N} (x_k - \overline{x})(y_k - \overline{y})}{N}$$

$$r = \frac{C_{xy}}{\sqrt{V_x V_y}}$$

It has been the author's observation that physical scientists are more demanding of r^2 being close to 1 than are social scientists. For the data in Figure 2.5, r^2 is 0.918. However, in correlating some question of human behavior with some characteristic such as age, education, or marital status, a correlation this high might seem definitive. Looking around the web, Porambu (Porumbu & Necşoi, 2013) has a sentence: "The results showed that the largest correlation was between parents' aspirations and expectations for children's education (average r = 0.40)... ." That's an r^2 of 0.16. A chemist or physicist would look at an r of only 0.40 and say, "The variables are barely related!" A social scientist would say, "Given all the confounding variables that also influence the outcome, this is an astonishingly strong relationship!" One of the friction points between physicists and social scientists is the demands that are placed on degree of correlation before recognizing that a useful research outcome has been obtained.

Insets A, B, and C in Figure 2.4 have r^2 of 0.0003, 0.9984, and 0.01356 respectively. Recall that the exact same pseudo-random numbers were used in generating each plot, but the slopes were substantially different. Scattered measurements can obscure small effects, but not large effects. Similarly, if someone claims a small effect with a lot of scatter in the data, be skeptical!

There are all sorts of libraries (compilations of many algorithms, all written with some internal notational and interface consistency) available for computers to do the arithmetic in these data processing formulas. The hard (and, therefore, fun and challenging) part is that when the numbers are just so, the computations don't work. In the fractions in equation (2.16), the denominator has to be non-zero to proceed. One way that the denominator can be zero is if the fitted line is perfectly vertical (equation of the line: x = constant). Another, non-intuitive, situation is when there are small differences between large numbers. As a human, it is easy to see that 1,111,111,111,111 − 1,111,111,111,110 = 1. Subtracting two 13-digit numbers isn't a huge problem. But for computers, it can be a problem. The earliest microcomputers had 8-bit words, so that integers could only be represented as −128 to +127 or 0 to 255. Then came 16-bit computers that worked from –32,768 to 32,767 or 0 to 65,537. 32-bit computers are limited to –2,147,483,648 to 2,147,483,647 or 0 to 4,294,967,295. Thus, on a 32-bit machine, if you try to take 1,111,111,111,111 – 1,111,111,111,110, you get zero! Such round-off error (if you treat the variables as real numbers) or truncation errors (if you treat them as integers) may be less likely for 64-bit or 128-bit machines, but they can still occur. Are you sure your math library knows this? How can you be sure? And if you aren't sure, how do you trust that your library gives you the right answer? Note that if the arithmetic is done incorrectly, you may think there's a correlation when there isn't or think there isn't a correlation when there is. "If it comes from the computer, it must be right" is a viewpoint that drives computer scientists, electrical engineers, and critical thinkers in general to madness. Similarly, "you just can't trust computers" drives them to madness. Every calculation needs to be run past a "sanity check": based on personal experience, is the output consistent with reality? If so, is there confirmation bias? If not, what may have gone wrong? Surprising results should be investigated, not categorically accepted or rejected.

2.5 Equal Spacing Simplification

What about simplifications? The most common simplification is if all the x values are equally spaced. Suppose $x_k = Sk$ so that we ignore a point at the origin, and every other data point is at a multiple of the distance from the origin of the first data point. The sums over x then become quick and easy to calculate.

$$\begin{aligned}
\sum_{k=1}^{N} x_k &= \sum_{k=1}^{N} Sk = S\sum_{k=1}^{N} k = S\frac{N(N+1)}{2} \\
\sum_{k=1}^{N} x_k^2 &= \sum_{k=1}^{N} S^2k^2 = S^2\sum_{k=1}^{N} k^2 = S^2\frac{N(N+1)(2N+1)}{6} \\
\sum_{k=1}^{N} x_k^3 &= \sum_{k=1}^{N} S^3k^3 = S^3\sum_{k=1}^{N} k^3 = S^3\frac{N^2(N+1)^2}{4} \\
\sum_{k=1}^{N} x_k^4 &= \sum_{k=1}^{N} S^4k^4 = S^4\sum_{k=1}^{N} k^4 = S^4\frac{N(N+1)(2N+1)(3N^2+3N-1)}{30}
\end{aligned} \tag{2.18}$$

These sums not only save a lot of looping in software, they also make calculation of the denominators in equations (2.15) and (2.16) rapid. For equation (2.15), the denominator is

$$\begin{aligned} &N\frac{N(N+1)(2N+1)}{6}S^2-\left(\frac{N(N+1)}{2}\right)^2S^2 \\ &=\frac{N^2(N+1)(2N+1)}{6}S^2-\frac{N^2(N+1)^2}{4}S^2 \\ &=N^2(N+1)\left(\frac{(2N+1)}{6}-\frac{N+1}{4}\right)S^2 \\ &=\frac{N^2(N+1)(N-1)S^2}{12} \\ &=\frac{N^2(N^2-1)S^2}{12} \end{aligned} \tag{2.19}$$

The more parameters one tries to fit, the uglier the algebra, but also the more worthwhile it is to simplify the calculation instead of endlessly adding up equally spaced x values. The denominator in equation (2.16) can also be simplified. Recall that a determinant can be computed by expanding its subdeterminants, or minors:

$$\begin{vmatrix} a & d & g \\ b & e & h \\ c & f & j \end{vmatrix} = a(ej-hf)-d(bj-hc)+g(bf-ec) \tag{2.20}$$

We can identify that

$$\begin{vmatrix} a & d & g \\ b & e & h \\ c & f & j \end{vmatrix} = \begin{vmatrix} N & \sum_{k=1}^{N} x_k & \sum_{k=1}^{N} x_k^2 \\ \sum_{k=1}^{N} x_k & \sum_{k=1}^{N} x_k^2 & \sum_{k=1}^{N} x_k^3 \\ \sum_{k=1}^{N} x_k^2 & \sum_{k=1}^{N} x_k^3 & \sum_{k=1}^{N} x_k^4 \end{vmatrix} \tag{2.21}$$

Thus, the simplification is

$$
\begin{aligned}
&N\left(\frac{N(N+1)(2N+1)}{6}\frac{N(N+1)(2N+1)\left(3N^2+3N-1\right)}{30}\right.\\
&\quad\left.-\frac{N^2(N+1)^2}{4}\frac{N^2(N+1)^2}{4}\right)S^6\,\frac{N(N+1)}{2}\\
&\left(\frac{N(N+1)}{2}\frac{N(N+1)(2N+1)\left(3N^2+3N-1\right)}{30}\right.\\
&\quad-\left.\left(-\frac{N^2(N+1)^2}{4}\frac{N(N+1)(2N+1)}{6}\right)S^6+\frac{N(N+1)(2N+1)}{6}\right.\\
&\left(\frac{N(N+1)}{2}\frac{N^2(N+1)^2}{4}-\frac{N(N+1)(2N+1)}{6}\frac{N(N+1)(2N+1)}{6}\right)S^6\\
&=\frac{N^3(N+1)^2S^6}{24}\left(\begin{array}{l}\dfrac{(N-1)(2N+1)\left(3N^2+3N-1\right)}{15}\\[2ex]+\dfrac{N(N+1)^2(N+2)}{2}-\dfrac{(N+1)(2N+1)^3}{9}\end{array}\right)
\end{aligned}
\tag{2.22}
$$

What if the points are equally spaced but they don't start at $x = 1$? Offset the starting point to 1, do the regression analysis, and then replace x in the fitted form by $(x - x_{offset})$. If $x_1 = 3$ and the points are spaced by 1.5 units, then $S = 1.5$ and $x_{offset} = 1$. It's a good idea to do the offset so that the sums aren't too large. Otherwise, the round-off/truncation errors already mentioned will occur. Incidentally, this approach to using integers to speed up calculating sums and regression coefficients is the basis for one of the most frequently used data reduction algorithms, the Savitsky-Golay smoothing and differentiation functions (Savitsky & Golay, 1964).

What if the uncertainty in x isn't small? There's a nice 2-page writeup on this situation in the *Journal of Chemical Education* (Irvin & Quickenden, 1983). More recently, Joel Tellinghuisen has written more detailed papers on this important topic (Tellinghuisen, 2018, 2020).

2.6 Linearizing Nonlinear Functions

What if the model isn't linear? For example, pseudo-first order chemical kinetics of a product P, concentration [P], forming starting at $t = 0$, changes from 0 to some maximum P_{max}, according to

$$[\mathrm{P}(t)] = P_{max}(1 - e^{-kt}) \tag{2.23}$$

with t the time, and k the constant describing the rate of reaction. What an experimentalist wants to compute from knowledge of $[\mathrm{P}(t)]$ are the two constants, P_{max} and k. There are two ways to do this. The simplest is to rearrange equation (2.23) to linearize the problem:

$$\begin{aligned}
&[\mathrm{P}(t)] = P_{max}\left(1 - e^{-kt}\right) \\
&P_{max} - [\mathrm{P}(t)] = P_0 e^{-kt} \\
&\ln\left(\frac{P_{max} - [\mathrm{P}(t)]}{P_{max}}\right) = -kt \\
&\ln\left(P_{max} - [\mathrm{P}(t)]\right) = \ln P_{max} - kt
\end{aligned} \tag{2.24}$$

While we don't know P_{max} at the outset, we can make an educated guess (just use the value of the biggest data point so that the argument of the logarithm is never negative, and omit using any point where the argument is 0), and now we're back to a linear equation with $\ln(P_{max})$ playing the role of b and $-k$ playing the role of m. After doing linear regression on this modified equation, plot the results and see if the fitted line threads through $\ln(P_{max} - [\mathrm{P}(t)])$. If yes, you have the numbers you were seeking. If no, look for where the precision of the data is poor (like Figure 2.4, insets B and C), omit those points, and try again. Furthermore, when recalculating, use the fitted value for P_{max}. It may take a few repetitions or iterations, but you should eventually get a useful result. Figure 2.6 Inset A shows simulated reaction data, and Inset B shows how small changes in P_0 show up in a semi-logarithmic plot of $P_{max} - [\mathrm{P}(t)]$. Looking only at the first 20 data points, r^2 for the three values of P_0 are at least 0.9999. It is high r^2 values like this that lead to skepticism among physical scientists of r^2's value in choosing best

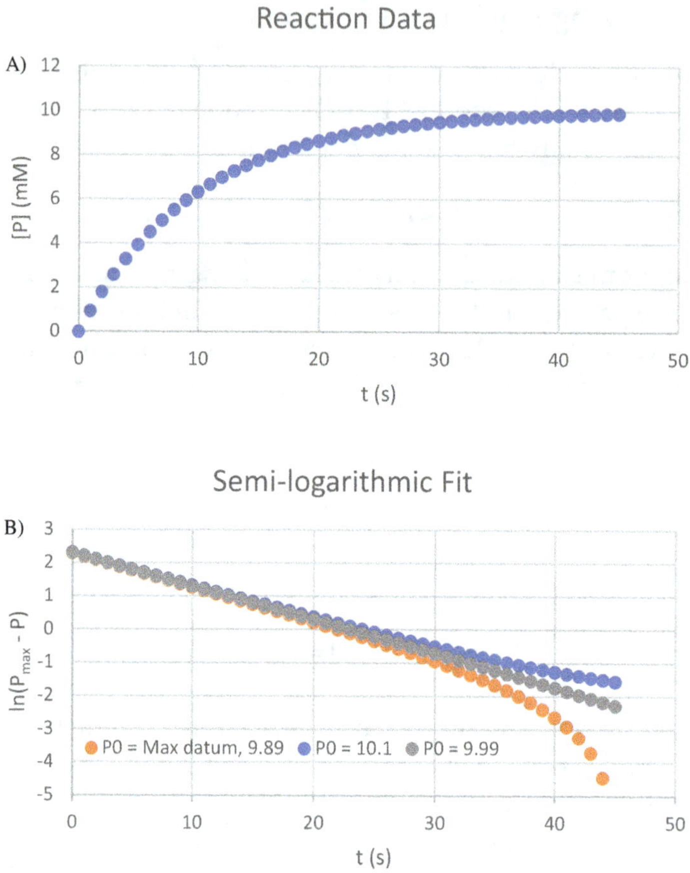

Figure 2.6. Fitting nonlinear reaction data by data linearization. Inset A shows simulated pseudo-first order reaction data, while Inset B shows the result of plotting $\ln(P_{max} - [P(t)])$ for various values of P_{max}. The optimum value of P_{max} gives the straightest line. To save space, the legend in the lower figure used P0 as a symbol instead of P_{max}.

fits. On the other hand, fitting only data points from $t = 24$ s to $t = 44$ s gives r^2 values of 0.9382, 0.9961, and 0.9999, which are more useful.

The other approach is to use an algorithm designed to work with nonlinear parametric fitting. One of the most cited papers in chemometrics (statistical analysis of chemical data) is that of

Levenberg (1944) as implemented by Marquardt (Marquardt, 1963). A useful description of how it works can be found in *Numerical Recipes*, available for several different computer languages; I'll cite my favorite edition (Press *et al.*, 1992). Many mathematics libraries including *SciPy* (for *Python*), *Mathematica*, and *ALGLIB* include a Marquardt-Levenberg algorithm.

Finally, why did I throw all those matrices and equations and details of detecting statistical correlation into a chapter that started with detecting temporal correlation, especially since all that algebra could be avoided either by automating solution through *Mathematica* or some other symbolic algebra program, or buried completely by using some software library? Not only did I want to force us to confront the confusion that comes from one word meaning multiple mathematical concepts, I also want to show you the inside of my brain. When I see a concept, I not only want to use it, but I want to dissect it to see how the equations work and to see what the simplifications and limitations may be. My favorite book on this part of my perspective on the world is Robert M. Pirsig's *Zen and the Art of Motorcycle Maintenance* (Pirsig, 1974). For him, a motorcycle was an entryway to understanding values, problem solving, and reality. For me, the junction between physics, chemistry, mathematics, and engineering serves the same purpose. So I tinker in my corner of the world just as Pirsig tinkered in his. Simplifying algebraic expressions and tuning an engine have a lot in common.

3

Noise

Imagine being all alone, floating on a raft in the middle of a lake on a windless day. The birds are taking a mid-day nap, it's early spring so there are no insects. It's quiet, so quiet that you can hear the blood pulsing through your ears. And then there's a rain drop that hits the surface of the lake. PLOP! You hear the splash, and your hearing guides you to look in the direction from which the drop came, so you can see the ripples propagating from where it hit. The sound of the drop hitting the water conveyed information.

But now it starts to rain harder. Each drop makes a PLOP!, but now before you can turn to see where one drop hits, another falls, here, there, everywhere. Eventually, the drops come down so fast that you can't count them. Instead, if you want to know how much it's raining, you get a bucket and a ruler and measure how much water falls from the sky in some period of time, and the sound is a continuous patter. The fundamental phenomenon is a series of individual events, but the overall effect is some mean rate of water condensing out of the sky. The average rate of water accumulation appears to be a continuous (or analog) variable, arriving at some number of milliliters per square centimeter per hour. But we know that in fact the rate is digital, drops per hour, with a large but countable number of water molecules in each drop. The fundamental phenomenon is digital, based on integers, and discontinuous. You cannot have half a water molecule.

"You should mention Plato's Analogy of the Cave here," said a reviewer. I looked this up on the Web, and thought, "Plato says many things that I am saying too — just without the math, and 2.4 millennia earlier." I have not read Plato. "How can you call yourself an educated person?" Please ask that question again after reading the rest of the book.

How precisely can you measure the rate of rainfall? What limits the precision of the measurement? There are many sources of fluctuations, and since those fluctuations obscure whatever it is you're trying to measure, they are, as a group, called noise. What we try to measure is called signal, which we look at in the next chapter. Every textbook I've ever seen puts the Noise chapter after the Signal chapter. I've reversed them for an important reason: a central theme of this book is that the real world obscures as much as it reveals, so I want to emphasize the difficulties in cutting through obfuscatory phenomena before I talk about what information we might be seeking.

We started by talking about items that can be counted. How hard can that be? Most youngsters can get to 100 pretty easily. For a real-world situation, think of a street with moderate traffic. How many vehicles go by in a day? If you sat in the middle of the block and counted the number of vehicles that came by in one-minute intervals, would you see the same number every minute? Unless there were at least 1,440 vehicles per day, you couldn't – 60 minutes/hour × 24 hours/day = 1,440 minutes per day, so anything less than 1,440 vehicles ensures that there will be minutes with cars and minutes without cars. You might expect lots of cars going by at the start and end of the school day, and at the start and end of the typical workday. There may even be predictable peaks when medical personnel go and come to the overnight shift at the hospital a few blocks away, and seasonal differences.

3.1 Shot Noise

There are two limiting cases for how to deal with the complexities here. One is to try to quantify all these influences. If we leave anything out, no matter how minor, then we still won't be able to describe what's going on exactly. The other limiting case is to assume that the number of vehicles coming along is random. The variance, the square of the standard deviation of the number of cars that we count, is equal to the number of cars that we observe. So if we count 100 cars during some period of time, the standard deviation or uncertainty is $\sqrt{100} = \pm 10$. So during that same hour, under similar conditions, we'd expect 68% of the counts to be between 90 and 110, and 95% of the counts to be between 80 and 120. If, on the other hand, we are at some major interstate highway choke point with 10,000 cars per hour, that would be 10,000 ± 100. The bigger the number, the larger the fluctuations in absolute terms, but the smaller in relative terms. Remember the raindrops? At 5 drops per hour, it's 5 ± 2. At 1,000,000 drops per hour, it's ±1,000, and the rain seems steady. When the count gets high enough, the rate seems almost constant.

> If the number of cars is very low (perhaps a side road in a rural area) such that the average number of cars is fewer than 20 per counting period, you'd need to use a Poisson distribution that insists that no count can be negative, rather than the Gaussian distribution employed here.

Counting fluctuations are given a name: shot noise. The source of the name is that when early electronics were used to monitor individual photons striking a detector, and the resulting electrical pulses turned into a sound, that sound reminded researchers of what lead shot would sound like striking a thin piece of metal. It also sounded like hail hitting a roof, but somehow that isn't the description that stuck! In any event, with the exception of some laser experiments where photons occur in bunches, almost all photometric experiments experience shot noise since packets of light are countable. Even when there is a lot of light, the photons are, in principle, countable. Similarly, if one is counting molecules (e.g., in a mass spectrometer), or asteroids (telescopic astronomy), or grains of wheat being harvested, the measurement precision is limited by shot noise if not something else. As we saw in the car-counting example, the fluctuations in counting measurements scale as the square root of the number of items counted.

Applying this to airline reservations, the seating capacity of planes like the Airbus A320 or Boeing 737–800 is about 160 passengers. Suppose 160 passengers make reservations. How many will actually show up? 160 ± 13, if there's nothing coherently encouraging everyone to appear. Maybe someone gets sick, or they have a change of plans, or they get caught in traffic on the way to the airport. So what is an airline to do? They don't make money on empty seats. They could only book 160 passengers, in which case there would be no chance of overbooking, but a significant chance of empty seats. They could book 173 seats, in which case there would be a 16% chance that everyone would get accommodated, but an 84% chance that some passengers would be bumped. If they overbook by 4 seats (1/3 standard deviation, shot noise limited), there's a 13% chance of overbooking. Overbook by just 1 seat? Now it's tricky. If all passengers are independent, there's only a 3% chance of overbooking, but if two people must travel together and they're the last ones to show up, then there's a 6% chance of a problem. Unless we know how many people are traveling singly and how many as pairs (or family groups), we really don't know how to figure out if there's a problem. Statisticians working for the airlines figure out the probabilities, and add in the cost (financial, regulatory, and reputational) of various booking levels. One suspects that business travelers and recreational travelers have different "no-show" rates, and that those rates are different for the Sunday after Thanksgiving than for a Tuesday in late July.

Shot noise applies not only to photons and people, but to any countable item. There is shot noise in electric current. At first glance, one might think that it is preferable to measure electrical potential (voltage) than current since electrical potential is an analog variable. Alas, Ohm's Law gets in the way. $V = IR$; potential is current times resistance. Current is made up of countable particles (electrons and holes), so voltage, too, is affected by shot noise, and the lower the current the worse the problem is.

Ohm's Law clues us in to another source of noise. What influence does the resistor have? There are at least two sources of noise. One is the random motion of electrons within the resistor, known as Johnson noise. The other is that a resistor heats up as it dissipates energy from current flowing through it. That heat has several effects. It changes the resistance (lowering the resistance in semiconductors, raising it in metals), it changes the temperature of other electronic components (giving rise to drift, the reason electronics need to be warmed up to reach some stable behavior), and it increases the Johnson noise. The amplitude of Johnson noise scales as the square root of resistance times temperature. Superconductors (low temperature, no resistance) do not suffer from Johnson noise.

3.2 Error Propagation

Ohm's Law is a good place to discuss how errors in various quantities combine to give errors in composite quantities. Noise, fluctuations, and errors occur on top of the mean values of variables. Typically, we build models of the world with enough of reality built into the models that the fluctuations and noise are small variations about mean values. We can thus start looking at how noise works by differentiating the model. In the case of Ohm's Law,

$$\begin{aligned} V &= IR \\ dV &= IdR + RdI \end{aligned} \tag{3.1}$$

Since noise is random, the differentials in equation (3.1) average to zero over time. To learn anything useful about average fluctuations, we need to square the two sides of the equation so that all contributions are non-negative.

$$dV^2 = (IdR + RdI)^2 = (IdR)^2 + 2IRdRdI + (RdI)^2 \tag{3.2}$$

Now average over some time period that is long with respect to the duration of the fluctuations. The squared terms do not average to 0. The *dRdI* term averages to zero if the correlation between resistance fluctuations are random with respect to current fluctuations (that is, dR and dI have opposite signs as often as they have the same sign, and their magnitudes are each random). We take that as correct, but with a caveat. If current fluctuations are slow, they can result in resistance changes due to changes in temperature induced by that current, so there could be a non-zero component of the middle term. Such cross-correlations complicate the formulas, but are typically sufficiently small or dealt with by adding nonlinear terms to the modeling equations that we won't worry about them. The average fluctuation or uncertainty is the standard deviation. Thus

$$\begin{aligned} \langle dV^2 \rangle &= \langle (IdR)^2 \rangle + \langle (RdI)^2 \rangle \\ \sigma_V^2 &= I^2\sigma_R^2 + R^2\sigma_I^2 \end{aligned} \tag{3.3}$$

(as in the previous chapter, angle brackets $\langle \ldots \rangle$ mean "average over all measurements.")

Divide both sides by V^2 and use Ohm's Law to simplify terms with more than one variable to get the standard form of the relationship:

$$\left(\frac{\sigma_V}{V}\right)^2 = \left(\frac{\sigma_R}{R}\right)^2 + \left(\frac{\sigma_I}{I}\right)^2 \tag{3.4}$$

There's a small subtlety here. The assumption is that we measure the uncertainty in R and I, seeking to compute the uncertainty in V. However, measuring current and voltage are direct observations, while R is computed from knowing I and V. In laboratory operation, the experiment is

$$R = \frac{V}{I} \tag{3.5}$$

Repeating the derivation, one gets:

$$\left(\frac{\sigma_R}{R}\right)^2 = \left(\frac{\sigma_V}{V}\right)^2 + \left(\frac{\sigma_I}{I}\right)^2 \tag{3.6}$$

At this point, the typical student or citizen compares equation (3.4) to equation (3.6) and says, "Which is it? How could both of these be true?" So glad you asked! The result of an experiment is less certain than the result of any of the constituent sub-experiments. Measurements are expressed on the right side of the equation and derived quantities are expressed on the left. So if we measure I and R and seek V, the precision of V is poorer than that of either I or R. Similarly, if we measure V and I, the precision of the derived quantity R is poorer than the precision of either V or I. This procedure, *Propagation of Error,* is central to understanding the measurements first highlighted in Chapter 1. In that chapter, we stated that measurements are a consequence of everything that precedes the measurement in time, integrated over all accessible space. Here, we recognize that much of that precedent cannot be exactly known, and so there is uncertainty. This is one of three types of uncertainty we encounter: quantum uncertainty and classical uncertainty are described later. Here we have statistical uncertainty. *Yet another instance where one word, uncertainty, has multiple meanings which are rarely highlighted and thus cause confusion.* (Is this the end of semantic blurring? No. The worst case in this book is the word "frequency." Stay tuned!)

What if the errors and y values are functionally related to each other? In this situation,

$$\langle \sigma_x \sigma_y \rangle \neq 0$$

In this case, during the derivation of the error propagation (see Chapter 3) equations, this cross-term must be included. As stipulated, there is some functional relationship between the two uncertainties, and thus the additional term can be expressed algebraically in terms of one or the other of the variables, i.e., something like

$$\left\langle \sigma_x \sigma_y \right\rangle = 0.2x\sigma_x^2$$

For this approach to work, there must be some experimental or theoretical basis for establishing the correlation in the noise. We'll give an example in Chapter 4.

Where were we? Oh, yes. Johnson noise. The voltage that is generated due to electrons randomly moving within a resistor is:

$$\sigma_V = \sqrt{4k_B TR\Delta f} \quad (3.7)$$

This says that even if the current is 0, a voltage noise of the above stated magnitude will appear across a resistor of resistance R ohms, temperature T in Kelvin, measured over a frequency range Δf, with the units conversion fudge factor k_B, the Boltzmann constant, equal to $1.38064852 \times 10^{-23}$ kg m^2 s^{-2} K^{-1} or, since 1 ohm = 1 kg m^2 s^{-3} A^{-2} (A = Amperes = 1 Coulomb s^{-1} past a given point, and 1 Coulomb = $6.241509074 \times 10^{18}$ unit charges). For a 1 megohm resistor observed across 10 kHz (about the frequency range of an AM radio station),

$$\sigma_V = \sqrt{4 \times 1.38064852 \times 10^{-23} TR\Delta f} = 13\,\mu\text{V} \quad (3.8)$$

A bit over 0.01 mV doesn't seem like much (after all, wall power in most of the world is 100 V, 120 V in North America). But when you figure that a 5 kW AM radio transmitter has an electric field of 390 V m^{-1} at 1 m from the transmitting antenna that falls off as 1/distance (*E Ham Radio ~ Ham Tools*, 2010), at 1 mile from the transmitter the field has fallen to 240 mV m^{-1}, at 100 miles it's 2.4 mV m^{-1}. A 0.1 m long antenna (the length of a cell phone) thus only generates 240 μV of initial signal and about 4% of the sound you hear is static (ignoring other noise sources like the spark plugs in your car engine or fields around lightning bolts).[1] And of course there's more than one resistor in the radio. If you're a fan of deep space probes, you know that the transmitters on missions like New Horizons and Voyager operate at about 5 W. Across billions of kilometers of space, how can such a weak signal be detected? The receiving antenna is maintained near T = 4 K, resistance is close to the impedance of free space, 300 ohms, and Δf is reduced to 100 Hz or less for the most distant, weakest probes. That lowers the noise to 2.6 nV.

[1] I chose these numbers for the example, as KDKA in Pittsburgh always had a lot of static when I listened to it from 100 miles away in the 1960s.

3.3 Other Noise Sources

What other noise sources are common? Shot noise is an example of white noise, i.e., noise that is present at all frequencies. Other noises are narrow band noise (power lines generating interference, radio stations clashing with laboratory instruments) and often can be blocked with appropriate electronics that deemphasize information at exactly the interfering frequencies. But there's another wide class of noise that is generically called "one over f" noise or noise that has high power at low frequencies and disappears at high frequencies. While it sounds like the noise power scales as $1/f$, in fact it scales as $1/f^{\alpha}$, where α is any positive number (with specific values for α depending on the noise source). Examples include earthquakes, volcanos, power outages, decaying batteries, corrosion, aging of circuits, electronics warm-up, and intermittent use of heavy equipment (which changes available electric power in a building). None of these occur on a fixed schedule, and all of them are quite disruptive.

A qualitative example may help. Remember Thomas Edison's incandescent lightbulb? Passing a current through the filament heated the filament, and the heating continued until the rate of heat radiation exactly balanced the resistive power dissipation. Since conductors have increasing resistance as temperature rises, and the power from the wall has fixed voltage, heating increases resistance and decreases current. Eventually, the heating causes a high enough temperature and low enough current at a fixed potential that the light output stabilizes. But we've left out three important considerations. 1) If someone turns on another light, the voltage drops slightly, so the first of the lights dims just a little. 2) The filament is not in open air; it is inside a glass globe. As the inside of the globe heats, it radiates heat back to the filament and conducts heat to the outside of the globe. Once the outside of the globe gets hot, it too radiates heat. In addition, air adjacent to the globe gets heated, setting up convection. For weak heating, the air may smoothly flow over the globe (laminar flow), and heat dissipation is constant. But more typically, heating will generate vortices, turbulence, and a gradually expanding region of convective cooling.

Thus, air currents, or someone breezing past the lamp, will change the envelope temperature and the filament temperature, which changes the heating, and round and round and round goes the system, never reaching steady state. The lamp is said to flicker. 3) As the filament temperature changes, its length changes and its thermal properties also change. Any change in size changes coupling to the envelope, and any change in length changes the surface area to volume ratio, which changes the resistance, which changes the current. What a convoluted mess!

This is a good place to show how much noise is floating around in the universe. We show how much electromagnetic radiation and other activity is going on from rare events to the background glow of the light left over from the Big Bang. Figure 3.1a shows frequencies corresponding to a century up to 1 GHz. The seasons cause changes as shown by the noise peak at approximately yearly intervals. The rhythms of the week and day appear, while hourly changes correspond to class changes in schools, shift changes in factories, and assorted appointments and meetings. At slightly higher frequency (~2–3 times per hour) are changes due to heating and cooling systems. The $1/f$ noise (plotted here with $\alpha = 1/2$) fades into white noise just above the frequency of power systems. While radio transmissions are allocated as low as 60 kHz (U.S. Department of Commerce, 2016), in the figure we only show U.S. AM, FM, and television broadcast bands, with the operating frequencies of magnetic resonance imaging and other nuclear magnetic resonance imaging instruments superimposed. Also not plotted in either inset are radio frequency bands used for industrial processes at 27.13 MHz, 54.26 MHz, and the ever popular 2.45 GHz employed in microwave ovens. Inset B shows radiation impinging on earth from all celestial objects. I_ν is the radiation intensity in watts meter^{-2} steradian^{-1} Hz^{-1}; the reason the ordinate is scaled by ν, or the frequency of the light, is so that the vertical axis reveals the power impinging on a fixed area over a defined solid angle rather than in photons per second. Light visible to humans is in the frequency range from 4 to 7.5 × 10^{14} Hz (Hill *et al.*, 2018).

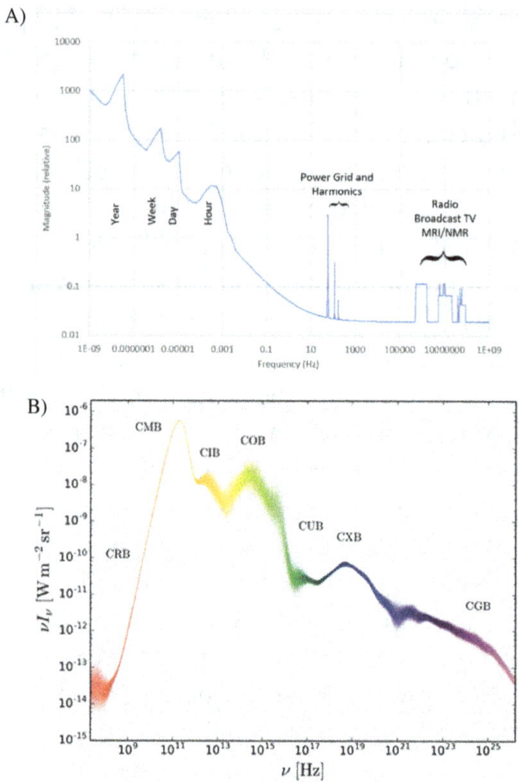

Figure 3.1. The electromagnetic background. Inset A shows the low frequency part of the spectrum. Inset B shows cosmic background radiation that impinges on everything in the universe (but materials that absorb at particular energies may shield the contents of sealed boxes from parts of this spectrum). Inset B acronyms: C = cosmic, B = background, R = radio, M = microwave, I = infrared, O = optical, U = ultraviolet, X = X-ray, and G = gamma. Inset B Credit: Figure 8 from Hill *et al.* (2018), reproduced with permission.

In addition to noise from countable particles and electromagnetic fields, there are fluctuations in atoms, molecules, and materials. Gas molecules in air are moving with a speed of about 500 ms^{-1}. They bump into each other, on average, after they've moved about 70 nm, or every 140 picoseconds. People don't notice this because our sensory systems respond too slowly and, averaged over the distance from one nerve ending to another, the fluctuations in pressure (the result of the bombardment by all those nitrogen and oxygen molecules) are vanishingly small. If, however, we look at airborne viruses responding to gas molecule collisions, the bombardment can adjust the trajectory almost continuously. We can visualize such motion if we generate a sheet of laser light,[2] then take pictures of dust motes (of which viruses are one example) rapidly and repeatedly. This Brownian motion results in particle trajectories that are not smooth curves, but rather a set of jagged segments between collisions. So motion can be noisy. On a much larger scale, in high traffic areas, the flow of traffic can be noisy as aggressive drivers weave from one lane to another (occasionally colliding with other vehicles moving at different velocities). This is noise in excess of the shot noise of how many cars are going by. Only on a single lane is there no lateral motion of the cars; even then, if someone drives the wrong way on that one lane, one-way road, there can be noise (when vehicles meet head-on, the near-instantaneous crunch is a high noise event!).

Slowly changing, drifting, gradually aging systems are classic examples of systems with $1/f$ noises. Any real system will exhibit white noise (within which shot noise is prominent) and some sort of $1/f$ noise. This makes it impossible to exactly measure anything because there is no single value for the measurement. There are many reasons that the speed of light has been defined as exactly 299,792,458 meters per second, but a primary reason is that at least some value is fixed in the midst of a gelatinous world. Experiments converged on that value based on the artifactual standard meter bar at the International Bureau of Weights and Measures in Paris and a value for the second derived originally astrometrically (1/86,400 day) and later by the radio frequency oscillations between the two lowest energy levels of ^{133}Cs which occur at 9,192,631,770 oscillations per second (a wavelength of 3.261225572 cm in vacuum). By defining the units of time using a frequency

[2]A laser usually produces a narrow beam, but with the right lenses, the beam can be formed into a thin, wide shape like a piece of paper — a light sheet.

standard slow enough to count individual oscillations, and defining distance based on a universal observable assigned a constant value, the uncertainties occur only in applying these reference values, not in the values themselves. But there is a catch. Showing that the speed of light is a constant in vacuum, independent of reference frame, was a major accomplishment in the 19th century. Making frequency counters that could operate at speeds greater than 10 GHz was a significant accomplishment of 20th-century electronics. But now our measurement systems assume that the speed of light is constant and that ^{133}Cs has properties that never change. In Chapter 14, we discuss why "but what if the assumptions are wrong?" can't be answered within the structure of modern measurement science — or any logical system.

As if all the above isn't complicated enough, please note that gradually since Samuel Morse (and others about the same time, 1844) invented the telegraph, we have become a digital species, encoding information as numbers and symbols, rather than continuous, analog quantities. If we have enough detected items that shot noise isn't limiting and we measure sufficiently rapidly that $1/f$ noise is not limiting, we eventually run into digitization noise. The problem isn't the size of computer words — it's the resolution of converters that read light intensity, voltage, temperature, or other physical quantities. These only display a certain number of digits or binary counts. The uncertainty from quantizing analog quantities to integers is plus or minus one count. Thus, if we convert the range 0 volts to 5 volts into a 16-bit (2^{16} = 65,536) word, the smallest increment in voltage we can read, ignoring all other noise sources, is 5/65536 V = 76 µV. That also means that the most precisely we can calibrate the converter is to within one count. So all digital readings of analog quantities have an uncertainty of at least ±1 count on top of any other noise. We'll talk more about this when we discuss signals in the next chapter and when we examine dynamic range in Chapter 9. Figure 3.1A will, in part, guide our understanding of measurement limitations. While there are many factors that limit how well we can understand the world, the ubiquity of noise is certainly an important factor. When we get to

Chapter 10, we will learn that our listing of noise factors here needs to be supplemented with additional noise-like behavior due to the complexity of the universe. We wait to discuss this until some additional concepts become familiar.

Let's talk some more about error propagation, since that's what couples noise in sub-measurements to overall uncertainty in complete observations. What we showed in equations (3.4) and (3.6) is that quantities that are multiplied have an error propagation rule that the square of the relative standard deviation or coefficient of variation (standard deviation divided by the mean measured value) for the product or quotient terms add. What happens if

$$z = x + y \tag{3.9}$$

Doing the same differentiate/square/average derivation we did for products of variables, we find that

$$\sigma_z^2 = \sigma_x^2 + \sigma_y^2 \tag{3.10}$$

Here, the variance (square of the standard deviation) adds. Whether x and y are added or subtracted makes no difference because variance is independent of whether the mean value of the variable is positive, negative, or zero.

Now we can look back at Chapter 2 and make sense of the scattered data that we used in seeing if there was a time-proportionate trend to data in Figure 2.4. For some number of measurements N, the mean value is

$$\bar{x} = \frac{\sum_{k=1}^{N} x_k}{N} \tag{3.11}$$

If we make N measurements, we can only extract N parameters from those measurements. The mean is one such parameter. Thus, if we want to know the variance, we've already used up one parameter (or what statisticans call a degree of freedom) so we're basing determination of the variance on $N - 1$ independent values. Thus, for repeated measurement of x,

$$\sigma_x^2 = \frac{N\sum_{k=1}^{N} x_k^2 - \left(\sum_{k=1}^{N} x_k\right)^2}{N(N-1)} \tag{3.12}$$

3.4 Significant Figures

We cannot talk about measuring variance from a single measurement (we'd be dividing by 0 in equation (3.12)). Two measurements give us a range of error, but we cannot know if that estimate is reliable. Even at three measurements, we are only vaguely estimating the variance. Typically, if we have 10 measurements, we can estimate the variance to one significant figure. I now take a moment of author's privilege to rant.

> FOR CRYING OUT LOUD, DON'T SHOW MORE DIGITS IN YOUR WRITING AND SPEAKING THAN IS STATISTICALLY JUSTIFIED!

I will quit shouting and explain. Since we know all measurements have uncertainties, we should only report to the world those numbers we can actually support. If someone asks, "how many bicycles are in your garage," you can count them and, exactly, report "2" or "3" or whatever the number may be. The number is exact. But if someone asks, "how much do you weigh?", the answer is fuzzy and uncertain. What sort of scale or balance was used to make the measurement? How accurate and precise is it? What time of day was the measurement made? You weigh more after a meal than before it. You weigh less after eliminatory activity (how's that for a euphemism?) than before it. You weigh less after you exhale than after you inhale. You weigh less if you take your shoes off or if you wear tennis shoes instead of hiking boots. "We can get around these problems," you say. "I will weigh myself at 10 AM every day for a week, wearing nothing." You have access to a balance with ¼ lb gradations (or, in most of the world, 0.1 kg gradations). Suppose

Table 3.1. Plausible weight for someone during their birthday week.

Day	Weight (lbs)	Weight (kg) (units converted)	Weight (kg) (if metric balance)
Sunday	150 ¼	68.15	68.2
Monday	150 ½	68.27	68.3
Tuesday	150 ¼	68.15	68.2
Wednesday (Happy Birthday!)	150	68.04	68.0
Thursday	150 ¾	68.38	68.4
Friday	150 ½	68.27	68.3
Saturday	150 ¼	68.15	68.2
Mean Column average	150.357143	68.20143	68.22857
Conversion of column 2		68.201	
Standard Deviation	0.244	0.112	0.125

your birthday is on Wednesday and you have a large slice of cake at dinner. Your weight might be as shown in Table 3.1.

The computed mean and standard deviation in the above are obtained by inserting the seven daily numbers in the columns into equations (3.11) and (3.12) and copying over what is displayed on a calculator or in a spreadsheet without any critical thought. In no case do we have more than four significant figures in the measurements. How on earth are we going to have more than four or five significant figures in the means? If we report your average weight as 150.357143 pounds, that means that you are claiming your weight is not 150.357142 pounds or 1530.357144 pounds, it's 150.357143 pounds. The scale only measured with a resolution of ¼ pound, so the unaveraged resolution is 0.25 lbs. We can directly read in increments of 0.25 lbs. The next better level of resolution we could get is 0.125 lbs (1/8 lb). So the resolution we actually have is about 0.2 lbs, not 0.000001 lbs. If the uncertainty is 0.2 lbs, we should report neither the mean nor the standard deviation to more than one place past the decimal point — anything more is posturing and puffery. For the first data column, your weight is 150.4 ± 0.2 lbs. By similar logic, your weight from either the second or third data column is 68.2 ± 0.1 kg. It is oh so tempting to copy the 15 digits that spreadsheets commonly provide you. But many of the digits are meaningless, since the last digit reported is a numerical artifact, not an observable. Politicians, economists, some psychologists, and alas some of my fellow chemists report far more digits than are sensible. If the Dow Jones Industrial Average changes from 26519.95 to 26519.94, has the stock market really gone down? Probably a few stocks went down, a few went up, and for all practical purposes, nothing changed. If a behavioral experiment looks at 23 people and 18 act the same way, 18/23 to many figures is about 0.7826087, but does that say that 78.26% of people act the same way? The implication is that 78.25% or 78.27% isn't the right answer. In fact, with only 23 subjects, the resolution of the experiment (a difference of one person) is about 4%. So you might say 78%, but I'd be more comfortable with 80% — one significant figure. And, of course, when someone suggests the economy will grow by 2.78% next year, they're implying it's not 2.77% or 2.79%, but history suggests that a pandemic, a major productivity increase, a peace treaty, or a trade war will knock those numbers silly. There's hubris in showing too many figures, humility and integrity in showing a statistically defensible number of figures.

And about that slice of cake — there's a short-term jump in your mass of 0.7 lbs or 0.4 kg. That's about three standard deviations, and there is about a 95% chance that the weight bump on Thursday was due to your indulgence on gâteau.

Disparaging the use of excessive significant figures is an early example of how physical scientists see the activities of other people in society. Claiming more precision than is plausible as a way to imply perspicacity looks artificial, just as my tendency to use overly flowery words (like perspicacity!) makes me sound like a thesaurus instead of an author of popular science books. It's not just the substance of what we say that matters, it's how what we say is perceived. To me, equations sing and lend a solidity to descriptions of interactions within the tangible world that qualitative descriptions lack. The reason I've included equations throughout this book is so that you too can join in the chorus if you wish.

Enough about noise for now. Rising out of the noise is what we perceive routinely — a signal.

4

Signal

In the last chapter, we outlined the many ways in which fluctuations occur globally. Whether by using our senses or using some sort of measuring device, we can observe those fluctuations. While noise can be measured everywhere, the magnitude will vary with location. The temperature is noisier on the surface of the earth than 500 feet underground because fluctuations due to weather, seasons, and surface activity are weakly and slowly communicated by thermal conduction through rock. Electromagnetic signals are noisier in the open air than inside a metallic box (a Faraday cage) that shields the inside of the box from surrounding electromagnetic fields. If we detect something which is at least three standard deviations above the noise floor at the frequency we observe, we call that something "signal." Signal is not some pure measurement; it is a deviation in a physical property above the background noise level, and it is, in turn, noisy. Wherever we look to make a measurement (Chapter 1) and detect correlations among those measurements (Chapter 2), we must overcome noise (Chapter 3) and deal with the added noise that is always part of the signal (this chapter). A few pages hence, we'll give a chemical example, based on the unfortunate lead contamination that ruined the municipal water supply in Flint, MI in the mid-2010s.

Electrical engineer and mathematician Claude Shannon wrote a paper in 1948, "A Mathematical Theory of Communication", that is central to understanding what a signal is (Shannon, 1948). Suppose that you use Morse code to communicate. Ever since the early 20th century, many people recognized that "dit dit dit dah dah dah dit dit dit" (3 short pulses, 3 long pulses, 3 short pulses) correspond to "SOS", and while purists may argue about whether SOS stands for "save our souls" or "save our ship" or "send out sassafras", most people recognize that whoever sent that pattern is in deep trouble. What happens if between two of the "dits" there is electrical noise so that the two "dits" are turned into a "dah"? Do it twice, and we have "dah dit dah dah dah dit dah", or NOA. Any guesses what that means? Clearly, the information has been corrupted. Shannon's paper deals with the use of redundancy and encoding to describe the limits of ambiguity in a link from a transmitter to a receiver. But we must be careful. "Transmitter" sounds like something a human might build to direct information to another human. It must take human intentions and transduce them so that the intentions can be conveyed across time and space. In fact, "transmitter" is any point in space-time from which information (particles, energy, and correlations between them) emerges, "receiver" is the point at which transduction occurs, and a channel is whatever is in between. In other words, Shannon gave the basic explanation of how what goes on at one position and time links to what happens at other positions and times, given that noise is added at some level in between.

When we judge (note that's subjective!) that background noise and fluctuation do not impede our ability to figure out what patterns are being transduced, we think we're getting clean, unambiguous signals. When we're dealing with digital 0s and 1s, as long as noise isn't enough to convert a 0 to a 1 or vice versa, we maintain clarity over long distances and time periods. However, embedded in those 0s and 1s are information carriers, typically photons or electrons. And we saw in the last chapter that these carriers are infected with shot noise. If we interpret that 100 photons is a logical 1 and 0 photons is a logical 0, then the shot noise in the 1 is ±10 photons. The shot noise in 0 photons is +1 (that is, any random photon isn't exactly an indication of 0). So we cleverly put the point of ambiguity somewhere between 0 and 100 photons. Maybe we put the threshold at 30 photons (close to three times the square root of the maximum signal). What is the probability that, at random, a 100-photon pulse will actually only have 29 photons, less than the threshold for distinguishing 0 from 1? Since a standard deviation is 10 photons, that's 7.1 standard deviations. The probability of a signal being 7.1 or more standard deviations below the mean is 6×10^{-13}.[1] Thus, there will be a false zero about once every 10^{12} bits, which is once every 100 megabytes. That sounds pretty rare, but given the petabytes that flow through the Internet, it's far from zero. Error detection and correction is essential, even in the digital world. And in the analog world? It's worse, much worse. Material and information moving from one place to another get contaminated by debris or noise, sometimes but not always with our knowledge or understanding. If we miss the fact that something is noise, not signal, we may act on the noise, not what should have been above the noise. Since brains use memory, any error, once recorded, may be used thereafter as fodder for a time-delayed response to a misconstrued signal, and the error propagates. Be cireful to avoid typos! (It is going to be interesting to see if that intentional typographical error survives editors, reviewers, and proofreaders.)

Shannon made a connection between information and entropy. Colloquially, many understand that entropy means disorganization, but it's more subtle than that. The field of statistical mechanics, the microscopic correspondent to thermodynamics, posits that matter is conserved, energy is conserved, and within those constraints all attainable microstates are equally likely to happen. If Jefferson had lived after Ludwig Boltzmann, he might have said: "We hold these truths to be self-evident, that all microstates are

[1]Here I have assumed a Gaussian distribution, standard deviation 10. I noted that 29 photons is the presumed mean of 100 minus 71, and then looked up the probability that a signal of mean 100, standard deviation 10, would randomly yield 29 or fewer photons, i.e., the integral of a Gaussian curve from minus infinity to −7.1 standard deviations.

created equal, and they are thus equally likely to be observed." Because many particle arrangements have the same energy, they are said to be degenerate, and the condition we observe for a macroscopic system is that corresponding to the most numerous degenerate states. Entropy thus tracks the number of accessible states, and that number (summed across the universe) only increases with time. A data channel carries more information if it has a large number of distinguishable states rather than a small number. Thus, counterintuitively, pure noise has higher entropy than signal! What humans perceive as signal is the absence of uncertainty, the absence of a torrent of unstructured information, the presence of pattern. If something is certain, there is no increase in information from re-observing what we already know. Only what isn't predictable contains information of value.

I'm an analytical chemist — a subspecies of chemists who takes great joy in measuring the composition and behavior of the material world. But I and my colleagues are not alone in making measurements. Everyone measures signals — what does the traffic signal tell us that we may or should do? What is that person trying to say? What does that body language indicate? Whether we use sensory-augmenting devices like spectrometers or microscopes or we use our innate senses to perceive, we derive information about our surroundings by sensing signals and determining correlation among those signals. Our first signal processing is, doubtless, *in utero*. At birth, there's the shock of temperature change and environmental change (suddenly, we need to breathe). Shortly thereafter comes hunger and the need to eat. In most cases, interaction with other people is also nearly instantaneous. So long before we have language, we communicate and sense. Analytical chemists are more formal in how they go about measuring and more likely to validate their measurement approaches than members of many other professions.

Henceforth in our discussion, think of signal as the magnitude of information perceived, whether by organisms or instruments. For a signal to be meaningful, it must be sufficiently above the noise that it is statistically unlikely that the sensor, automaton or living being is instead detecting only noise. Furthermore, to interpret the signal requires some conceptual framework. Someone who reads English can perceive Chinese characters, but without training those characters are just so many lines or strokes. Similarly, someone who can read Chinese can sense Roman characters, but may have no idea how to impute meaning to the shapes. A camera records light. But does that light mean that you've captured a selfie, watched the glint of sunlight off the water, or measured the amount of lead in drinking water? The camera, lacking cognition, knows none of this. It simply records that more photons arrived than are consistent with the shutter being closed. The interpretation of the signal requires intelligence.

Now perhaps you sense why I discussed noise before signal. I wanted to emphasize that there's a lot of preconception that goes into measurement, and every individual, every culture, and every device has a lot of preconception built into it. When I taught Quantitative Chemical Analysis, Instrumental Methods of Chemical Characterization, and other courses, I didn't mention the biases except as a trap to be avoided, and I taught about several types of signals before discussing noise as something that limits the utility of signals. The danger of that approach is seen in the attitude many of my colleagues (and I as well for most of my career) have about chemistry, physics, and engineering: we record reality, and anything real has some way of being observed. We then develop refined means to characterize that reality. For many types of problems, this works phenomenally well. Want to know what the composition of Pluto is? Send instruments (in the form of the New Horizons spacecraft) to go take a look. Want to know if you have a disease? Develop a test for it, and if the noise is so big that too many errors are made in diagnosis, devise a better test. Fear you have lead in your drinking water? Measure the amount of lead in the water in a way where even lawyers can't deny its presence. We will pursue this approach for a while, but we will be just as interested in its limitations as in its successes. We will find that the assumptions that precede the measurements are as critical to the results as the measurements themselves. Furthermore, whether measurements should be made at all also has a cultural basis. We explore that topic later in this book.

Discussing signals in the abstract can get confusing rather quickly. You may find that as we get specific, complexity leads to confusion too. To provide a concrete example, let's narrow our focus. Let's choose a problem whose solution involves generating a signal highly correlated with the amount of some substance, and then describe how to make that measurement. We'll include discussion of some of the complications in order to decide whether the measurement can actually solve the problem. I'll choose a problem where my first choice of approach will fail because there is too much noise, then choose a second approach that will work.

Let's look at the problem of lead in the drinking water in Flint, Michigan. According to the EPA website on 11/1/2020, if at least 10% of tap water samples show at least 15 parts per billion (ppb) of lead, enforcement action is appropriate (https://www.epa.gov/ground-water-and-drinking-water/basic-information-about-lead-drinking-water#regs). 15 ppb means 15 nanograms of lead per gram of water (which is roughly 15 nanograms per milliliter. Why is 15 ppb the regulated level? Good question, but a topic for another book). One can look carefully at how the density of water varies with temperature and convert nanograms per gram to nanograms per milliliter, but let's not get into that detail for now. Instead, let's assume we take a one-liter (about one quart) sample of water. The regulation means that there should be less than 15 micrograms of lead in the water. Since the density of lead is 11.4 g cm^{-3}, that's a volume of metallic lead of about 1.3×10^{-6} cm^{-3} or a speck under 0.011 cm on a side. That's about the thickness of a sheet of laser printer paper. How can we detect that amount of lead reliably? The first thing to realize is that lead in water can be in at least two forms: suspended particulates and dissolved ions. Because the particulates may be soluble in stomach acid, we really want to know the total amount of lead, not just the concentration of dissolved ions.

Lead determination was thoroughly reviewed by Fitch in 1998 (Fitch, 1998). We'll only look at two of the methods she describes, and not necessarily the ones best suited to municipal water systems. Rather, I want to show how two types of signals are generated and measured, and what limits their utility.

For a good part of the 20th century, the standard way to determine lead was to dissolve a sample in nitric acid, then extract the lead ions into an organic solvent to form a dithizone complex. While there are a number of ways lead can appear in water, we'll assume that our pre-treatment leaves it all as lead nitrate, $Pb(NO_3)_2$. If we have 15 micrograms per liter of Pb, we have 24 micrograms per liter of $Pb(NO_3)_2$. Since this compound has a formula weight of 331 g/mole, the concentration we need to detect is 7 nanomolar (nM). "Nano sounds small," I hope I hear you think. And you're right. To the human eye, a solution of 7 nM lead looks no different than a solution with effectively no lead in it. If we extract the lead into an organic solvent as the dithizone complex using 100 mL of organic solvent per liter of water, and if all the lead is extracted (a big if!), then concentration in the organic solvent is 70 nM. "Why not extract it all into 1 milliliter? Then you'd get 7 micromolar (μM) which would be a lot easier to work with!" Organic solvents are slightly soluble in water, just as water is slightly soluble in organic solvents, so knowing the volume of organic solvent floating on top of the water or sinking to the bottom of the container (depending on the density of the solvent compared to water) is tricky if the volume of the solvent is small. One of the noise sources in handling solutions is uncertainty in the volumes of sample and other liquids; if the volume of the organic solvent is imprecisely known, the concentration of lead in that solvent is also imprecise, and we won't be able to make a measurement that has a known relationship to what we started with. If the solubility of some solvent in water is about 0.5 mL per liter of water, using only 1 mL of solvent means there's a 50% shrinkage of organic solvent volume and a factor of 2 error in the concentration of lead in solution, while for 100 mL of the same solvent, the shrinking is only to 99.5 mL and the error is half a percent. The tricky part is that the solubility of the solvent depends on what sorts of solutes are in the water, so using a reasonable amount of organic solvent also protects us against compositional surprises in the sample.

Choosing a solvent is a problem. Originally, when dithizone methods were first used in 1925, chlorinated hydrocarbons were employed. These are now frowned upon because of their environmental impact. Carbon disulfide, CS_2, is a possibility, although it's somewhat toxic. It can be disposed of by incineration. Its solubility in water is 2.1 g L^{-1} (https://www.who.int/ipcs/publications/cicad/en/cicad46.pdf, p. 5, 11/3/2020) or, given a density of 1.26 g mL^{-1}, 1.6 mL of CS_2 can dissolve completely in a liter of water. To avoid having to use such a solvent, I'll describe a dithizone method that was published in 2006 by some authors from Bangladesh (Khan *et al.*, 2006).

Before we get even deeper into the weeds, let me outline where the rest of this chapter is going. We'll go through the chemistry, physics, and engineering of the optical spectrometer that allows us to make a measurement. We'll then figure out if the dithizone method can usefully measure the lead in Flint's water. By the time we finish, you are likely to join me in saying, "that's a lot of work — surely there must be a better way." At which point we'll discuss the chemistry, physics, and engineering of a mass spectrometer that allows measurement directly from the original aqueous solution. "Then why talk about the optical approach?" Because the optical approach uses much less expensive equipment and consumables, provided whoever does the work has adequate expertise. Remember the integrals from Chapter 1? We are trying to get to a particular result, but numerous functions f and g are available to get there. If you want to know about even more paths to a useful result, either read Fitch's lead article or download the free textbook, *Analytical Chemistry 2.0* (Harvey, 2009) or its 2016 successor.

4.1 Spectrophotometry

To review from Chapter 1, get some water and some food coloring. Put the water in a glass with some space to spare. Look through the glass at a light (not the sun — never look directly at the sun without filters designed specifically for the purpose). What do you see? Depending on whether it's an incandescent lamp, fluorescent lamp, or LED, it's probably some shade of white (if you are color blind, my descriptions won't match what you sense). Add a drop of food coloring. The color of the lamp will have a slight tinge of the color you added. Keep adding drops and mixing, and the color deepens. What is happening? The food coloring is absorbing some of the light coming out of the lamp, leaving only the color you perceive. Food coloring does not generate color — it absorbs colors other than the one you see.

And so it is for spectrophotometric measurement of any compound that absorbs light. We don't look at wavelengths corresponding to the color we see — we look at wavelengths that are blocked by the compound. If a compound looks red, that means green light is absorbed and we should look between 480 nm and 570 nm, where humans perceive green. If the compound is blue, we should look at red (and maybe green) wavelengths. Further, we need to know how much light is detected absent the compound of interest so that when the compound is present, we know how much light is blocked.

Compared to many modern instruments, a spectrophotometer looks simple. In reality, there is significant complexity, so much so that whole books are written on what I will describe in a few paragraphs. If you want to get really techie, see my article (Scheeline, 2017). Davis Baird has opined: the most compact expression for how an instrument works and what it means is the instrument itself (Baird, 2004). Any words or diagrams are incomplete.

A spectrophotometer is an instrument that determines how much light is transmitted through a specimen at a selected wavelength (or over a limited range of wavelengths near a chosen wavelength). It requires a light source, a set of optics to direct light to where it is needed and prevent light traveling along unwanted paths from interfering with the measurement, a specimen and holder for that specimen, a means of breaking up white light into its various wavelengths and selecting the desired subset of those wavelengths, a transducer to convert light intensity to an electrical signal, and a means to convert that electrical signal into a form, usable by humans, to complete the measurement. Since about 1960 (research) or 1980 (commercial), that processing has involved converting electrical signals to numbers and then processing the numbers through a computer.

Since the dithizone complex absorbs visible light, let's use a white LED as the light source. We'll carry the light to an observation housing with a fiber optic cable, collimate the light with a half-ball lens, pass the light through a cuvette (a clear glass, square container with inside width 1 cm), then refocus the light with another half-ball lens, carry it to the spectrograph through another fiber optic cable, and pass the light through an entrance aperture into the spectrograph. The light will hit a concave diffraction grating and fall on a silicon array detector. The charges induced in the detector will generate an electrical potential which is digitized, displayed as a spectrum, and processed as we will explain shortly. A sketch of the apparatus is shown in Figure 4.1.

In Chapter 1, we explained Beer's Law, using CO_2 absorption in the infrared as an example. Here, the measurement approach is

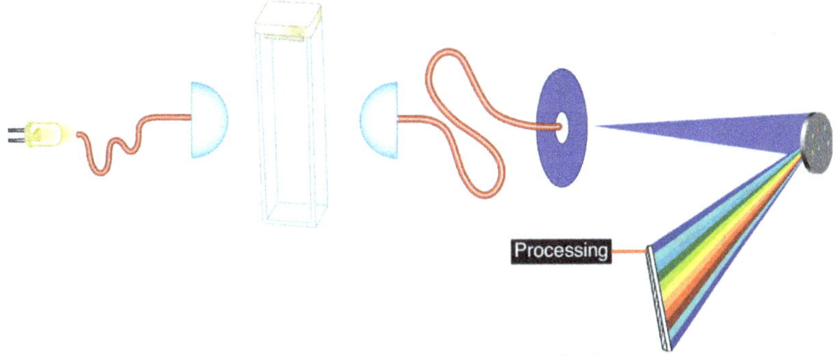

Figure 4.1. Visible spectrometer. Starting at the left, light is generated by an LED, carried through a fiber optic to a collimating lens, transits a specimen container/cuvette, is refocused by another lens to another fiber optic, from which it exits through a pinhole into a spectrometer consisting of a diffraction grating and photodiode array. The blank, and then the sample solution, are observed by placing them, sequentially, into the cuvette.

the same, but the wavelength is different. And now we know enough to ask how precisely we can measure absorbance, what may be misleading about the measurement, and how confident we can be in the result. We are trying to measure the concentration of lead, so we're trying to evaluate

$$C_{meas} = \frac{A}{\varepsilon(\lambda)b} = \frac{\log_{10}\frac{I_0(\lambda)}{I(\lambda)}}{\varepsilon(\lambda)b} \tag{4.1}$$

Equation (4.1) conceals three assumptions. First, it assumes that the only light intensity signal reported is that due to light at the wavelength we desire, having passed from the light source, through the sample, and to the detector without taking any stray paths. Second, it assumes that the only phenomenon to change between the sample signal and the reference signal is that the sample absorbs light. Third, it assumes that if we turn off the light source, the detected signal is zero. All of these assumptions are approximate, not exact. And that means we need to expand equation (4.1) to include additional complexity if we want to get the most precise and accurate answer.

Light that doesn't follow our preconceived path is called stray light. It may refract around a sample rather than through it, or scatter off dust on the grating and hit an inappropriate pixel, or enter the instrument through a gap in the lid. Thus all the intensities need to include a term expressing the influence of stray light. The sample may fluoresce or phosphoresce, generating light at one wavelength based on illumination at a different wavelength. Not much of this light is picked up by the observation system, but it doesn't take much to offset the intensity noticeably. And that assumption of zero signal in the absence of illumination? Remember that detectors all have non-zero noise, so there's always an offset, which is either a dark current or dark charge depending on whether we're monitoring photocurrent or the accumulated charge from integrating signal for a fixed period of time. That gives us

$$C_{meas} = \frac{\log_{10} \frac{I_0(\lambda) - I_{stray} - I_{fluor\_sample} + I_{dark}}{I(\lambda) - I_{stray} - I_{fluor\_bkrnd} + I_{dark}}}{\varepsilon(\lambda) b} \tag{4.2}$$

Since I_{dark} is included in each of the non-dark measurements, any single subtraction automatically cancels the mean dark current without ever measuring it explicitly. Here we do two subtractions, so we actually have to add the dark current back in once to fully cancel its magnitude. Often, measuring stray and fluoresced light is difficult. If it's ignored, we get a nonlinear relationship between absorbance and concentration. There will be a minimum absorbance we can reliably measure, based on how little $I(\lambda)$ has to change from $I_0(\lambda)$ to be detectable, and there will be a maximum based on how close $I(\lambda)$ can be to 0 but distinguishable from that nominal level. I was fortunate to be in the research group where the details of these limitations were worked out (although I had nothing to do with that work). The key paper is Rothman *et al.* (1975). That paper doesn't mention fluorescence explicitly; adding it in here just complicates the propagation of error calculation a little.

What about the denominator in equation (4.2)? We use a calibration curve to determine $\varepsilon(\lambda)$, which means that photometric errors in making the measurement contaminate the accuracy of any measurements that employ the Beer's Law curve that we fit to the calibration data. Then there's *b*. One expects that all 1 cm cuvettes have the same width. They're close, but not exact. More problematic is that any rotation of the cuvette about its vertical axis refractively offsets the light beam and changes the path length as shown in Figure 4.2. This is one source of sample cell positioning error. The other is that the walls of each cuvette may contain imperfections, bubbles, scratches, and small departures from flatness. So that cuvettes can be removed from their molds, all cuvettes have some slight slope or draft to the walls, making the path length slightly non-uniform across the beam. If the walls were perfectly parallel, they'd form a Fabry-Perot interferometer (look it up if interested; details add to complexity of analyzing this problem without adding essential insight).

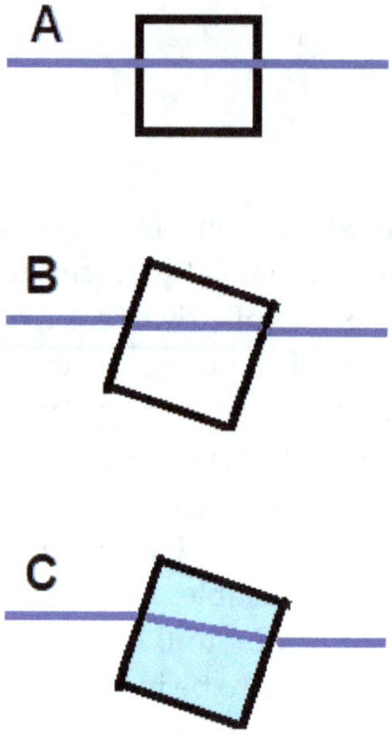

Figure 4.2. Effect of cuvette rotation on light beam path.

Inset A: perfectly aligned cuvette. Regardless of contents, collimated light goes straight through, undeviated. Cuvette may act as a Fabry-Perot interferometer, modulating throughput as a function of wavelength.
Inset B: rotated cuvette filled with air. Beam is translated, path length increases, but interference effect is reduced.
Inset C: Contents of cuvette have refractive index different from air. Beam translates, path length increases and is a function of wavelength since refractive index changes with wavelength.

The offset and path length for the rotated cuvette depends on wavelength thanks to Snell's Law. For light not normally incident on (perpendicular to) an interface,

$$n_1(\lambda)\sin\theta_1 = n_2(\lambda)\sin\theta_2 \tag{4.3}$$

Going through a cuvette, there are at least two media, air (or, in some cases, vacuum where $n(\lambda) = 1$), and the wall material of the cuvette. If the cuvette is filled with air, the light emerges from each wall at the same angle it entered, but translated slightly. If an instrument is perfectly aligned for a squared-up cuvette, then there is slight misalignment if the cuvette is rotated. But if the cuvette is filled with something other than air (which it typically is — it has a sample inside or why would we be using the cuvette in the first place?), then the path length through the liquid increases with cuvette rotation. Further, since the sample, like all materials, has a wavelength-dependent refractive index, the path length is also wavelength dependent. Ignoring non-uniformity in the cuvette walls,

$$b(\theta_1,\lambda)=\frac{b_0}{\cos\theta_2}=\frac{b_0}{\cos\left(\arcsin\left(\frac{n_1(\lambda)\sin\theta_1}{n_2(\lambda)}\right)\right)}=\frac{b_0 n_2(\lambda)}{\sqrt{(n_2(\lambda))^2-(n_1(\lambda)\sin\theta_1)^2}} \tag{4.4}$$

While, for many purposes, $n_1(\lambda) = 1.000$ in air, the value is not exactly 1 and the effect of non-unity refractive index in air is readily observed in atomic spectroscopy. If we use the unity refractive index approximation for air, then for water in a 1.00 cm cuvette, rotated 1°, the path length increases by 7.6 μm for $\lambda = 200$ nm while increasing by 8.6 μm at $\lambda = 700$ nm. This is less than 0.1% larger than the nominal path length, and so matters little for many routine measurements. However, for the highest precision measurements, it is measurable (Rothman *et al.*, 1975).

And then there's another problem due to refractive index. Any time light travels between media, some of the light is reflected, some transmitted, some scattered, and (potentially) some absorbed. So the assumption that only absorbance occurs is almost never true. The best one can hope for is that the solution employed in measuring $I_0(\lambda)$ is close in refractive index to that used for measuring $I(\lambda)$ so that reflective losses and optical path length are indistinguishable between sample and reference. Considering that refractive index variation can be used to detect compounds at modest concentrations, this often-ignored parameter is actually critically important. Omitting the effect of refractive index leads to baseline offsets and, of course, additional noise.

When all of this is taken together, the useful absorbance range for common spectrophotometers is $0.02 < A < 2.0$. There are specialized situations where A as low as 10^{-6} can be reliably measured, as can absorbances up to 6, but without exquisite control of temperature, solution composition, vibration, and light source stability, the useful range is narrower. I have personally never measured an absorbance less than 0.0001 nor one higher than 4.

Now let's see how to measure lead in Flint tap water.

4.2 Dithizone Determination of Lead

1,5-Diphenylthiocarbazone or dithizone is a commercially available reactant. Thus, while we could talk about how it is synthesized, we won't. To avoid the need for large amounts of organic solvents and a lot of messy sample handling, the reactant is first dissolved in 2-propanol (isopropyl alcohol) and the compound stabilized in water by using cetyltrimethylammonium bromide or CTAB for short. CTAB is a cationic surfactant — the organic part of the molecule has a positive charge. Most people are more familiar with anionic or neutral surfactants: soap and detergent. CTAB keeps the otherwise insoluble dithizone suspended in solution (once the dithizone plus isopropanol are added to the sample, the dithizone would precipitate without CTAB). So that $Pb(dithizone)_2$ forms to (or mostly to) completion, there must be about a factor of 100 excess dithizone. Since we know that the safe lead level is below 7 nM and we know that at times Flint's tap water was more than a factor of 20 above that level, we can make a decision on whether the water is safe, slightly unsafe, or undrinkable if we target measuring lead up to 140 nM, meaning the dithizone needs to be 28 μM in the analysis solution (140 nM lead times 100 = 14 μM, but since 2 dithizone moieties complex each lead ion, we need twice as much or 28 μM in complexing agent). This sounds feasible.

However, other metal ions can also react with dithizone. Specifically, other ions likely to be in tap water including Fe^{3+}, Cu^{2+}, Ni^{2+}, and Zn^{2+} will react. While iron may make the water look brown, it isn't harmful (in fact, it's an important nutrient). Zinc is used in throat lozenges and shampoo, so it's not a health risk (if not consumed in excess). A little bit of copper and nickel are also needed for nutrition. But if there's a large amount of these metals, they could react with all of the dithizone, and then there's little left over for the lead. Sodium tartrate (similar to potassium tartrate, otherwise known as cream of tartar) can be used as a masking reagent for interfering levels up to 10 times the lead level, but iron is likely to be at levels far higher than this — the Environmental Protection Agency standard for allowable iron in tap water is 300 ppb (https://www.epa.gov/sdwa/drinking-water-regulations-and-contaminants#List, 11/10/2020). There are plenty of additional parameters to be optimized. See Table 1 of Khan's method if you care about the details. We'll jump to the absorbance measurement.

The optimum wavelength is 500 nm (green). Khan doesn't specify whether he used 500 ± 1 nm or 500 ± 100 nm. He says $\varepsilon(\lambda) = 3.99 \times 10^5$ L mol^{-1} cm^{-1}, implying that this molar absorptivity is known to three significant figures, but gives no data to defend that precision. But what he does state is that if one has no other measurement problems, complications, or limitations, the concentration of lead that gives $A = 0.001$ in equation (4.1) is 10 ppb. Without preconcentration (which we ruled out because of toxicity and environmental impact limitations), an unhealthy level of lead gives a signal so weak that the Khan method can't detect it. This variant of the dithizone method for lead cannot provide a useful measurement.

And you, dear reader, are likely fuming: "Then why did you go into all this detail about spectrometry and chemistry and interferences when you knew you'd end up saying, 'method...cannot provide a useful measurement' at the necessary level?" A snarky answer would be: why do detective mysteries seek to have the identity of the criminal materialize from an odd direction in the last chapter? But a more justifiable answer is: without doing a deep dive on a measurement to see how well it works, one cannot judge whether it's a useful approach to pursue. Cost, availability, and long establishment of the method all suggested, "let's do it," but without deep knowledge (and I left a lot of stuff out!), one ends up making technically correct but useless measurements. The signal is there, but it is insufficient. The reason Alanah Fitch could write an entire book on lead is that there are many ways to sense the element, many of which are appropriate under specific circumstances, but not under all circumstances. If we were trying to quantify lead between 20 and 2,000 ppb, the dithizone method might work well (although at the high end of that range, one might not have enough excess reactant to keep the Beer's Law plot linear — it would start to approach some asymptotic maximum absorbance). So what can we do for the good citizens of Flint to check on the lead in their water?

4.3 ICP-Mass Spectrometry

What happens when you put a charged object in an electric field? Positive ions (cations) accelerate towards the negative side of the field while negative ions (anions) move to the positive side. The dynamics can usually ignore relativity and use Newton's equations of motion:

$$\mathbf{F} = m\mathbf{a} = q\mathbf{E} \tag{4.5}$$

where **F** is force in Newtons, m is mass in kg, **a** is acceleration in m s^{-2}, q is charge in Coulombs, and **E** is electric field in volts m^{-1}. If we generate ions that stand still, then pulse an electric field to some value for a short period of time T, then turn the field off, we can provide constant acceleration for that brief time.

$$\begin{aligned}
\mathbf{a} &= \frac{q}{m}\mathbf{E} \\
\mathbf{v} &= \int_0^T \frac{q}{m}\mathbf{E}dt + \mathbf{v}_0 \\
\mathbf{v} &= \frac{qT\mathbf{E}}{m} + \mathbf{v}_0
\end{aligned} \tag{4.6}$$

The initial velocity, $\mathbf{v}_0$, is the velocity with which the ion enters the electric field. It's often assumed to be 0, but in fact there's usually thermal motion as the ions are in the gas phase. Even if the average $\mathbf{v}_0$ is 0, there will be thermal motion around 0, so different nominally identical ions will have slightly different velocities.

How long does it take for the ion to get some distance d from where it was when the field turned off?

$$t_{transit} = \frac{d}{|\mathbf{v}|} = \frac{m}{q} \frac{d}{T|\mathbf{E}|} \tag{4.7}$$

The charge on any ion is some integer multiple of the charge on an electron, the distance, pulse time, and electric field are all independent of ion mass, so the transit time is proportional to the mass of the ion. One cannot easily tell the difference between two isotopes $^{65}Cu^+$ and $^{65}Zn^+$, but distinguishing $^{63}Cu^+$ from $^{65}Cu^+$ is easy. Doing exactly this experiment is time-of-flight mass spectrometry.

As you might imagine, there are all sorts of combinations of electric and magnetic fields that can be used to steer ions once they're accelerated, and the sorts of arguments we've made so far about noise, and getting a signal above that noise, are among the factors to consider for selecting among these various techniques. Many of the specifics haven't been given yet (see the next few chapters), so we won't be quite as critical of mass spectrometry as we were about optical spectrometry and the sample preparation that goes with it. It turns out that time-of-flight mass spectrometry is one of the ways we might look for lead in drinking water, but another approach is more common: triple quadrupole mass spectrometry. For what may be the only time in this book, I will spare you the equations (if curious, look up Mathieu equations). Figure 4.3 shows the parts of the instrument, but not in a lot of detail.

The solution containing the sample is vaporized with an ionized argon plasma as described in the next paragraph. The resulting vapor cloud is sprayed at a pinhole inlet that admits the atoms and ions to a region where the air and water vapor from the solution are pumped away. The bare ions are focused into a quadrupole (four rods used to generate a time-dependent, shaped electric field), and only a narrow range of masses gets through that quadrupole without being steered out of the ion beam. The ions then pass through a region with a low pressure of ammonia or helium

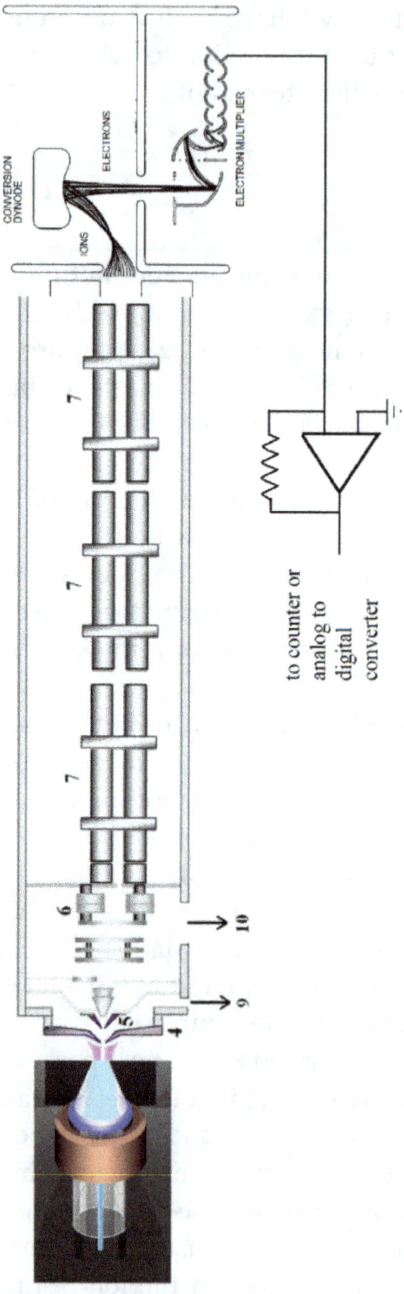

Figure 4.3. Inductively coupled plasma triple quadrupole mass spectrometer for trace metal analysis.

gas so that any ions carrying small molecules or other atoms with them are broken apart into atomic ions, and then another quadrupole separates the mixture so generated. The ions are detected with a device called an electron multiplier. The ion crashes into the first metallic electrode of the electron multiplier just like a bowling ball hitting the pins. The electrons (analogous to the pins) go flying. They in turn hit another electrode held at a positive potential compared to the first electrode. The crash/electron ejection happens again. This happens on 8–10 electrodes, so that a single ion generates a pulse of several thousand electrons, enough that an amplifier can recognize that something crashed into the electron multiplier to begin the avalanche. By counting how many pulses occur, one detects how many ions of the chosen mass get through the instrument. Of course, one can tune to any reasonable number of mass intervals and look at the composition of all the ions flooding into the inlet. If there are too many pulses to distinguish them, one can simply measure the average current. In some sense, this is no different than the rain drop analogy at the beginning of the noise chapter, except that instead of rain drops we start with ions.

Let's discuss how ions are generated. Why not just spray water into the instrument? After all, lead in solution is already a positive ion, Pb^{2+}. The debris typically in drinking water would prevent us from seeing a lot of the lead. Bacteria or viruses might adsorb lead ions, or particulates might not vaporize, trapping some of the lead. The most common way to vaporize the metals and turn them into (typically, singly charged) cations is with a fancy blowtorch called an inductively coupled plasma (ICP). A 1 kW radio frequency transmitter is attached to an induction coil and a stream of argon gas directed through the center of the coil (the gas stream is usually confined inside a quartz tube). The electromagnetic field in the inductor accelerates any ions in the argon stream and breaks the argon gas into electrons and argon ions. These in turn can be accelerated by the field, and eventually one gets an argon flame, bright blue in color, and many thousands of degrees in temperature. The water sample is pumped through the center of this flame. The water evaporates, molecules break into individual atoms, and particulates vaporize as well. Mind you, getting this process so it works just right has taken research from the mid-1960s onward, but it is now commercially routine.

If you have a spare hundred thousand dollars or more, you can get a combination of an ICP and mass spectrometer (MS) to detect and quantify metals and ions in water. You'll need liquid argon to supply the carrier gas for the argon flame, vacuum pumps for the mass spectrometer, and plenty of electricity. It would be a good idea to learn of all the complications in making sure the ions are easily detected, and of course you'll need standard solutions whose lead content is carefully controlled (just as we needed CO_2 standards to measure levels of that species). But it's doable, for a price.

4.4 Direct Assay of Lead in Water by ICP-MS

The good news is that mass spectrometry coupled to an ionization source can detect metals at levels not just of parts per million or parts per billion, but often at parts per trillion. The bad news is that one does not (yet?) have one ICP-MS per home, nor one per block, nor usually one per large-sized town. They are operated by skilled technicians and scientists trained in their idiosyncrasies. The EPA method for lead in water runs 57 pages (https://www.epa.gov/sites/production/files/2015-06/documents/epa-200.8.pdf, 11/10/2020), but is capable of quantifying lead in water at concentrations less than 1 ppb up to hundreds of ppm. It is noteworthy that while the EPA method goes into great detail about handling and preserving the sample, in making standards and calibrating the instrument, it says very little about the instrument itself. In other words, it assumes that a signal is obtained and presumes the engineers got the instrument design right. The method says what to do, but does not explain why. If something goes amiss, how will the user know? How will the person submitting the specimen know?

Thus, determining if lead contamination is a problem ceases to be a measurement problem. Instead, it becomes a problem of resources: instruments, personnel, time and means to send samples to the instrumented laboratories, and communication of the results to those concerned. Further, people who wonder if their water is clean have to wait for a water sample to be taken to the lab, measurements made, and results returned. Getting water from source to lab entails preserving the sample. For example, if the sample is transported in a glass bottle, ions may stick to the glass, and at low levels may actually be cleared away from the solution. If the sample is transported in a plastic bottle, plasticizers may diffuse into the solution and complex (surround and bind with) some of the metal ions. Metallic containers cannot be used — metals will leach into the solution. While careful adjustment of acidity may preserve the sample optimally, there's always a worry that delay may alter the results. And then there's a matter of trust. The Flint water problem was, at root, a political problem, where minimizing cost overwhelmed sound engineering and public health. If the same people who caused the problem tell you they've solved it, would you believe them? They're also the people paying for the analyses.

4.5 Correlated Noise Example

As promised in Chapter 2, we just slipstreamed an example of a system with correlated noise (or a system with high covariance — the terminology varies by field) into the book, and if I had wanted to, I could have snuck it right past you! That inductively coupled plasma? It's a treasure trove of coupled fluctuations. The amount of sample entering the plasma is proportional to the speed of the pump feeding sample into the uptake tube. The plasma of course heats the solution as it sprays into the plasma, but the sprayed solution cools the plasma. Thus, temperature fluctuations depend not only on the behavior of the power supply, but also on the sample feed rate. Since the extent of sample ionization influences the proportion of lead (or anything else) that vaporizes and ionizes, there is coupling between solution uptake, temperature, and signal. Because the solution breaks into droplets, the plasma cannot be spatially homogeneous or even smoothly changing in temperature; it will be coolest near the vaporizing drops — exactly where it needs to be hottest to ensure sample vaporization! This coupling has been studied since the 1960s (at the risk of leaving out many important authors, look up: Gary Hieftje, Gary Horlick, John Olesik, Paul Farnsworth), and there is still much being learned (for example, vaporization of samples containing organic solvents is different than vaporization from aqueous solutions, and mixed solvents are really complicated). There is yet another coupling that was difficult to spot initially, but once you read about it, it will look obvious in retrospect (being obvious in retrospect but not in prospect is the mark of discovery — and we'll see in Chapter 11 that unpredictability is built into the structure of the universe). The plasma spins on its axis, so that there are noise components depending on the coupling of gas flow with sample flow and alignment of all the mechanical components (Belchamber & Horlick, 1982). Thus, there is a non-zero correlation between sample input rate and gas input rate on the ion signal, even though one would think that these two variables would be independent.

Covariance isn't limited to chemical measurements. Few people in the U.S. contracted Ebola during its various outbursts. Those who did were people who were in Africa, helping to suppress the outbreak. Such individuals doubtlessly had above average numbers of frequent flyer miles. I don't know if anyone did a statistical study of the correlation between frequent flyer miles and probability of getting Ebola, but I suspect that it would be higher than the correlation between playing poker and getting Ebola. Failure to search for primary causes of phenomena, particularly where there is high covariance, can lead people in wild directions (it is all too easy to imagine someone generating a web meme: flying causes Ebola!). If the covariant parameter is one that excites people with an ax to grind, much destruction can result. Continuing the Ebola example, some environmentalists would like to see international air travel decrease to reduce CO_2 injection into the atmosphere and to cut down on propagation of communicable diseases. If "flying causes Ebola" were true, that would support both arguments. In fact, flying helped to bring medical staff from all around the world to end the virally caused disease outbreak, and excessive travel could have spread the virus. "It's more complicated than it first appears." Covariance can be a false source of signals.

4.6 Summary

In seeking to understand a part of the world, we design experiments to pile up events which, individually, might be perceived as noise, but, because of their correlation with the question we're asking and the way we're manipulating the world, we construe to be signal, a measure of a desired quantity. The physics, chemistry, or biology at the root of the matter is transduced to electrical quantities and then digitized into numbers, the meaning of which are putatively related to the original question. We have seen that even when the measurement is carefully designed, it may not solve some specific problem, and even when the details of a measurement are not described in great detail, we still may learn what it is we seek. This is a hint at where we are headed: how much information can we have, how much information do we need to have, and how much is inaccessible in our attempt to understand and control our lives? It's slightly too soon to answer that question, but at least we're beginning to sense glimmers.

But we can also perceive why there are limits to understanding by individuals, societies, and all of humanity. Information is often hierarchical. The family in Flint who sees their children being poisoned knows that Someone Should Do Something. But what? How? The person fabricating the electron multiplier for the instrument that will make the measurement that will convince the Water Department to talk to the politician who will have to sell a bill to the legislature to pay for repairing the damage has skills unlike those of anyone else along the chain of information. If there's a flaw in the design, fabrication, shipment, installation, or use of that electron multiplier, people will die. Even if there *isn't* a flaw in the electron multiplier, there are many other failure points to overcome before the problem is solved. In a society that is efficient at finding people to blame and inefficient in helping develop mutually supportive teams to seek out, propose, fund, and execute solutions to problems, it is wise to remember that every step from causing the problem to maintaining a solution once it's in place requires much information, many measurements, and many people, all in communication. Getting signal above noise is difficult, even in simple circumstances (remember those raindrops?). How can we lower the noise without squelching the signal? That's a subject for a different book.

5

Uncertainty – Quantum and Classical

The presence of noise means we aren't quite sure what the mean value of a measurement may be. This sort of uncertainty can be thought of as being due to subtle differences from one measurement to another from all sorts of perturbations and uncorrelated influences on a rigorously valid procedure. There are, however, uncertainties that are fundamental. Three such sources are: quantum uncertainty, bandwidth uncertainty, and nonlinear uncertainty. The latter two are considered classical since they are independent of the two most prominent early 20th-century physics revolutions of quantum mechanics and relativity. However, nonlinear uncertainty was researched by Henri Poincaré in the early 1900s and is a third 20th-century physics revolutionary idea, less discussed than the ideas stemming from Einstein's Annus Mirabilis of 1905, but perhaps more important on a day-to-day basis. Let's see how each of these works.

5.1 Quantum Uncertainty

For a quantum particle, momentum and position cannot be simultaneously known to better than the value of Planck's constant. That is, if particles have a mass m, conventionally (since the time of Isaac

Newton) one would expect them to have a momentum $\mathbf{p} = m\mathbf{v}$ with units of kg m s^{-1}. However, if one starts with the presumption that particles are also waves, the expression for momentum is

$$\mathbf{p} = -i\hbar\nabla = -i\hbar\left(\hat{x}\frac{\partial}{\partial x} + \hat{y}\frac{\partial}{\partial y} + \hat{z}\frac{\partial}{\partial z}\right) = -i\hbar\left(\hat{r}\frac{\partial}{\partial r} + \hat{\theta}\frac{1}{r}\frac{\partial}{\partial \theta} + \hat{\varphi}\frac{1}{r\sin\theta}\frac{\partial}{\partial \varphi}\right) \tag{5.1}$$

where (x, y, z) are Cartesian coordinates, (r, θ, φ) are spherical coordinates, h is Planck's constant, $6.62607004 \times 10^{-34}$ kg m^2 s^{-1}, $\hbar = h/2\pi = 1.05457180 \times 10^{-34}$ kg m^2 s^{-1}, and the gradient operator ∇ can be expressed in any convenient coordinate system with symmetry appropriate to a problem. This leads to the uncertainty one faces in trying to simultaneously measure momentum and position or energy and time:

$$\begin{aligned} \Delta p \Delta x &\geq \hbar \\ \Delta E \Delta t &\geq \hbar \end{aligned} \tag{5.2}$$

One can experimentally see the blurring of energy when using very short (small Δt) laser pulses to measure optical spectra. The values Δp, Δx, and so on, are the ranges of the respective parameters that can be measured or computed, given the uncertainty in the complementary parameter. Thus, if you know that an atom is located somewhere inside a box with side 1 nm, you can measure its momentum with uncertainty of 1.05457×10^{-34} J s/10^{-9} m = 1.05×10^{-25} kg m s^{-1}. For a molecule with a mass of 100 atomic mass units or 1.66×10^{-25} kg, if momentum were only due to classical linear motion, the velocity would be constrained only to ± 0.6 m s^{-1}, the pace of a comfortable stroll. Yet molecules are often confined to locations a lot smaller than 1 nm on a side for billions of years. What's missing? Momentum need not only be bulk motion; there can be internal angular and spin momenta that don't depend on mass.

Because h seems small on a human scale, one might think that this sort of uncertainty doesn't matter except in exotic, small-scale situations. In fact, the quantum limitation, at least for the form of the energy expression in equation (5.2), is clearly evident in the operation of the internet, broadcast radio, and auditory communications. We brought up the quantum phenomena not because we're going to discuss them further, but to point out that quantum uncertainty is not where humanity finds most of its constraints in understanding the world. Rather, classical uncertainty makes the world sufficiently fuzzy that both what is knowable and the rate at which we can learn what is known are limited and constrained.

5.2 Classical Bandwidth Uncertainty

The essential mathematics covered here were studied by 19th-century mathematician Jean-Baptiste Joseph Fourier and 20th-century electrical engineer Harry Nyquist.

Suppose you observe a signal for a fixed period of time T. There are several possibilities of how the signal changes during the observation time. It could be constant. It could have one value for most of the time interval and then a different value for the rest of the time interval. It could change several times during T. Or it could be varying so rapidly that no matter how fast you look at it with available equipment, every measurement is different. If it is changing every instance you examine the signal, is that variation due to noise or due to the process you're trying to characterize? And how do you distinguish the source of variation in each instance?

Fourier looked at flipping the viewpoint from seeing a series of measurements at $t = 0$, $t = t_1$, $t = t_2$, ..., $t_N = T$ to a view of the frequency make-up of the data. In other words, instead of looking at a sine wave like in Figure 5.1, he looked at it like in Figure 5.2.

In Figure 5.1, I plotted $y = \sin(2\pi t/20)$, listing times in 1 ms increments from 0 to 160 ms. In Figure 5.2, I plotted the signal as a function of frequency. The sine wave oscillates once every 20 ms, or 50 times per second, or 50 Hertz (Hz). The amplitude is 1 at 50 Hz, and 0 everywhere else. Notice how compact this representation is. A single amplitude/frequency combination summarizes an infinite amount of data, were that data plotted as a function of time.

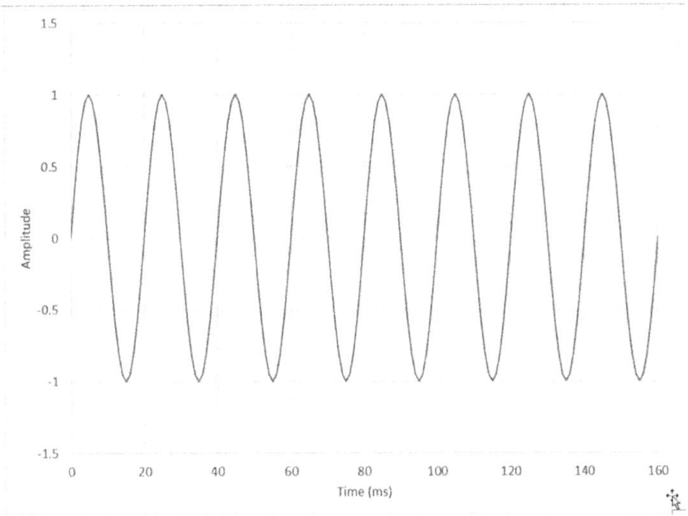

Figure 5.1. Sine wave as a function of time.

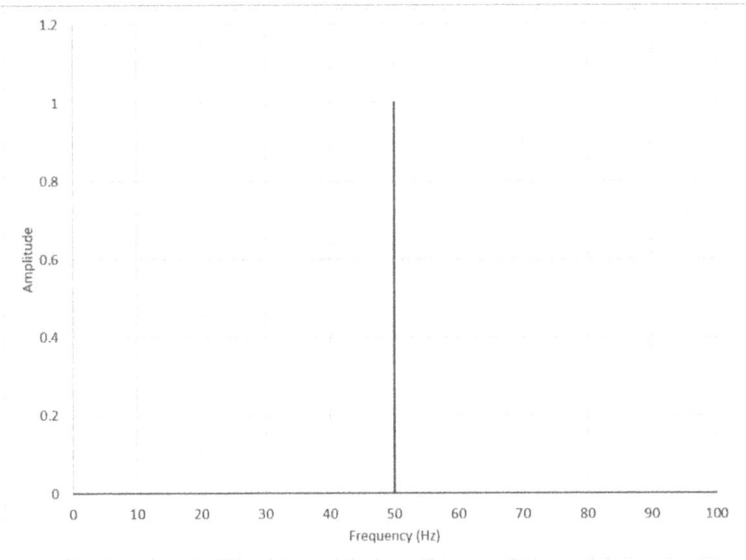

Figure 5.2. Sine wave as a function of frequency.

Frequency

This is a good time to talk about the many meanings of the word "frequency." We will frequently (often) use the word, but because it can have so many meanings, it can be confusing. Frequency means:

1. 1/period of a periodic function.
2. How many times in a fixed interval a repetitive event (dubbed a pulse) occurs.
3. Speed of light divided by wavelength.
4. For a stream of pulses with gaps in the pulse stream, 1/time between when the groups of pulses start. Thus there is a frequency inside each group of pulses and a second frequency describing the repetition rate of the groups.
5. For each pulse in a group, 1/pulse width is the lowest frequency that can be represented by that pulse.
6. For nearly periodic waveforms where the amplitude is not constant, frequency can be 1/period of the wave, absent modulation (modulation is the variation of waveform amplitude), 1/period of modulation, the sum of carrier and modulation frequencies, or the difference between those frequencies.
7. How often a measurement is made in a specific time interval.
8. For a stream of particles (typically ions, electrons, or photons), how many are produced or pass a given point per unit time.
9. In summary, frequency represents a count of some phenomenon within a fixed measurement interval.

We will frequently use the word "frequency" henceforth. Please see the box above that discusses the many ways "frequency" is used.

What is consistent in all the definitions and explanations is that frequency (either f or ν, depending on whether an author prefers

Latin or Greek alphabets and whether f has some other meaning in a context) has units of 1/time or 1/distance. Yes, there can be spatial frequency as well as temporal frequency. Which brings to mind several other symbols: $\omega = 2\pi\nu$, which gives frequency in radians per second instead of cycles per second, $k = 2\pi/\lambda$ (usually combined with a directional vector to indicate the direction of wave propagation), and $\bar{\nu} = 1/\lambda$, the wavenumber. Further confusing everyone is that the metric named unit for wavenumbers is the Kayser, not in m^{-1} but in cm^{-1}. Why? Convenience. 500 nm light, in the middle of the green part of the visible spectrum, is at 20,000 cm^{-1}. This corresponds to 2,000,000 m^{-1}. In the infrared part of the optical spectrum, energies are between 400 and 4000 cm^{-1}. These CGS units have been so pervasive for so many years that there's no motivation to move the decimal point two places just for consistency. It's a habit!

Back to the main thrust here, note that for a measurement of duration T, the lowest frequency one can measure is $1/T$. What happens if the process being studied is at a lower frequency?

What can one make of the plot in Figure 5.3? While the caption tells you how I made it, if you ran into this without me telling you what I did, all you'd know is that there's a hump of data. Is it a single pulse? Part of a train of pulses? Part of a sine wave? An inverted parabola? You can't know. One of the well-recognized ways data can be deceptive is if one assumes that data outside the observation window has some presumed shape or value. Extrapolation is dangerous. It should only be done when there is strong reason to believe the extrapolation is valid, based on similar experiments where additional measurements showed the form expected outside a narrower window. For a 200 ms window, the lowest frequency one can work with is 1/200 ms = 5 Hz. (It turns out there are upper limits too, but understanding that has to wait for Chapter 6!).

Which is where Fourier comes into the picture. He looks at data as shown in Figure 5.3 and asks, "what is the frequency makeup of

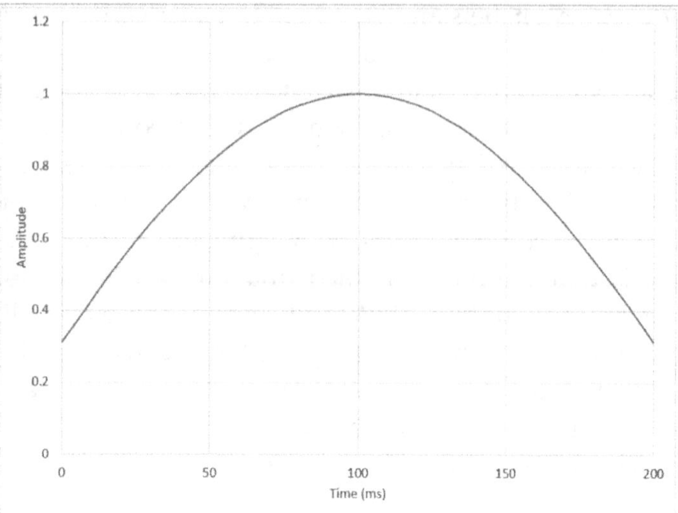

Figure 5.3. 2 Hz data observed for 200 ms starting 25 ms after the sine crosses 0.

that waveform?" There is an average signal level S_0. There's a component at the lowest frequency one can have in the time window available or the fundamental frequency $f_1 = 5$ Hz. And then there are contributions at higher frequencies or harmonics of the fundamental: $2 \times f_1 = f_2 = 10$ Hz, $3 \times f_1 = f_3 = 15$ Hz, and so on. How do we determine the contribution at each frequency? By carrying out a Fourier transform, as first mentioned in Chapter 2. There are two ways to describe the Fourier transform for continuous functions as in Figure 5.3. One uses only real numbers and the other uses complex numbers. Most undergraduate textbooks I have seen use real numbers because they are more familiar to people, but electrical engineering texts almost always move to complex numbers because the manipulations are more efficient. I will choose complex numbers here because common spreadsheet software such as *Microsoft Excel* has a Fourier transform function available in the Data Analysis Add-in. (I wish the default was to install the Add-ins during program installation, but it isn't. On the File menu drop-down,

Options at the bottom brings up a list, of which Add-ins is the last, and Data Analysis can be installed into the Data tab by activating that Add-in. *XLMiner* is a *GoogleDocs* analog to Data Analysis.). After transforming, you can get back to a real spectrum (see Ng & Horlick, 1981 for details), but you can't avoid dealing with complex numbers.

We start with Euler's formula:

$$e^{ix} = \cos x + i \sin x = 1 + ix - \frac{x^2}{2!} - \frac{ix^3}{3!} + \frac{x^4}{4!} + \frac{ix^5}{5!} \pm \cdots \tag{5.3}$$

and $i = \sqrt{-1}$. Further,

$$\cos x = \frac{e^{ix} + e^{-ix}}{2} \qquad \sin x = \frac{e^{ix} - e^{-ix}}{2i} \tag{5.4}$$

As long as you're happy that i is simply a way to express the square root of −1, a number that can't be computed using only real numbers, everything else works just the way any other number works in ordinary algebra. It follows that harmonics are orthonormal and sines and cosines of the same frequency are orthonormal. "Orthonormal?" The integral of a function times its complex conjugate across one period is 1 (or can be made 1, i.e., "normalized" by multiplying the function by a constant), while the integral of a function times any other function in the set under consideration (harmonics, sin or cos of a given harmonic) is 0.

$$\int_0^T e^{i(\omega_0 t+\varphi)} e^{-i(\omega_0 t+\varphi)} dt = \int_0^T dt = T$$

$$\int_0^T e^{i(n\omega_0 t+\varphi)} e^{-i(\omega_0 t+\varphi)} dt = \int_0^T e^{i((n-1)\omega_0 t)} dt = \left.\frac{e^{i((n-1)\omega_0 t)}}{i(n-1)\omega_0}\right|_0^T = \frac{e^{i((n-1)\omega_0 T)} - 1}{i(n-1)\omega_0} = \frac{1-1}{i(n-1)\omega_0} = 0$$

$$\int_0^T \sin\omega t \cos\omega t\, dt = \int_0^T \frac{e^{i\omega t} - e^{-i\omega t}}{2i} \frac{e^{i\omega t} + e^{-i\omega t}}{2} dt = \int_0^T \frac{e^{i2\omega t} - e^{-i2\omega t}}{4i} dt = \left.\frac{e^{i2\omega t} - e^{-i2\omega t}}{-8\omega}\right|_0^T$$
$$= \left.\frac{\sin 2\omega t}{-4}\right|_0^T = 0 \tag{5.5}$$

Thus, the normalization constant for $e^{i(\omega t+\varphi)}$ is $T^{-1/2}$, and we can find the contribution of any harmonic to a given waveform by carrying out:

$$f(t)=\sum_{n=-\infty}^{\infty} c_n e^{i(n\omega_0 t)}$$

$$\int_0^T f(t)e^{-i(m\omega_0 t)}dt=\int_0^T \sum_{n=0}^{\infty} c_n e^{i(n\omega_0 t)}e^{-i(m\omega_0 t)}dt=\int_0^T c_m e^{i(m\omega_0 t)}e^{-i(m\omega_0 t)}dt=c_m T$$

$$c_m=\frac{1}{T}\int_0^T f(t)e^{-i(m\omega_0 t)}dt$$

(5.6)

We can get all the complex coefficients c_m just by integrating the original function, multiplied by complex exponentials of the harmonics. Whether you use *Mathematica, Macsyma, R, Wolfram Alpha,* or your favorite hard-copy integral table (Gradshteyn & Ryzhik, 1980 is mine), it's quite straightforward from here. The case $m = 0$ is special because the integral always gives a real number — the average value of the function in the observed interval. In the case of the function in Figure 5.3 where $T = 0.2$ s, we already know that $f(t) = \sin(2\pi(2t + 1/20))$ because I told you, but the time over which we plotted data isn't long enough to see that that's the form of the function. Doing the necessary integrals, we find:

$$c_0=\frac{1}{0.2}\int_0^{0.2}\sin\left(2\pi\left(2t+\frac{1}{20}\right)\right)dt=-5\frac{\cos\left(2\pi\left(2t+\frac{1}{20}\right)\right)}{4\pi}\Bigg|_0^{0.2}$$

$$=5\frac{\cos\left(\frac{2\pi}{20}\right)-\cos\left(\frac{2\pi*9}{20}\right)}{4\pi}=5\frac{2*0.9510565}{4\pi}=0.756827 \qquad (5.7)$$

For all the other harmonics, we take the fundamental frequency as $1/0.2$ s = 5 Hz.

$$
\begin{aligned}
c_m &= \frac{1}{0.2}\int_0^{0.2} \sin\left(2\pi\left(2t+\frac{1}{20}\right)\right)e^{-i2\pi m5t}dt \\
&= \frac{1}{0.2}\int_0^{0.2} e^{-i2\pi m5t}\,\frac{e^{i2\pi\left(2t+\frac{1}{20}\right)}-e^{-i2\pi\left(2t+\frac{1}{20}\right)}}{2i}dt \\
&= -2.5i\int_0^{0.2}\left(e^{i2\pi\left(2t+\frac{1}{20}\right)}-e^{-i2\pi\left(2t+\frac{1}{20}\right)}\right)e^{-i2\pi m5t}dt \\
&= -2.5i\int_0^{0.2}\left(e^{i2\pi\left(t(2-5m)+\frac{1}{20}\right)}-e^{-i2\pi\left(t(2+5m)+\frac{1}{20}\right)}\right)dt \\
&= -2.5i\left(\frac{e^{i2\pi\left(t(2-5m)+\frac{1}{20}\right)}}{i2\pi\,(2-5m)}+\frac{e^{-i2\pi\left(t(2+5m)+\frac{1}{20}\right)}}{i2\pi\,(2+5m)}\right)\Bigg|_0^{0.2} \\
&= -\frac{2.5}{2\pi}\left(\frac{e^{i2\pi\left(t(2-5m)+\frac{1}{20}\right)}}{(2-5m)}+\frac{e^{-i2\pi\left(t(2+5m)+\frac{1}{20}\right)}}{(2+5m)}\right)\Bigg|_0^{0.2} \\
&= -\frac{2.5}{2\pi}\left(\frac{(2+5m)e^{i2\pi\left(t(2-5m)+\frac{1}{20}\right)}+(2-5m)e^{-i2\pi\left(t(2+5m)+\frac{1}{20}\right)}}{4-25m^2}\right)\Bigg|_0^{0.2} \\
&= \frac{2.5\left(\begin{array}{l}(2+5m)e^{i2\pi\left(0.2(2-5m)+\frac{1}{20}\right)}+(2-5m)e^{-i2\pi\left(0.2(2+5m)+\frac{1}{20}\right)} \\ \quad -(2+5m)e^{i2\pi\left(\frac{1}{20}\right)}-(2-5m)e^{-i2\pi\left(\frac{1}{20}\right)}\end{array}\right)}{2\pi\left(25m^2-4\right)}
\end{aligned} \tag{5.8}
$$

This can be further simplified.

$$c_m = \frac{2.5\left((2+5m)e^{i2\pi\left(0.2(2-5m)+\frac{1}{20}\right)} + (2-5m)e^{-i2\pi\left(0.2(2+5m)+\frac{1}{20}\right)} - 4\cos\left(\frac{\pi}{10}\right) - i10m\sin\left(\frac{\pi}{10}\right)\right)}{2\pi\left(25m^2-4\right)}$$

$$= \frac{2.5}{2\pi\left(25m^2-4\right)}\left(\begin{array}{l} -4\cos\left(\frac{\pi}{10}\right) - i10m\sin\left(\frac{\pi}{10}\right) \\ (2+5m)\left(\cos\left(2\pi\left(0.2(2-5m)+\frac{1}{20}\right)\right)\right. \\ \quad \left.+\, i\sin\left(2\pi\left(0.2(2-5m)+\frac{1}{20}\right)\right)\right) \\ +\,(2-5m)\left(\cos\left(2\pi\left(0.2(2+5m)+\frac{1}{20}\right)\right)\right. \\ \quad \left.-\, i\sin\left(2\pi\left(0.2(2+5m)+\frac{1}{20}\right)\right)\right) \end{array}\right) \tag{5.9}$$

Several important points follow from equation (5.9). First, as m gets larger, the magnitude of terms falls off as $1/m$ for some and $1/m^2$ for others. The magnitude of high harmonics is small, but it never goes to 0. Secondly, for a given harmonic $m\nu_0$, both $+m$ and $-m$ terms are combined (thus allowing sines and cosines to be pulled from the complex expressions). Thus

$$f_{|m|} = c_m e^{-i|m|\omega_0 t} + c_{-m} e^{i|m|\omega_0 t} \tag{5.10}$$

Third, because of the symmetry of the function around its peak, the function is even and only cosine terms will survive the combination in equation (5.10). Fourth, the sudden termination of the function at the ends of the interval mean it will be comparatively easy to model the slow changes (low frequency) in the middle of the function, but difficult to model what's happening at the edges. Let's write out expressions for the amplitude and phase of each harmonic.

$$
\begin{aligned}
f_{|m|} = {} & \frac{2.5e^{i2\pi m5t}}{2\pi\left(25m^2-4\right)}\left(\begin{array}{l}
-4\cos\left(\frac{\pi}{10}\right)-i10m\sin\left(\frac{\pi}{10}\right) \\
(2+5m)\Big(\cos\Big(2\pi\Big(0.2(2-5m)+\frac{1}{20}\Big)\Big) \\
\quad +i\sin\Big(2\pi\Big(0.2(2-5m)+\frac{1}{20}\Big)\Big)\Big) \\
\quad +(2-5m)\Big(\cos\Big(2\pi\Big(0.2(2+5m)+\frac{1}{20}\Big)\Big) \\
\quad -i\sin\Big(2\pi\Big(0.2(2+5m)+\frac{1}{20}\Big)\Big)\Big)
\end{array}\right) \\
& +\frac{2.5e^{-i2\pi m5t}}{2\pi\left(25m^2-4\right)}\left(\begin{array}{l}
-4\cos\left(\frac{\pi}{10}\right)+i10m\sin\left(\frac{\pi}{10}\right) \\
(2-5m)\Big(\cos\Big(2\pi\Big(0.2(2+5m)+\frac{1}{20}\Big)\Big) \\
\quad +i\sin\Big(2\pi\Big(0.2(2+5m)+\frac{1}{20}\Big)\Big) \\
\quad +(2+5m)\Big(\cos\Big(2\pi\Big(0.2(2-5m)+\frac{1}{20}\Big)\Big) \\
\quad -i\sin\Big(2\pi\Big(0.2(2-5m)+\frac{1}{20}\Big)\Big)\Big)
\end{array}\right)
\end{aligned}
\tag{5.11}
$$

Now combine terms, and suddenly the expression looks a lot cleaner.

$$f_m(t) = \frac{5}{2\pi\left(25m^2-4\right)}\left(\begin{aligned}&\left(-4\cos\left(\frac{\pi}{10}\right)+(2+5m)\cos\left(2\pi\left(0.2(2-5m)+\frac{1}{20}\right)\right)\right.\\&\left.+(2-5m)\cos\left(2\pi\left(0.2(2+5m)+\frac{1}{20}\right)\right)\right)\cos(2\pi m5t)\\&+\left(10\sin\left(\frac{\pi}{10}\right)+(2-5m)\sin\left(2\pi\left(0.2(2+5m)+\frac{1}{20}\right)\right)\right.\\&\left.-(2+5m)\sin\left(2\pi\left(0.2(2-5m)+\frac{1}{20}\right)\right)\right)\sin(2\pi m5t)\end{aligned}\right) \tag{5.12}$$

Even this can be cleaned up, using trigonometric identities.

$$f_m(t) = \frac{20}{2\pi\left(25m^2-4\right)}\left(\left(\left(\cos\left(\frac{9\pi}{10}\right)\right)-\cos\left(\frac{\pi}{10}\right)\right)\cos(2\pi m5t)\right) \tag{5.13}$$

Now we see the terms fall off as $1/m^2$. Had the waveform not been symmetrical about its midpoint, the $\sin(2\pi m5t)$ term would not have disappeared. Some people would use the identity for $\cos a - \cos b = 2\sin((a+b)/2)\sin((b-a)/2)$. Because the sum of the arguments equals π, that's likely a good idea.

$$\begin{aligned}f_m(t) &= \frac{-20}{2\pi\left(25m^2-4\right)}\left(\sin\left(\frac{8\pi}{5}\right)\cos(2\pi m5t)\right)\\&= \frac{-6.0546138}{25m^2-4}\cos(10\pi mt)\end{aligned} \tag{5.14}$$

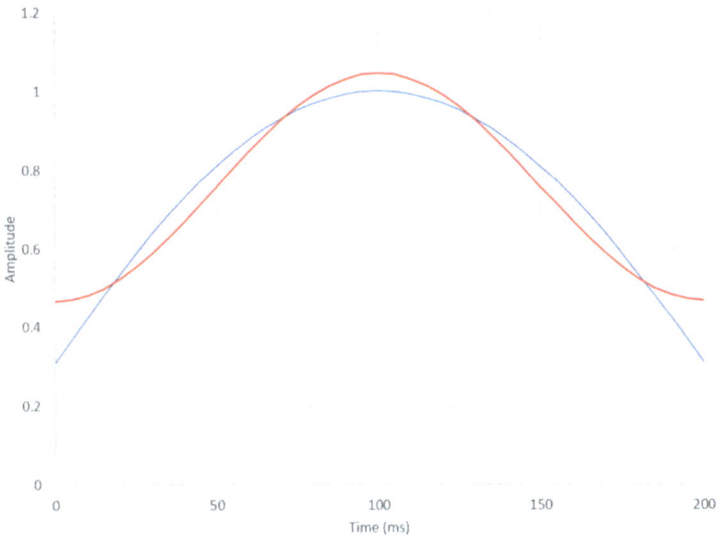

Figure 5.4. Approximating Figure 5.3 using only two Fourier terms, $m = 0$ and $m = 1$.

For $m = 0$, equation (5.14) gives an answer twice as large as we found in equation (5.7). Why? Because we used both positive and negative values of m in deriving equation (5.14) which means if we uncritically employ equation (5.14), we're using both $m = 0$ and $m = -0$. That's double counting! So now let's overlay the approximation from just the $m = 0$ and $m = 1$ terms on Figure 5.3.

Figure 5.4 looks like a fairly good approximation. What happens if we sum up to $m = 5$?

Figure 5.5 shows that a five-term Fourier series is an even better approximation to that 2 Hz sine wave within the observation window. In fact, if there's any significant amount of noise overlaid on the observation, we'd have no way to distinguish this 2 Hz data from a superposition of harmonics of 5 Hz data.

So let's plot the spectrum of these data (Figure 5.6). While this spectrum falls off cleanly, if there were 1% white noise, all data would approach an asymptotic high frequency level of just below 0.01 rather than continuing to fall as $\sim 1/m^2$.

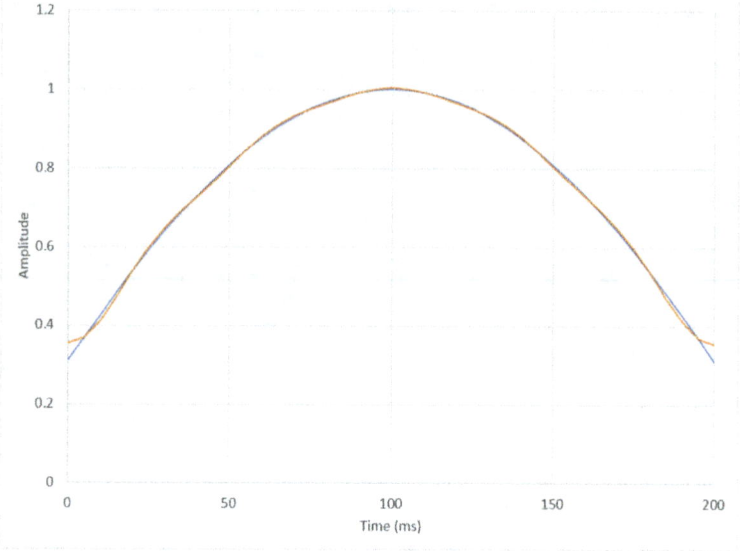

Figure 5.5. Approximating Figure 5.3 using Fourier terms through $m = 5$.

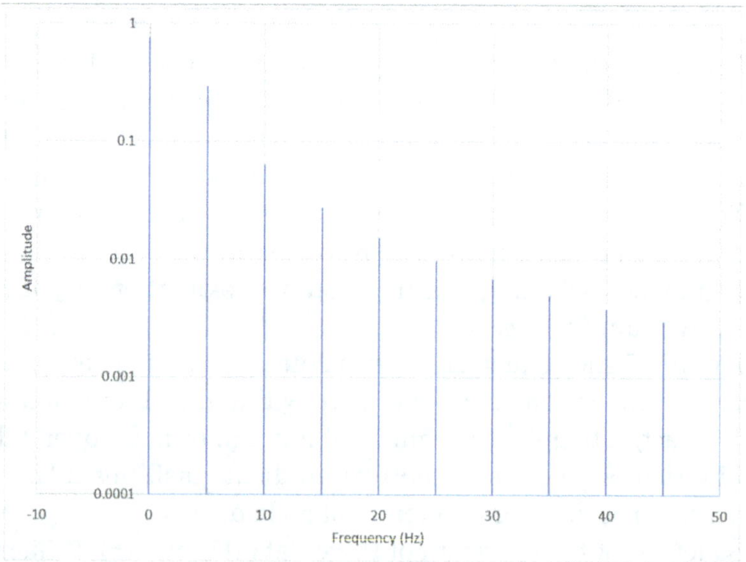

Figure 5.6. Spectrum of 2 Hz sine wave observed for 0.2 s. There is no evidence of any data at 2 Hz because the observation is too brief. Note that amplitude is shown on a logarithmic scale.

Now do you see the problem? Every experiment humans have done is of finite duration. The lowest frequency we can see in data is $1/T$, the duration of the experiment. We cannot know what is happening beyond our experimental window. The longest continuous experiment of which I am aware is a study of viscous flow started by Thomas Parnell in 1930, studying the viscosity of pitch (Wikipedia gives a good enough description). Thus, T as of this writing is ≤92 years. This sets a minimum on the frequencies we can observe directly. The classical uncertainty relationship is:

$$\Delta\nu\,\Delta t \geq 1 \tag{5.15}$$

Notice that this does not mean we cannot observe frequencies smaller than $1/T$, but that we cannot observe them cleanly. As we saw above, a 2 Hz waveform appeared to be a mixture of waveforms with a fundamental frequency of 5 Hz when observed for only 0.2 s ($\Delta t = 0.2$ s, so $\Delta\nu > 5$ Hz). When a signal has a frequency ν_0, but it appears to an observer to be at a frequency $\nu' \neq \nu_0$, the signal is said to be *aliased*. This can sometimes be quite useful. AM radio works by aliasing sound frequencies (32 Hz to 20 kHz) up to the AM radio band (530 kHz to 1600 kHz), transmitting the signal, and then aliasing the sound information back to audio range. Similarly, many instruments including magnetic resonance imaging cameras and stroboscopic motion monitors move frequencies around for various purposes, including signal gathering where interactions are strong, signal digitization within a frequency range that employs economical components, and shifting information to frequency bands where noise is minimal. A particularly ingenious way to make white light is to start with short-pulsed green light and shorten the pulse to broaden the spectral coverage. 500 nm light has a frequency of about 6×10^{14} Hz. If the pulse is compressed to a duration of 10^{-13} s (0.1 ps), then $\Delta\nu$ must be at least 10^{13} Hz, or 5.95–6.05 $\times\ 10^{14}$ Hz. These frequencies correspond to 496–504 nm. Compressing to 5 fs forces $\Delta\nu$ to 2×10^{14} Hz and a wavelength range from 430 to 600 nm, most of the visible spectrum. Operationally, the easiest wavelength to produce near 500 nm is 532 nm, half the wavelength of the 1.064 μm Nd:YAG laser, which, if compressed to 5 fs, gives a continuum from 452 to 646 nm, rich in red, but poor in blue. Look up mode-locked lasers for details.

5.3 Classical Nonlinear Uncertainty

This is going to start out looking easy. It ends up being mind-boggling.

Suppose you have a sequence of numbers: $x_0, x_1, x_2, \ldots x_n$. All the numbers are between 0 and 1. x_0 can be any real number in the allowed range. The sequence is computed using equation (5.16).

$$x_{n+1} = 4\lambda x_n(1 - x_n) \tag{5.16}$$

The equation is a parabola with a peak at $x_n = 0.5$ and a height of λ, $0 \leq \lambda < 1$. The graph of the equation is known as the logistic map. If x_n were ever identically 0 or 1 on any iteration, it would collapse to 0 and stay there forever. Zero is thus a stable fixed point — once you get there, you never leave. What other fixed point is there? A fixed point is where $x_{n+1} = x_n$, so stipulate that condition and solve. A little algebra reveals

$$x_{fp} = 1 - \frac{1}{4\lambda} \tag{5.17}$$

For $0 < \lambda \leq 0.25$, $x_{fp} < 0$ and so 0 is the only realizable fixed point; starting at any allowed x_0 will eventually lead to $x_{fp} = 0$. For $0.25 \leq \lambda \leq 1$ there's a non-zero solution to equation (5.17). For $0.25 \leq \lambda \leq 0.75$, starting at an arbitrary x_0 gives the same fixed point as equation (5.17). But for $0.75 \leq \lambda \leq 1$, the behavior gets more complicated and more interesting. Try using $\lambda = 0.8$. From equation (5.17), $x_{fp} = 1 - 1/(4 \times 0.8) = 1 - 1/3.2 = 0.6875$. Pick an x_0. I'll choose 0.2. Starting at x_2, the even numbered points are near 0.799, while the odd numbered points are near 0.513. By the time one reaches points 14 and 15, the pattern is: even numbered points = 0.79945549, odd numbered points = 0.51304451. Where did the fixed point go? If I insert $x_0 = 0.6875$ into equation (5.16), $x_1 = 0.6875$ as expected. Yet, if I insert 0.687501, iterate 72 is 0.79934 and we are nearly to the place where we're oscillating between the two values we saw at points 14 and 15 when starting at 0.2. What happened? At $\lambda = 0.75$, the fixed point became unstable and the alternating fixed points, one above and one below the original fixed point, became stable. A single-word explanation is that the system *bifurcated*.

If bifurcation happens once, what's to keep it from happening again? Nothing. In fact, the system bifurcates an infinite number of times until the system becomes chaotic — one variety of random. Continuing to increase λ past the initial chaotic transition, one goes through inverse bifurcations until a window with period 3 appears. Then the period 3 behavior breaks down through bifurcations. As one gets asymptotically close to $\lambda = 1$, the logistic map becomes a random number generator. Don't believe me? Using *Excel* and an initial point of $x_0 = 0.5$ (so you can compare what you get to what I do), Table 5.1 shows points 50–55.

The values are all over the place. What if we have $\lambda = 0.9999$ and choose different values for x_0 (Table 5.2)?

A change of initial value even as small as 0.001 completely changes the sequence! This is called sensitivity to initial conditions. What we have seen is that for sufficiently nonlinear systems, small changes in parameters can result in a huge change in outcome, even within a bounded system. This was noticed in predictions of planetary orbits by Henri Poincaré in the early 20th century and first reported in digital computer output by Ed Lorenz in 1963 in

Table 5.1. Iterates, starting from $x_0 = 0.5$, for various values of λ.

Point # λ	0.99	0.999	0.9999	0.99999
50	0.505713	0.004018	0.259248	0.886242
51	0.989871	0.015993	0.768077	0.403264
52	0.039706	0.062885	0.712467	0.962559
53	0.150991	0.235485	0.819349	0.144155
54	0.507643	0.719408	0.592006	0.493492
55	0.989769	0.806633	0.966043	0.999821

Table 5.2. Iterates, starting from various values of x_0 for $\lambda = 0.9999$.

Point # x_0	0.2	0.5	0.8	0.801
50	0.979778	0.259248	0.986655	0.999861
51	0.079243	0.768077	0.052662	0.000558
52	0.291826	0.712467	0.199534	0.002229
53	0.826571	0.819349	0.638816	0.008894
54	0.573348	0.592006	0.922828	0.035254
55	0.978383	0.966043	0.284837	0.136033

computations of atmospheric flow (Lorenz, 1963). Tiny perturbations (a butterfly flapping its wings in Brazil) can, eventually, make weather forecasts a hemisphere away unreliable. This is not noise — it is absolutely predictable if one controls the number of significant figures during calculations. It is not uncertain — for the same parameter values, you get identical numbers to as many significant figures as you can see every time. But if you have a system that is well-modeled by this sort of simple equation, and the parameters are in an appropriate range, the outcome of any experiment is pseudo-random within constraints (in the case of the logistic map, all x's are between 0 and 1). This sort of uncertainty is called chaos and its understanding is complicated by the finite precision of every measurement. In Table 5.2, we saw that a change of 1 part in 800 in initial conditions could make the numerical sequence vary unrecognizably in short order; imagine what happens after a few hundred iterations. Had we had the two λ values the same to 4 or 8 or 12 significant figures, any difference would have eventually led to a lack of coherence between the two columns of numbers.

And yet, there's hidden structure. What happens if we plot x_{n+1} vs. x_n? Of course — we'll get the parabola of equation (5.16). Plotting all the iterates (not just the ones in Table 5.2) for $\lambda = 0.9999$, there are four colors for the four initial conditions, and the map structure is clear (Figure 5.7).

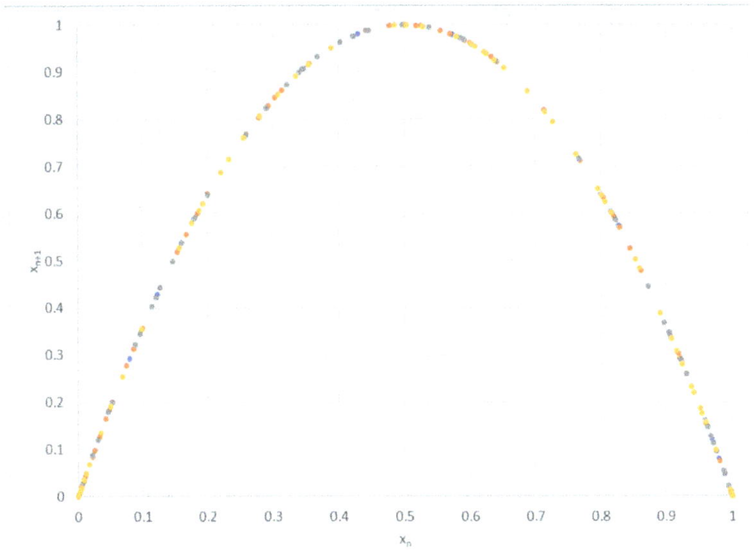

Figure 5.7. The logistic map for $\lambda = 0.9999$. Four colors are for four different initial conditions as per Table 5.2.

Notice that near the fixed point computed in equation (5.17), there is a gap. The map actively avoids its own fixed point and all its periodic iterates (i.e., the twin fixed points that appeared after the first bifurcation, the period 3 points, and so on). A structure that has gaps between every pair of points is a Cantor set, and multidimensional Cantor sets are called *fractals*. The curve or surface along which points place themselves is an *attractor*. The early guru of fractals was Benoit Mandelbrot, whose beautifully illustrated book the interested reader should enjoy (Mandelbrot, 1982).

Our concern here isn't beauty. It's what we can learn about the world. If such simple nonlinear systems as the logistic map can demonstrate so much complexity, is nonlinear uncertainty overwhelming compared to noise, quantum uncertainty, and classical uncertainty? Astonishingly, the answer is a hopeful "it depends." An important difference in this section compared to prior sections is that we are looking at discrete events. Event 0 is the initial value. Event 1 is what happens as a consequence of event 0, and so on. Thus, each event is the integral of a large amount of information in the real world. Each event might be one month's activity, or one year's, or one lifetime's. It could also be one lightning flash in a thunderstorm, and then another. Physicists would call this integration of data over a long period or of space over a significant extent "coarse-graining," that is, looking at an overall effect, not the microscopic behavior femtosecond by femtosecond. When such a distant view is taken, behavior looks less predictable than when one is looking at smaller, simpler, more linear regions of systems. We can model biological processes using linear approaches, but systemically, we know there are at least two highly nonlinear processes for every organism: birth and death. As we will see in Chapter 11, iterated maps have been used to model populations of herbivores, plants, and predators. Excess herbivores destroy plants and feed predators. Excess predators destroy herbivores, thus allowing plants to rejuvenate. Iterated maps have something in common with the game rock-paper-scissors!

Furthermore, not all chaotic or divergent behavior is due exclusively to nonlinearity. In fact, a calculation that diverged was what drew my attention to iterated maps in the first place. Let's look at the behavior of weak, dissociating acids to make the point.

Suppose you have a weak, monoprotic acid, perhaps acetic acid (the acid in vinegar). Use the shorthand HA for the acid; it dissociates into protons and anions, H^+ and A^-. If you make a solution with G grams of acid in 1 L of water, the molarity $[HA] + [A^-] = C_A = G/M/(1\ L)$, where M is the molecular weight of HA (for acetic acid, 60 g/mole). What are the concentrations of the various species in the solution, H^+, A^-, and HA? This isn't as easy to compute as you might think. Do we include the effect of the dissociation of water? Do we include the changes in solution energetics from the electrostatic forces the ions exert on each other (commonly called activity corrections)? For now, let's not. Let's just say that all the bare protons $[H^+]$ come from dissociation of HA into $H^+ + A^-$. Then:

$$\begin{aligned} [\mathrm{HA}] &= C_A - x \\ [\mathrm{H}^+] &= [A^-] = x \\ \frac{[\mathrm{H}^+][A^-]}{[\mathrm{HA}]} &= K_a \end{aligned} \tag{5.18}$$

with K_a called the dissociation constant. What is x, which then allows us to compute all the other concentrations?

$$\frac{x^2}{C_A - x} = K_a \tag{5.19}$$

There are two ways to solve equation (5.19). One is to remember the closed form solution for quadratic equations from algebra class and say:

$$\begin{aligned} x^2 &= K_a(C_a - x) \\ x^2 + K_a x - K_a C_a &= 0 \\ x = [\mathrm{H}^+] = [\mathrm{A}^-] &= \frac{-K_a + \sqrt{K_a^2 + 4K_a C_a}}{2} = \frac{K_a}{2}\left(\sqrt{1 + \frac{4C_a}{K_a}} - 1\right) \end{aligned} \tag{5.20}$$

Another way to solve the same problem is to realize that, typically, $x << C_a$. So we make an initial guess for x: $x_0 = 0$. We then restate the first equation in (5.20) as

$$x_{n+1} = \sqrt{K_a(C_a - x_n)} \tag{5.21}$$

If, in fact, x is small, equation (5.21) converges rapidly to a fixed point.

$$\begin{aligned} x_1 &= \sqrt{K_a(C_a - x_0)} = \sqrt{K_a C_a} \\ x_2 &= \sqrt{K_a(C_a - x_1)} \\ x_3 &= \sqrt{K_a(C_a - x_2)} \end{aligned} \tag{5.22}$$

Given how easy it is to work with equation (5.20), *successive approximation calculations* as illustrated in equation (5.22) seem unnecessarily complicated, or at least time consuming.

What happens if we have a diprotic acid, one that releases two hydrogen ions? This would be something like ascorbic acid (vitamin C) or carbonic acid (what we get if CO_2 is dissolved in water).

$$[\mathrm{H_2A}] + [\mathrm{HA^-}] + [\mathrm{A^=}] = C_A \tag{5.23}$$

So that the net charge in solution remains 0, and ignoring $[OH^-]$, $[H^+] = [HA^-] + 2[A^=]$. Let's keep $x = [H^+]$, add $y = [A^=]$ and $z = [HA^-]$, and see what we get:

$$\frac{[H^+][HA^-]}{[H_2A]} = K_{a1}$$
$$\frac{[H^+][A^=]}{[HA^-]} = K_{a2}$$
$$\frac{xz}{C_A - z - y} = K_{a1} \tag{5.24}$$
$$\frac{xy}{z} = K_{a2}$$

If you like algebra, this looks like fun. And if not? It's still fun!

$$x = z + 2y$$

$$z = \frac{xy}{K_{a2}} = \frac{y(z+2y)}{K_{a2}} \qquad z\left(1 - \frac{y}{K_{a2}}\right) = \frac{2y^2}{K_{a2}} \qquad z = \frac{2y^2}{K_{a2}\left(1 - \frac{y}{K_{a2}}\right)} = \frac{2y^2}{K_{a2} - y}$$

$$x = 2y + \frac{2y^2}{K_{a2} - y} \qquad x(K_{a2} - y) = 2y(K_{a2} - y) + 2y^2$$

$$0 = -2yK_{a2} + xK_{a2} - xy \qquad y = \frac{xK_{a2}}{x + 2K_{a2}}$$

$$z = \frac{2\left(\frac{xK_{a2}}{x+2K_{a2}}\right)^2}{K_{a2} - \frac{xK_{a2}}{x+2K_{a2}}} = \frac{2K_{a2}^2x^2}{K_{a2}(x+2K_{a2})^2 - xK_{a2}(x+2K_{a2})} = \frac{x^2}{x+2K_{a2}}$$

$$K_{a1} = \frac{\frac{x^3}{(x+2K_{a2})}}{C_A - \frac{x^2}{x+2K_{a2}} - \frac{xK_{a2}}{x+2K_{a2}}} = \frac{x^3}{C_a(x+2K_{a2}) - x^2 - xK_{a2}}$$

$$K_{a1}\left(C_a(x+2K_{a2}) - x^2 - xK_{a2}\right) = x^3$$
$$0 = x^3 + K_{a1}x^2 - K_{a1}(C_a - K_{a2})x - 2K_{a1}K_{a2}C_a \tag{5.25}$$

If we can figure out x by solving the last of these equations, computing y and z is just a matter of back-substitution. There are formulae for solving cubic equations. There are even formulas for solving quartics in closed form, but it has been proven that pentics and higher degree polynomials cannot, except in special cases, be solved in closed form. Did I mention that there are triprotic acids (citric acid, phosphoric acid) and other, higher polyprotic acids? If we're going to deal with those, and add in the influence of water's dissociation, there is no way around it: in general we must be able to solve equations of such high degree that we can't do it in closed form. Successive approximation calculations are going to have to be in our toolkit.

Here's where the calculations get funky. Which rearrangement do we want?

$$\begin{aligned} x_{n+1} &= \sqrt[3]{2K_{a1}K_{a2}C_A + K_{a1}(C_A - K_{a2})x_n - K_{a1}x_n^2} \\ &= \sqrt[3]{K_{a1}}\sqrt[3]{2K_{a2}C_A + (C_A - K_{a2})x_n - x_n^2} \end{aligned} \tag{5.26}$$

or

$$\begin{aligned} x_{n+1} &= \sqrt{\frac{2K_{a1}K_{a2}C_A + K_{a1}(C_A - K_{a2})x_n - x_n^3}{K_{a1}}} \\ &= \sqrt{2K_{a2}C_A + (C_A - K_{a2})x_n - \frac{x_n^3}{K_{a1}}}\,? \end{aligned} \tag{5.27}$$

Here's a hint. In equation (5.26), it is possible for an iterate of x_n to be less than 0, a physical impossibility (the amount of H^+ can't be negative). Further, there is a positive feedback loop; in the limit of small K_{a2} and small x, x_{n+1} increases approximately as the cube root of x_n. If either of these situations happen, the calculation may diverge (i.e., head for plus or minus infinity, also physically impossible). In equation (5.27), x_{n+1} is always positive, and the calculation converges.

In January 1981, I did not realize what I just told you. I used equation (5.26) when I should have used equation (5.27), and the end of my lecture diverged as surely as the iteration. I was saved by the bell, walked across the University of Iowa campus to the Van Allen Physics Building to attend Plasma Physics Seminar. There, Dwight Nicholson talked about Mitch Feigenbaum's work on period-doubling bifurcations to chaos and universality (Feigenbaum, 1980, 1983), the rate at which bifurcations converge to chaos. Because I was sensitized to the instabilities of iterated calculations, I paid attention. And that was an important waystation of the path that led to this book!

The combination of a research program in plasma chemistry, teaching about weak acid dissociation, and iteration resulted in a ternary collision. Was this serendipitous? Random? Preordained? We'll get to that. But notice that had I not learned a lot about numerical analysis, analytical chemistry, electronics, plasmas, and several other topics, I wouldn't have been in Nicholson's seminar. The uncertainty of one's trajectory through life parallels the uncertainty of measurement, fluctuations, noise, and chaos. But the extent of divergence is contained. No human has yet been more than 250,000 miles from home. No human has lived more than 122.5 years during times when records could be reliably checked. We have only modeled planetary orbits as ellipses since the early 1600s. While writing goes back thousands of years, mass production of printed material dates only from Gutenberg's combination about 1450 of moveable type (originated in East Asia) with the printing press. Without Gutenberg or some similarly inspired inventor, none of the math in this chapter would likely have been derived, nor would I have encountered it, nor would you be able to download it from the publisher (either on dead trees, DVDs, or as bytes). The frequency of communications is exploding and, as we saw earlier, as $\Delta\nu$ has increased, Δt has decreased. Can this continue without limit? If I were to be consistent with the title of this chapter, you'd expect the answer to be "I'm not sure." But, in fact, I am sure. There are limits to how much can be learned. While noise and chaos reduce that limit, the ultimate limit is bandwidth. Humans are Fourier limited in the longest time they can access, and as we will see in the next chapter, they are also sampling limited in the shortest time they can access. Total information transfer to one person in one lifetime is constrained. Information can be produced more rapidly than it can be consumed. Relative to the amount that there is to be known, we humans are losing the race to keep up with all the information we and the non-human universe can generate, and so are our tools, computers and networks.

6

Sampling

Don't blink or you'll miss it!

If something happens faster than it can be sensed, information about what happened is obscure. Until mechanical and electronic timing devices became available in the late 19th century (Canales, 2011), time perception was limited to the range from 0.1 s to a century or two (with somewhat longer perception linked to written traditions such as holy books or histories). In recent years, attosecond (10^{-18} s) experiments have been performed. As measurement granularity has increased, the range of processes of which humans are aware has exploded. Instrumentation has revealed everything from microscopic life to the nature of chemistry, the structure of atoms, and the quantized nature of the energy of electrons bound to atoms or molecules.

Typical human hearing extends from 20 Hz to 20,000 Hz. Some people I know claim they perceive frequencies up to 50,000 Hz. Since sound is pressure waves in air, that means that human perception does not sense pressure that varies at greater than 30,000 times a second (no, the 3 isn't a typo — you'll see why later in this chapter); the individual pressure waves blur into sensation at a slower speed. The typical march is performed at 120 beats per minute or 2 beats per second, so the booming of the base drum outputs a sound pulse of a few tens or hundreds of Hertz at a 2 Hz rate. A roll on a snare drum outputs sound in the hundreds of Hertz perhaps 10 times a second. Ordinary English speaking sounds painfully slow at one syllable per second which is about 30–40 words per minute. You can hear for yourself at https://clearly-speaking.com/what-is-the-ideal-rate-of-speech/. I find that 180 words per minute sounds about right (and my students used to tell me I talked too fast).

What about sight? Standard video at 30 Hz doesn't flicker for most people, and it doesn't flicker at 60 Hz for an even larger fraction of the populace. Gaming PC displays refresh at up to 360 Hz according to my local computer store. We can't conceptualize pictures at even 10 frames per second; it takes several seconds to look at a scene and render into thoughts and active memories many of the details we see. In other words, we don't continuously stream sights, feelings, sounds, smells, or taste. We sample the world, break what we sense into discrete nerve firings, perceptions, memories, and actions, and thus only operate at a finite rate. In this chapter, we look at the details of sampling events that bombard us, and in the next chapter, the central concept of the book, we look at how what we have learned constrains human, and even automaton, intelligence, learning, and action.

In the early days of electronic measurement, devices were comparatively slow and their response fell off quickly at high frequencies. People thus extended the speeds and reduced the time intervals at which measurements could be made without instruments, but extremely fast phenomena were still hidden. Then along came Bell Laboratories, Harry Nyquist (who worked at Bell Labs), and Harold Edgerton; high speed measurement changed. Let's look at Nyquist and his theorem first.

Suppose one is looking at a 5 Hz sine wave, measuring the amplitude of the wave once every 20 ms. A device called a sample-and-hold amplifier picks off the voltage in a matter of a few nanoseconds and holds that voltage at a constant value while an analog-to-digital converter (ADC) reports the voltage as an integer. That integer gets stored and, 20 ms after the first data point is

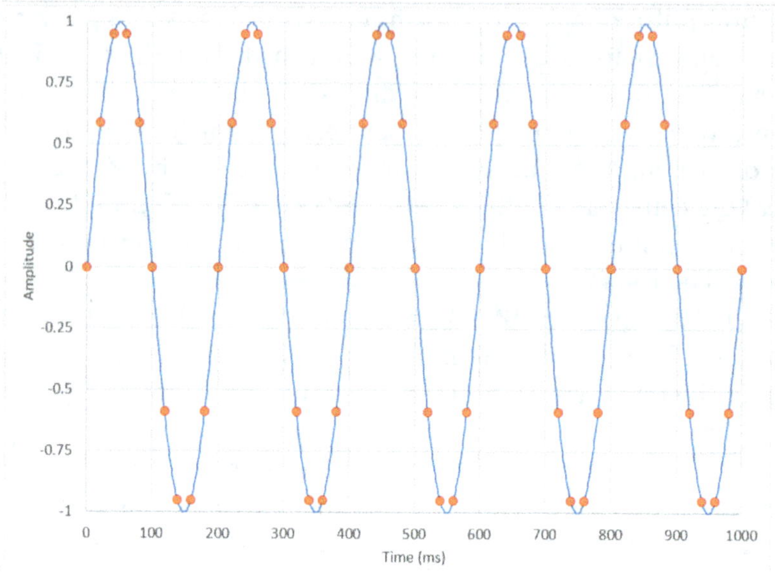

Figure 6.1. 5 Hz sine wave sampled at 50 Hz. Orange dots are the sampled points, while the smooth, blue curve is the parent sine wave.

taken, the next one is snatched. This continues, and the result is shown in Figure 6.1. The dots show the values obtained by the sample-and-hold plus analog-to-digital converter, while the blue curve is the 5 Hz sine wave, going on its merry, analog way.

It's fairly clear that the sampled points fall along the 5 Hz curve. We could probably figure out a least-squares approach to measuring amplitude, frequency, and phase of the sine wave just from looking at the sampled points. If we had more points, it would be easier, perhaps, but there's nothing misleading about just the sampled points. If I were fitting the waveform, I'd see that the waveform goes through 0 at $t = 0$, that it's sinusoidal and periodic, so most likely $f(t) = A \sin(2\pi\, t/T)$, the $(t, f(t))$ pairs are the measured points, T is the time between alternate zeros, and so the only fitting parameter is A. Find the mean of $f(t)/\sin(2\pi\, t/T)$ at all points other than where $f(t) = 0$, and we've estimated A. Easy, fast, and, alas, not a particularly general situation.

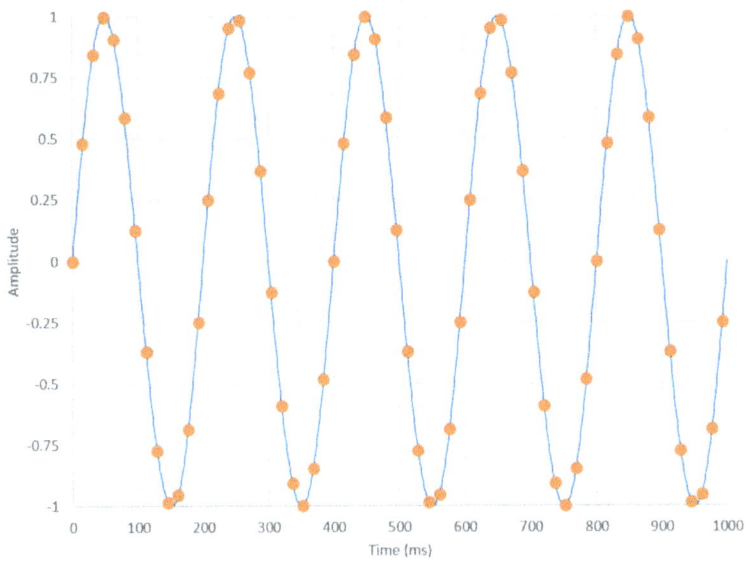

Figure 6.2. 5 Hz sine wave sampled at 62.5 Hz. Orange dots are the sampled points, while the smooth, blue curve is the parent sine wave.

Many times, one doesn't know the frequency of the waveform being measured until after the measurement is made. So let's look at that 5 Hz waveform in Figure 6.2 where, instead of sampling at 50 Hz (one point every 20 ms), we sample at 62.5 Hz (one point every 16 ms). This is close to sampling once every 16.666 ms, or 60 Hz, the frequency of the electric power grid in North America (though not most of the rest of the world).

Now we have more data points, and we can see that we get 2 cycles of the sampled waveform in 400 ms, which indeed is 5 Hz. One of the ways to have confidence in a measurement is to get the same shape, period, and amplitude when sampling at different frequencies. Perhaps fitting the data isn't quite as easy as in Figure 6.1, but the answer is the same, with greater statistical confidence because we have more data points.

Now we ask The Limbo Question: "How Low Can You Go?" (https://www.lyrics.com/lyric/7025945/Chubby+Checker, 21/11/2020). What is the fewest number of points one can measure to analyze a waveform? It isn't 1. If we measure a single point and learn V = 0.5 V, we have no idea what happened before or after the moment of sampling. Is the waveform constant in time? Is it a sine wave and, if so, what is its frequency? We know nothing. How about two points? Two points can be used to determine the slope and intercept of a line, but they cannot reveal if a signal is varying periodically.

Nyquist showed that the slowest sampling that can measure the frequency of a waveform is sampling at twice the frequency of the waveform. Even then, there is a 50/50 chance that one will be misled. Think of a 1 Hz sine wave. The theorem says we must sample at 2 Hz. If we sample at $t = 0$ and $t = 0.5$ s, we will measure 0 both times and think that nothing is happening. However, if we sample at $t = 0.25$ s and $t = 0.75$ s, we will measure amplitudes of $+A$ and $-A$, alternating, and that will tell us that there is an oscillation at 1 Hz, or perhaps a linear change in potential with a slope of $-2A$ in 0.5 s or 4 A s^{-1}. If we measure at the same rate and phase repeatedly, we will indeed see measurements of $\pm A$ alternately and know that there is a periodic waveform.

In the last chapter, we learned about aliasing, and aliasing is the bane of sampling waveforms. Let's go back to the 5 Hz sine wave. We know we should sample it at 10 Hz or more to get an unaliased measurement of frequency and amplitude. What happens if we sample it at 4 Hz? Figure 6.3 shows two possible sampling patterns: in A, the 4 Hz sampling occurs synchronized to a zero crossing of the sine wave, while in B, there's a 40 ms delay from the zero crossing.

If we connect the dots, in Inset A, we see a 1 Hz sine wave, while in Inset B, it's not quite clear what is happening. Is there a straight line, with a negative-going noise spike at about 540 ms? Is it a sine wave? We don't know. In both cases, we say the parent 5 Hz sine wave is undersampled. 5 Hz, sampled at 4 Hz, gives an apparent sine frequency of 1 Hz. At first glance, it looks like $\nu_{waveform} - \nu_{sampling} = \nu_{apparent}$. Actually, it's slightly more complicated.

$$\begin{aligned} \nu_{Nyquist} &= \nu_{sampling} / 2 \\ \nu_{aliased} &= \left| m\nu_{sampling} - \nu_{waveform} \right| \end{aligned} \tag{6.1}$$

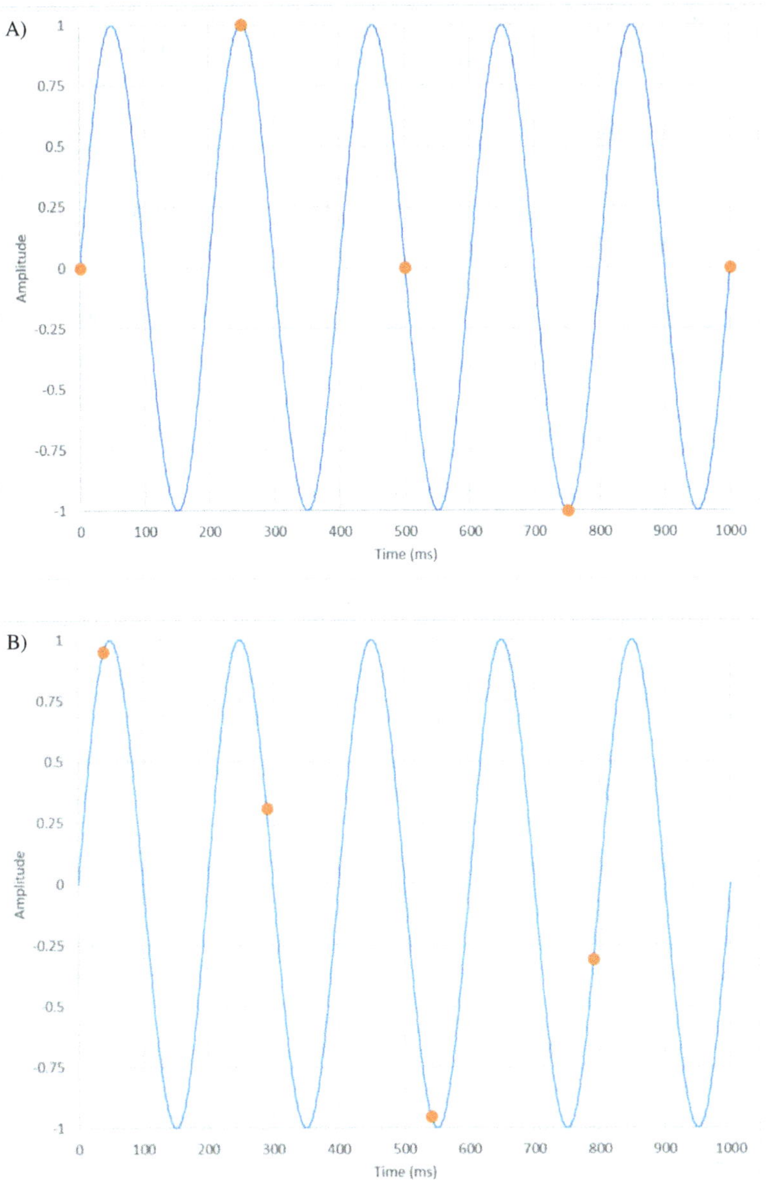

Figure 6.3. Sampling a 5 Hz sine wave at 4 Hz. Inset A: first sample occurs at a zero crossing. Inset B: First sample delayed 40 ms from a zero crossing.

The integer m is chosen so that $\nu_{aliased}$ is between 0 and $\nu_{Nyquist}$.

Combining what we have learned so far in this chapter with what we learned in the last chapter, every experiment has a minimum frequency $1/T$ that can be measured, and a maximum unaliased frequency $\nu_{Nyquist}$. There may be a variety of experimental factors that reduce information content to less than this range of frequencies, but nothing that can increase it. If we alias from 100 MHz down to 10 kHz and $\nu_{Nyquist}$ is 20 kHz, we will only measure information at 100 MHz ± 5 kHz or 100 MHz to 100.01 MHz, depending on how the aliasing is done.

6.1 Granularity

There's more to sampling than how often we look at data. There's the resolution with which we measure that data. If someone says "one volt", do they mean 1 volt, or 1.0 volts or 1.0000000000 volts? If they claim they mean 1.0000000000 volts, does that mean they can distinguish that potential from 1.0000000001 volts? I would find that to be surprising; the difference is 0.1 nV, meaning they claim to measure potential to 10 significant figures. This is approximately the precision with which the volt is defined in the 2019 International System of Quantities (the agreed-upon SI units). A 32-bit, unsigned number has a magnitude just over 4×10^9, so claiming a potential with resolution to 10 decimal places means measurement precision to 33 or 34 bits. Such extraordinary precision is difficult to realize — temperature and atmospheric pressure must be stringently controlled, power supplies must be rock stable, shielding against electromagnetic interference must be rigorous, and a variety of effects that can be ignored in day-to-day measurements must be compensated. Outside of the laboratories where standards are defined and maintained, it would take extraordinary evidence to convince me that anyone measured an analog quantity with a precision of 32 bits.

On the other hand, people measure potential with a precision of 24 bits routinely. The digitizers for electronic music typically are 24-bit (or higher) ADCs, operating at 96 kHz (or higher). Imagine my astonishment that a 32-bit ADC was available in November 2020 from the well-known electronics distributor Digikey for $63 (https://www.digikey.com/en/products/detail/analog-devices-inc/LTC2500CDKD-32-PBF/6670442, 11/21/2020). It operates at up to 1 MHz. What's the catch? The very first line on the specification sheet (https://www.analog.com/media/en/technical-documentation/data-sheets/250032fb.pdf, 11/21/2020) says "Integral nonlinearity ±0.5 ppm". In other words, while one can get 2^{32} different signal levels, the accuracy is only 1 part in 2 million or 21 bits. Full scale error is guaranteed to be no more than 100 ppm (0.01%) and is typically 10 ppm, but that is far, far less precise than 32 bits. So, no, you can't measure to 32-bit accuracy on the cheap (to which someone who believes Moore's Law on the perpetual improvement of integrated circuits might add: "yet!").

On the other hand, optimizing the number of useable bits is central to knowing how precise a single measurement may be. In Figure 6.4, we plot that same 5 Hz sine wave we've been looking at, using simulated ADCs with various numbers of bits.

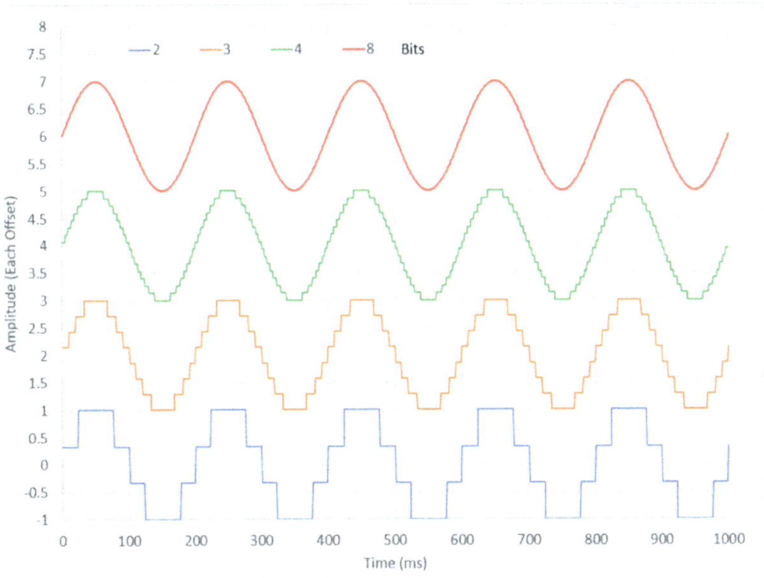

Figure 6.4. Effect of resolution of digitized sine waveform. Only the lowest granularity waveform is shown centered at 0 V. The others are offset, 2 V per waveform, for clarity.

Note the stairsteps in the lower few waveforms. The blue line is for a 2 V peak-to-peak sine wave digitized with a 2-bit ADC. The binary codings for a 2-bit number can only be 00, 01, 10, and 11. These correspond either to 0, 1, 2, and 3 (straight binary), or 0, 1, −2, −1 (two's complement binary). As the plot shows, the sine wave is coded as four observable levels. The next higher plot is for a 3-bit converter, where the output is one of 000, 001, 010, 011, 100, 101, 110, or 111, representing either the integers 0 to 7 (straight binary) or −4 to 3 (two's complement binary). Is this waveform a triangle wave or a sine wave? It's hard to tell. By the time we get to 4 bits, it's clear there's some curvature to the waveform (there's no pointed top or bottom), and at 8 bits, where there are 256 different levels, to the naked eye it's clear this is a sine wave. At 24 bits, there are 4 million different digitization levels, and even at 24 bits there are some musical purists who claim they can hear the jumps in sound level as each bit clicks over; they prefer analog sound which they claim is cleaner. As I, alas, lack this auditory acuity, I will simply wonder how humans can have such refined ability to distinguish so many levels. Nevertheless, at some point, there are differences in sound pressure that are too fine for electronics or humans to distinguish.

6.2 Aliased Sampling

How do we study extremely fast processes, processes that are over in less time than it takes to do a single analog-to-digital conversion? That's where Harold Edgerton and aliasing come in. For a repetitive phenomenon, we can use a stroboscope to slow down the apparent motion from its actual speed to something more tractable. Think of a horse galloping on a treadmill — it stays in place and the movement of its legs is repeated. We flash a bright light when the left rear hoof hits the treadmill belt and get a picture of the beginning of a cycle. Store that picture, then when the left rear hoof hits again, wait 1 microsecond, flash the lamp again, and get an image of how far the leg moved in 1 microsecond. Of course, if the horse is galloping at 4 strides per second, it's actually a bit over 250 milliseconds between images, but relative to the start of a stride, the delay is 1/250,000 of a stride. Each stride, delay an additional microsecond.

The horse will tire before one has pictures of all 250 ms of a single stride. If the horse can run for 3 minutes, that's 180 s or 720 strides, we'll only cover a bit over 700 microseconds. But since we can choose the frame-to-frame delay, we could get a coarser measurement to cover a longer portion of the stride if we wished. To capture a full stride by taking 720 photos in 3 minutes, we'd need to increment the delay time by 250 ms/720 photos ~350 μs for each increment. There's a trade-off: more detail of a brief part of a stride or less detail of a longer portion. The number of images we can take before the horse is winded is roughly constant.

Suppose something happens 10^9 times per second and each of those events lasts 0.1 ns. If we make an optical measurement lasting 0.1 ns and synchronize it with the beginning of each event, we can signal average for many seconds to build up a signal aliased to DC. Suppose something happens 10^6 times per second, and we want to study it with ~ nanosecond resolution. As long as we can trigger our observation devices precisely, we can average at the moment the event starts for several seconds, then start adding delays to gradually sample later parts of the repetitive phenomenon. Either a xenon flash (Edgerton's approach in the 1930s) or a pulsed laser (after 1960) can take sub-microsecond portions of a phenomenon and generate enough fluorescence or scattering to be readily recorded. We thus sample and alias to bring the data we collect into a comfortable frequency range. These techniques for down-sampling have various names such as boxcar averaging, lock-in amplification, gated image intensification, time-delayed integration, and parallel strobed digitization. With suitable time increments in shifting offsets for observing repeated events, phenomena can be measured with time increments and durations ranging from attoseconds to years.

6.3 Human Perceptual Limits

How fast can humans take in information? Here are some estimates of rates and rationalizations for the values.

Sight: While there are millions of nerves, rods, and cones on the retina (Koch *et al.*, 2006; Potter *et al.*, 2014), the retina pre-processes raw transduced information before trans-shipping it to the brain. Each optic nerve has fewer than 2 million fibers (https://pubmed.ncbi.nlm.nih.gov/1582806/) which transmit data at 80 Hz or less. While an image flashed for 13 ms can be described, one cannot perceive detail in such a brief image. Then there's the problem of how wide a range of intensities can be perceived at once. Having seen examples of 16-bit CCDs that could detect planets against a blue, daylight sky when humans could not, let's guess that each neuron can communicate 1.5 bytes or less at 80 Hz, or each eye can feed the brain at 250 MB s^{-1} or less. The two eyes together would thus seem to feed 500 MB s^{-1}, but typically they share at least parts of their field of view. But now let's do a sanity check (defined as comparing a number with everyday experience and seeing if it makes sense). A high-definition TV screen is about two megapixels with 24-bit color, refreshed 30 times per second. That's 180 MB s^{-1}. If the TV fills my field of view, my perception is that the TV resolution is better than what I can see (but I'm near-sighted). I tend to focus on only a portion of the screen if I'm trying to see details. So while there are situations where the eye can convey rapid information or detailed information, it seems unlikely that sustained data input is as fast as 500 MB s^{-1}. But one must be a little careful here; is it that we can't perceive that fast or that we can't push that much information into memory that fast?

Smell: less well understood than other senses, the chemicals sensed as odors typically enter the nose with each inhalation, roughly 10 times/minute.

Touch: various Google hits say Braille reading can be 200–400 words per minute. Other inputs are slower and subject to interpretation.

Taste: personal experience suggests 1/second. To fully appreciate the finish on a fine wine, I recommend sipping at considerably less than once per second.

Balance: it takes a fraction of a second to feel when balance is lost. As with seeing and hearing, response is on the order of milliseconds.

Hearing: while we can distinguish sounds from 20 Hz to 20 kHz, we are limited to fewer than 100 independent auditory events per second. Musically, sixteenth notes at 200 beats per minute occur at

3200/60 = 53 Hz. The speed of sound is about 1,000 feet per second, so an orchestra spread across 100 feet of stage can only be "simultaneous" within 0.05 s to the conductor.

Early in this chapter, I suggested that auditory input was limited to less than 30,000 Hz, even if an acute listener could detect 50,000 Hz sound. To notice a stimulus takes more than one cycle of a sine wave; even a 50 kHz listener, with infinitely rapid brain, would require at least two cycles of the sound wave to be sure the stimulus wasn't a noise spike. So the true limit isn't 30 kHz, it's 50 kHz/2 = 25 kHz, absent brain limitations. But we already have seen that brains are considerably slower than transducers. While we can detect a wider range of tones, translating them into actionable information (Stay? Flee? Dance to the music?) cannot happen at the oscillation frequency of the sound waves. In fact, while hearing for warning can elicit sub-second response, language response is less than 10 phonemes per second.

The six senses (including balance) are the only ways we have to learn from the world. Some maintain that there is a connection to non-physical (spiritual) information sources. These are problematic. How can one check the accuracy or reality of such claims, absent a way to measure that is independent of the person claiming the observation? Yet such claims are sufficiently widespread throughout history, so how can one discount them? We address these questions only at the end of the book. For now, we confine ourselves to explicit information, that conveyed by light (or, more broadly, electromagnetism), pressure (sound, touch, balance/kinesthetic sense), and chemicals (taste, smell). How much information can we integrate, evaluate, and retransmit? What are the practical integration limits on the measurement integrals and judgment integrals we discussed in Chapter 1? How many correlations can we detect, how many of those can be evaluated as to whether they are ethereal or indicative of causation? What noise gets in our way, and what signals emerge from that noise? We know that the longest awareness we have is of the order of a century, and that the shortest moments we sense without instrumental assistance are of the order of 0.1 s. In one century, there are approximately $10^{10.5}$ tenths of a second. Thus, we are ready to see how bandwidth constrains humans.

7

Bandwidth

This is the heart of the matter. Since we know there is a maximum time over which we can measure, a maximum frequency within that time that we can sense the external world, and a limited number of sensory channels, how much can one person measure, learn, know, and retransmit? What are the limits of human communications, and what does this say about how physics constrains life?

Let's start with a simple idea. Each person is unique. Really? How do we know? Have you met every person in the world and compared each to every other one? I haven't. As I write this, the population of the world is reputed to be about 8 billion people. To decide if each one of these people is unique, I'd have to at least meet every one of them. For how long would I need to interact with them? Probably for quite a while; I've been married for 38 years, and I'm still learning details about my wife. But let's keep it simple. Let's suppose that I only have to see each other person for 1 second and I can tell if they're unique, or at least get a picture of them so I can let some computer sort through and tell me if it finds two people who are superficially identical. How long would that take?

8 billion seconds = 133 million minutes = just a little more than 2.222 million hours = 92,593 days = 254 years (ignoring the average of 1/4 day per year that comes from leap years). 254 years of doing nothing but meeting people currently alive, one per second. I don't know about you, but I'd like to stop every so often to eat, drink, sleep, and maybe even do something besides seeing one person with whom I establish the shallowest of relationships every second. Considering that no one in modern times has been documented to live as long as 125 years (I make no claims for pre-mass media times), there's the slight problem that half the people I would want to meet would die before I could get to them, and that ignores that I have less than 50 years left to live. It is physically impossible for me, or anyone else, to meet every human with whom I share the planet.

I go back to Chapter 1 and look at the integrals. The speed of light is not what limits how many people I can meet. Distance isn't a factor either. It's the sheer number of people involved. Each one of those people knows something. Maybe what they know is something I can't even conceive of, or maybe what they know is a subset of what I know. The problem is: I don't have measurement speed to find out, and neither does anyone else. "So get a computer to do it for you." What do I tell the computer? The question isn't "do I have a clone?" but "are any two of these people non-unique?" How will the computer figure that out? It too will need to obtain data and make comparisons. Let's suppose every human has a connection to the internet (not yet the case, but reasonably close. By 2017, there had been at least one cell phone manufactured for each human on earth, so connectivity is at least physically plausible if not yet accomplished). Each person takes a 1-megapixel selfie and uploads it. That's 8 terabytes, a drop in the bucket as it were (a statement that would have appeared absurd only a few decades ago. According to one website (https://www.pingdom.com/blog/amazing-facts-and-figures-about-the-evolution-of-hard-disk-drives, 11/22/2020), the first 1 TB hard drive shipped in 2007.). But now comes the big problem: how do we make comparisons? Do we extract features of each picture and compare those tabulated features? Compare every image to every other image? How do we account for differences in lighting or clothing? After all, if we don't account for that, with two well-posed photos, I could fool the system into thinking I'm different from myself!

Before we get distracted into search algorithms and extraction of facial features, let's refocus. Even if two people look superficially the same, have they had identical life experience? Have they read the same books, had the same teachers, played the same games, suffered the same setbacks? My grandsons are identical twins, born moments apart. How can two people be more identical than that? I assure you that their personalities are utterly distinct, even though they've had the same tennis lessons, the same swimming lessons, and been in the same classrooms through the third grade. So it's obvious — if they aren't identical, then no two people are identical. But there's a problem with that jump. You used your experience in life (deftly abetted by your mischievous author) to model how people behave and then used that experience to short-circuit the evaluation of other people's identities. I led you to extrapolate, "if even identical twins aren't actually identical, then no two people are identical, so you don't have to waste time making the measurements, you can simply conclude the answer and move on." In other words, rather than collecting the data and evaluating it, you convinced yourself (with a little underhanded help) that you didn't need the data, that you already had the answer. But how did you develop the ability to draw that conclusion? From collecting unrelated data to unrelated questions, building a model of the world, and then consulting that model to reach a conclusion. Instead of:

> Data → Information → Hypothesis → Measure correlation → Compare to expectation → Conclusion

you carried out:

> Hypothesis → Consult existing model/notion/bias → Reach conclusion → Avoid gathering data

But where did the hypotheses and existing models come from? Pre-existing knowledge. Where did that come from? There are three possibilities. One is that the knowledge is transmitted at conception. A second is that the knowledge is obtained *in utero*, so that it pre-exists language and independent mobility. The third is that one obtains knowledge by measurement, correlation of measurements, storage of those correlations, and then recall when desired. Once hearing develops *in utero*, it is plausible that learning may begin before birth. Anyone who has felt a fetus respond to voices or music knows that some trans-abdominal communication occurs.

Hypothesis generation using language is confined to a small number of species, but the process of alingual hypothesis generation is common to most living creatures. A bird will soar first one way, then another, searching for prey. That can be construed as hypothesizing that since there is no prey within sight looking in one direction then the direction should be changed. A bacterium searching for a food source moves randomly, but is biased to swim uphill in a chemical gradient, looking for ever higher amounts of nutrients. But then terminology and behavior get messy and controversial. Is that bacterium thinking? Is it feeling? Does it have a soul? If not, how complex must an organism be to think, feel, or have a spiritual dimension? We'll return to these issues at the end of the book, but let's get back to the original problem of this chapter: if we can't even meet everyone on earth in several lifetimes, how do we take into account their circumstances, insights, knowledge, feelings, and ingenuity?

7.1 Language and Information

By saying that we can't get all the information we'd like from a serial (one at a time) connection with each person, we are saying that serial communications has insufficient bandwidth to get us all the information we'd like to have. There are several ways to increase bandwidth. One is to measure at a higher frequency — what if we saw each person for only 0.1 s? Instead of 247 years, we'd get done in 24.7 years, and that's (marginally) plausible. How could we learn as much about someone in 0.1 s as we did in 1 s? We could add data acquisition channels, i.e., make parallel measurements. Humans already do that, because we have multiple sensing organs, functioning together. In American society (and some others), prior to COVID and the necessity of social distancing, the standard introduction ritual went something like:

"Person 1, this is person 2. Person 2, meet person 1." The people shake hands and look each other in the eye. They typically say something, ranging from "It's a pleasure to meet you, Person 2" to "How ya doin'?" or "Yo, bro!" or "I've heard so much about you." In just seconds, we get an initial impression from seeing, hearing, feeling the handshake, and comparing what we sense with our cultural standards. That comparison is also a measurement, but it's a consequence of earlier measurements. In other words, there is a feedback loop, where the result of an earlier measurement impacts what we measure later and how we interpret that later measurement. Figure 7.1 explains what is happening:

The first four measurements (starting from the top of the diagram) innocently probe the world and lead to correlations. These correlations lead to hypotheses for future measurements *which are then interpreted in light of the hypothesis*. Thus, earlier measurements bias both what is to be measured and the interpretation of what has been measured. The old measurements are implicit in interpreting the new measurements.

One has access to more information inside their head than from observing the immediate environment, but what's in their head

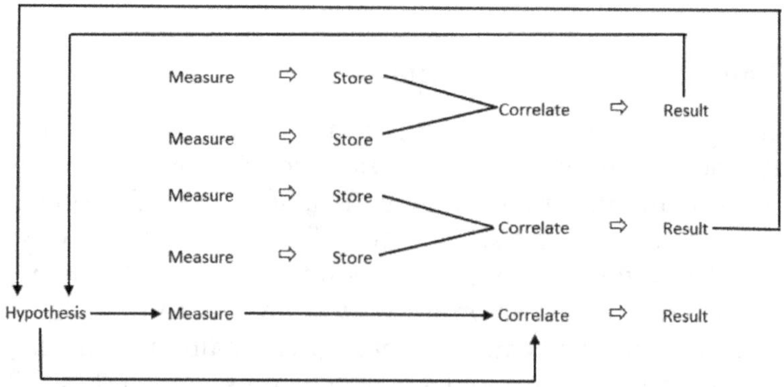

Figure 7.1. Measurements lead to correlations which inform hypotheses that bias measurements and later correlations.

came from previous observations. Figure 7.1 might be criticized for not putting all the "Measurement" events on the left side of the diagram rather than embedded in the middle of it, but what was missing in Chapter 1 is emphasized above: all measurements, other than very early ones, are made in a context of prior measurements. This allows a greater amount of information to be brought to bear on a decision than just what is immediately sensible at a given moment. Thinking of those 8 billion people, some vague acknowledgment of all the other people on earth is embedded in the phrase "8 billion people." What is lacking is detail. Do those details matter? Only if we measured something about a select few of those people could we begin to figure that out.

And now we're right back to the problem of not being able to see them all in a lifetime, yet having some information about them available inside our heads. The number and speed of our senses form a choke point. The speed of our thinking is a choke point. The number of prior measurements is a choke point.

ALL MEASUREMENTS ARE DESIGNED BASED ON LIMITED INFORMATION because we don't have time or bandwidth to bring in enough prior perspective.

ALL HYPOTHESES CONTAIN BIASES because they are based on an incomplete view of the world.

ALL CONCLUSIONS ARE DRAWN BASED ON INCOMPLETE INFORMATION because we lack the ability to acquire enough data due to limited measurement speed and limited experiment duration.

ALL CONCLUSIONS ARE BIASED BY EXPERIMENTAL DESIGN because what we observe and how we interpret it is based on the limited data available to us.

These statements are true of all life and thus all people. Among the phrases that have been used to criticize approaches to identifying or solving problems have been buzzwords such as "silo thinking," "broad but shallow," "what about?", "unfocused," "perspective too narrow," "doctrinaire," "biased," "parochial," and "narrow-minded." All of them are, to some degree, accurate. What they omit is that they describe not only the person, group, or situation being described, but also the person or group providing the critique. There's always missing information. A legitimate question is, "Does the missing information matter?" An illegitimate statement is, "I know everything I need to know to make a good decision." No one can prove that last statement, because there's always unknown information!

Donald Rumsfeld, U.S. Secretary of Defense during the invasion of Iraq in 2003, was mocked for splitting information into four bins: known knowns, known unknowns, unknown knowns, and unknown unknowns. Given what we now recognize about the ability to gather information, we can recognize that his characterization is an alternative summary of this chapter. Everyone who is reading this paragraph, with some level of comprehension, in the language in which it was first written, is literate, at least to a degree, in English. The statement is self-evidently true, and the person who reads it knows that it is true. I have no way to know if the reader speaks or reads Arabic — I don't even know who you are, dear reader, so I know that I don't know anything about you. That's a known unknown. Another way of saying "unknown known" is when someone has tacit information, information not necessarily rendered in language, but useful nevertheless. When my youngest daughter was learning to ride a bicycle, at one point the bike fell over. Without even thinking, she jumped out of the way of the falling velocipede and landed on her feet. She didn't realize she knew how to avoid being hurt — but to everyone's astonishment, she got it right the first time. None of us knew that she knew how to stay unhurt — an unknown known. And then there's almost everything else. There are languages I've never heard of, so while I know, in general, that such languages exist, I have no specifics on which languages I don't know. There are professions I've never heard of, so I don't know that I'm lacking in their expertise. There are people with experiences I'll never have and insights I lack, but since I'll never meet those people, I'll never know it. The vastness of the universe is filled with unknown unknowns. While some people go to great lengths to conceal information in order to manipulate the world, thus creating unknown unknowns, the limitation on our ability to measure ensures that, even with the purest of intents and greatest efforts to advise others of information, there will be unknown unknowns. Add noise, and connections are even less reliable or efficient.

This has not stopped people from thinking they have all the answers. If one is unaware of unknown unknowns, it can seem as if the universe of knowledge is already effectively in one's grasp, and that all expressable questions can be answered from the available store of knowledge. For much of human history, this perspective was defensible. If a group of people is isolated from most interaction with other, distant people, then the community wisdom is finite, all that wisdom can be conveyed in a single lifetime, reinforced as it is reconveyed within the group, and the wisdom is appropriate for survival and even flourishing in a fixed environment. Prior to the advent of writing, while there were unknown unknowns beyond the horizon, within a given community it was feasible to share essentially all knowledge.

Such isolation is no longer the norm. I will confine my description to Euro-American lore, as I have not read enough of Oceania, Asian, or African history to be able to comment intelligently (a known unknown). According to some, approximately 10,000 years ago, writing began in the Middle East. Cuneiform tablets are heavy and brittle, but they can hold information over long periods and in large volumes which need not be conveyed in person to a subsequent reader. Papyrus and sheepskin were lighter materials that came into later use. By the time ancient Egypt was at its height, folklore could be conveyed in writing and art such that ideas could spread rapidly and to significant distance. Rather than isolated cultures, connected with low-bandwidth descriptions by travelers, one could now leave written materials to convey information other than in person. And it is at this time that cross-fertilized ideas of commerce, culture, and religion took root. Whether one traces Western religions to Mesopotamia 5,000 years ago, Egypt 3,500 years ago, or the Eastern Mediterranean after Persia allowed Jews to return to Judea about 2,500 years ago, the growing facility of sailors, traders, and book/scroll sellers to convey information increased bandwidth among settlements. Of course, the rate at which information conveyance was required also increased, and from then until now, there has been a continued competition among production, storage, transportation, organization, and consumption of information. 10,000 years ago, there were no speed readers because writing had not yet been invented. Today, speed reading is essential if there is to be any hope of mastering vast portions of knowledge.

In Europe, by the end of the Middle Ages, ships and what remained of Roman roads limited information transport. Replication of written knowledge was manual, so the typical individual could not obtain knowledge beyond that conveyed by apprenticing or from religious texts whose content was largely unchanged over centuries and thus copies of manuscripts could accumulate. An educated person in 1430 and an educated person in 430 had much the same knowledge (although history of the intervening 1,000 years might have been a significant added burden to convey and learn). And then came Gutenberg.

7.2 Accelerated Communication

Since Gutenberg combined moveable type (of which he learned from traders who came from East Asia) and flat bed presses, the volume of information, the speed of its dissemination, and the fraction any one person could know has explosively increased, exponentially increased, and decreased, respectively. By 1500, the number of distinct tracts printed somewhere in Europe, Incunabula, were in the tens of thousands. Could one person access, read, and absorb all this information? Was it even worth doing? Thus, about the time that Spain and Portugal set out to expand their control into the Western Hemisphere, the amount that was known, the amount knowable, and the amount that was "out there" but not known to each individual expanded. If in 1493, no one in England knew that Christopher Columbus had returned from the islands just east of what would later be called America, were they ignorant? What about in 1494? By the time Magellan's voyage had circumnavigated the globe in 1522 (sans Magellan, alas), all of Europe could know there was a continent beyond their western horizon. Until the Conquistadors started wreaking havoc in the Americas, how much were the native people aware of Europe, its civilizations, religions, armaments, and attitudes?

The Gregorian calendar, now the common calendar of societies deeply influenced by Europe, was set in 1588. At that time, modern mathematics did not exist, nor did chemistry, electronics, combustion engines, flight, or high speed communications. The idea that the earth orbits the sun was controversial; that orbits were elliptical was not yet known. The Reformation was approximately 70 years along, and it would be another 60 years before Western Europe, tired of religiously justified conflict, would sign the Treaty of Westphalia, stabilizing disparate interpretations of Christianity across the continent. Thus, only 430 years before I got the idea to write this book, a mere 22 generations, much (most?) of what is currently considered essential knowledge did not exist, with the exception of religious texts (and even there, English versions were still in the future). Those who knew a profession, plus a religious canon, thought they, together with their similarly educated neighbors, knew everything.

Figure 7.2 shows the rather battered copy of the 1911 edition of the *Encyclopedia Britannica* that graces my home bookshelves. The set was purchased by my grandparents, and I was told that, in its

Figure 7.2. All but four volumes of the 1911 *Encyclopedia Britannica*.

day, it covered all human knowledge, or at least all knowledge of which the English-speaking world was aware. The pictured shelf excludes the last three substantive volumes and the index. Ignoring for the moment the question of whether the volumes are comprehensive, it was nevertheless the conceit of the time that it was possible for an educated person to know, or at least know of, everything. Read the Britannica, read the Bible, and read the daily newspaper. That was it. Fiction? Know Shakespeare, read the English and American novelists (and maybe a French or Italian author or two), and be cognizant of opera. Music? Beethoven, Bach, Brahms, Dvořák, Mozart, Tchaikovsky, Gilbert and Sullivan, and maybe the dissonance of the new renegades, Mahler and Schoenberg. Ignore that horrible popular music coming from Tin Pan Alley and the ragtime coming from bordellos. What about the expertise that went into manual labor, building railroads, forging steel, farming, or ranching? That wasn't necessarily considered knowledge. Even then, "knowing everything" wasn't knowing everything; declarative knowledge was different than tacit expertise.

In 1911, high speed communication meant steam-powered ships, express trains, and telegraph lines. Phone exchanges were local (the first transcontinental phone call did not happen until after the Great War, later renamed World War I). It would be one more year before Arizona became the 48th U.S. state.

Contrast this with the situation 109 years later (I'm drafting this in November 2020). I have the preconceived notion that Wikipedia is the biggest widely known encyclopedia. I asked Google, "How many topics are covered by Wikipedia?", and a few clicks later get to https://en.wikipedia.org/wiki/Wikipedia:Size_comparisons. It has a graphic, dated August 2010, purporting to show how big Wikipedia had become in terms of Britannica volumes. It was about 135 times bigger than the space shown in Figure 7.2 (although the font was likely larger in the comparison volumes). And then I Googled "Size of Wikipedia" and got a different article (https://en.wikipedia.org/wiki/Wikipedia:Size_of_Wikipedia) that shows the rate of growth of the site and the sizes of the various language editions, together with a graphic dated March 2020 of the

English version's size that shows 2,647 volumes covering almost 143 shelves. As of Thanksgiving 2020, the English version has 6,197,253 articles containing over 3.7 billion words.

However, what we have just shown is that not all of those articles have unique information; there is redundancy. Suppose we wrote a computer program to exclude redundancies and to provide a new Wikipedia article as soon as we finished each one. Could a person read all the articles in Wikipedia? At 300 words per minute (Wikipedia's estimate of typical reading speed with comprehension) and assuming that 3 billion words are non-redundant (and that we don't look at pictures, listen to audio, or watch video), that's 19 years of reading, or 38 years of reading at 12 hours per day. It is physically possible for someone to read it all — provided no more articles are written (how likely is that?). But even if every word were read and understood, there are still all the maps to see, images to study, music to hear, and that would, likely, overwhelm a lifetime. Of course, Wikipedia is not all human knowledge or even all English language knowledge. The articles come with footnotes that link to other websites, to scientific articles, to newspaper articles, and to speeches where copyright restrictions prevent quoting them *in toto*. We thus have demonstrated again:

> IT IS PHYSICALLY IMPOSSIBLE FOR ANYONE TO KNOW EVERYTHING THAT HAS BEEN EXPRESSED IN THE ENGLISH LANGUAGE.

Of course, there are numerous other languages (Google says there are approximately 6,500 languages spoken. Some are dying, some have no written equivalent, and some can be written in multiple ways.). It is trite but true that northern indigenous peoples have more detail in their language for frozen water than indigenous people in the tropics, just as tropical peoples have more to discuss about heat and humidity than their northern indigenous neighbors. None of this can be adequately expounded upon solely in English.

Just because there are huge gaps in what we know individually, that does not stop people from acting on the premise that they know enough to make good judgments on various topics. This is most famously explained by the Dunning-Kruger Effect (Kruger & Dunning, 1999). Any philosopher reading this book will, justifiably, note that I am sufficiently ill-read in philosophy that this book is a classic example of someone who doesn't know a field expounding on it anyway. But even in my own field of analytical chemistry, I frequently feel like I don't know enough. The day I knew the most in all my life was in 1976, the day after I took my preliminary examination, the oral exam that admits a Ph.D. student to degree candidacy. I had written a research proposal and survived a grueling cross-examination by a panel of four erudite faculty members. I was there! I was certified! Of course, I kept learning thereafter. At that time, I had done no reading about nonlinear dynamics, ultrasonically levitated drops, nanotechnology (the field didn't yet exist), or pedagogical theory. I had never used an electronic camera (CCDs had only been invented a few years before). All of these areas are ones to which I later made contributions, at least in small measure. And yet, in '76, I thought I knew it all. If there was so much I didn't know in an area where I had read paper after paper and combed the scholarly literature in detail, what about the areas where I didn't even know there was a literature? And you, dear reader, are equally unknowledgeable overall, even though there are areas in which I am sure you know vastly more than I do.

It's even worse than that. Because of the feedback loop as shown in Figure 7.1, we cannot learn as fast as we can measure or observe. Prior knowledge biases what we choose to explore and alters how we interpret what we encounter. Thus input bandwidth, how many bytes of data can transit into our heads, sets a ceiling on how much we can learn. Reinforcement learning, building on prior knowledge, is faster and easier than novel learning, learning that requires building of new perspectives or disrupting old ones. We'll see more about this in Chapter 11 on nonlinearity.

The feedback loops are a double-edged sword. When we learn something correctly, the feedbacks lock in the knowledge, making employment of the knowledge efficient and rapid. Yet, if we need to change assumptions, they make relearning difficult. Have you ever been present for a child's first independent steps? They've been crawling and cruising for weeks. They've held on to tables or parental hands and learned that legs can propel them. But they fall over because they haven't gotten coordination figured out. And then they do figure it out. It's instantaneous. It's digital (or at least it was for my youngest daughter). One minute, it seems like the brain/leg coordination isn't there. The next, she's toddling from room to room. Once talking starts, vocabulary explodes to several hundred words quickly (although "no", "mom", and "up" or some similar demand to be carried are prominent). The downside? Once a pattern is set, changing it is extraordinarily hard. Watch someone trying to learn to walk again after surgery, a military injury, or a stroke. Try learning a second language if you're 50 (it's a lot easier at 5). Similarly, when stimuli are flooding the learner, processing slows down if there is a mismatch between hypothesis and result. The equations in Chapter 1 need a "sticking factor," a filter on input data that says whether the sensed parameter can be included in short-term thinking, or whether the measurement fails to be recorded in a useful form.

First with radio, then with television, then telephone modems, and finally the internet, humanity has developed ever faster ways to move information. When I started in graduate school, the 1200 baud modem on our terminal connected to the main University computer seemed outlandishly fast. I was used to a 10-character-per-second (about 80 baud) teletype. I now have upwards of 225 megabits per second download speed and 13 megabits per second upload speed. I can receive data over 10 times as fast as I can send it, but I can send over 10,000 times as fast now as I could 45 years ago. Can I learn 10,000 times faster? No. I can harvest raw data much faster thanks to Google, Duck Duck Go, Wikipedia, and a myriad of curated databases available through my local library. While memorizing may be good mental exercise, it is now so easy to look up physical constants, equations, poems, songs, and works of art that instantaneous recall is now more of a parlor trick than a necessity. But this speed highlights yet another set of problems.

7.3 Someone, Everyone, or No One Knows

If learning facts and memorizing artifacts of a culture is no longer necessary to access either facts or artifacts, what does it mean to be educated? When *Mathematica* can take integrals, simplify expressions, and solve equations (not to mention drawing graphs) almost faster than one can supply problems that used to stump 7th through 12th grade students for days, where's the motivation to learn mathematical manipulations? Yet, without doing and understanding the manipulations, will anyone know what questions to ask the programs? Is modern technology the next-to-last gasp of intellectual growth of the last 500 years, to be followed by a return to a technology-free culture because too few engineers know how to do what was so laboriously learned in half a millennium? A friend, upon hearing I was going to mention this concept, pointed me to a novella from 1909, E. M. Forster's *The Machine Stops*. In ten minutes of web searching I couldn't find a complete citation, but found that reprints are widely available (including PDF downloads — it's out of copyright), there are modern updates, critical comments, a small ecosystem that you can find by searching online faster than I can write to explain what you'll see. But do you have time to find it? Read it? Think about it? Or is merely knowing that *Brave New World* (Huxley, 1932) was hardly the first book to worry about technology swallowing humanity enough?

Here's a tiny corner of the problem. Much of modern electronics is based on complementary metal oxide semiconductor circuits, CMOS. The first step in making CMOS is to make ultrapure, single crystal silicon. Ideally, one wants silicon in which there are no impurity atoms (impurities will later be doped into the silicon intentionally, with fine spatial tolerances, and careful control of amounts). How pure? In the early days (the 1940s), silicon that was 99.999% pure was considered quite clean. By the 1950s, impurities were reduced below 1 part per billion, or silicon was 99.9999999% pure. In some cases, even higher purities are needed and produced. Can you grow silicon that pure? Neither can I. Modern civilization featuring cellular telephones, bright, thin panel displays, video games, and the internet are utterly dependent on being able to make high-purity silicon. How many people need to know how to do this? 1 billion? Probably not. 1 million? Probably not. 100? Maybe. 10? Surely. 1? That would be living dangerously. If the only person who knows how to make really clean silicon retired, all the tacit knowledge required to make the processes work would be lost. All the scholarly articles in all the journals would be useless until another person read enough papers and played with the processes sufficiently to relearn what to do and how to resolve the inevitable problems and errors that are encountered. Artificial intelligence and good documentation may help, but it's not the same as being able to do the job. How do the billions of people on the planet ensure that enough, but not too many, people have the required skill and experience? How do we identify the right people? What criteria should we use? How will the people know if they're right for the job? What fulfillment is there in doing one critical job extraordinarily well for decades? What compensation is appropriate? Given that I am a North American retired academic, am I even asking a broad enough set of questions, given that the right people might be living in a country that I wouldn't name in the first 50 that come to mind?

While we are living in an age where communications bandwidth seems to increase without limit, we will eventually reach some point where transistors can get no smaller and no faster, communications channels can be no more numerous and no faster, and there is so much information that it cannot be rapidly accessed. We will then be back to where we were before Gutenberg, though at a high level. There will be knowledge saturation and communications saturation. I have no idea who said it first, but my colleague Larry R. Faulkner was the first person whom I heard observe, "We lose more information in the library each year than we add to it." A quick Google search reveals that every minute, about 500 hours of YouTube videos are uploaded. We are generating information and storing it faster than it can possibly be accessed with comprehension. The result is that while much is known, in the sense that someone has generated a document recording the information, most possible information is not known in a place and time where it is needed. Yet people act based on what they know (or at least think they know). A tiny subset of the knowable is the basis for each culture. All sorts of thought leaders advocate for specific ways of addressing the world. All of them, working from an information deficit, are leaving out important perspectives. Where has data generation, storage and retrieval been most effective? Where the problems are, comparatively speaking, simple. "Any culture that can land a man on the moon can surely …" Any completion of that sentence that involves anything other than rocketry and space exploration is misguided. Landing someone on the moon is a convergent activity; many pieces of a problem are put together sequentially to achieve a narrowly defined goal. But the usual predicates to the just-quoted sentence fragment are divergent activities: curing cancer (a whole set of diseases), ending poverty (a complex set of behaviors, conditions, and interactions), or cleaning up the environment. Environmental cleanup is an entropy reduction process — we are trying to remove dispersed, unwanted components from a complicated, spatially extended mixture. Inherently this requires expenditure of energy, but energy generation is always less than 100% efficient, creating undesirable environmental impacts!

Now that you're hopeless that you can know enough to comprehensively address any issue, let us continue with what physical science knows about measurement. In navigating the world, you now have the benefit of a mindset that may or may not have previously been part of your thinking. At least you can bring one more perspective to bear on life's vicissitudes.

8

Detection Limit

Polyfluorinated alkyl substances, PFAS, are toxic; they disrupt endocrine function. They are found in drinking water. How much would you like to have in your drinking water? Before you say "zero, of course!" read this chapter.

Start with a glass full of your favorite flavored drink (preferably non-alcoholic; you need to be thinking clearly). Take a sip, and note the flavor. Get an empty glass, pour a splash of the drink into that glass, and fill the second glass ¾ full of water. Stir. Take a sip. It will still taste a little like the original drink, but it will be weaker. Now repeat, taking a splash of the weakened (diluted) drink, pouring it into an empty glass, adding water, and tasting. How many times do you have to dilute the drink before you taste nothing but water? At the point where you can just barely taste the flavor, you have reached your personal detection limit for your favorite flavor.

Would some instrumentation still be able to detect that flavor? It's the Chubby Checker limbo question all over again: how low can you go? Suppose you like sugary soda (bad for your teeth and waistline, but pleasing on the palate). The nutrition information for Coca Cola says that there are 39 grams (140 calories) of carbohydrates in a 12-ounce (355 mL) serving (https://www.

myfitnesspal.com/nutrition-facts-calories/coca-cola-12oz-serving-whole-can, 11/27/2020). I am not privy to Coke's secret formula, but sucrose is sweet, inexpensive, and weighs in at 4 calories per gram (https://sugar.ca/sugar-basics/uncover-the-truth-about-sugar, 12/1/2020). Within round-off error, it looks like Coke uses sucrose (molecular weight 348 g/mol), and its concentration is 0.3 molar (to one significant figure). If at each transfer/dilution step, you reduce the concentration to 1/3 of its previous value, the sequence of concentrations (all to 1 significant figure) would be: 0.1 M, 30 mM, 10 mM, 4 mM, 100 µM, 40 µM, 10 µM, 5 µM, 200 nM, 50 nM, 20 nM, 6 nM, … . At what point can you no longer taste the sweetness? (*Scientific American* has a slightly more rigorous approach to the question: https://www.scientificamerican.com/article/bring-science-home-taste-thresholds/).

Let's suppose a mouthful of soda is about 20 mL. What if there were just one sugar molecule in that volume? From what we learned about shot noise, we'd know that would be 1 ± 1 molecule; there'd be about equal likelihood that there would be 0 or 2 molecules in that volume. We couldn't be sure what would happen. In an instrument that could reliably tell whether it had spotted a single sugar molecule, we would still require at least 9 molecules in the sample, since that would be shot noise limited signal of 9 ± 3. 9 molecules in 20 mL is a concentration of 7.5×10^{-22} moles per liter. That's 13 orders of magnitude more dilute than 1 nM.

After years of analytical chemists arguing over how precise a measurement should be in order to establish that something is present, that it has been detected on a statistically sound basis, perhaps in exhaustion, the decision was that the signal from the molecules present had to exceed the noise sensed in the absence of the molecule by a factor of 3. This corresponds to a signal level that gives a 99% probability that the signal is due to the sought-for substance, not random noise. "Why not 2 standard deviations (95% probability the signal isn't random)?" "Why not 1 standard deviation (67% probability the signal isn't random)?" When I was an undergraduate, I attended the Pittsburgh Conference on Analytical Chemistry and Applied Spectroscopy, and heard people passionately asking exactly those questions. The smaller the number of standard deviations, the less reliably anyone can assert "I found it!" The higher the number of standard deviations, the less impressive the number claimed as the detection limit sounds. My colleagues decided that reliability was more important than impressive, but shaky, claims.

No one calls the Pittsburgh Conference by its full name anymore. Everyone calls it Pittcon. It hasn't been in Pittsburgh since 1967, but it's still run by scientists headquartered there.

But all the puffery has not disappeared. Because DL is easy to confuse with dL (deciliter – 1/10th liter or 100 mL), a different name was needed so that "detection limit" could be abbreviated. Some wag dreamed up "limit of detection", LoD, and that's what you'll see in much modern literature.

So back to our original question: what is "zero" for PFAS? Let's look at two techniques, and discuss each technique's LoD.

A PFAS has lots of carbon-fluorine single bonds. How can we see evidence of such bonds? The two we'll consider are nuclear magnetic resonance (NMR) spectroscopy and LC-MS/MS, liquid chromatography followed by two sequential mass spectrometers. They sound high tech, and both are. The literature says both will work, but in practice one is clearly preferable.

NMR magnets are frequently built as superconducting magnets, maintained at liquid helium temperatures. The cost of the liquid helium and liquid nitrogen to keep the magnet cold is lower than the cost of electricity and cooling for an ordinary electromagnet, and it doesn't hurt that, once cooled and magnetized, the superconducting magnet may be more stable.

8.1 The NMR Approach

In NMR (Figure 8.1), the spinning nuclei of atoms in a sample interact with an external magnetic field

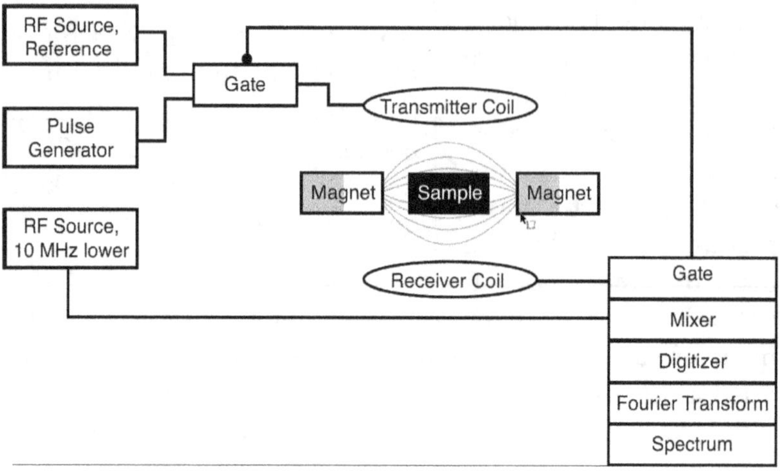

Figure 8.1. NMR spectrometer.

imposed by a large electromagnet. The nuclear magnets align with the magnet's field. Radio waves flip the nuclear magnets out of alignment with the field; the nuclei then return to alignment, emitting energy in the form of radio waves as they get back in order. The absorption and emission occur at an energy that is the difference between having the nuclei line up with the field or opposite the field. The bigger the external field, the higher the energy difference and the higher the radio frequency. The more nuclei involved, the higher the signal. And, it shouldn't surprise you, different nuclei have different spin, and so different energy. Fluorine has an ease of measurement second only to hydrogen. However, to sense the nuclei, there has to be sufficient energy difference so that the spin flips can be detected. If the anti-aligned energy and the co-aligned energy are the same, the population of the two alignments will be the same, the radio waves will simply interchange these co-energetic, or degenerate, sets of spins and no net signal will arise. There has to be a population difference to see a signal, and the population ratio is

$$\frac{P^*}{P_0} = e^{-E^*/k_B T} \tag{8.1}$$

where P stands for population, E is energy, * is the higher energy state, T is the temperature of the probed material (not the temperature of the magnet!), and k_B is Boltzmann's constant, still $1.38064852 \times 10^{-23}$ J K^{-1}.

NMR has a reputation of having poor detection limits. This is because E^* in equation (8.1) is fairly small. The gyromagnetic ratio of ^{19}F is about 25.18×10^{-7} rad $Tesla^{-1}$ s^{-1}. In an 11.74 Tesla magnet, common for 500 MHz hydrogen NMR, that means that E^* for fluorine is 25.18×10^{7} rad $Tesla^{-1}$ s^{-1} $\times$ 11.74 Tesla $\times$ 1.05457×10^{-34} J s (using $\hbar$ since we have to cancel radians to clear units), or 3×10^{-25} J. To maintain a population difference, we need the exponent in equation (8.1) to be as big as possible, which means keeping the temperature low. Practically, that means liquid nitrogen temperature or 77 K. The population ratio is thus $\exp(-3 \times 10^{-25}/(77 \times 1.38 \times 10^{-23}))$ or $1 - 3 \times 10^{-4}$. That means only 0.03% of the nuclei will flip (and if the temperature is higher, the population is even less amenable to measurement). Is it any wonder that NMR has the reputation of being good for elucidating structures of pure compounds, but is not good for trace analysis? And yet, with the cleverness of chemists, physicists, and engineers, it can do the job.

The key is not to use NMR in isolation. If all the PFAS in a large volume of water can be scavenged into a small volume and then observed in that small volume, such preconcentration can raise the signal intensity. If we require 10 μL of 1 mM PFAS to easily see it, that's only 10^{-8} moles. If a typical compound has a molecular weight of 400, and we start with 1 L of water, we're looking for 4 μg of fluorinated compounds in that liter of water. 4 parts per billion. If we looked directly in the water, it's hopeless. But if we pass all that water over a material that adsorbs the PFAS (think of it as flypaper for fluorinated chemicals) and then release all of the PFAS into a tiny volume of a solvent that doesn't get in the way of the NMR measurement, we have what we need. And, sure enough, that's what Cain and Powers (Cain & Powers, 2020) did.

At least, with a clean laboratory sample, that's what they did. But as was observed by G. E. F. Lundell in 1933 in "The Analysis of Things as They Are" (Lundell, 1933), real samples do not come neatly prepared for the analyst. They come from a messy, complicated world. If anything in the sample sticks to the adsorber material better than PFAS, and there's enough of the competing material, the PFAS will not be retained and the NMR data will make it look like the water is clean, even if it isn't. It's just like theater seating. Once I get to a movie, I find an empty seat and plop into place. After that, I don't move. But if all the seats are filled when I get there, it doesn't matter how immobile I would be if I got a seat — I turn around and walk out. PFAS is no more aggressive at jousting for surface adsorption space than I am.

Thus, while we could use NMR, we're totally dependent on adsorbing and desorbing the molecule of interest, and on the precision and accuracy of both processes (go read the paper for demonstration that less than 100% of the PFAS is released, even under optimal circumstances). So now we fall back on mass spectrometry. To be preferable to NMR, it has to be able to detect a smaller amount of PFAS, even in the presence of other compounds that complicate the measurement. It's not just "how low can you go," but "given that there's other substances and interactions that get in the way, can you reliably go low enough?"

8.2 The LC-MS Approach

Liquid chromatography separates molecules by passing them through a tube filled with a solid (or thin film of liquid sticking to the solid) that differentially retains compounds of interest. For the sorts of columns used for PFAS determinations, the solid phase would attract the hydrophobic alkyl regions of the PFAS compounds and ignore charged ions or highly polar portions of molecules like aldehydes, ketones, and amines. That means the polar compounds will come out of the column quickly, but the PFAS compounds and many other organic molecules will elute more slowly. That will clean up the sample. Then we squirt the column effluent into a mass spectrometer. What does it do? And why do we need two mass spectrometers in sequence? And didn't we talk about ICP-MS two chapters ago, so why am I bringing this up again? Which reminds me — why not just use ICP-MS and quantify the fluorine? Excellent questions! Let's discuss how molecular mass spectrometry works, and then go back and explain why ICP-MS isn't the method of choice.

The first thing that happens is that we turn molecules into ions. Yes, I know I just said that ionic compounds are not retained by the liquid chromatograph; the PFAS compounds are neutral in aqueous or alcoholic solution. But once they're sprayed into the vacuum in which the main parts of the mass spectrometer are located, we can shoot electrons at the molecules and ionize them. In fact, since there's a lot of fluorine around, we could end up with either positive cations or negative anions. Alternatively, if there are free protons in the solvent, we can form a protonated adduct. If M is a neutral molecule, then

$$\begin{gathered} M + e^- \rightarrow M^+ + 2e^- \\ or \\ M + e^- \rightarrow M^- \\ or \\ M + H^+ \rightarrow [M{+}H]^+ \end{gathered} \tag{8.2}$$

Formation of cations is more common, but mass spectrometry can work with either type of ion. Of course, we choose whichever one gives us a lower detection limit. As we'll see shortly, we can also form the cations in solution, evaporate the solvent, and shoot the dry ions into the vacuum. That's called electrospraying, a process also used in painting (charge the paint positively, the part being painted negatively, and the paint is attracted to the part).

Once we have an ion in a vacuum, it acts just like a bowling ball. It travels in a straight line until it hits something, subject only to the pull of gravity. But we don't leave the ion alone — we manipulate it with electric fields (actually, the earliest mass spectrometers used magnetic fields as well, but instruments using electric fields can be made more compactly, so magnetic instruments are becoming less common). There are many ways to manipulate the ions, but three have emerged as most cost effective: time of flight (described in Chapter 4), quadrupole (Figure 4.3), and Orbitrap™. The most common for LC-MS/MS (Figure 8.2) uses quadrupole mass

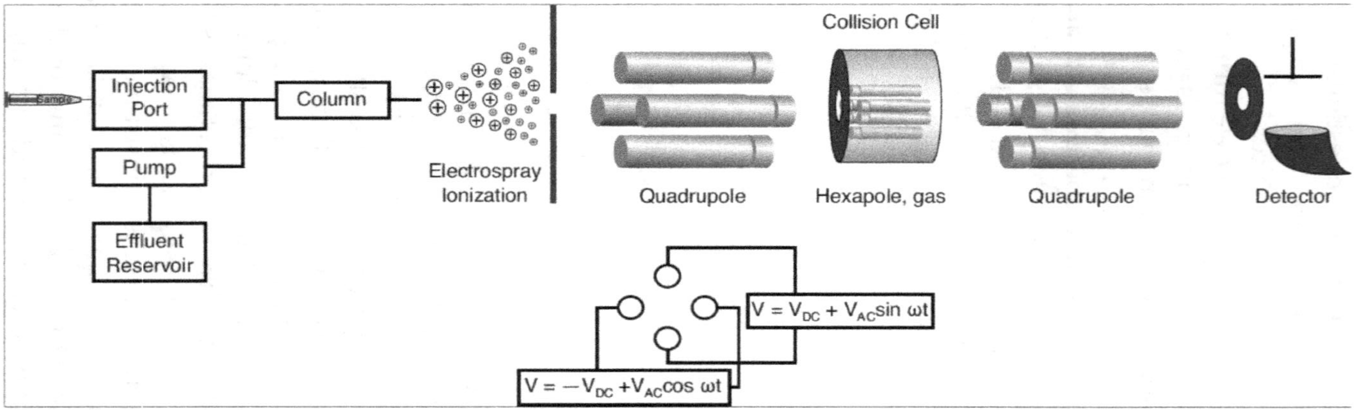

Figure 8.2. LC-MS/MS. The lower sub-diagram shows an end-on view of the potentials imposed on the four quadrupole rods.

spectrometers, which rapidly scan from about 10 Daltons (atomic mass unit, defined as 1/12 the mass of a ^{12}C atom) to 1,000 Daltons, about 1,000 times per second. The resolution is also about 1 Dalton. Suppose that the particular fluorinated compound of interest is perfluorooctanoic acid (PFOA), $C_8F_{15}O_2H$, nominal molecular weight 414. We would expect that either the cation $C_8F_{17}O_2H^+$ or $C_8F_{17}O_2H_2^+$ would form. We'd look for a peak at mass-to-charge ratio of 414 or 415. And, of course, we'd see a peak there. But how do we know it's due to PFOA? Is that the only molecular ion with a molecular weight of 414 or 415 Daltons? Of course not. If I look for molecules with molecular weight 414 that might behave similarly to PFOA on a liquid chromatography column, they would have formulas like $C_{28}O_2H_{46}$ or $C_{26}O_4H_{38}$. Lupulone, an example of the latter, isn't a primary carboxylic acid, so it probably wouldn't elute at the same time as PFOA, but 5-cholestene-3-carboxylic acid probably would. If we put an even number of nitrogens into the formula, we could come up with additional compounds, so in a sample from natural waters, where there are many living organisms, some polypeptide would interfere. Are we doomed?

No! We can break up whatever shows up near $m/q = 414$ or 415 by colliding the ions with a puff of gas (helium, argon, ammonia, maybe even xenon), and then look at the mass spectrum of the pieces that are broken off. By analogy, if we started with a car, accelerated it to 1,000 mph, hit it with an air-to-ground missile, and then found a chunk of metal on the ground with a nameplate that said "Corolla," we'd have a pretty good idea that we'd just destroyed a Toyota. Similarly, if we fragment something with a mass to charge ratio of 414 or 415 and find fragments that look like fragments of a known PFOS, we can guess we've found one. The number of ions we get (or the charge collected by an electron multiplier) is proportional to how much material is present. We can quantify the amount of PFOS.

Well, let's be careful. We can ALMOST quantify PFOS. If I told you that you detected 100 ions with m/q characteristic of some specific PFOS, would you know the concentration in the original solution? No. Why not? Because you don't know what fraction of ions made it into the mass spectrometer, what fraction was ionized, what fraction was broken up in the collision cell, and what the ion collection efficiency at the detector may be. You don't know how much of the sample made it into the vacuum and how much was lost. So there's one more trick: before we start the analysis, we add a known quantity of something that elutes at a slightly different time than the PFOS substances but whose mass spectrum we know. We then measure the ratio of the signal from the PFOS fragment to the signal from the reference compound. If the ionization efficiency or detection efficiency changes, as long as it changes for sample and reference to the same degree, the ratio will be a reliable indication of the amount of the PFOS. This approach is called "using an internal standard." It's not internal to the original water — it's added at the earliest possible stage of analysis.

A common sample size for LC-MS/MS is 10 μL. If we started with 1 ng/L of PFOS (one-fourth of what we used in the NMR example, and below the LoD for NMR), we have 10 fg (10^{-14} g) of PFOS in the sample. If there are 10 different PFOSs in the sample, we'd have about 10^{-15} g of each. For a typical molecular weight of 400, that gives us 1.5 million molecules going into the experiment. The column transmits most of them and 1% of those get into the mass spectrometer. Perhaps half get ionized. Of those, 50% come out of the first quadrupole, 10% get fragmented, and 50% of those get detected. So we're down to 200 ions, specific to one PFOS that get detected. But, remembering that shot noise goes as the square root of the signal, we'll have a precision of 10:1, and can

> There are techniques for getting more than 1% of the LC output into the mass spectrometer. Drew Sauter has a patent on injecting 100% of the ions into a mass spectrometer from an LC (Sauter & Sauter, 2018; Sauter, 2016). My students used these droplet launchers in a completely different context — launching sub-microliter droplets into ultrasonically levitated drops. The chemistry we were studying was interesting, and the associated videos (https://pubs.acs.org/doi/full/10.1021/ac403968d) are entertaining. Think of them as electrohydrodynamic basketball (Chainani *et al.*, 2014)!

reliably quantify the compound. Recalling that there were 9 other PFOSs in the sample, we're actually looking at about 1 fg of the specific PFOS in the 10 μL sample, and there could be additional PFOSs at other masses. We could have a factor of three lower in just this compound and still detect it with a certainty of 99%, even if there were no other PFOSs present. So our LoD is well below 1 ng/L and, unlike the NMR, we can have all sorts of other compounds in the sample and not worry about them. LC-MS/MS has the detection limit and specificity we need to look at truly tiny amounts of PFOS.

While LC-MS/MS allows measurement of molecular weight, you may still have a nagging feeling that ICP-MS might have allowed us to identify fluorinated compounds, and maybe that's good enough for determining if water is contaminated. Why not do so? First, fluoride from fluoridation would swamp any signal from PFOS; indeed PFOS may have formed from some of that fluoride reacting with organic compounds in the water. To distinguish between isolated fluoride ions and PFOS, some sort of separation is required. There are LC-ICP-MS instruments, so just the separation issue isn't justification enough, and not all problems require molecular identification for solution; simply knowing that there are fluoridated compounds might be adequate. Still, ICP-MS is unlikely to be helpful here. The problem is that fluorine is difficult to ionize. Fluorine atoms are the strongest oxidizing neutral atoms known — they attach electrons to form F^-. ICP-MS is most often used to detect cations (since most of the periodic table is made of elements that, when heated to several thousand degrees, release electrons). How much energy does it take to release an electron from an atom? It's E^* for ionization, analogous to E^* for magnetic spin flip energy in equation (8.1). The ICP is typically operated using argon as the plasma gas. Argon requires 15.76 electron volts to ionize. Most metals require a lot less, so iron, sodium, calcium, etc., wafting through an argon plasma will be ionized by colliding with energetic electrons. Fluorine, however, has an ionization potential of 17.42 electron volts. Few electrons will be energetic enough to ionize fluorine atoms, so only a tiny fraction of the fluorine will be ionized, making mass spectrometry a poor means of detection. We can get around this issue by running the plasma on helium, with ionization energy 24.59 electron volts, and some people have done that. However, 1) helium is less effective in vaporizing, fragmenting, and atomizing molecules than is the heavier argon, 2) maintaining a stable helium plasma is more difficult than maintaining an argon plasma, and 3) helium is comparatively rare. Which is a better use of resources — doing elemental analysis (when there are alternatives) or saving the helium for use in superconducting magnets for magnetic resonance imaging instruments for medical diagnosis? Until we can mine Jupiter or Saturn for helium, being judicious in its use here on earth is wise.

8.3 What Does "Zero" Mean?

Finally, we can get back to how little PFOS you're willing to tolerate. If we use an ordinary LC-MS/MS, we see that we can readily detect below 1 part per trillion of PFOS. But is that zero? If we inject 100% of the LC effluent into the MS, we can probably detect 10 parts per quadrillion. Is that zero? If we only have 10 molecules of a particular PFOS in the 10 μL specimen we inject into the LC and we get 100% of the molecules to the MS detector and recognize it as a PFOS with a shot noise limited signal-to-noise ratio of 3, is that zero? 10 molecules per 10 microliters is 10^6 molecules per liter, which corresponds to 1 attomolar or 1 part per quadrillion. That's as low as LC-MS/MS can go with a 10 μL sample, but is that zero? "Zero means none — not even one molecule." But there's no way to measure at that level. If there were only one PFOS molecule in the Pacific Ocean, you'd have to run the entire ocean through an instrument, but if you got a signal from a purported PFOS molecule, it would be 1 ± 1, and thus not statistically significant. When we count, zero has an intuitive meaning, but in chemical measurement, zero means "undetectable." But as we've seen with just two instruments for comparison, "detectable" means "can be measured with statistical significance under defined circumstances with characterized methods, specimens, and instruments." The LC-MS/MS would give a non-zero reading at a lower PFOS level than the NMR. Gas chromatography with an infrared absorbance detector would give a zero reading at a higher level than that. Gas chromatography with a thermal conductivity detector would give a zero reading at an even higher level. Suddenly, the detection limit of one or another instrument has policy implications. How can you know if something matters if you can't detect it? How do you know if something matters at a low level if you do detect it? If one part per million of something, consumed daily, sickens 10% of a population after one year, would 0.1 parts per million (100 parts per billion) sicken 1% of a population in a year, or 10% of a population in 10 years, or no one?

When I started into this chapter, I knew I would cite https://www.vanishingzero.org/. The author, John Long, was a Champaign, IL native who was lead chemist at the G. F. Smith Chemical Company. Smith, in turn, was an analytical chemistry professor at Illinois from 1922 to 1961, a key player in designing what is still the standard curriculum in learning about analytical chemistry, and co-founder of the company that bears his name. He and graduate student Charles Goetz invented spray whipped cream and the aerosol dispenser industry. Smith was an advocate for the use of perchloric acid to prepare specimens for analysis, because perchlorate could oxidize almost any organic chemical. Aside from perchlorates used for rocket fuel, I believe that GFSChemicals Inc. is still the largest manufacturer of perchlorates in the world. So when it was alleged that perchlorates could displace iodine in the thyroid gland and thus were health hazards, GFSChemicals was worried for obvious reasons. That's when Long put the website together. And you can guess the immediate back-reaction that elicited: GFSChemicals had a huge financial stake in not having their perchlorate business shut down. Since GFSChemicals supported a chemistry conference I attended each year and a descendent of Smith's supported an annual lecture at the Illinois Department of Chemistry, I had more than passing sympathy for their concern. And I suspect every environmentalist reading this paragraph just decided I have limited credibility because of the obvious conflicts of interest.

There are people who passionately think differently about what happens when detection limits reveal trace amounts of material that previously were invisible (http://tenovin-1.com/2019/05/21/the-concept-of-the-vanishing-zero-which-was-first-discussed-50/, 12/2/2020). There are at least some substances that are toxic at high concentrations that are essential nutrients at low concentrations (selenium, copper, molybdenum) so that extrapolating behavior to sub-detection-limit levels may be destructive of health and welfare. If you can't detect it, you can neither fear, appreciate, nor regulate a substance. But just because you can detect something also should not dictate whether you fear, appreciate, or regulate it.

When we calibrate analytical instruments, one of the samples that is run is a reagent blank. That is, we do all the manipulations we will do when looking for a target compound, except we leave that target compound out. How do we know that there is none of the target compound present? Of course, we don't. We can try to prepare a specimen that lacks whatever we're trying to measure, but we can't know that we've succeeded. Thus we have to assume that a working curve will have a non-zero blank. In fact, the blank can be negative as well as positive. If the compound we care about sticks to the walls of the apparatus, we might need some minimum amount before the compound shows up above the noise. Instead of zero being a hard, intuitive number, it's fuzzy.

Suppose we wanted to remove one part per quadrillion of a substance from water. How could we do it? There are many ways to separate chemicals: precipitation, distillation, adsorption, reaction into something less noxious. What cannot be done, however, is to make chemical species completely vanish. The fluorine in PFOS, once the PFOS is decomposed, will be an inorganic fluoride, F_2 gas, HF, or an organic fluoride. Thus, "get rid of contaminants" isn't physically possible. We can change their form, we can in many instances change their location, but the atoms we start with are the ones we end with unless there is nuclear fission or nuclear fusion, and nuclear processes add radiation and radioactivity to the list of complications. The reasonable question is: given the presence of some compound as demonstrated by valid measurement, what is the most desirable or least undesirable way to handle the substance? Once we ask that question, we need to look at the energy required to carry out a transformation, what products will result, what environmental impact those products will have, or what constructive uses they may have. Detoxification and purification are systems or optimization problems, not component problems. If we remove the offending material from water, what do we do with it? Is it more or less harmful in its next context than in its original context? How much energy and how many materials are required to remove the offending substance? Taking these externalities into account, are we overall better off trying to remove the trace impurity or leaving well enough alone? Unless we look at the engineering specifics, these questions are unanswerable.

Because of the vagueness of what "zero" means, and because the signal-to-noise ratio at the detection limit is three, the detection limit should never be specified to more than one significant figure. If I say that the detection limit is one part per billion, then that means I can tell that 1 ppb is different from 0. Were I to say that the detection limit was 1.1 parts per billion, then the implication is that I can tell that 1.0 ppb is below the detection limit, but 1.1 is above that limit. In turn, that means that I can detect a signal that is 10% different for 1.1 ppb compared to 1 ppb, and at 10% precision, I'm actually able to quantify the compound. Such numerical niceties escape many people, but those who've worked in statistics or in quantitative measurement feel such issues intensely. It's part of the culture of measurement science.

8.4 Bias and Offsets

So far, we have talked about detection limits in terms of how little of a specific molecule we can detect, and noted that we have to be aware of the effect of other chemicals, or residual amounts of the same specific molecule, in the sample matrix and reactants. But there's an additional aspect of detection limits. For each method we use, there's a low limit on whether we can distinguish any signal at all from what the instrument indicates in the absence of any analyte. In the case of a mass spectrometer, we know we need at least 10 analyte counts during the observation window, but that assumes that if we had no sample there at all, we would see zero counts.

In practice, there is a low signal absent any analyte ions, a dark current (a term that arises from first seeing such signals in optical spectrometers when all the lights were out). As soon as there is a non-zero instrument bias, seeing a signal requires that the putative signal appear at least three standard deviations of the bias above the mean bias. If a mass spectrometer sees 16 counts per second of ions in the absence of specimens, the standard deviation is 4 counts, and the signal has to be high enough that the overall standard deviation of (signal + bias) – bias is at least 3 × 4 counts = 12 counts. Using propagation of error computations:

$$\begin{aligned} S_{net} &= S_{gross} - S_{dark} \\ \sigma_{net}^2 &= \sigma_{gross}^2 + \sigma_{dark}^2 \\ \frac{S_{DL} - S_{dark}}{\sigma_{net}} &= 3 = \frac{S_{DL} - S_{dark}}{\sqrt{\sigma_{gross}^2 + \sigma_{dark}^2}} = \frac{S_{DL} - S_{dark}}{\sqrt{S_{DL} + S_{dark}}} \end{aligned} \tag{8.3}$$

If there is excess noise in either the gross or dark signal, the expression in the denominator in equation (8.3) will be more complicated. For the circumstances we're describing here, with S_{dark} = 16 counts,

$$\begin{aligned} &9\left(S_{gross} + 16\right) = \left(S_{gross} - 16\right)^2 \\ &9S_{gross} + 144 = S_{gross}^2 - 32S_{gross} + 256 \\ &0 = S_{gross}^2 - 41S_{gross} + 112 \\ &S_{gross} = \frac{41 \pm \sqrt{41^2 - 4*112}}{2} = \frac{41 \pm \sqrt{1681 - 448}}{2} = \frac{41 \pm 35}{2} = 38 \end{aligned} \tag{8.4}$$

The net signal at the detection limit is 38 – 16 = 22 counts from the detected molecule. Compared to the 9 counts that were needed against a zero dark signal, we need over twice as many detected ions. Whether in mass spectrometry, amperometry, or photometry, suppressing dark signal, blank, and background are critical for getting low detection limits.

For measurements that measure against a low, nearly zero bias, the instrument detection limit may be close to the shot noise limit. However, many instruments do not run against a zero bias. Amperometric instruments have double layer charging current. Absorbance spectrometers measure signals in comparison to 100% transmittance which is typically a high signal level. Gas chromatography thermal conductivity detectors measure signal in comparison to the thermal conductivity of pure helium. We could go off on flights of fancy looking at the lowest absorbance one can sense, or the lowest change in thermal conductivity. But that leads us away from our central theme. It pains me to not share the details of how analytical instruments have informed my interest in understanding all the gritty little details of measurement, but if I tell you that, I'll never have room to talk about the social implications of what you're reading; we'd lack the bandwidth!

When quantifying analytes, the low quantity end of the working curve is anchored by the blank and the detection limit. What about the other end of the curve?

> Postscript: After I finished this chapter, I saw a news story that U.S. EPA was considering lowering the allowed amount of PFOS in drinking water to 0.02 parts per trillion (20 parts per quadrillion) and some other fluorinated hydrocarbons to even less than that. In light of what you've read, is this low detection level realistic?

9

Dynamic Range

Once you know how low you can go, how high can you fly?

Along the highways, there are occasionally truck weigh stations. "All trucks over six tons must weigh," says the sign. An 18-wheeler may tip the scales at 80,000 lbs, with a precision (accord to NIST (National Institute of Standards and Technology) Standard HB44) of ±160 lbs. The corresponding OIML (International Organization of Legal Metrology) standard is ±40 kg. Would you want to use this scale to see how you're doing on your diet?

Similarly, a kitchen scale that works only up to 7 pounds (3 kg) is useless for weighing people, horses, or trucks. The range over which a measurement is useful is the dynamic range. It can be expressed as a range, a ratio, or the logarithm of a ratio. For an analytical balance that has a minimum useful mass of 1 mg (resolution of the readout is 0.1 mg) and a maximum of 160 g, the useful range is 159.999 g, the ratio of maximum to minimum mass is 160 g / 0.001 g = 1.6×10^5, and the range in decibels is 20 $\log_{10} m_{max}/m_{min}$ = 104 dB. "Why the factor of 20? 10 would make sense." The concept of decibels comes out of

> An alternative wording:
> If $V_2 = 10\ V_1$, then
> $\log_{10}(V_2/V_1) = \log_{10}(10V_1/V_1)$
> $= \log_{10}(10) = 1$.

communications, and 10 dB is one order of magnitude in power. The power dissipated in an electrical circuit scales as V^2 or I^2. So if V changes by one order of magnitude, $\log_{10}V$ changes by 1, but power changes by $2 \times \log_{10}V$ or 2. So that the number to the left of the decimal point in a voltage or current reading typically shows up as an integer, the extra multiplication by 10 appears, and thus either $P_{dB} \sim 10 \log_{10} P_0$ or $P_{dB} \sim 20 \log_{10} V$.

Suppose, as in a mass spectrometer, we have a method that can detect a small number of ions. How high can the signal go before the instrument fails? Each detected ion produces a pulse of several tens of thousands to several million electrons, and the pulses are counted. The pulses are not instantaneous; they have a duration that, depending on the electronics, may last from 1 ns to 20 ns (there's nothing to prevent adding capacitance to generate longer pulses, but no one wants excessively long pulses in this context). The ions arrive at the detector randomly, and to accurately count pulses, we need to avoid pulse pileup, i.e., having a second pulse arrive before the first pulse is counted and the charges cleared from the circuitry. For full details see Chaplin *et al.* (2013), but for pulses that aren't too closely overlapping, the true arrival rate, R_{true}, can be deduced from the observed arrival rate, R_0, if the pulse width τ is known:

$$R_{true} = \frac{R_0}{1 - R_0\tau} \tag{9.1}$$

Clearly, since a high enough R_0 will yield division by 0 and then negative numbers, this correction cannot work when pulses are closely packed. If τ is 10 ns, then R_0 should likely be limited to 10^7 s^{-1} or less (a 10% correction). In this case, the dynamic range is 10^6 or 120 dB. Shorten the pulses to 2 ns, and the limit increases to 5×10^7 s^{-1}, a dynamic range of 5×10^6, or 126 dB. However, we can keep going by switching from counting pulses to measuring current. If each detected ion generates (on average) 10^5 electrons, then at 10 ions s^{-1}, the current is 10^6 electrons s^{-1} or 6×10^{-12} A, 6 pA. This can be measured, but obviously it's noisy, since there are 10 spikes of

100,000 or so electrons with long pauses in between. If at 10^6 pulses per second we switch to measuring current, the mean current is 0.6 μA, easily followed with an inexpensive operational amplifier. We can use this sort of circuit up to a mean current of perhaps 10–100 mA. Why this limit? Typically, we want to observe an analog signal by digitizing a voltage. If an analog-to-digital converter has 16 bits (common and inexpensive), we want the signal to be big enough that we get 3 or 4 significant figures to the digitization. A 16-bit converter has $2^{16} = 65{,}536$ values, so at the low end of measurement, we probably want 500 or 1,000 counts. If the full-scale range of the converter is 5 V, then 1,000 counts is 1000 / 65536 × 5 V = 76 mV. So we design the current-to-voltage converter to turn 0.6 μA into something like 76 mV. Let's keep it simple: 0.6 μA gets converted to 60 mV, and the resistor that does that conversion is 6×10^{-2} V / 6×10^{-7} A = $10^5\ \Omega$. 100 kΩ, 1% precision resistors only cost a few cents each. However, at 65 times that signal, the analog-to-digital converter will saturate, i.e., it will hit a count of 65,535 and it can't go any higher. Before we get a signal that big, we'd better use a smaller resistor to keep the signal in range of the converter. At 30 μA (or above), when the digitizer count exceeds 50,000, switch to a 1 kΩ resistor (autogain amplifiers can be bought or built), the count drops to 500, and we can run up another factor of 100 in signal to 3 mA. At this point, the pulse arrival rate at the detector is 6500×10^6 per second or 6.5×10^9. Now we have a dynamic range of 6.5×10^8. We might push it farther, but now another problem shows up. The power dissipated in the current-to-voltage conversion resistor is high enough to dissipate significant heat. 3 mA across 1 kΩ is 3 V, and V^2/R = power = 9 mW. If we use a 0.5 W resistor and heat-sink it to keep it cool, that's not a problem, but if we switch to a 100 Ω resistor to push the dynamic range to 6.5×10^9, we're pushing 30 mA across 100 ohms, dissipating 90 mW, and we need a 1-Watt, heat-sunk, precision resistor. This is getting expensive, difficult to engineer precisely, and the ion current at 1 nA, unamplified, is going to start doing serious damage to the detector if the current is sustained. The point is, at such high currents, we've reached the end of the line. A mass spectrometer's dynamic range (when we detect ions by crashing them into a metal detector plate) is limited to about 10^9. Using similar logic, optical measurements are frequently limited to 8 or 9 orders of magnitude. This is not to say that clever people haven't made wider dynamic range instruments under special circumstances, but rather to indicate what is practically attainable for a reasonable budget.

While the ADC range in the previous paragraph was 16 bits, and we already mentioned the 24-bit converters used for audio recording, doesn't that leave you wondering how many bits are ultimately achievable? Of the 17,555 analog-to-digital converters at the widely known parts source, Digikey, in September 2021, 14 have a resolution of 32 bits, and they're not particularly expensive (none cost even $100). That's a resolution of 1 part in 4 billion. If a least significant bit is 1 nanovolt, then full scale is 4 volts. Would any wider scale be useful? At the nanovolt level, Johnson noise as discussed in Chapter 3 is likely to be significant. Analog electronics up to 15 V are common. Power outlets have outputs ~ ±100 V. Much above 100 V, voltages may prove lethal if accidentally contacted (and even 5 V can be lethal if there's enough current). Thus, a range of 40 bits covers the entire range of analog potentials that one is likely to encounter in terrestrial electrical measurements. Counting measurements can cover a greater range. One mole of material is 6.02×10^{23} particles, $\sim 2^{79}$.

But it's not just the instrument dynamic range that limits our ability to characterize drastic differences in amounts. Chemistry and physics have a way of getting complicated when we go from dilute to concentrated mixtures or solutions. Let's look at an example: the use of chemical derivatives to increase or shift dynamic range. But first, I'll discuss a method that can be performed manually and show its limitations.

9.1 Titration

Almost always the assumption of linearity breaks down over wide ranges of concentration or signal magnitude. As soon as a working curve becomes nonlinear, there's a worry whether simply fitting that nonlinearity is sufficiently accurate to allow measurements to remain valid, or whether to shift to a less responsive measurement that deals better with larger quantities. Suppose we want to measure the concentration of acetic acid in aqueous solution. Look at a typical bottle of vinegar — it's 4% acetic acid. That's 4% by volume. In 1 liter of vinegar, there are 40 mL of 17.4 M glacial acetic acid (actually, vinegar is fermented; concentrated acid isn't diluted with distilled water in any quality food product. But we can do the calculations as if that was where the acetic acid came from.). Thus, the expected concentration is 0.04 L × 17.4 mol L^{-1} = 0.7 M. How might we measure if an aqueous solution contains acetic acid and, if it does, what concentration it has, provided there are no other major constituents? For vinegar, the concentration is high enough that I thought about suggesting near infrared (NIR) absorbance spectroscopy. But after I looked at the literature, it turned out that the spectra are so complicated that it looked like NIR would be more trouble than it was worth. So I decided to stick with what many readers may have done if they took high school or college chemistry: titration, using a pH electrode to monitor the acidity of the solution. I'll simulate the results, taking activity corrections into account. For pure vinegar, we'll titrate a 5 mL aliquot with 0.1 M NaOH. The expected endpoint is at

Definitions

Endpoint: where during a titration there is an indication that the amount of titrant and the amount of titrand match.

Equivalence point: where during a titration the number of moles of titrand molecules and the number of titrant molecules required to react with the titrand without excess or shortfall are equal.

Ideally, the endpoint is at the equivalence point.

$$\begin{aligned} 5\,\text{mL} * 0.7\,\text{M} &= x\ \text{mL} * 0.1\,\text{M} \\ x &= 35\,\text{mL} \end{aligned} \tag{9.2}$$

We'll then dilute by factors of 10 until titration doesn't work anymore, choose another technique, and keep going. If I need to change any other conditions to make the experiment work well, I'll do so and tell you what I did and why. Since I'm including activity corrections (as mentioned in Chapter 5) and want to use formulas to calculate activity coefficients, I have to keep ionic strength below 0.1 M. See the box on the right for details. To have room for a practical experiment (I'm going to assume equipment that's macroscopic rather than using the modern microfluidic approaches), we'll add the specimen to 50 mL of distilled water to start. We'll ignore changes in partial molar volume of solutions as they mix. So that measurement of titrant volume contributes a constant error, we'll dilute NaOH to the same extent that we dilute the vinegar (so when we dilute 9:1, the stock vinegar will drop to 0.07 M and we'll use 0.01 M NaOH. The equivalence point will thus remain at 35 mL.).

> Activity is related to concentration, but does not change linearly with concentration. Charged particles can interact at a distance, so the energy of interaction changes nonlinearly with concentration. Classically, Debye and Hückel modeled activity corrections to equilibrium behavior in the early 20th century. Later, Stokes and Robinson devised empirical extensions that worked in concentrated solutions, and Ken Pitzer added quantum mechanical rigor. In calculations here, I've used the Debye-Hückel Extended Equation.
>
> Ionic strength $\mu = \frac{1}{2}\sum_i C_i Z_i^2$, with C_i the concentration of a specific ion and Z_i the charge on that ion.
>
> Activity of an ion, [X], is then approximated as γ_X[X] with γ the activity coefficient. The diameter of the solvated ion, a_X, is an empirically observed constant. At 25°C,
>
> $$-\log_{10}\gamma_X = \frac{0.5085 z_X^2 \sqrt{\mu}}{1 + 0.328 a_X \sqrt{\mu}}$$

Figure 9.1 shows several titration curves. It shows how calculations that ignore activity corrections differ from calculations that include the effect of such corrections. Such corrections are only

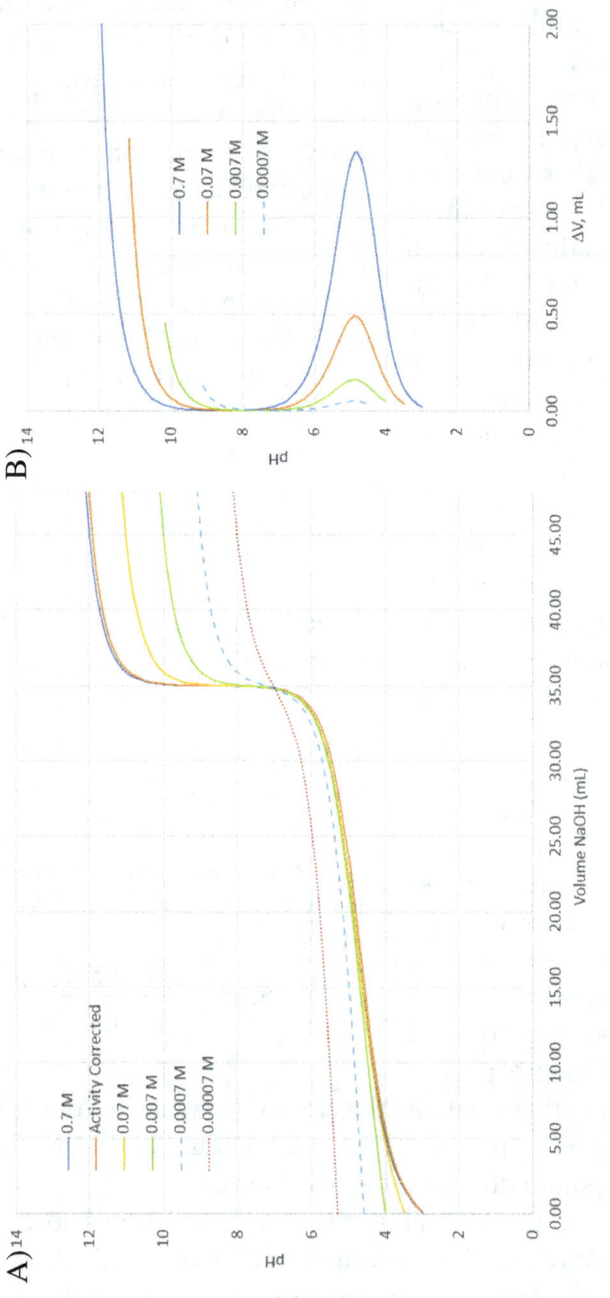

Figure 9.1. Titration for acetic acid in vinegar and diluted vinegar. A) Titration curves. B) Shift in volume at which a particular pH is reached if activity corrections are included.

visible for a significant portion of the titration curve for the highest concentration shown, which is why an inset is needed to demonstrate the effect for more dilute solutions.

Visually, we hit the equivalence point at 35 mL fairly closely, even for a factor of 10,000 dilution. The volume at which we arrive at various pH values is less affected by activity corrections as the system becomes more dilute, as we would expect. But now we have to point out the problems. To qualitatively identify a weak, monoprotic acid, a common procedure is to measure the pH halfway from the start of the titration to the equivalence point, or at 17.5 mL. We expect that to be 4.75, the pK_a of acetic acid. Once the acid concentration is less than 7 mM, we never see such a low pH. While we get an equivalence point, other than trusting the label on the bottle, what evidence do we have that we are titrating acetic acid? A typical pH meter with glass electrode has a measurement resolution of 0.01 pH units and is reliable only to 0.02 pH. A pH jump at the equivalence point less than 2 units will be difficult to fit precisely. 70 μM is close to the lower limit for such an increase. We have ignored the effects of contaminants, including CO_2 that can suppress the peak pH of the titration curve. While titration will work up to 98% glacial acetic acid, the low end of reliable titrimetric measurement is roughly 70 μM, for a dynamic range of 17.4 M/70 μM = 2.5×10^5 or 106 dB. Considering that titrations have been performed since at least the 18th century and that the glass electrode, allowing direct pH monitoring, dates to the early 20th century, it is little wonder why scientists continue to use this venerable method. There are autotitrators that eliminate the need for manual dexterity. But close examination shows that the obvious isn't quite as obvious as it seems.

If someone wishes to avoid instrumentation, there are indicators that change color at a particular pH. Looking at the titration curves, the pH at the equivalence point looks to be about 8.7. But what is it really? Table 9.1 shows some comparative data.

By construction, the equivalence point is at 35.00 mL. For 0.7 M acetic acid, diluted into 50 mL of water and titrated, this is precisely achieved. At 0.07 M, the same pH is achieved at 35.04 mL, essentially an additional drop of titrant, just over 0.1% higher than expected, and probably statistically irrelevant. As the acid is

Table 9.1. Acetic acid titration for various dilutions (theoretical).

Starting acid concentration (M)	V (pH 8.7), mL	V (pH 7.7), mL	V (pH 9.7), mL	δV_{ep}, mL	$\frac{\delta V_{ep}}{V_{ep}}$	pH_{ep}	Fixed pH overshoot
0.7	35.00	34.96	35.045	0.085	0.0024	8.7	0
0.07	35.04	34.965	35.45	0.485	0.0138	8.2	0.1%
0.007	35.45	35.0	39.75	4.75	0.1340	7.7	1.3%
0.0007	39.74	35.4	—			7.255	13.5%

further diluted, pH 8.7 is achieved at ever higher volumes. Using a colored indicator such as phenolphthalein, the equivalence point would be overshot. Avoiding that problem by choosing an indicator that changes color at a slightly lower pH (perhaps neutral red) would lead to a color change slightly too early, for minor undershoot at high concentration. The pH meter makes colorimetric endpoints moot, but a pH meter is more expensive than a drop of indicator solution. With a pH meter, the equivalence point is most easily determined by the mid-point of the pH jump near that point. Taking a 2 pH jump as indicative of where an equivalence point occurs, we see that the volume range for such a change varies from 85 microliters for 0.7 M acid to 4.75 mL for 0.007 M acid. For 700 μM acid, the equivalence point is at pH 7.255, and the 2-pH range runs from 33.45 mL to 36.63 mL, a range of 3.2 mL, or almost 10% of the titration volume. Titrations work well at high concentration, but at even minor concentration, they degrade. They don't work for trace analysis, at least in this form. There are methods for titrating reactive groups on surfaces where there are tiny amounts of material, but those don't use burettes, glass electrodes, or drops of solution to deliver and detect titrants and conditions.

9.2 Derivatization

Below 1 mM, how can we expand the dynamic range for acetic acid? You might guess the use of electrospray mass spectrometry, as discussed in the previous chapter. But that won't work. One of the common buffers used for electrospray is ammonium acetate because the buffer dissociates into ammonia and acetic acid, both neutral molecules. Electrospraying dilute acetic acid will give no direct acetate signal. Further, acetic acid is so light (formula weight for $C_2H_4O_2$ is 60 Dalton) that there is a significant problem with crowding of the spectrum with fragments of heavier ions and potential interference from, e.g., ^{60}Ni. Yet, there's an easy way to do electrospray detection of acetic acid and any other carboxylic acid: derivatize the acid in a selective manner. More generally, if you can't answer a question, change the question! Here, we link a bigger molecule to the acetate to take it into a range where mass spectrometry works well. Adding 2-hydrazinoquinoline (Lu *et al.*, 2013) to acetic acid produces a compound, 2-hydrazinoquinoline acetate, that has a mass-to-charge ratio of 202 and can readily be detected by electrospray mass spectrometry. From data I could find in the literature, I don't know whether the reaction goes to completion, so I don't know if the detection limit will be set by background, shot noise in the signal, or the completeness of the reaction. However, the detection limit will surely be sub-nanomolar. If we have an internal standard, we can do quantitative work, and now the dynamic range is extended to at least 10 orders of magnitude. If the reaction goes to completion, we might be able to detect picomolar or even smaller quantities of acetate. Why does the equilibrium constant matter?

> "If you can't answer a question, change the question." Or change the approach to answering the question. Or change your perspective on what the problem actually is so that you can solve the revised problem rather than the original problem. But don't stay stymied. A significant part of learning how to do research is figuring out when to refine an approach, when to abandon one approach for another, and when to change the question to one that can be answered and is useful in the context of the original problem.
>
> A more colloquial way to say the same thing: "If you can't raise the bridge, lower the river."

Suppose we start with a solution of 1 mM 2-hydrazinoquinoline. Any acetate solution more concentrated than this will use up all the reactant, so 1 mM, 10 mM, and higher concentrations of the acetate will all look like 1 mM at most. If we have sub-millimolar acetate, plausibly all the acetate can react. But what is the equilibrium constant for compound formation?

Acetate + 2-hydrazinoquinoline ↔ aceto2-hydrazinoquinoline, with formation constant K_{eq}. (The symbol ↔ means "in equilibrium with").

Suppose the formation constant is 10^6. Then

$$\frac{[\text{aceto-2-hydrazoquinoline}]}{C_{acetate}[\text{2-hydrazoquinoline}]} = K_{eq} \tag{9.3}$$

I have assumed that both acetic acid and acetate will react, so that only the total amount of analyte matters and the pH is set to maximize K_{eq}. If we start with 1 mM reactant and 1 μM acetate, then the reactant concentration is almost unchanged, and

$$\begin{gathered}\frac{[\text{aceto-2-hydrazoquinoline}]}{C_{acetate}10^{-3}} = 10^6 = \frac{x}{\left(10^{-6}-x\right)10^{-3}} \\ 10^3 = \frac{x}{\left(10^{-6}-x\right)} \qquad 10^{-3}-10^3x = x \qquad x \sim 10^{-6}\text{M}\end{gathered} \tag{9.4}$$

For all practical purposes, x is within 1 part per million of 10^{-6} M, for a complete reaction. What could possibly go wrong? At low concentration, the derivatization reaction is slow. The fastest any reaction can go is if every collision between reactants immediately produces the product. In aqueous solution, except for proton-water collisions, the rate constant is 10^8 $M^{-1}s^{-1}$ or slower. If both reactants start out millimolar, and we ignore reverse reactions, then

$$\begin{gathered}\frac{d[\text{product}]}{dt} = k[\text{R}_1][\text{R}_2] \\ \frac{dP}{dt} = k\left([\text{R}_1]-P\right)\left([\text{R}_2]-P\right)\end{gathered} \tag{9.5}$$

In the second equation, I use P as shorthand for the concentration of product. If $[R_1] = [R_2] = R_0$ then

$$\int_0^T \frac{dP}{\left(R_0 - P\right)^2} = \int_0^T kdt$$

$$kT = \left.\frac{1}{\left(R_0 - P\right)}\right|_0^T = \frac{1}{\left(R_0 - P(t)\right)} - \frac{1}{R_0}$$

$$kT = \frac{P(t)}{R_0\left(R_0 - P(t)\right)} \qquad kTR_0\left(R_0 - P(t)\right) = P(t) \tag{9.6}$$

$$P(t)\left(1 + kTR_0\right) = kTR_0^2$$

$$P(t) = \frac{kTR_0^2}{1 + kTR_0}$$

Can we say that a reaction is complete when $P(t) = 0.99\ R_0$? Then, at millimolar R_0, the reaction is over when $t = 1\ \mu s$. Effectively, it's instantaneous. But what happens if $R_1 >> R_2$ so that R_1 (the concentration of the derivatizing agent) is effectively constant?

$$\frac{dP}{dt} = k[R_1][R_2] = kR_1\left(R_0 - P\right) \tag{9.7}$$

$$P = R_0\left(1 - e^{kR_1 t}\right)$$

Now how long does it take to get to 99% reacted? $0.01 = e^{-kR_1 t}$ or $\ln(0.01) = -4.6 = -kR_0 t$. Now $t = 4.6 \times 10^{-8}/R_0$. For micromolar acetate, the reaction completes in less than 50 μs, hardly an issue. But for 10 picomolar (pM) acetate, it takes over an hour. Picomolar or less? Who has the patience? The expectation is that the detection limit for electrospray mass spectrometry is 10 pM if one can wait an hour from adding derivatizing agent to measurement (and assuming the reaction is rapid!), and less dynamic range if the analyst is in a hurry.

Perhaps you now see why chemists in particular and physical scientists in general are always saying "except that...", "but if ...", "depending on ...". If you only read the discussion of detection limits in the last chapter, you'd think that electrospray mass spectrometry could detect attomolar amounts of anything. Here we have an analyte where even 10 pM is hard and 1 nM (where 99% reaction completion takes less than a minute) is what works reliably. It's not just about noise (though noise matters). It's not just about detection limit (though instrumental performance matters). It's not just chemical kinetics or equilibrium constants or interferences or selectivity. A measurement, to be valid, has to be looked at from many perspectives. Thinking back to Chapter 1, we cavalierly said that what we decide is based on measurement, which it is. But making a valid measurement is hard. We can only see data from within the relativistic light cone (see box on next page), but actually we see a lot less than that. The rate at which we can obtain information, whether valid or not, is limited by experiment duration and instrument response speed or sampling speed. Our perspective is constrained no matter how unbiased we are because the information we have is limited. Whenever we expand dynamic range, by improving instruments or improving chemistry or inventing new technology, we remove a little of that limitation. As we gain greater understanding and capability, the time required to wisely select among the possible approaches increases. The point of the next several chapters is to expand on the types of integrated knowledge we can obtain and to understand the limitations of such knowledge. First we look at the mountains and valleys in our understanding of the world that limit us to particular points of view. Then we pick up with iterated maps and differential equations where we left off in Chapter 5. Just as the *Encyclopedia Britannica* after 1911 could no longer encompass all knowledge even of the English-speaking world, so the scientific world discovered about the same time, from the work of Henri Poincaré, that our ability to predict the future, even with the best possible knowledge of the current state of the universe, was limited.

Light cone: that portion of the universe, as seen by some observer, for which the time interval available for collecting information, Δt, limits from how far away the information can come. $x_{max}^2 + y_{max}^2 + z_{max}^2 \leq c^2 \Delta t^2$. This looks like a sphere. First, time can only be sensed in the past, which limits the volume of space-time producing detectable information to a hemisphere. Second, when the Special Theory of Relativity was new, it was easier to sketch the concept for two-dimensional space plus time rather than three-dimensional space. In this case, $x_{max}^2 + y_{max}^2 \leq c^2 \Delta t^2$, and the radius one can see, $\sqrt{x_{max}^2 + y_{max}^2}$, grows linearly in time. If one draws a three-dimensional plot with axes x, y, t, the volume swept out by the circle in x,y projected along t has a conical shape.

10

Potential Wells

"I'm trapped in my job and I can't get out!" is all too common a feeling among employees. After searching for a better position, the worker moves, and initially, the new job feels so much more rewarding. But then later, the worker once again feels trapped. Why can't we wander from one job to another, one place to another, or one situation to another? Each ongoing situation is at the local minimum of a potential well, similar to the gravitational potential well created by massive objects or the electrostatic potential well created by atomic nuclei. Exiting such wells requires climbing out, tunneling through the walls, or randomly being ejected. People act like particles orbiting in those wells. When life's conditions change, the parameters describing the orbits change, sometimes making the binding stronger, sometimes weaker, and sometimes breaking the links entirely.

When babies are born, they appear to be pre-wired for some behaviors, but their declarative knowledge is non-existent. It takes about a year before children start talking. During that year, what language do they learn? Whatever they're exposed to. If they're in a monolingual home, they learn the language that's spoken there. A bilingual home? They pick up two languages. While they're young, they can learn additional languages facilely. But then it gets tougher. By the time they're adults, learning a new language is quite challenging. How might we envision this?

At the moment the child is born, that child will likely have heard language from the surrounding world, but the sounds likely mean little because there is no touch, smell, or sight of what the sounds refer to. The landscape of languages may look something like Figure 10.1.

There are thousands more languages, of course, but for a newborn there's no bias or preference for any of them.

Suppose the only language the newborn hears is Arabic? After one year, the situation might look more like Figure 10.2.

The little dashes at the top left of Figure 10.2 are to indicate that there might be vague awareness that perhaps not everyone in the universe speaks Arabic, but everyone nearby does, whatever is said in Arabic is comprehensible, and the language, culture, and understanding of the universe is wrapped in a close pocket around the child. The child sees a world defined by Arabic. It is in an Arabic potential well — to get into any other language or culture, the child would have to climb out of the only world they would have known, travel across the landscape, and find another region filled with the language and culture of some other linguistic group. That takes significant effort and energy. The idea of a potential

Dari	Telugu	Ladino	Portuguese	Turkish
German	Eastern Punjabi	Gujarati	Hausa	Latin
Pashto	Italian	Hakka Chinese	Western Punjabi	Burmese
Hindi	Korean	English	Aramaic	Javanese
Russian	Vietnamese	Thai	Zulu	Yiddish
Japanese	Arabic	Marathi	Wu Chinese	Persian
Swahili	Kurdish	Spanish	Mandarin Chinese	Yue Chinese
Bengali	Hebrew	Ukrainian	Romanian	Tamil
Urdu	Khymer	Navaho	Polish	Czech
Hungarian	French	Sunda	Hawaiian	Bhojpuri

Figure 10.1. Languages on an isoenergetic landscape. Because there is nothing to distinguish one condition from another (no energetic differences), the arrangement is meant to display no discernable order.

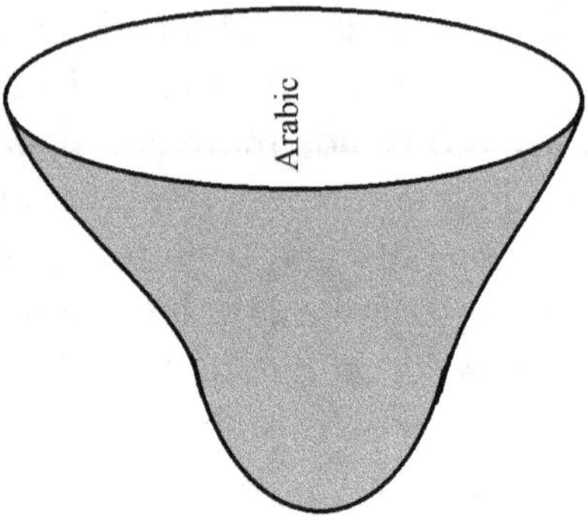

Figure 10.2. The language world as seen by a one-year-old who has only heard Arabic.

well, in fact, comes from physics, so let's look at potential wells before we come back to the societal relevance of the concept.

10.1 Forces and Wells

Both electrostatics and gravity act according to inverse square laws. That is,

$$F_G = \frac{Gm_1m_2}{r^2} \qquad F_E = -\frac{\varepsilon q_1 q_2}{r^2}$$
$$U_G = -\frac{Gm_1m_2}{r} \qquad U_E = \frac{\varepsilon q_1 q_2}{r} \tag{10.1}$$

F stands for force, *U* for energy, G for gravity, *E* for electrostatic, *m* for mass, *q* for charge, and ε for dielectric constant. Masses attract each other. Like charges repel, opposite charges attract. The equations are more complicated if the masses and charges are free to move (so that they have kinetic energy) and if there are more than two point masses or point charges involved (the multipole expansion is discussed as an aside at the end of this chapter). The conversion of potential energy to kinetic energy is work, the integral of the force through a distance, so while force falls as $1/r^2$, the magnitude of the energy falls as $1/r$. At infinite separation, both force and energy are zero. As masses or opposite charges get closer, the energy is reduced; the particles can't get away from each other.

So why doesn't the entire universe collapse into a point? In response to force, the particles accelerate. They now have kinetic energy. If there were only two particles, they'd aim straight for each other and eventually collide. But there are more than two particles, which means the force is not purely centrosymmetric. If there's a third body pulling on the first two particles, the particles will have some non-radial motion and will typically zoom past each other. If particles accelerate as they move closer, they decelerate after passing each other. For a particle to escape a potential well, it has to have enough energy so that the kinetic energy is greater than 0 at $r = \infty$. At least, that's the case for classical physics and a single potential well. But the world isn't that simple.

It will not escape the reader's attention that $U_G = -\infty$ at $r = 0$. However, no real pair of particles ever coincide with each other. Particles are larger than points, so they collide at $r = r_{min} > 0$. Typically, one particle moves rapidly with respect to the other, so that the lighter particle either passes the heavier particle once (on a hyperbolic or parabolic orbit) or orbits continually (elliptical or circular orbit). At the closest distance between the particles, the lighter particle moves at its highest speed. How might we redraw a potential well to capture such behavior? Here are two common models. One approximates the potential well as a parabola, $U = U_0 + kr^2$. If $U_0 < 0$, we cut off the parabola at $U = 0$, and above that level, the moving particle can fly free. If the kinetic energy of the particle at the center of the well is less than $|U_0|$, the particle will remain trapped in the well, while if it has greater energy, it will fly out of the well. A second model, rarely used for gravitating particles, approximates the potential energy when two atoms approach each other. Far apart, they don't interact and the energy is 0. At a short distance, the electron clouds around the atoms interact, possibly forming a chemical bond at a distance corresponding to a potential minimum. Try to get too close, however, and the nuclei repel each other, giving rise to a repulsive wall. While the exact

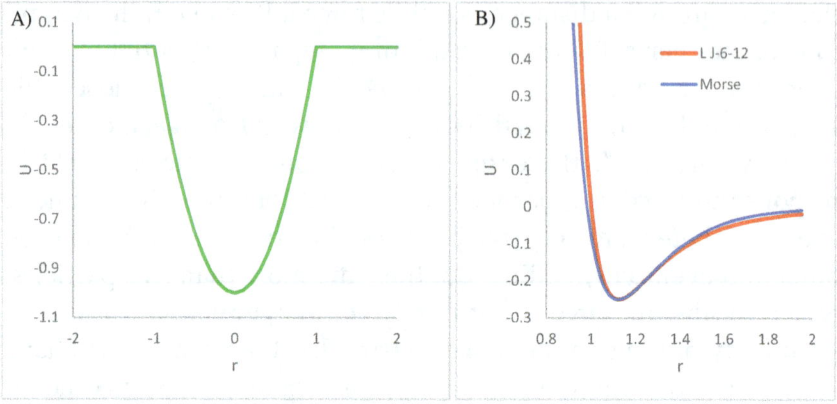

Figure 10.3. Common potential wells. A) Parabolic well. B) Lennard-Jones and Morse potentials.

shape of such a well depends on the details of electron orbitals and the number of nuclei, a reasonable approximation is to say that the repulsive force falls off as $1/r^{12}$, while the attractive force decreases as $1/r^6$. It's called a Lennard-Jones 6–12 potential. A related approximation, for which I omit the equation, is the Morse potential, where energy changes exponentially with distance. All three approximate forms are shown in Figure 10.3.

10.2 Multiple Wells

Let's build on the parabolic well. What happens if two of them are next to each other?

As in Figure 10.4, if we put a particle in either well, it will stay there. If we start a particle moving from the left edge towards the right and there is no friction, the particle will drop into the first well, pop back out, head through the second well, and disappear past the right edge. However, if there is friction, the particle might get trapped in one of the two wells, and once it's in the well, it will stay there, gradually settling to the bottom. Using our language analogy, a person typically falls into the first language/culture combination to which they're exposed. There are other cultures nearby, but once in a particular culture, getting out is rare and difficult.

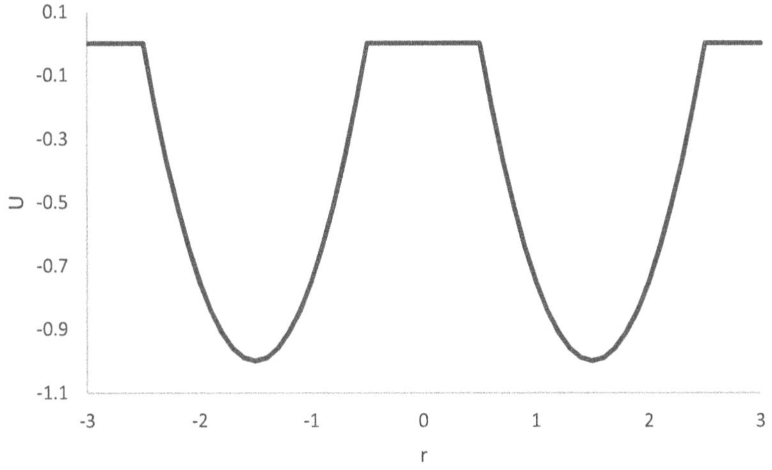

Figure 10.4. Pair of parabolic wells.

But we do know that people learn multiple languages and participate in multiple cultures. Is our analogy bogus, or do we just need to adjust it a little? There are five changes we could make:

1. Reduce the separation between the wells until they merge, leaving only a single well.
2. Make the walls porous so that information can diffuse back and forth between the wells.
3. Take quantum mechanics into account so that information can tunnel between the wells.
4. Make parametric adjustments so that the height of the wall between the wells can be changed.
5. Instead of having Newtonian motion, subject to frictional loss, allow Brownian motion with a Maxwell-Boltzmann energy distribution so that, as long as the temperature isn't absolute zero, there is a computable probability that the occupant of one of the potential wells will have enough energy to pop out of the well, randomly explore the potential environment, and randomly fall into an adjacent well.

Since item 1 is self-explanatory, let's take these one at a time, starting with 2.

Think of a chain link fence. A human can't go through it (except at a gate), but pollen goes through almost as if the fence isn't there. There is a characteristic size, the pore size, below which atoms, molecules, and small particles can get through a barrier, while larger entities are blocked. If the wall between the potential wells is porous, then the contents of the wells can mix. Suppose the wall has a thickness L. If the holes are too small, nothing will go through the holes, but if the holes are sufficiently large, random motion of the particles will allow diffusion between the two wells. The bigger the particle, the smaller the diffusion coefficient D. For one-dimensional motion, the distance d that a particle can move in a time t is

$$d = \sqrt{2Dt} \tag{10.2}$$

For glucose in water at room temperature, $D \sim 10^{-5}$ cm^2 s^{-1}. Thus, in one second, a glucose molecule could pop through a membrane 4.5×10^{-3} cm, or 45 micrometers, thick. If the wall is 0.1 cm thick, then diffusion would require $t = 500$ s or a bit longer than 8 minutes. Diffusion coefficients in air are larger than in water by about 10^4, so the distance covered in a fixed amount of time is about 100 times greater.

If we pressurize one side of the inter-well membrane, we can cause fluid to pass from one well to the other. Pressure-driven, or Poiseuille, flow can be far faster than diffusion, but requires an external energy source, whereas diffusion is an isoenergetic, or isothermal, process. The social analogies are that if people just mix and mingle, they'll share language, cuisine, style, and at equilibrium will have a mixed culture. Only impervious barriers can prevent diffusive mixing.

If we were interested in small-scale dynamics, for example in integrated circuits or batteries using graphene oxide as a dielectric, we could go into great detail about a subtle and non-intuitive topic, quantum tunnelling. Because my main interest is in human-scale physics and chemistry, I'm going to gloss over tunneling, as a means of connecting potential wells. We are used to thinking of walls as impenetrable. Actually, walls are assemblies of electron clouds and atomic nuclei (often further arranged into molecules). What that means is that if we bring another collection of electrons and nuclei up to a wall, we expect the electrons to mutually repel, keeping one solid or liquid from going through another. However, if the wall is sufficiently diffuse or thin, the electron repulsion is insufficient to keep other electrons from occasionally shooting through to the other side. Similarly, nuclei can get through if the potential within the wall is low enough. It's analogous to a youngster on a tricycle facing a speed bump. If the youngster is going slowly, they start up the bump, come to a stop, and drift backward. Go fast enough, and they can get past the bump. It's also analogous to light interacting with a transparent window. The refractive index of the window is different from the surroundings (for ordinary plate glass, refractive index is about 1.5 in the visible region of the spectrum. Water has a refractive index of 1.33, while air has a refractive index close to 1.). At such a speed bump for light (well, it's more complicated than that. See Feynman's discussion of refractive index, https://www.feynmanlectures.caltech.edu/I_31.html.), some light gets transmitted and some is reflected (which is why you can use an ordinary window as a mirror, provided the far side of the glass is not illuminated). The reflectance at an interface between two media with refractive index n_1 and n_2, e.g., air and glass, if we're looking perpendicular to the interface, is

$$R_{\perp} = \left(\frac{n_2 - n_1}{n_2 + n_1} \right)^2 \tag{10.3}$$

which for glass and air (or vacuum) is about 0.04. Analogously, matter waves hitting a boundary are partially reflected and partially transmitted. In the case of running into a well-built brick wall, the transmittance fraction is, for all practical purposes, zero (although the transport fraction to the hospital is close to 1!), but for electrons approaching thin layers of semiconductors, the transmittance is non-zero and can be controlled by adjusting the electrical potential of each layer of the semiconductor.

10.3 Parametrized Wells

Many potential wells are controlled by parameters that can be adjusted by circumstances. Take, for example, a potential well where the potential energy V is given by:

$$V = V_0 + V_2x^2 + V_4x^4 \qquad V_{\text{min}} = 0 \tag{10.4}$$

If $V_0 = V_2 = 0$, then the potential well is a pure quartic, and appears as the blue curve in Figure 10.5. If we make $V_2 < 0$, the potential has a local maximum at $x = 0$ and local minima at $x = \pm\sqrt{|V_2 / 2V_4|}$. In turn, to meet the condition that $V_{min} = 0$, $V_0 = V_2^2/4V_4$. We have defined a potential well where V_4 sets the steepness of the walls, V_2 controls the height of the barrier at $x = 0$, and V_0 ensures that the minimum potential is 0. If we wanted to scale the width of the well, we could substitute $x' = kx$, with $k > 1$ to compress the well width or $0 < k < 1$ to spread the plotted lines out. V_2 can be regarded not only as a barrier height adjustment but also

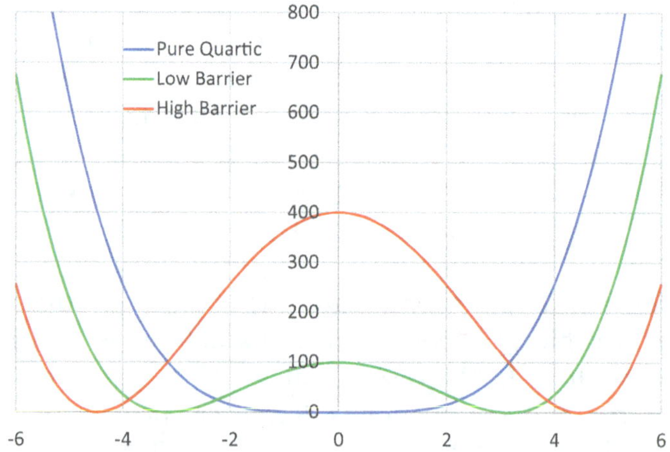

Figure 10.5. Quartic potential wells.

as a bifurcation parameter. If $V_2 > 0$, the well does not have a central bump or barrier. Once $V_2 < 0$, there are two subwells within the larger overall well.

Suppose a particle is sitting at the bottom of the blue potential well and V_2 is set to any value less than 0. The particle perches on a point. Any small move to the left sends the particle to a minimum where $x_{min} < 0$; any small move to the right sends it to a minimum where $x_{min} > 0$. The change in V_2 is said to be symmetry breaking. If V_2 is continuously changed from greater than 0 to less than 0, the shape of the potential well changes and the behavior of anything in the well changes. Although there is no x dependence to any of the constants, there is an x dependence to behavior after V_2 changes sign. Changing V_2 is thus a way to change a global parameter to influence local behavior.

In Figure 10.5, there is nothing to bias whether a particle that starts in the center will end up to the left or right of center when V_2 changes. If we decenter V_2 (i.e., make the quadratic term $V_2(x - x_0)^2$ rather than V_2x^2), a bias appears. As shown in Figure 10.6, we now choose V_0 so that $V = 0$ and $dV/dx = 0$ for the same x. Finding V_0, however, is hard to do explicitly. I can't resist trying!

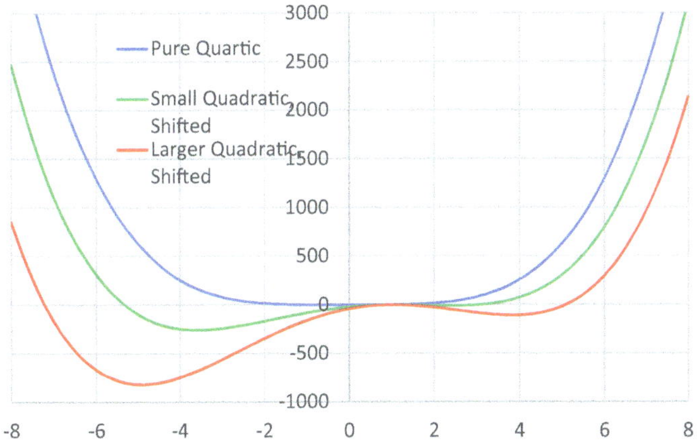

Figure 10.6. Quartic potential well with decentered quadratic perturbation.

$$V = V_0 + V_2(x - x_0)^2 + V_4 x^4$$
$$\frac{dV}{dx} = 2V_2(x - x_0) + 4V_4 x^3 = 4V_4 x^3 + 2V_2 x - 2V_2 x_0 \tag{10.5}$$

The problem is that we now need to solve a cubic equation to find x such that $dV/dx = 0$. We see there are three values of x where the derivative is 0 and we know all three places have real values for x. If we put the form $2ax^3 + cx - cd = 0$ into the formula solver at alpha.wolfram.org (or, equivalently, in *Mathematica*), we find the three solutions as follows:

$$\begin{aligned}
x &= \frac{\sqrt[3]{9a^2cd + \sqrt{3}\sqrt{27a^4c^2d^2 + 2a^3c^3}}}{\sqrt[3]{36a}} \\
&\quad - \frac{c}{\sqrt[3]{6}\sqrt[3]{9a^2cd + \sqrt{3}\sqrt{27a^4c^2d^2 + 2a^3c^3}}} \\
x &= \frac{\left(1 + i\sqrt{3}\right)c}{2\sqrt[3]{6}\sqrt[3]{9a^2cd + \sqrt{3}\sqrt{27a^4c^2d^2 + 2a^3c^3}}} \\
&\quad - \frac{\left(1 - i\sqrt{3}\right)\sqrt[3]{9a^2cd + \sqrt{3}\sqrt{27a^4c^2d^2 + 2a^3c^3}}}{2 \times \sqrt[3]{36a}} \\
x &= \frac{\left(1 - i\sqrt{3}\right)c}{2\sqrt[3]{6}\sqrt[3]{9a^2cd + \sqrt{3}\sqrt{27a^4c^2d^2 + 2a^3c^3}}} \\
&\quad - \frac{\left(1 + i\sqrt{3}\right)\sqrt[3]{9a^2cd + \sqrt{3}\sqrt{27a^4c^2d^2 + 2a^3c^3}}}{2 \times \sqrt[3]{36a}}
\end{aligned} \tag{10.6}$$

Substituting $a = V_4 = 1, d = x_0 = -1$ (what was used for Figure 10.6), we get

$$x = \frac{\sqrt[3]{\sqrt{3}\sqrt{27V_2^2 + 2V_2^3} - 9V_2}}{\sqrt[3]{36}} - \frac{V_2}{\sqrt[3]{6\sqrt{3}\sqrt{27V_2^2 + 2V_2^3} - 54V_2}}$$

$$x=\frac{\left(1+i\sqrt{3}\right)V_2}{2\sqrt[3]{6}\sqrt[3]{\sqrt{3}\sqrt{27V_2^2+2V_2^3}-9V_2}}-\frac{\left(1-i\sqrt{3}\right)\sqrt[3]{\sqrt{3}\sqrt{27V_2^2+2V_2^3}-9V_2}}{2\sqrt[3]{36}}$$

$$x=\frac{\left(1-i\sqrt{3}\right)V_2}{2\sqrt[3]{6}\sqrt[3]{\sqrt{3}\sqrt{27V_2^2+2V_2^3}-9V_2}}-\frac{\left(1+i\sqrt{3}\right)\sqrt[3]{\sqrt{3}\sqrt{27V_2^2+2V_2^3}-9V_2}}{2\sqrt[3]{36}}$$

(10.7)

On inspection, it looks like the second and third solutions might be complex, yet looking at the plot in Figure 10.6, we know that all three points where the derivative is 0 are real. Substituting $V_2 = -20$ and simplifying, we find, to 7 significant figures,

$$x=\frac{\sqrt[3]{124.9i+180}}{\sqrt[3]{36}}+\frac{20}{\sqrt[3]{6*124.9i+1080}}=\left(\frac{219.09e^{0.60661276i}}{36}\right)^{1/3}$$

$$+\frac{20}{\left(1314.534e^{0.60661276i}\right)^{1/3}}$$

$$=-1.82574*2*\cos\left(-0.20220425\right)=\mathbf{-3.57709}$$

$$x=\frac{-\left(1+i\sqrt{3}\right)20}{2\sqrt[3]{6}\sqrt[3]{124.9i+180}}-\frac{\left(1-i\sqrt{3}\right)\sqrt[3]{124.9i+180}}{2\sqrt[3]{36}}$$

$$=\frac{-40e^{1.047197755i}}{2\sqrt[3]{6}\left(219.09e^{0.60661276i}\right)^{1/3}}-\frac{2e^{-1.047197755i}\left(219.09e^{0.60661276i}\right)^{1/3}}{2\sqrt[3]{36}}$$

$$=-1.82574e^{0.844993i}-1.82574e^{-0.844993i}=2*1.82574\cos(-0.844993)$$

$$=\mathbf{2.42362}$$

$$x=\frac{-\left(1-i\sqrt{3}\right)20}{2\sqrt[3]{6}\sqrt[3]{124.9i+180}}-\frac{\left(1+i\sqrt{3}\right)\sqrt[3]{124.9i+180}}{2\sqrt[3]{36}}$$

$$=\frac{-40e^{-1.047197755i}}{2\sqrt[3]{6}\left(219.09e^{0.60661276i}\right)^{1/3}}-\frac{2e^{1.047197755i}\left(219.09e^{0.60661276i}\right)^{1/3}}{2\sqrt[3]{36}}$$

$$=2*1.82574\cos\left(-1.24940\right)=\mathbf{1.153466}$$

(10.8)

If you carefully look at equation (10.8), you will see I cheated. Why did I choose negative angles and positive magnitudes rather than positive angles and negative magnitudes when converting complex exponentials to trigonometric forms? Since $\cos(-x) = \cos(x)$, whether the angles are positive or negative are ambiguous. But the plot in Figure 10.6 makes it evident that two of the three x values where the derivative is 0 are at $x > 0$. Only the sign choice I made gives the correct symmetry. Given these x values, we can see that to get $V(1.153466) = 0$, V_0 for $V_2 = -20$ is -1.3. Similarly, the three points at which the derivative is 0 for $V_2 = -40$ are at $\{-5.054, 1.05946, 4.24264\}$, and V_0 for $V_2 = -40$ is -1.118.

So now we have a one-parameter system where we can make potential wells of different depth, and a two-parameter system where we can make the subsidiary wells asymmetrical. If a particle gets trapped in the shallower well, it may never get to the deeper well; once it's in the deeper well, it isn't going to get to the shallower well unless enough material gets into the deeper well that the deeper well overflows. However, in the real world, that's a more static description than what actually happens. The problem is that particles, once in a well, do not stand still (except if the temperature is absolute zero, and even there quantum uncertainty forces there to be "zero-point energy" where the particles aren't perfectly still). Now we add the influence of random particle motion, and the potential wells come to life.

10.4 Migrating Between Subwells

Recall that temperature is a parameter that summarizes the kinetic energy density in a bolus of matter. Each particle of a given mass and internal structure has some amount of energy, but averaged over a macroscopic amount of material, the mean energy per particle is temperature T, measured in Kelvin for most of the world or Rankin for those still using English units. How is energy distributed? Let's assume we have three particles with a total energy of 3 Joules. If two particles are stationary, the third has all 3 Joules. If the particles are moving at the same speed and in the same direction, each particle has 1 Joule. They could be moving at different speeds, but the sum of the energies would be the same. Statistical mechanics looks at the many ways a set of particles (fixed number of entities) and a fixed total energy (conservation of energy) can be distributed. The usual hypothesis for equilibrium systems is that each of the arrangements that conserve matter and energy are equally probable. However, some of the states are degenerate — there are many ways to arrange the individual particles while having the same energy. For example, if one particle has 1 J, a second particle has 2 J, and the third particle has 0 Joules, there are six possible ways to combine particle identification and energy distribution (0, 1, 2), (0, 2, 1), (1, 0, 2), (1, 2, 0), (2, 0, 1), (2, 1, 0). Scale that up, and recognize that for motion not in highly confined geometries, energy can be assumed to be a continuous variable, and the number of ways to distribute a fixed amount of energy is vast. Fortunately, the probability that a particular state is populated scales exponentially.

$$P \sim P_0 e^{-E/k_B T} \tag{10.9}$$

P is the population of a specific state, P_0 is the population of the lowest or ground state (or, at $T = 0$, the total population), E is the energy of the state in question, T is temperature, and k_B is Boltzmann's constant. This looks like equation (8.1), and is nearly identically derived. What is most important here is that not all particles have identical energy. In a pool (or potential well), some particles have high energy, some have low energy, and there's an exponential falloff in the number of rapid, hot particles as energy increases. Because molecules move in three dimensions, their mean energy scales as $3/2k_BT$. At room temperature, roughly 300 K, the energy per particle is about 6.2×10^{-21} Joule. On a human scale, this seems negligible. However, if we look at a nitrogen molecule, molecular weight 28 Dalton, we find the kinetic energy and corresponding molecular speed are

$$\begin{aligned} &\frac{1}{2}mv^2 \sim 6.2\times10^{-21}\,\text{J} \\ &m \sim \left(2*14/6.022\times10^{23}\right)\text{g} = 4.65\times10^{-23}\,g = 4.65\times10^{-26}\,\text{kg} \\ &v \sim \sqrt{2*6.2\times10^{-21}/4.65\times10^{-26}}\,\text{ms}^{-1} = 517\,\text{ms}^{-1} \end{aligned} \tag{10.10}$$

Oxygen has an atomic weight of 16 (atom) or 32 (diatomic molecule), which gives it a typical speed of $(14/16)^{1/2} \times 517$ m s^{-1} or 483 m s^{-1}. What is the speed of sound in air? 343 m s^{-1}, roughly 2/3 of the speed of a molecule with the mean energy. Do any room temperature molecules reach escape velocity from the earth's gravity potential well, 11.2 km s^{-1}? For a nitrogen molecule, 11.2 km s^{-1}/0.4 km s^{-1} = 28 times the mean room temperature speed or 784 times the mean energy. For convenience in integrating, rather than measuring energy in Joules, measure it in $k_B T$.

$$P_{escape} = \frac{\int_{784kT}^{\infty} e^{-\frac{E}{k_B T}} dE}{\int_0^{\infty} e^{-\frac{E}{k_B T}} dE} = e^{-784} = 3 \times 10^{-341} \qquad (10.11)$$

Clearly, this is negligibly small. To have even 0.1% of the molecules energetic enough to escape gravity, E must be no more than 7 $k_B T$. That means $k_B T$ corresponds to a molecular speed of $11.2/7^{1/2}$ = 4.23 km s^{-1}, $k_B T = 4.1 \times 10^{-19}$ or $T \sim 30{,}000$ K. The plasma in the Van Allen radiation belt can get that hot, and the solar wind is hot enough to remove the outer portions of planetary atmospheres. At earth's surface, we aren't in any immediate danger.

While phase changes (solid to liquid, liquid to gas) are a topic deferred to Chapter 12, we can use the exponential dependence of equilibrium on temperature to understand evaporation. At sea level, the pressure of water vapor above a pool of pure water is 1 atmosphere, 760 torr, at 100°C. At room temperature, 25°C, the vapor pressure is about 23.7 torr. Ignoring all sorts of nonidealities, and changing to P meaning pressure instead of probability,

$$P = P_0 e^{-E/k_B T}$$

$$\ln P = \ln P_0 - \frac{E}{k_B T} \qquad (10.12)$$

$$\begin{aligned}\ln 23.7 &= \ln P_0 - \frac{E}{k_B 298}\\ \ln 760 &= \ln P_0 - \frac{E}{k_B 373}\\ \ln \tfrac{760}{23.7} &= \frac{E}{k_B}\left(\frac{1}{298} - \frac{1}{373}\right)\end{aligned} \tag{10.13}$$

From this, we learn that the energy of vaporization of water is 7.1×10^{-20} J per molecule, or 43 kJ/mole, or 10.3 kcal/mole (the *Handbook of Chemistry and Physics* lists the heat of vaporization of water as 549 cal/g at 100°C or 9.9 kcal/mole. The two-point approximation and the fitted value based on many temperature/pressure measurements agree within 4%.). The relative humidity at any temperature is the actual humidity divided by the vapor pressure of water at the same temperature in a closed container first evacuated and then partially filled with water. The highest-energy molecules in a drop of water will vaporize first, removing both matter and energy from the liquid, and thus cooling the liquid upon vaporization. Similarly, if water vapor condenses, the pool of liquid increases in temperature. Cool air condenses water; the common sentiment that rain cools off the air has it exactly backwards. Random molecules at the liquid/air interface have sufficient kinetic energy to vaporize. The rate of evaporation is a shot noise limited behavior since individual molecules are the desorbed species.

Whether the atmosphere is gravitationally trapped or departs, whether one water molecule or another in a puddle evaporates, selecting which molecules leave is random. Similarly, if we have a pair of potential wells, as long as there is motion within those wells, some denizens of the well will have enough energy to pop out, explore the energy landscape, and randomly fall into either the well originally occupied or some adjacent well. This is the means by which potential wells most often exchange occupants. If all the wells have the same depth, at equilibrium all will be filled to the same height; any filling mismatch will be annealed to equality. If some wells are deeper than others, then the energy needed to leave those wells will be greater and the shallower wells will be depleted as the deep ones fill up.

Let's use the deepest asymmetric curve in Figure 10.6 to illustrate what happens. We take the red curve and put a collection of energetic substances into the well.

In Figure 10.7, inset A, the articulation at the bottom of the potential well is irrelevant. Both subwells are full, the outer walls of the well are high, so everything is trapped in the $V = V_0x^4$ potential. In inset B, the well is filled just to the point where the filling touches the boundary between the two wells. While hot particles in either well may temporarily vaporize into the headspace above $V = 0$, neither well fills nor empties. On average, if one particle goes from left to right, another will go from right to left, maintaining a flat distribution across the well. In inset C, the behavior gets interesting. The left-hand subwell is less than full, while the right-hand subwell is full to the brim. If a particle vaporizes into the headspace, it might condense to the left of where it started, and either roll down the edge of the potential subwell into the left-hand pool of particles or directly condense into the left-hand pool. However, once a particle gets to the left, it is unlikely to move back to the right. Moving right is an uphill climb. Thus, over time, the right-hand pool will empty due to the random motion of the particles.

10.5 Connecting Wells to Bandwidth

How does this relate to bandwidth? Particles carry information. More energetic particles are more likely to evaporate, and if they recondense, they are more likely to do so at a lower energy. Even when there is an internal energy barrier, particles, and information, flow downhill. However, information that might motivate change on a planar energy surface may be insufficient to cause change when people are in wells of preconceived notions. The deeper the well, the greater the energy required to escape the well. That either means a high temperature or achieving the rare event of a lot of information being concentrated into a single particle. For routine matters, having deep wells to retain information is useful. Retaining information limits how much bandwidth we require to obtain information at any moment. What we already transduced and retained remains available. However, if we have learned counterproductive

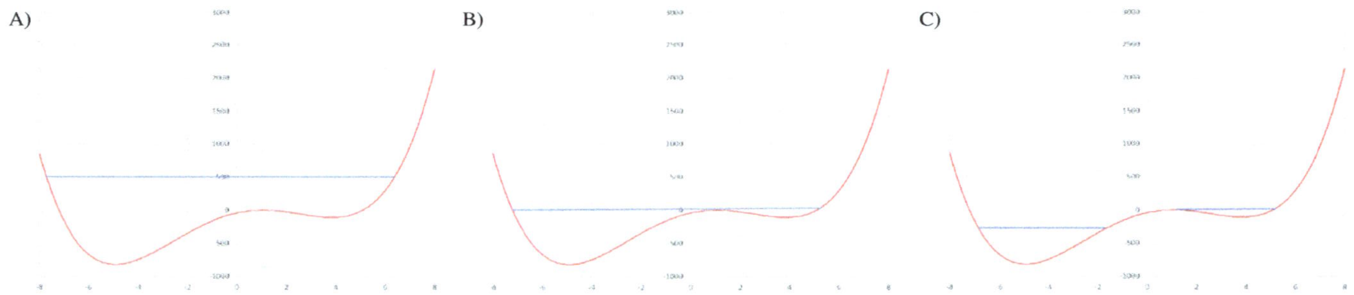

Figure 10.7. Material in an asymmetric potential well. What happens to hot particles? A) Particles overfill the subwells. B) Particles just fill the subwells. C) Smaller well full, larger well contains more particles but is not full.

behavior, the difficulty in unlearning the behavior is a serious impediment. The same physics applies in either case.

If parameters were static, and wells were deep enough, groups of particles would settle to the lowest available subwell. If this were how societies worked, sooner or later a society would become homogeneous with everyone viewing the same information, believing the same information, and having uniform distribution of assets both tangible and intangible. The dream of many societal leaders is exactly such behavior — uniform rules, uniform beliefs, uniform behavior. But such uniformity will always be imperfect for temperatures above zero, because there will be at least some probability that some highly excited states will be populated. Some individuals will rise above the pools of uniform behavior and either condense in adjacent subwells or leave an energy well entirely if the walls aren't too high. Further, parameters can change, shifting the shape and depth of wells, and thus moving behaviors from one regime to another.

Migration of people across borders may also be thought of as a vaporization/condensation problem between potential wells. Think of desirable countries as having deep potential wells, while troubled countries have either shallow wells or even potential hills or mountains from which people desire to leave. If there are no barriers to migration, people will naturally gravitate to those potential wells they believe are optimal. Any barriers (physical or legal) that are small compared to the depth of the destination potential well will slightly lower the rate of vaporization/departure from the country of origin or slow/delay arrival at the destination, but the potential gradient will still ensure that the net motion of people will be towards the optimum location. The main mechanism by which migration can be halted is by having either a world free of potential minima (i.e., all places equally desirable to live), having all potential minima at the same level (a strategy attempted by the European Union), or by making a country so undesirable a place to live that its own population starts to leave. What constitutes "troubled" is to some extent subjective. For example, some people find Florida to be attractive in the winter, while I find its humidity much of the year to be oppressive. Nevertheless, the Florida potential well is deep (especially during Spring Break) until a hurricane arrives when the locals head north if they can't ride out the storm in place. Given the migration between Central and North America, it appears that the U.S. is a potential well deeper than, e.g., El Salvador or Nicaragua. Attempts to prevent migration that rely on walls or border zones may change the migration kinetics, but they don't change the potential well differences and thus fail to adjust the equilibrium condition (no net migration in either direction). To reach equilibrium, all countries involved would need to be perceived by the typical individual as equally desirable to live. Thinking of migration as a physics problem rather than a cultural problem suggests that improving living conditions in countries experiencing outflows is a way to limit such outflows. Given recent labor shortages (spring 2022) in the U.S., it is not obvious whether limiting immigration is desirable.

Making analogies between human behavior and molecular diffusion may sound fanciful, but one of the important steps in turning polymer chemistry into biochemistry seemingly follows the pattern described. When proteins are made in cells, they are linear strings of amino acids. When they function, they have been folded to a quite specific shape which allows them to act as structural or catalytic components of life. How does the folding happen? In some cases, there are chaperone proteins that aid folding. In other cases, the protein is modified after it is synthesized and chemical bonds modified to lock a particular spatial relationship in place. But generally, the protein flops around in the cell, exploring the energy landscape. If two parts of the protein chain interact but only weakly, they can easily pull apart; the potential well binding those two parts together is shallow. If other regions interact and that interaction is strong, forming a deep potential well, the components stick. However, since the temperature is well above absolute zero, even after the associations form, they come apart every so often, and if the potential well of the interaction isn't too deep, the regions pull apart and flop around some more, looking for an even lower energy arrangement. Because the distances are short and the reptation of the chain is rapid, many arrangements can be explored in a short time. If the cell were static, eventually the protein would fold into the absolutely lowest state possible, and if the temperature were then lowered to absolute zero, it would stay in that shape forever. However, exploration of the energy landscape is fastest at high temperatures, but the rate of escape from shallow potential wells is also highest at high temperatures. There is a tradeoff between temperature and folding optimality, between rapid assembly into a nearly optimal form and slower exploration of even more optimal forms. Protein folding on energy landscapes has a vast literature, and while I cite a 1997 paper (Onuchic *et al.*, 1997) and a 2016 paper (Mallamace *et al.*, 2016), a Scifinder search on "protein" and "energy landscape" on March 20, 2021 found 94,222 documents, of which 97% were in English, 373 were Ph.D. theses, and the most prolific author was Harold Scharaga, with 180 entries. I won't consume bandwidth delving in any farther.

It strikes me that finding a mate has similar dynamics. If someone moves too slowly, too few possible pairings are explored. If they move too fast, they may miss learning someone else's characteristics. Some interactions are weakly attractive and perhaps the couple goes on a date or two. Other interactions are stronger, and the potential well binds two people more closely. The divorce rate indicates that not all apparently (or initially) optimal pairings actually are optimal, yet for some fraction of the populace, once a pairing happens, the bonds are sufficiently attractive that people do not evaporate out of the well to explore adjacent possibilities, and the confines of the well are small enough that others (except offspring!) do not enter. The internet has destroyed many spatial walls of community and neighborhood, allowing a search over a vast geographical range.

Parents and societies often work hard to indoctrinate youth in specific ways. They are attempting to push the young into potential wells of which the parents or other institutions approve. Such effort has variable success. To what extent do your values mirror your parents' values? Their cultural tastes? Their geographic choices? Their religion and politics? Those who conform poorly to the boundaries others tried to establish for them as youngsters can variously be viewed as adventuresome, energetic, revolutionary, rebellious, nonconformist, and probably other descriptors. We know that humans have $T > 0$, because some fraction of the populace ends up in behavioral potential wells other than those to which they were first exposed. Saying that indoctrination "chills" individuality is a case where sociological and physicochemical languages have similar meaning.

Recasting chemical or sociological behavior as random events in a multi-parameter energy space may strike some readers as a bit of a stretch. Yet, if we look at how materials interact and look at how people interact, we can recast the people's behavior in ways that allow abstraction and detached, careful thinking and simulation. The bandwidth consumed in learning physical chemistry can assist in making sense of an often chaotic world. Any time a concept can be used in multiple contexts, that saves communication bandwidth. By seeing society as governed by varying energy landscapes across which people diffuse, and with those same people manipulating the parameters, we see society dispassionately, even as various interactions are felt to be desirable or horrific. If we don't like the structure of a society, the routes to change are either to alter the rules (the potential landscape), to move to a different potential well (select a different, pre-existing set of rules), or to travel and become exposed to a variety of rules. Indeed, travel in search of optimality nicely aligns with protein folding as a means to maximize utility and stability while avoiding undesirable traps.

Maxwell, Schrödinger, the Multipole Expansion, and the Structure of the Hydrogen Atom

I thank my late colleague Klaus Schulten for relating this story. In the 19th century, one forefront of physics was gaining an understanding of electric and magnetic fields. James Clerk Maxwell unified electromagnetics with his famous equations (shown in Gaussian or CGS units. Electromagnetic units inconsistency is enough to drive teetotalers to drink):

$$\begin{aligned}
\nabla \mathbf{E} &= 4\pi\rho \\
\nabla \mathbf{B} &= 0 \\
\nabla \times \mathbf{E} &= -\frac{1}{c}\frac{\partial \mathbf{B}}{\partial t} \\
\nabla \times \mathbf{B} &= \frac{1}{c}\left(\frac{\partial \mathbf{E}}{\partial t} + 4\pi\,\mathbf{J}\right)
\end{aligned} \tag{10.14}$$

(*Continued*)

(*Continued*)

where **E** is the electric field, **B** the magnetic field, **J** the current density, ρ the charge density, c the speed of light, and ∇ the gradient operator. (To get as clear an understanding of the ∇ operator as you can with the least amount of pain, get a copy of *Div, Grad, Curl and All That* (Schey, 2004)). Working out the electric field and potential from a distribution of charges led to the multipole expansion (Jackson, 1975), and for a pair of charges, Maxwell figured out that the angular parts of the solution could be described by spherical harmonics and the spatial parts by Laguerre polynomials. Thus, by early in the 20th century, every college physics major knew about these functions.

In 1923, Pauli deduced that what had classically been considered particles could also be considered as waves. In 1925, Born and Heisenberg cast quantum phenomena as matrix mechanics. Thus, Schrödinger became aware of the quantum momentum operator,

$$\mathbf{p} = -i\hbar\nabla \tag{10.15}$$

Schrödinger also was familiar with Lagrangian and Hamiltonian expressions of classical dynamics. The classical Hamiltonian expresses conservation of energy as:

$$\frac{1}{2}mv^2 + V = \frac{p^2}{2m} + V = E \tag{10.16}$$

That is, the sum of kinetic and potential energy is total energy.

Substituting de Broglie's wave function for system state, the quantum momentum operator for momentum, and the potential of charge interaction into equation (10.16), Schrödinger deduced the expression governing the quantum hydrogen atom. Given all the manipulation in solving the equation, I suspect that modern students would expect that solving that equation would have taken him quite a while. In fact, it took only one evening.

(*Continued*)

The Schrödinger equation for the hydrogen atom and the multipole expansion of the electromagnetic field are identical except for the constant in front of ∇^2! The Schrödinger hydrogen atom equation:

$$\left(-\frac{\hbar^2}{2m}\nabla^2+\frac{ze^2}{r}\right)\psi = E\psi \qquad (10.17)$$

The equation for the electric field generated by charges in motion in a non-magnetic medium is:

$$\left(\nabla^2+k^2\right)\mathbf{E} = -ik\mu_0\mathbf{J}-i\frac{\mu_0}{k}\nabla(\nabla\bullet\mathbf{J}) \qquad (10.18)$$

J is non-zero when charges are moving — for example, when a molecule vibrates or rotates, current is driven through an antenna, or an electron is orbiting a nucleus. $\mathbf{E}(r,t) = \mathbf{E}_0(r)e^{-i\omega t}$. The wavenumber $k = 2\pi/\lambda$. In equation (10.18), the electric field has the same role as the wavefunction has in equation (10.17). The constants are in different places, but they can be rearranged to be in nearly identical form just by multiplying both sides of equation (10.17) by $-2m/\hbar^2$.

Thus, while solving the Schrödinger equation is typically challenging to chemistry students who have not taken a course on classical electromagnetic theory before learning quantum mechanics, for Schrödinger it was a trivial revision to his course notes. The flip side of this astonishing realization is that if Maxwell had known that $\mathbf{p} = -i\hbar\nabla$, the structure of the hydrogen atom could have been computed half a century earlier!

11

Nonlinearity, Complexity, Chaos

When I discussed noise, I mentioned the logistic map and the apparently random or chaotic behavior that can be seen even in a simple iterated system. We now revisit nonlinearity and learn some of its implications.

Suppose we launch a rocket from earth. We put it into orbit around the sun so that its aphelion is slightly outside earth's orbit and its perihelion is slightly inside earth's orbit. If the period of that orbit is 365.256 days to 6 significant figures, it matches the orbital period of the earth within 0.001 days. 0.001 days is 1 minute, 26.4 seconds. The earth's orbital speed varies from 29.29 to 30.29 km s^{-1}. Thus, on average, even when we know the time to orbit the sun within 3 parts per million, we have uncertainty in the earth's position after one orbit of 86.4 s × 29.79 km s^{-1} = 2,574 km or about 1,600 miles, $1/5^{th}$ of the planet's diameter. What happens when the rocket returns to the vicinity of earth after a year? With the information presented, we can't know if it will crash into the planet, miss it by 1,600 miles, or something in between. If it misses just in front of the planet, it will lose orbital speed, have its perihelion lowered, and perhaps head off to Venus. If it misses just behind the planet, it will gain speed and perhaps head for Mars or the asteroid belt. Tiny changes in initial conditions have a huge influence on what happens in the future.

Over short periods, trajectories change gradually, but over really short times, they behave almost linearly. In fact, we can formalize how two adjacent trajectories behave. Trajectory T_1 and trajectory T_2 are separated only by a distance x_0 in some direction x (let's not worry about whether that's a Cartesian x or just some distance in an abstract sense). Over short periods and distances,

$$x = x_0 e^{\lambda t} \tag{11.1}$$

How does x change in time?

If $\lambda < 0$, the trajectories grow together so at long times $x_1 = x_2$.

If $\lambda = 0$, the trajectories stay the same distance apart.

If $\lambda > 0$, the trajectories separate or diverge.

As with many variables, λ has a name: the Lyapunov (or Liapunov, depending on the transliteration) exponent. Depending on its value, paths either can converge from various trajectories to a single trajectory ($\lambda < 0$), diverge to quite different trajectories ($\lambda > 0$), or be in an unstable condition where no divergence or convergence occurs. Since the real world always is noisy, $\lambda = 0$ is not a stable condition; any fluctuation will drive the system to converge or diverge.

Lyapunov and his contemporary, Poincaré, were thinking about orbital mechanics and why planets had the orbits that they do. They worried about the stability of the visible structure of the solar system. If we think about the rocket whose launch we described in the second paragraph of this chapter, when the rocket returns near earth, $\lambda > 0$. If the orbit is just so, the rocket will reenter the atmosphere at the trailing edge of the earth and crash into the ground, ocean, or ice cap. If it arrives only 8 seconds later, it will be about 240 km behind the planet, will miss the atmosphere, but have its trajectory bent, experiencing a gravitational speed boost. Depending on the exact alignment and relative velocity, that change could boost (or reduce) the speed of the rocket, relative to the sun, by a large fraction of the earth's speed around the sun. When the Cassini spacecraft passed the earth for the last time in August 1999, as far as an observer on earth was concerned, it came in moving at 15.9 km s^{-1} and left with the same speed. However, relative to the sun, the spacecraft's speed was increased by 5.5 km s^{-1}, about 20% of the earth's orbital velocity around the sun (https://en.wikipedia.org/wiki/Timeline_of_Cassini%E2%80%93Huygens, 12/11/2020).

Imagine if the spacecraft had approached from in front of the earth instead of from behind it and had the same minimum altitude and same angular offset from the sun/earth line, but on the opposite side. The spacecraft would have lost 5.5 km s^{-1}, and instead of heading for Jupiter, it would have been orbiting the sun at 11 km s^{-1} too slowly to reach Jupiter; in fact, it would have barely reached the orbit of Mars. In other words, depending on the initial orbital period changing by about 6 minutes out of an entire year (0.1 hour or 1 part in 87,660), we vary the asymptotic result among Jupiter, Mars' orbit (whether or not Mars itself is in the vicinity), or burning up in the atmosphere. That is clearly sensitive dependence on initial conditions! And that corresponds to a highly positive Lyapunov exponent.

In contrast, imagine two pendula. Each has a 1 kg bob. One has a length of 1.000 m and the other has a length of 1.210 m. Since the period of the pendulum is $2\pi(l/g)^{1/2}$, the two pendula oscillate with a time per swing ratio of 1.1, 10% different. But since they're oscillating in earth's atmosphere, there's friction with the air, and the pendula take smaller and smaller swings as time advances. At $t = \infty$, both are hanging straight down, motionless. Their motion converges. The Lyapunov exponent describing their relative motion is negative. Whether or not they are synchronized at the moment they start, whether they're even started in the same year doesn't matter; asymptotically, they converge to a fixed behavior. There is weak dependence on initial conditions.

But what if time ran backwards? Now the roles of positive and negative Lyapunov exponents exactly reverse. For a positive Lyapunov exponent, we can precisely determine what the past looked like, while for a negative Lyapunov exponent, it's easier to see what the future will be. If we think about life as a trajectory through reality, it has a huge, positive Lyapunov exponent! We can know the past rather precisely (unless someone intentionally, yet unobtrusively, distorts the historical record), but the future is fuzzy. That's why hindsight is 20/20, but foresight is excruciatingly difficult.

Lyapunov exponents can be different locally and globally. Those rockets? Their trajectory when they got near the earth exhibited a large positive λ. However, as none of the post-encounter speeds generated sufficient velocity to escape the sun, globally the trajectories are bounded and λ is negative. The trajectories are never farther apart than the diameter of Jupiter's orbit.

What happens when trajectories diverge locally but are constrained globally? The trajectory is neither fully convergent nor fully divergent, but sits on a manifold (a geometric surface that, over small regions, behaves according to Euclidean geometry). If the trajectory closes on itself, the orbit on the manifold is periodic. If it doesn't quite close, it may be quasi-periodic or chaotic. As we already know, if it's chaotic, we can't predict its future precisely because we can't characterize where it is at any moment with sufficient precision. The difference between chemists and mathematicians in describing such surfaces is that the mathematicians describe neighborhoods δ of a point, while chemists speak of measurement precision σ. The chemists figure they can't know anything to infinite precision, while the mathematicians envision (some) entities that are infinitely precise, whether or not that precision can be measured. In fact, given a point in space, they may compute backward (exploiting the convergence at negative times for positive Lyapunov exponents) in time to find out where a point came from.

Complexity occurs not only in orbital mechanics but, more profoundly, in life. One of the common observations made about governmental or corporate policies is the Law of Unintended Consequences. This law states that unpredicted effects of any new rule will be important, and often more important than the intended consequences. As an example, being humane by ensuring that the unemployed do not starve sounds ethical. How is this accomplished? If it's via unemployment insurance, perhaps an unintended consequence is that higher wages are needed to lure people back to work. It is controversial as to whether subsidizing the unemployed reduces work incentives, but is a plausible example of attempting to achieve one outcome and ending up with another. Large divergence from predicted trajectories corresponds to large, positive Lyapunov exponents.

11.1 Wrestling with Rössler

Let's look at a three-dimensional situation. Consider an ecosystem of humans, corn, and rootworms. Humans and rootworms eat corn, humans eat foods other than corn if the rootworms are too aggressive, and rootworms eat other plant material, but don't thrive, on vegetation other than corn. We can imagine a situation where all species are in balance or dynamic equilibrium. But we can also see that the equilibrium is easily disrupted. Too many rootworms kill the corn, but then the rootworms starve. The human population will oscillate depending on how much corn it can eat. The original modeling of ecosystems like this was done by Lotka in the early part of the 20th century, and the Lotka-Volterra predator-prey model is the classical example of simple competitive ecology. Rather than show such a system, we use a three-species example for several reasons. 1) You can read about Lotka-Volterra dynamics on Wikipedia. 2) A two-species system can vary in time periodically, but it cannot have more complicated dynamics. I want to show complicated dynamics, so I need three competing species. 3) I'm lazy! I am actually relabeling one of the earliest examples of a chaotic set of orbits, described by Otto Rössler in 1976 (May, 1976; Rössler, 1976). He modeled chemical reactions and his attractor was described by my colleague and recent World Scientific fellow author Raima Larter in her book (Larter, 2021), but here we connect equations to phenomena that are at least somewhat intuitive. Anyone who has farmed corn is familiar with the interactions of rootworms, people, and corn. In fact, any three-species cross-linked system may have dynamics similar to those we are about to see here.

Rössler's equations are:

$$\frac{dx}{dt} = -y - z$$
$$\frac{dy}{dt} = x + ay \tag{11.2}$$
$$\frac{dz}{dt} = b + z(x - c)$$

Notice that there is only one nonlinear term: zx. Were it not for that term, (x, y, z) as a function of time t could be solved exactly in closed form. I'd probably find the solution using Laplace transforms, but I only name-drop that tool to bait you into looking it up.

Now we modify the notation slightly to use Rössler's equations to emulate the behavior of our three interacting species. Humans eat corn after it's grown, rootworms eat corn while it's growing. Let's be clear — no one is claiming that equation (11.2) describes all the complexity of agriculture, or everything about soil biology that influences corn growth, or the feeding habits of rootworms. However, with this oversimplified biology, the description of this ecological niche can be no simpler than equation (11.2). Let's recast the equations so that C is the amount of corn growing, H is the human population in the vicinity (farmers, agronomists, elevator operators, feedstore owners, and their families), and R is the rootworm population.

$$\frac{dC}{dt} = -H - R$$
$$\frac{dH}{dt} = C + aH \tag{11.3}$$
$$\frac{dR}{dt} = b + R(C - c)$$

> Don't you hate it when capitalization is all that distinguishes two values? If so, never program in C or C++.

Translating equation (11.3) into English, corn is eaten by humans and rootworms. Humans eat corn, and having a community of humans typically attracts more humans (the constant a tells how successfully one set of humans attracts others). Rootworms migrate from surrounding territory at a rate b, eat corn (so having lots of rootworms and lots of corn means even more rootworms, the fundamental nonlinearity in the model), but if the amount of corn drops to c, the rootworms quit growing locally and only increase at rate b. So that we don't have to deal with negative populations (I don't believe in ghost rootworms, do you?) we'll offset the plotted data so that all the numbers we display are greater than or equal to 0. Thus, instead of (C, H, R), we plot $(C + C_0, H + H_0, R + R_0)$, and we choose the zero subscripted variables so the populations are non-negative. Had we not made this choice, C, H, and R would have indicated departures from steady state, time-invariant behavior.

The dynamics we can observe depend on the initial values of the populations and the values of the parameters a, b, and c. Rössler mapped out the dynamics as a function of these values. What I want to show is a subset of what he showed. The message is: if even this simple model gives complicated dynamics, imagine how much more complicated the real world is. Nevertheless, complicated dynamics can be obtained from fairly simple interactions, and the complexity isn't necessarily due to noise. It can be deterministic. Figuring out whether messy-appearing data are random or deterministic is an interesting, even compelling, scientific challenge.

Let's choose $a = b = 0.2$, and use these values throughout. That is, human behavior and corn growth are unchanging, and the rate at which rootworms sneak into a field is also constant. The only parameter we'll vary is c, how much corn has to be present to keep the rootworms growing. If the corn can defend itself against rootworms, as some genetically modified corn strains can, what's being changed is c. "The bigger c is, the harder it should be for the worms to mess up the corn yield" seems pretty intuitive. Is it right?

Start with $c = 1.0$. Figure 11.1 is a plot of the populations as a function of time.

We see that all the populations oscillate periodically, with corn feeding people and rootworms. It looks like a time of 0.4

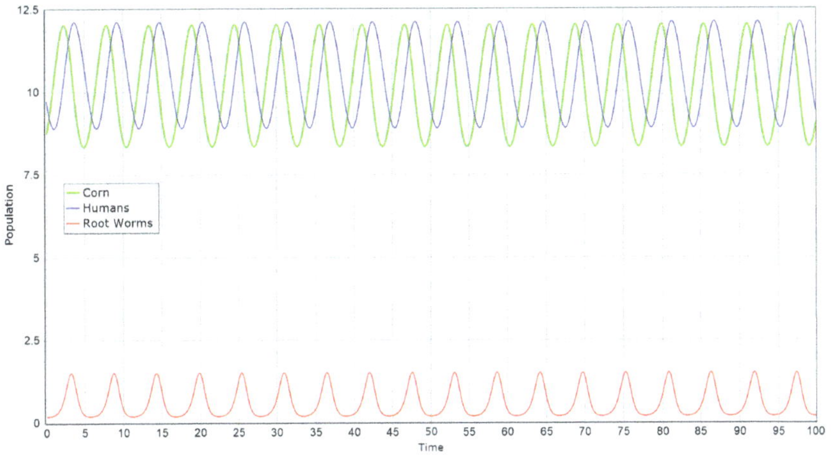

Figure 11.1. Corn, human, and rootworm populations as a function of time for $c = 1.0$.

corresponds to a single growing season. Could we plot these data in a different way to show the periodicity without having to show the behavior over a prolonged period of time? How about plotting the three populations as a function of each other, leaving time as an implicit variable (Figure 11.2)?

Now increase c to 3.0 (Figure 11.3). For the rootworms to multiply, more corn has to be growing. What happens?

At first glance, it looks like the growing season is half as long, but then something really strange is more striking. All the populations vary alternately. There's a large rootworm population, then a smaller population. There's a higher corn peak population, then a lower peak, while humans have a lower peak followed by a higher peak. The oscillations are flipping behavior alternately. We can see why the mathematicians call this "period 2" — a periodic oscillation where alternate cycles are similar or identical.

What does this look like in 3D?

The trajectory is no longer a circle (or, perhaps, a distorted circle). It's an interlinked loop (Figure 11.4). The trajectory has bifurcated — it has to go through two rotations to reconnect to itself.

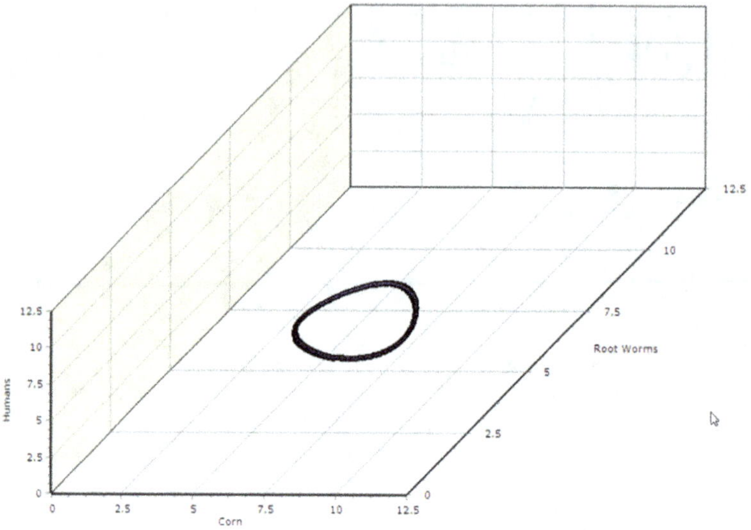

Figure 11.2. Corn, human, and rootworm populations plotted vs. each other for $c = 1.0$.

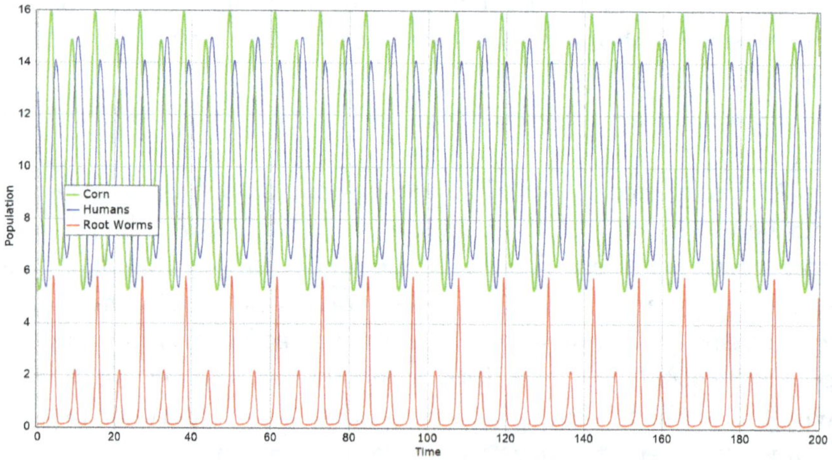

Figure 11.3. Corn, human, and rootworm populations as a function of time for $c = 3.0$.

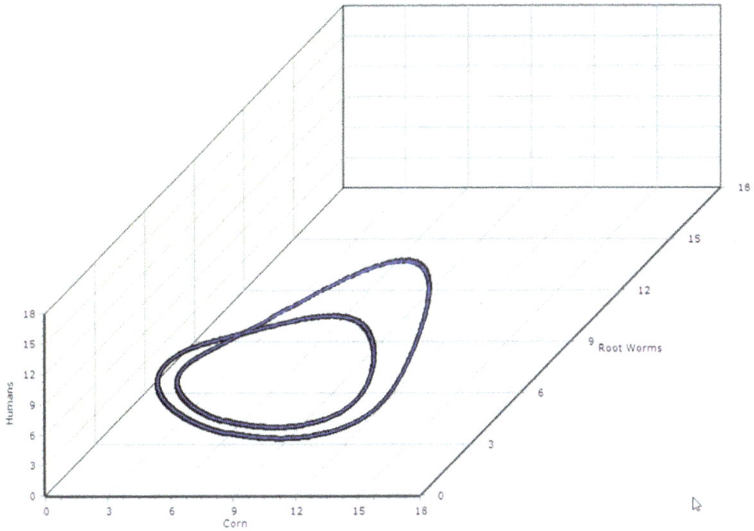

Figure 11.4. Corn, human, and rootworm populations plotted vs. each other for $c = 3.0$.

Perhaps this is easier to see if we look through the face of the human/corn viewing plane (Figure 11.5).

What happens if we increase c again? We can get chaotic oscillations. Figure 11.6 is an example when $c = 5.72$.

The pattern is completely non-periodic. What does the parametric plot look like? See Figure 11.7.

We can gain some insight if we look top-down on these data. We look towards the corn/rootworm plane (Figure 11.8).

We see that the rootworm population rises when corn population is high, then plunges when the corn population drops below 16. In what order do the various corn/rootworm trajectories occur? We could show this as a movie (very trendy for websites), but we'll use a different approach. Figure 11.8 contains 13,439 data points. We'll extract those points where the trajectory pierces a plane at Corn = 14.5 with corn population decreasing. This return map, a plot of rootworm population on successive orbits, is shown in Figure 11.9.

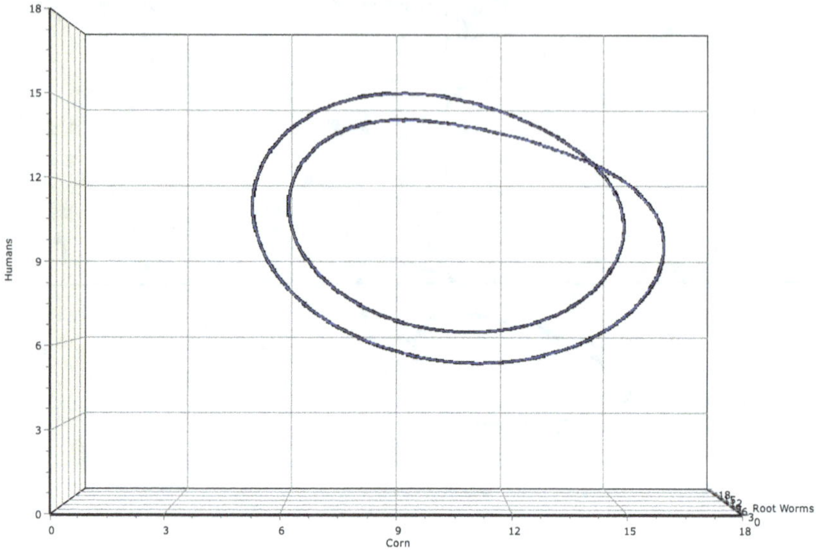

Figure 11.5. Same as Figure 11.4, viewed face-on.

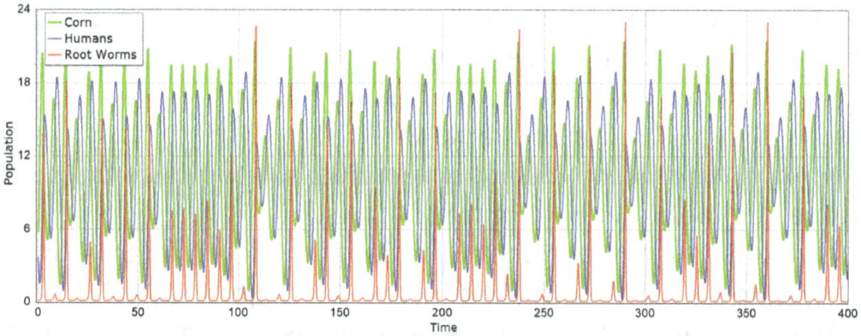

Figure 11.6. Corn, human, and rootworm populations as a function of time for $c = 5.72$.

Notice that while the time series looks noisy, there's a pattern underlying the noise; the orbits spiral out, then drop back towards the unstable fixed point, then spiral out again. If we start at low amounts of corn, succeeding growth accelerates. We pass a peak because for Corn > 1.5, $dR_{n+1}/dR_n < 0$. While the relationship among species shown in Figure 11.7 looks disorganized, chaotic,

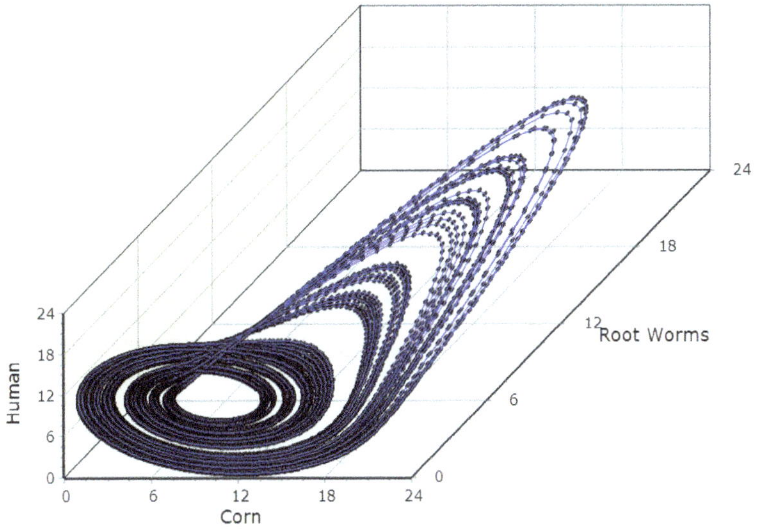

Figure 11.7. Corn, human, and rootworm populations plotted vs. each other for $c = 5.72$.

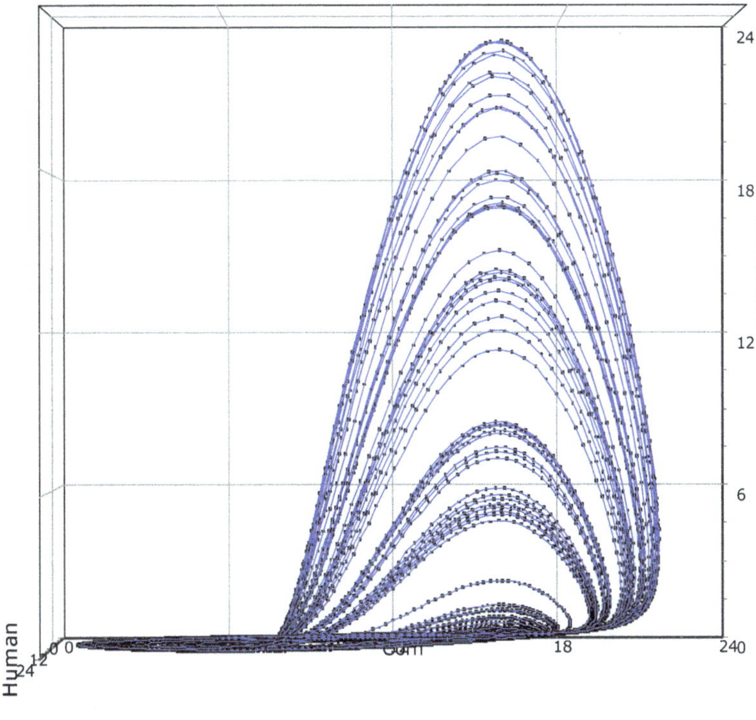

Figure 11.8. Same as Figure 11.7, viewed from the top.

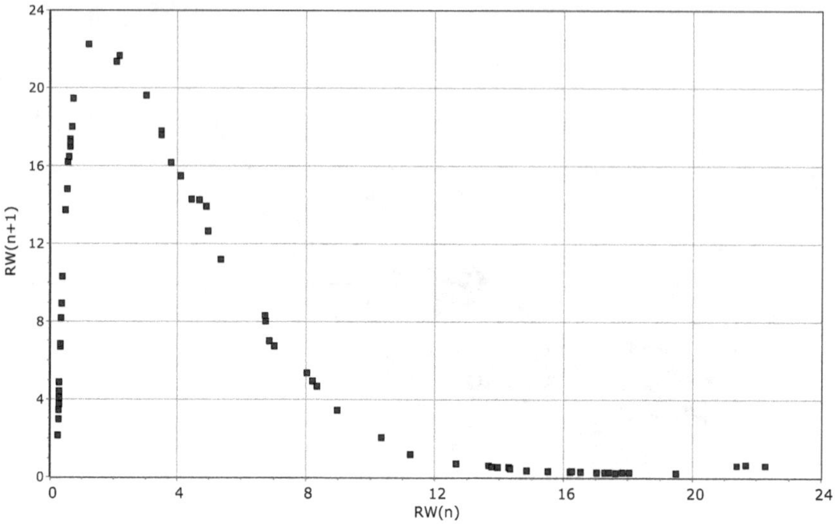

Figure 11.9. Return map for data in Figures 11.7 and 11.8.

and maybe even random, we see in Figure 11.9 that there's a pattern that's simple to discern. We can even imagine some simple function that could distort Figure 11.9 into Figure 5.7.

11.2 Poincaré, Lorenz, and Chaos, Oh My!

Contrast the nonlinear behavior above to what we saw about noise in Chapter 3. The worry in Chapter 3 was that people would discern patterns where there are none, while here the worry is that we'll miss patterns when they are there for the finding. Until the work of Henri Poincaré in the late 19th and early 20th century, science expected that all deterministic behavior would be stable or periodic. It was Poincaré's work on planetary orbits that showed deterministic trajectories could be noisy. This all sounds dense and abstract. In fact, it can be highly political.

The modern fascination with chaos was not kindled by Poincaré, whose focus on the gravitational challenge known as the "three-body problem" meant his work was studied almost exclusively by mathematicians and physicists. Until people started sending rockets into the cosmos, there was theoretical interest in the stability of planetary orbits, but no terrestrial process seemed connected to nonlinear esoterica. That changed in 1963 with the work of Edward Lorenz on atmospheric circulation or, more generally, Rayleigh-Benard convection (the transport of energy and mass in an initially uniform fluid, heated from below). The Lorenz equations abstract convective transport and temperature gradients in an atmosphere heated by the ocean or land below. We restate them here so you can compare the Lorenz equations to the Rössler equations, equation (11.2).

$$\begin{aligned}\frac{dx}{dt} &= a(y-z) = ay - az \\ \frac{dy}{dt} &= x(b-z) - y = bx - xz - y \\ \frac{dz}{dt} &= xy - cz\end{aligned} \tag{11.4}$$

Here, x is the rate of convection, y is the horizontal temperature variation, and z is the vertical temperature variation. Instead of one nonlinear term, there are now two. For simplicity, the atmosphere is two-dimensional. Absent temperature differences, there is no convection (the wind doesn't blow). Since we have already seen that just one nonlinear term is sufficient to lead to chaos, is it any surprise that two nonlinear terms also display such behavior? There are important consequences to the chaos associated with atmospheric heat and mass transport.

- Long-term weather forecasting in minute detail is difficult. We need data on a fine grid in both space and time to have any hope of computing atmospheric behavior. Data precision requirements are also exacting. Satellites and ground stations help, but eventually there simply isn't enough information density $I(x, y, z, t)$ to allow precise prediction of weather at a time t', $t' >> t$.
- However, because the atmosphere is constrained in space and time, and the parameters constraining energy transfer within the atmosphere are either constant or vary in a smooth way over relevant temperature and pressure ranges, the attractor on

which behavior evolves is simpler than the exact values of temperature, pressure, humidity, and so on. While we can't predict weather accurately for more than 10–15 days in advance, we know what seasonal variations to expect, and we know the rules governing chaotic changes.

- As we saw in the figures earlier in the chapter, even when the time series look incomprehensible, if we extract the behavior by removing time as an explicit variable (as we did in Figures 11.4, 11.5, 11.7, 11.8, and 11.9), we can see overall patterns even when we can't know exact values ahead of time.
- We thus see one reason why "climate change" or "global warming" are often confusing to the public but widely accepted by atmospheric scientists. If we look only at isolated data points, we miss patterns. If we look at overall patterns, we can't necessarily make point-by-point predictions.

The Lorenz equations are the source of the common meme that a butterfly, flapping its wings in the Amazon rain forest, may lead to a tornado in Illinois. But, equally, we see that temperature differences are critical to exacerbating short-term uncertainty, and the higher the CO_2 content of the atmosphere, the higher the energy input to, and mean temperature of, that atmosphere. With limited energy input, polar vortices are stable (as we can observe on Venus, Jupiter, and Saturn). With higher energy input, the polar vortex may bifurcate, and this is how great waves of frigid air migrate from the poles to the temperate zones. Fluid movements need not be on the scale of entire atmospheres to see these effects. A common science toy, the lava lamp as shown in Figure 11.10, shows the same thing.

In the lamp, a light bulb heats wax above its melting point. The solid wax is denser than the liquid in the lamp, but heated wax is less dense. So the liquid wax rises, cools, sinks, and repeats, but the rate of cooling depends on the rate of heating (how much heat the light bulb produces), the rate of cooling (thermal conductivity of the lamp and the internal liquid, external air temperature, and perhaps convective cooling if the lamp is placed in a drafty location), and the surface area to volume ratio of the wax drops. Rather than

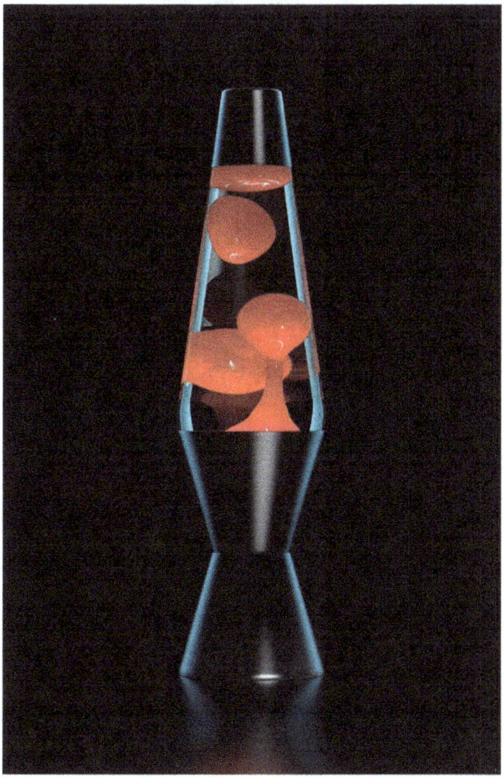

Figure 11.10. A fluid mechanical toy that illustrates chaotic fluid motion: the Lava Lamp.

horizontal and vertical convective rolls, as are found in the atmosphere under weak heating, we get rising and falling wax drops. But the essential multi-parameter, non-repeating character of mesmerizing movement is the same.

For small temperature gradients, the Lorenz differential equations have stable fixed points and conduction maintains a linear temperature gradient with no fluid convection. As the temperature difference increases, stable convection cells evolve — updrafts carry warm air upward to cool, and downdrafts bring that cooled air back to ground level. But at high enough temperature difference, the convective rolls become chaotic. It's the same thing with the polar vortex and jet stream. If the heat from the sun is weakly absorbed, the poles are cold, the temperate latitudes warmer, and the tropics warmest. Everything stays stratified. But with high [CO_2], the atmosphere becomes anomalously warm, the jet stream kinks, the polar vortex can break out into temperate latitudes, and Greenland can be warm while Texas freezes. Intuitively in Texas, residents might think, "global warming — what a hoax, I'm freezing to death!". However, looked at more globally, the situation is, "overall warming, and frigid air is being transported farther south than it should be!" Since temperature is a measure of mean energy content, increased atmospheric temperature corresponds to greater convection and greater movement. That's why the oceans (on average) are warmer and hurricanes or typhoons more energetic and more numerous (on average) than in the past.

One can see nonlinear effects in fluid behavior in contexts independent of energy transport in the atmosphere. The Rayleigh Taylor instability leads to viscous fingering in thin layers of immiscible fluids with different density, and flow of a stream of liquid into air or other low viscosity medium leads to droplet formation because of interfacial instability. I can recall a science toy from the 1960s, a Hele Shaw cell, that demonstrated this instability. The only web example I was able to find is at https://instructional-resources.physics.uiowa.edu/demos/2c4090-shock-wave-fronts-rayleigh-taylor-instability. My guess as to why such an inexpensive and vivid demonstration has disappeared is that the fluids were likely fluorinated hydrocarbon oils that are now frowned upon as potential pollutants, capable of causing ozone depletion (if transported into the atmosphere), endocrine disruption (in drinking water), or cancer (PFAS — polyfluorinated alkyl substances, https://dceg.cancer.gov/research/what-we-study/pfas).

Nonlinear models are descriptive of a more complex reality than linear models. Humans, however, often look at the world in linear terms. People typically look at a trend, then extrapolate it as if it will never end. After all, age only increases with time.

Temperature noisily increases from winter to summer, pauses, then noisily decreases from summer to winter. Learning is cumulative, so knowledge for each individual only increases (absent stroke, dementia, or trauma). Yet, real life is full of complexity. For example, the stock market goes up — and investors and pundits expect it to continue to climb. Cash flows in and out of investments; in some ways, money acts as a fluid. But disruptive events or nonlinear behavior can reck havoc with predictions. The stock market high of September 3, 1929 was not reached again until after the Second World War. The bull market following the Great Recession of 2008–2009 steadily increased (except for a shock implosion at the start of the COVID-19 pandemic) until the beginning of 2022, when it started sliding, allegedly due to increasing interest rates and the Russian invasion of Ukraine. Will it now decrease forever? I am confident the answer is no, but I have no way to parametrically predict when the reversal will come. However, some of the earliest people to apply chaos to markets may have enough data that they can make such a prediction. See the box below.

The Right Place, the Right Time

In 1986, Stephen Wolfram moved to the University of Illinois at Urbana-Champaign (UIUC), attracted by his ability to organize the Center for Complex Systems Research (CCSR). At that time, I was already interested in nonlinearity and chaos, and heard that Wolfram and a bunch of young physicists were gathered in a small building on Wright St., Urbana. Wolfram had assembled some of the hottest chaos hotshots together, including Norm Packard, Tom Meyer, Jim Crutchfield, and Chris Shaw. My contribution at that point was having co-authored what I believe was the first paper in the journal *Analytical Chemistry* to show a return map (analogous to Figure 11.9) in a paper about capacitor charging in spark sources (Hardas & Scheeline, 1984). Wolfram only stayed at CCSR and in the UIUC Department of Mathematics for two years. He then founded Wolfram Research and developed *Mathematica*. Meanwhile, the Beckman Institute

(*Continued*)

opened on campus, and CCSR was an early resident collaborative, cross-disciplinary program. The weekly seminars by some of the above-named people plus Atlee Jackson, Shau-Jin Chang, Jay Mittenthal, Paul Newton, and later Gottfried Meyer-Kress, Peter Jung, and Alfred Hubler made for most stimulating discussion. My hybrid approach of chemistry and measurement cloned onto nonlinear dynamics was already evident then, though I always felt like a bit of a pygmy among intellectual, or at least mathematical, giants. Norm Packard moved to the Santa Fe Institute, reunited with lifelong compadre Doyne Farmer, built the Prediction Company (Bass, 1999, 2000), and helped seed the development of automated securities trading. Eventually, CCSR shrank and my nonlinear connections were mostly with oscillatory reaction chemists and biochemists from across the world — Stanford University, Odense University, Waterloo, York, Toronto, and Sudbury in Canada, and the conveniently nearby Indiana University–Purdue University at Indianapolis.

11.3 Self-Organization

One more phenomenon demands our attention in describing the nonlinear world. Self-organization and nucleation generate structure while minimizing free energy and maximizing entropy. Has there been a more jargon-filled sentence in this book than the previous one? Let's take it apart and make sense of it.

Entropy is a measure of disorder. There are lots of ways to organize particles while maintaining conservation of energy and conservation of matter. Take a look at the air in front of you right now. Interchange the position of one nitrogen molecule and one oxygen molecule. Did the energy change? No, but the exact arrangement of molecules did. You have thus imagined two isoenergetic (same energy) states but in slightly different arrangements. If we list all the different arrangements that have identical energy, we are looking at all the degenerate, isoenergetic arrangements. The more such states there are, the higher the entropy. As temperature increases, systems can access more different states, and so have higher entropy. Free energy (well, Gibbs free energy; there's also Helmholtz free energy) is the difference between the energy internal to matter and the energy due to non-zero temperature and the large number of arrangements of molecules that have a particular internal energy.

$$G = H - TS \tag{11.5}$$

That is, the energy available to do work, G, is the enthalpy (internal energy plus pressure times volume) H minus temperature T times entropy S. Systems at equilibrium minimize energy and maximize entropy. At equilibrium, there are no externally discernable macroscopic changes in the system with time. If a system does change with time, it is not at equilibrium, in which case it is increasing entropy and decreasing free energy.

Suppose we dissolve salt in hot water. We then let the water cool. Eventually, the water will be cool enough that the salt cannot stay dissolved. If the system were at equilibrium, it would have solid salt at the bottom of the container and saturated salt water in the rest of the container. If there is no vibration, no dust in the water, and no scratches on the walls of the container, there is no way for precipitate to form, as there is no location where a slight release of energy to form a tiny crystallite can occur. If there is some small anomaly, a few salt aggregates can form there. Once this crystallite is seeded, a crystalline precipitate can readily form, and the system proceeds to equilibrium. To get to equilibrium, therefore, we need not only minimum energy and maximum entropy, but we need a mechanism by which the system can pass from disequilibrium to equilibrium. Often there are multiple mechanisms available, and the fastest path is the one the system follows. Once a path to equilibrium exists, only continual input of energy, matter, or both can keep the system away from equilibrium.

So now we have part of the jargon sentence explained: nucleation (seeding a crystal) is one way to release energy, increase entropy, and proceed to equilibrium. But what is self-organization? It's the formation of structures while staying far from equilibrium. A common example is the formation of a Langmuir-Blodgett layer

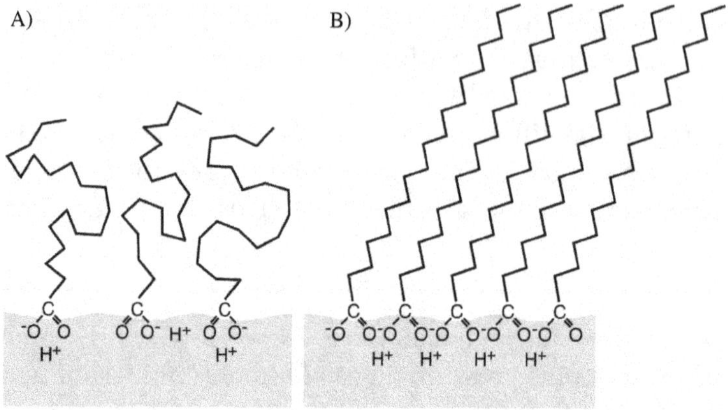

Figure 11.11. Formation of a Langmuir-Blodgett monolayer. A) Uncompressed layer, with molecular tails randomly oriented. B) Compressed layer with aligned tails.

on the surface of water, as shown in Figure 11.11. Start with water (or buffer, so that the acidity is controlled), and put one drop of a surfactant on the surface. Perhaps the compound is stearic acid, $C_{17}H_{35}COOH$. In basic solution, the proton is removed to form a stearate ion, $C_{17}H_{35}COO^-$. In the acid form, the COOH group takes up a lot of space, and because it is the most polar part of the molecule, it associates with the air/water interface, while the alkyl tail (the $C_{17}H_{35}$) sticks up in the air. In base, the negative end of the molecule is even more strongly preferred at the interface. However, the negative charges repel each other, spacing the stearate ions apart. Thus, when the amount of stearic acid or stearate is small, the compound only slightly dissolves in water; most of it sits on the surface of the water as an undissolved drop, or it spreads out as a monomolecular layer.

Once the monomolecular layer is present, the molecules can move around freely on the surface. Now start restricting the area the stearate can cover. Compress the layer with a scraper that penetrates the air/water interface and pushes the stearate towards one end of the container in which the stearate floats. The space between stearate molecules gets smaller. Eventually, the molecules run into each other. One thing that could happen would be for the molecules to pile up and make a stearate drop, floating on the water, and for neutral molecules that can happen. But for stearate ions, the molecules arrange themselves geometrically to pack into a crystalline form with the tails aligned.

Molecules are brainless, and scrapers lack molecular tweezers. The molecular tails line up so as to minimize the interaction energy between the molecules. At first, the alignment is poor, but if we compress the molecules slowly enough, they can wiggle around enough to anneal, that is, to fill in any gaps between molecules and to get any misaligned tails to straighten up. That gradual removal of defects and imperfections in molecular orientation is self-organization. If the temperature is high, the tails wiggle a lot, but that may lead to new defects as old defects fill in. If the temperature is low, the tails don't wiggle as much, but rearrangement is slower. It's the same behavior we discussed concerning protein folding and escape from potential wells; both kinetics and equilibrium are influenced by k_BT. We can only be completely defect-free at $T = 0$ Kelvin, but removing defects at that temperature takes forever. However, at temperatures considerably above 0 K, we can remove most of the defects in a reasonable time.

Self-organization is more than just spontaneous molecular arrangement. It's the formation of atmospheric convection cells to transport heat away from the earth's surface (sometimes leading to formation of thunderstorms and tornados). It's forming soap bubbles, vesicles, or micelles when surfactants, water, and gas are mixed. It's consuming water, sunlight, soil nutrients, and carbon dioxide to form a plant. It's starting with a fertilized egg and ending up with a fully formed animal. Self-organization is what happens when spatiotemporally organized chemical reactions generate highly structured outcomes while passing mass and energy through a dynamical system. Self-organization is epitomized by proteins translating nucleic acid codings into proteins, which in turn convert various small molecules into larger molecules or large molecules into smaller molecules, all the while creating or maintaining non-crystalline spatial forms. Your fingerprints? Self-organized. Facial features? Same. The three billion base pairs of your DNA specify the possible chemical structures of a human being. Modifications of that DNA by methylation, mutation, and regulation (often in company with histone proteins and geometrical constraints of DNA or RNA with catalytic proteins and nucleic acids) control spatial characteristics of molecular arrangements in cells and different types of cells in relationship to each other.

Society self-organizes as well. Imagine identical twins. They have the same parents, typically go to the same schools, have many of the same friends, participate in many of the same activities. Through some point in their schooling, they have the same advantages and liabilities. Suppose further that they go to the same college, get the same grades, and have the same interests. They apply to the same graduate school and both are admitted. They apply for the same fellowship. Only one is available. One gets the fellowship and goes straight into doing research. The other has to be a teaching assistant for two years and gets a slow start to research. For the rest of their research careers, barring some lucky break or unexpected insight by the twin that got the teaching assistantship, the fellowship-winning twin is going to have a leg up (if only because they will have the fellowship on their resume!). The moment at which the fellowship winner is chosen is a bifurcation point. The rest is self-organization. Winners keep winning. Self-organization and the accumulation of success to the successful is the physics of privileged members of society.

The same is true of the effects of economic or educational deprivation. Suppose parents are illiterate. They can't read to their children. The children get to school with less background in language and reading than their more advantaged contemporaries. Starting behind the others, they not only have ground to make up but lack the resources at home to accelerate that makeup. The longer the educational deficit persists, the more likely is discouragement, educational limitation, and continuation for a succeeding generation of lesser educational attainment. Of course this logic works symmetrically. Children of highly literate adults are read to, have language skills, are prepared for school, are pressured to achieve, and are likely assisted with outside enrichment or tutoring if shortcomings are found. Success begets success; limitation begets further limitation. Both privilege and the lack thereof can be viewed as either residency in potential wells (last chapter) or self-organization that stabilizes one's personal situation (this chapter).

Just as it is inevitable that a saturated salt solution, when cooled, will precipitate solid salt, so it is inevitable that complicated organic chemical mixtures will generate predictable, spatially patterned structures. If the number of different chemical species is limited, then the complexity of the structures is also limited. But from this perspective, life is not somehow miraculous; it is the inevitable consequence of organic chemistry, electrostatics, polymerization, and phase separation between hydrophilic and hydrophobic substances. Where scientists and theologians may collide is if the previous sentence is truncated to exclude the initial qualifying clause. Similarly, scientists may become irate if the qualifying clause is omitted from a sentence with the opposite meaning: Life is miraculous if one ignores its chemical nature. In the concluding chapters of this book, we will focus on these sorts of conflicting perspectives. If someone never studies science, understandings that include scientific perspectives are outside the thinker's bandwidth, yet they can still comprehend parts of the world. If someone never immerses in religious thinking, they can still comprehend parts of the world. As we have already seen, no one has universal knowledge, and so different weighting of such perspectives is inevitable. Just as the structure of salt and water depends on the ratio in which they are mixed, so one's explanations of the world depend on the ratio of various perspectives which mix in a single thinker. Just as the components of living systems spatially organize based on entropy maximization and energy minimization, so social interactions lead to clustering of perspectives and the formation of social groups, cults, factions, and denominations. Self-organization is the mechanism by which the energy landscape discussed in Chapter 10 develops minima, and once settled into a minimum, significant energy must be added to have populations escape one minimum and search for another. It is at the point of self-organization that a physicochemical view of the world and a sociological view overlap most closely. For an additional speculation on how human relationships can be abstracted as iterated interactions, see Appendix 2.

Self-organization is at odds with linear, Newtonian thinking. For Newton, initial conditions occur at $t = 0$, after which a system mechanically evolves to some steady state (uniform motion, zero kinetic energy, or periodic cycling being common). Because self-organization results in regular structure starting from random initial conditions, the final assembly appears to have resulted from some intentional construction. In fact, there is no "intention," only energy minimization consistent with other basic physical principles. As we discuss in the next chapter, structures on a large scale must behave in ways consistent with the rules for smaller-scale phenomena. However, such emergent behavior is not necessarily easy to predict. Life is an emergent behavior of molecular assemblies. Prior to the fusion of inorganic and organic chemistry into just chemistry, and the emergence of biochemistry as a subfield within chemistry, life appeared to be a separate realm, and to many it remains so. However, coupling self-organization to chemistry provides an alternative perspective: life is inevitable, is an automatic consequence of the inverse square law of electrical interaction coupled to the discrete nature of charges, and should be anticipated to occur anywhere that temperature and composition allow for sufficiently complex and facile self-assembly. Signals propagating through such assemblies that correlate with characteristics of the surroundings constitute information, and structures that respond to that information form the basis of intelligence. Such perspective is at odds with any theology common prior to the 20th century. While some scientists look upon evolution and self-assembly as tools of a Creator, others deduce that these dynamics eliminate the need for a creative intelligence. It will be several more chapters before we can critically discuss the collision of these viewpoints.

12

Markov Processes and Renormalization

What's going to happen next? Mostly, it's a matter of what is happening now, constrained by the laws of physics. If there are no new interactions, processes will keep progressing as they have. If there is a new interaction, then the way processes end up are a function of what's happening now (the initial conditions) and the nature of the interactions. If we break from the paradigm of a continuous world into a quantized world, we have a set of N particles, all interacting with each other, and a set of equally spaced times, t_k. If the behavior of the world is W, then

$$W(t_{k+1}) = f(W(t_k)) \tag{12.1}$$

Further,

$$W\left(P_n\left(t_{k+1}\right)\right) = \sum_m f_m\left(P_m\left(W\left(t_k\right)\right)\right) \tag{12.2}$$

"We blindly apply rules." This is the essence of a reductionist view of science: set up the initial conditions, hit "start", and watch what happens. For rocket trajectories where the rules are understood and the noise sources limited, this approach works well. For social interactions? Not so much. A highly cited source on symmetry breaking and emergent behavior was written by Phillip Anderson (1970).

That is, the state of the world at a subsequent time t_{k+1} is a function of the interactions of all the particles P_m at a previous time, based on the rules f_m, some of which are independent of particles, some of which depend only on the state of isolated particles, and some of which depend on interaction between two or more particles. As long as the behavior at t_{k+1} depends only on the behavior at time t_k and not on behavior at t_{k-1}, t_{k-2}, etc., we call the descriptions in equations (12.1) and (12.2) Markov processes. These equations are deterministic to the extent that we know $W(t_k)$ precisely and the behavior of the particles precisely. Because of measurement uncertainty, there are always uncertainties in applying these equations, and so Markov processes are often studied using statistical averaging over many approximate initial states near a particular $W(t_k)$. If something happens at t_{k-m}, there is a probability that it will give a fixed result until t_k, so long-term memory is simply a matter of having some state that was reached at t_{k-m} remaining static until t_k. At steady state or equilibrium, $W(t_{k-m+1}) = W(t_{k-m})$, at least in the absence of fluctuations. In trying to figure out where a system will evolve if we know the transition rules f, we blindly apply rules. However, those rules are probabilistic, so we treat rules as noiseless but probabilities as random. In a sense, this is the inverse of theistic philosophy, where an external force makes all events certain, but the rules are probabilistic, controlled by external forces that humans cannot influence.

Markov processes are frequently used in modeling microscopic systems, but the analogy to human-scale systems is easy to see. Each human is an individual. Each place that a human occupies in space excludes occupancy by other humans (except during pregnancy — and even there, we can use topology to model that fetus and mother are adjacent). If we coarse-grain time (that is, using clocks that work in units of years, decades, or centuries, rather than seconds), we could even have each human represented by a single point in a Markov process. We might describe life as: two humans collide, yielding a third (or, in the case of twins, a third and fourth). With some probability, the subset of humans remains closely associated in space and time for some period, after which one or more of them detaches in space, diffusing into the vicinity of many other humans, to one or several of whom the diffusing human closely sticks, repeating the cycle. While this may seem like a rather inhuman model (since personality, thoughts, and appearance are all ignored), on the scale of billions of people, it can yield reasonably useful characterizations. What happens in crowds? What happens during migrations? What happens during pandemics? Markov modeling provides a way to find out.

Closely related to Markov processes are cellular automata. These are binary numbers that are transformed by binary rules. Invented by John von Neumann, they have caught the imagination of physicists and mathematicians as abstractions of rule-based existence. Steven Wolfram in particular has written extensively on cellular automata in *A New Kind of Science* (Wolfram, 2002), followed by a somewhat controversial book, *A Project to Find the Fundamental Theory of Physics* (Wolfram, 2020), treating all of existence as describable by cellular automata, suitably construed.

How do we connect our perception that time is continuous to the discrete time of Markov processes? We can apply a continuous model over a short time to determine what will happen over that short time. If we are accurate in our short-time simulation, then repeatedly applying the calculation will move us along the time steps. Let's start with a simple example: first order chemical kinetics.

In this example, a reaction occurs to convert a starting molecule, A, to a product molecule, B. A common example is the

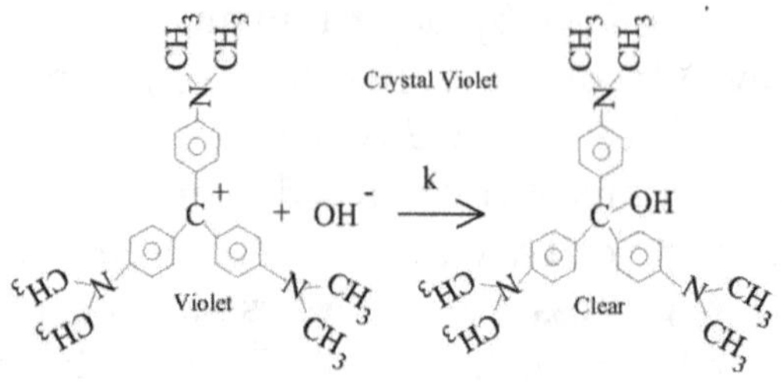

Figure 12.1. Crystal Violet hydrolysis reaction.

hydrolysis of Crystal Violet to a colorless carbinol (or, as shown in Figure 12.1, from a violet solution to a clear solution: Beach *et al.*, 1999; Turgeon & LaMer, 1952).

Overall, the reaction appears to be second order, as two entities, the Crystal Violet and the hydroxide ion, interact to form the product, a carbinol. If, however, the hydroxide is in excess so that its concentration changes imperceptibly during the reaction, then the reaction rate is proportional only to the concentration of Crystal Violet and is first order in that species.

As an aside, if Crystal Violet is placed in water, it can slowly react to give the carbinol, releasing H^+ and thus titrating endogenous OH^-. If we abbreviate the Crystal Violet cation as CV and the corresponding carbinol as CVC, we actually need to consider:

$$\begin{aligned} CV^+ + OH^- &\rightleftharpoons CVC \\ CV^+ + H_2O &\rightleftharpoons CVC + H^+ \\ H^+ + OH^- &\rightleftharpoons H_2O \end{aligned} \tag{12.3}$$

Typically when the hydrolysis reaction is presented to beginning chemistry students, only the first of these reactions is considered, as the reaction is carried out in alkaline solution so that the other reactions are slow or are at equilibrium and can, to a reasonable approximation, be ignored. To simplify matters even more, the reverse reaction (CVC dissociating to CV^+) is often ignored. So let's look at this as a Markov process, connect it to a continuum process, and finally show how to model the entirety of equation (12.3).

The simplest case is that CV^+ converts to CVC with a probability p_{12} and remains as CV^+ with a probability $1 - p_{12}$. We ignore the back reaction. If the initial number of CV^+ molecules is N_1, then, after a single step, the number of remaining CV^+ molecules is Round($(1 - p_{12})N_1$) and the number of CVC molecules is Round($p_{12} N_1$), where we round the numbers because p is real but N is an integer. Clearly, p_{12} is closely tied to the common reaction kinetics idea of a rate constant. The rate of a reaction in moles per liter per second can be converted to molecules per Markov step by:

$$\frac{d[\mathrm{CVC}]}{dt} = k\left[\mathrm{CV}^+\right] = kC_1 = \frac{k}{6.022\times10^{23}}\frac{N_1}{V} \tag{12.4}$$

We have converted moles per liter to molecules per liter using Avogadro's number and discretized time. A little rearranging gives:

$$N_1(t_2) = (1-p_{12})N_1(t_1) = (1-p_{12})6.022\times10^{23}VC_1(t_1)$$
$$N_2(t_2) = p_{12}N_1(t_1) = 6.022\times10^{23}VC_1(t_1)p_{12} = 6.022\times10^{23}V\int_{t_1}^{t_2}kC_1(t)dt$$
$$p_{12} = \frac{6.022\times10^{23}V\int_{t_1}^{t_2}kC_1(t)dt}{6.022\times10^{23}VC_1(t_1)} = \frac{k\int_{t_1}^{t_2}C_1(t)dt}{C_1(t_1)} \sim k(t_2-t_1) \tag{12.5}$$

The last equation in the set of equations (12.5) presents a problem, since p_{12} now depends on t_2, whereas for the Markov model of reality, time is discretized and so is given as a step number, which is unitless. Newton comes to the rescue; we set $t_2 - t_1$ to a sufficiently small value that $C_1(t)$ changes imperceptibly between t_1 and t_2. Harking back to the earliest chapters of this book, we measure concentration change over shorter and shorter time periods to find k (until the time is so short that measurement precision suffers, indicating that shorter measurement times will make precision worse), then choose $t_2 - t_1$ to be less than this limiting, minimum measurement time. Since a first order reaction slows down over time, having the initial time step so short that we can't measure the change in concentration ensures that p_{12} is small, its imprecision minimal, and $N_1(t_1) - N_1(t_2)$ is small compared to $N_1(t_1)$.

Now we express the values of N_1 and N_2 as a matrix multiplication recurrence relationship:

$$\begin{pmatrix} N_1 \\ N_2 \end{pmatrix}_{n+1} = \begin{pmatrix} 1-p_{12} & 0 \\ p_{12} & 1 \end{pmatrix} \begin{pmatrix} N_1 \\ N_2 \end{pmatrix}_n$$
$$\begin{pmatrix} N_1 \\ N_2 \end{pmatrix}_m = \begin{pmatrix} 1-p_{12} & 0 \\ p_{12} & 1 \end{pmatrix}^m \begin{pmatrix} N_1 \\ N_2 \end{pmatrix}_0 = \begin{pmatrix} 1-p_{12} & 0 \\ p_{12} & 1 \end{pmatrix}^m \begin{pmatrix} N_1 \\ 0 \end{pmatrix}_0 \quad (12.6)$$

As long as $p_{12} > 0$, eventually, $N_{2,\infty} = N_{1,0}$. We don't know which of the N_0 reactant molecules will become product molecules for any given step m, but we do know that, sooner or later, all will transform. We have also shown how to link an iterated, probabilistic process to a macroscopic, continuous process.

If we look at the continuous model for a first order reaction, the differential equations are easily solved (doing so is typically an early exercise in a differential equations or physical chemistry class). In summary,

$$\frac{d[\mathrm{CV}^+]}{dt} = -k[\mathrm{CV}^+][\mathrm{OH}^-] = -k'[\mathrm{CV}^+]$$
$$[\mathrm{CV}^+] = [\mathrm{CV}^+]_0 e^{-k't} \quad (12.7)$$
$$[\mathrm{CVC}] = [\mathrm{CV}^+]_0 (1 - e^{-k't})$$

If we have large numbers of molecules, discussing the reaction as a discrete process produces concentration curves indistinguishable from those of the continuous model. What about when the number of molecules is small? Let us assume that $p_{12} = 0.01$ and we start with 100 molecules. What would the number of product molecules look like as a function of time? We'll use a random number generator giving numbers uniformly on the interval [0,1] and, for each molecule at each step, show reaction of CV^+ to CVC if the random number is 0.01 or less, while leaving the reactant as CV^+ otherwise. Setting this up in *Excel*, Figure 12.2 is a snapshot of one

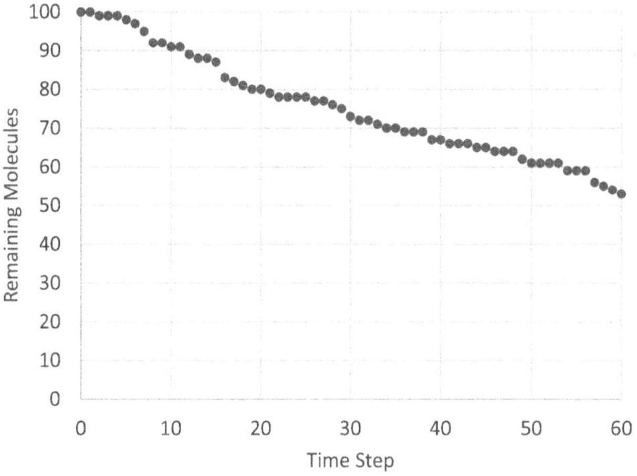

Figure 12.2. An example of a first order reaction modeled as a Markov process.

run where the horizontal axis is step number and the vertical axis is the number of remaining CV^+ molecules.

We see that the decay looks roughly exponential, as expected, but the change from step to step is noisy and a bit random. As stated above, when the number of molecules is small, a Markov process exhibits fluctuations due to the randomness of individual reaction events. "Is that realistic?" you may ask. Consider a biological cell. While cells range in size from 100 nm to 10 μm, let's model one as a 1 μm square box (real cells don't have sharp corners; a 1 μm sphere would be somewhat realistic, but then cells distort to fit snuggly against their neighbors. Let's not use more significant figures or more detailed geometric constraints than are realistic). A typical atom is 0.05 nm in diameter. Thus a 1 μm/side cube = 1000 nm/side, and a cell holds roughly $20{,}000^3 = 8 \times 10^{12}$ atoms. The human genome is made of about 3×10^9 nucleotides (single chain), each with about 30 atoms per nucleotide, in a double strand, so that accounts for 2×10^{11} atoms. The cell membrane is a bilayer with 50 atoms per lipid molecule and about 1×10^7 lipid molecules in the membrane. Membranes inside the cell are at least as large as the cell membrane, so 10^9 atoms are in membranes. This leaves 7×10^{11} atoms for proteins and small molecules. If there are 100 small molecules (100 atoms each) per protein/enzyme molecule

(10^6 atoms each), that means there are 10^5 protein molecules and 10^7 small molecules per cell. Some of those proteins are structural; histones are the spools on which the DNA in the chromosomes are wrapped. Some form fibrils that give the cell and its membranes stiffness. There are dozens of reactions to catalyze. Thus, there may be only 1–10 enzyme molecules of a particular type in a cell, or only a few dozen membrane proteins to sense the presence of signaling molecules in the surrounding space. Working with small numbers of molecules is thus typical of cellular systems, and Markov modeling of chemistry in single cells is more realistic than is continuous, differential equation modeling.

Looking back at equation (12.3), how do we model all three relevant reactions? First, let's make a model using ordinary differential equations, and assuming that the rate of aqueous hydrolysis, in acid, is so slow as to be irrelevant (consistent with experiment; I have seen year-old Crystal Violet solutions that are still deeply violet):

$$\begin{aligned}
\frac{d\left[\mathrm{CV}^{+}\right]}{dt} &= -k_1\left[\mathrm{CV}^{+}\right]\left[\mathrm{OH}^{-}\right]+k_{-1}[\mathrm{CVC}]\left[\mathrm{H}^{+}\right] \\
\frac{d[\mathrm{CVC}]}{dt} &= k_1\left[\mathrm{CV}^{+}\right]\left[\mathrm{OH}^{-}\right]-k_{-1}[\mathrm{CVC}]\left[\mathrm{H}^{+}\right] \\
\frac{d\left[\mathrm{OH}^{-}\right]}{dt} &= -k_1\left[\mathrm{CV}^{+}\right]\left[\mathrm{OH}^{-}\right]+k_{W,d}-k_{W,a}\left[\mathrm{H}^{+}\right]\left[\mathrm{OH}^{-}\right] \\
\frac{d\left[\mathrm{H}^{+}\right]}{dt} &= -k_{-1}[\mathrm{CVC}]\left[\mathrm{H}^{+}\right]+k_{W,d}-k_{W,a}\left[\mathrm{H}^{+}\right]\left[\mathrm{OH}^{-}\right] \\
\left[\mathrm{H}^{+}\right]\left[\mathrm{OH}^{-}\right] &= K_W = \frac{k_{W,d}}{k_{W,a}} \\
K_{f,CVC} &= \frac{k_1}{k_{-1}} = \frac{[\mathrm{CVC}]}{\left[\mathrm{CV}^{+}\right]\left[\mathrm{OH}^{-}\right]}
\end{aligned} \tag{12.8}$$

Among the approximations in equation (12.8), we ignore activity corrections to reaction rates and equilibria. Upon realizing that water dissociation is rapid, we can further simplify the problem as:

$$\begin{aligned}
\frac{d\left[\mathrm{CV}^{+}\right]}{dt} &= -k_{1}\left[\mathrm{CV}^{+}\right]\left[\mathrm{OH}^{-}\right]+k_{-1}[\mathrm{CVC}]\frac{K_{W}}{\left[\mathrm{OH}^{-}\right]} \\
\frac{d[\mathrm{CVC}]}{dt} &= k_{1}\left[\mathrm{CV}^{+}\right]\left[\mathrm{OH}^{-}\right]-k_{-1}[\mathrm{CVC}]\frac{K_{W}}{\left[\mathrm{OH}^{-}\right]} \\
\frac{d\left[\mathrm{OH}^{-}\right]}{dt} &= -k_{1}\left[\mathrm{CV}^{+}\right]\left[\mathrm{OH}^{-}\right]+k_{-1}[\mathrm{CVC}]\frac{K_{W}}{\left[\mathrm{OH}^{-}\right]}
\end{aligned} \tag{12.9}$$

Now we have to make a choice. Do we buffer the solution, effectively setting base concentration constant, or do we avoid buffering, allowing base concentration to vary? Let's not buffer the solution. Seeing that all the same terms occur in the reaction rate for all three species (except for sign changes), we can cast the problem as:

$$\frac{d\left[\mathrm{CV}^{+}\right]}{dt} = -k_{1}\left[C_{0,\mathrm{CV}^{+}}-x\right]\left[C_{0,\mathrm{OH}^{-}}-x\right]+k_{-1}[\mathrm{x}]\frac{K_{W}}{\left[C_{0,\mathrm{OH}^{-}}-x\right]} \tag{12.10}$$

At equilibrium, the rate is 0. At the start, $x = 0$, while at equilibrium, x satisfies:

$$\frac{k_{1}}{K_{W}k_{-1}} = \frac{[\mathrm{x}]}{\left[C_{0,\mathrm{OH}^{-}}-x\right]^{2}\left[C_{0,\mathrm{CV}^{+}}-x\right]} \tag{12.11}$$

Now, which is easier, solving equation (12.10) in closed form, solving equation (12.10) numerically, or making a Markov model where there are two probabilities, that of CV^{+} reacting with OH^{-} and that of CVC dissociating spontaneously or reacting with a proton? The latter is:

$$\begin{aligned}
N_{1,n+1} &= \left(1-p_{12}N_{3,n}\right)N_{1,n}+p_{21}N_{2,n} \\
N_{2,n+1} &= p_{1,2}N_{1,n}N_{3,n}+\left(1-p_{21}/N_{3,n}\right)N_{2,n} \\
N_{3,n+1} &= \left(1-p_{12}N_{1,n}+p_{21}K_{W}N_{2,N}/N_{3,n}^{2}\right)N_{3,n}
\end{aligned} \tag{12.12}$$

Species 1 is CV^+, species 2 is CVC, and species 3 is OH^-. Because of the nonlinearity in the second and third equations (dynamic variables in denominators), it's not easy to see how to recast this as a matrix formulation, but programming it is straightforward. The beauty of Markov modeling is that, once we specify the probabilities, we turn on the random number generator, throw a few thousand starting molecules into the initial conditions, and punch "go." It's a lot easier than numerical integration. Relating the probabilities to rate constants and choosing the time interval that corresponds to one iteration are the biggest remaining headaches.

I was going to be a wise guy and solve equation (12.10) in closed form. Since x is the amount of CVC formed, we can rearrange the problem:

$$-\frac{dx}{dt} = -k_1\left(C_{0,CV^+} - x\right)\left(C_{0,OH^-} - x\right) + \frac{k_{-1}K_W x}{C_{0,OH^-} - x}$$

$$\frac{dx}{k_1\left(C_{0,CV^+} - x\right)\left(C_{0,OH^-} - x\right) - \dfrac{k_{-1}K_W x}{C_{0,OH^-} - x}} = dt$$

$$\frac{\left(C_{0,OH^-} - x\right)dx}{k_1\left(C_{0,CV^+} - x\right)\left(C_{0,OH^-} - x\right)^2 - k_{-1}K_W x} = dt \tag{12.13}$$

$$\int_0^T dt = T = \int_0^X \frac{\left(C_{0,OH^-} - x\right)dx}{k_1\left(C_{0,CV^+} - x\right)\left(C_{0,OH^-} - x\right)^2 - k_{-1}K_W x}$$

$$= \int_0^X \frac{\left(C_{0,OH^-} - x\right)dx}{k_1(C_{0,OH^-}^2 C_{0,CV^+} - \left(C_{0,OH^-}^2 + 2C_{0,CV^+}C_{0,OH^-}\right)x + \left(2C_{0,OH^-} + C_{0,CV^+}\right)x^2 - x^3) - k_{-1}K_W x}$$

(Continued)

(Continued)

This is typically tweaked to read

$$k_1 T = \int_0^X \frac{\left(C_{0,\mathrm{OH}^-} - x\right)dx}{\left(C^2_{0,\mathrm{OH}^-}C_{0,\mathrm{CV}^+} - \left(C^2_{0,\mathrm{OH}^-} + \frac{k_{-1}K_W}{k_1} + 2C_{0,\mathrm{CV}^+}C_{0,\mathrm{OH}^-}\right)x + \left(2C_{0,\mathrm{OH}^-} + C_{0,\mathrm{CV}^+}\right)x^2 - x^3\right)} \tag{12.14}$$

In turn, this is broken into two integrals, one with a constant term in the numerator and the other with the term linear in x in the numerator. The integrals we need are:

$$\int_0^X \frac{dx}{A + Bx + Cx^2 + Dx^3}$$
$$\int_0^X \frac{xdx}{A + Bx + Cx^2 + Dx^3} \tag{12.15}$$

Conveniently, $D = -1$. This should be simple. Surprise! https://alpha.wolfram.com tells us the first (indefinite) integral is

$$\sum_{\{\omega : A + B\omega + C\omega^2 - \omega^3 = 0\}} \frac{\ln(x - \omega)}{B + 2C\omega - 3\omega^2} \tag{12.16}$$

One has to solve a cubic in order to evaluate this integral. When I asked Wolfram to solve the integral with xdx in the numerator, it choked. It may be possible to do the integral by integrating by parts:

$$\int udv = uv - \int vdu$$

$$u = x \quad dv = \frac{dx}{A + Bx + Cx^2 - Dx^3}$$

(*Continued*)

$$\int \frac{x\,dx}{A+Bx+Cx^2-Dx^3}$$
$$= \sum_{\{\omega:A+B\omega+C\omega^2-\omega^3=0\}} \frac{x\ln(x-\omega)}{B+2C\omega-3\omega^2} - \int \sum_{\{\omega:A+B\omega+C\omega^2-\omega^3=0\}} \frac{\ln(x-\omega)}{B+2C\omega-3\omega^2}dx$$
$$\int \Omega \ln(x-\omega)dx = \Omega((x-\omega)\ln(x-\omega)-x)$$
$$\Omega = \frac{1}{B+2C\omega-3\omega^2} \quad (12.17)$$

Equation (12.17) is still incredibly ugly — writing out the solution would fill pages. But it can be done. But it's a lot more painful than just using equation (12.12). Simplicity also reduces the likelihood of programming errors.

If we hypothesize that the reaction goes to completion so that $k_{-1} = 0$, the integral is routinely solvable in closed form.

$$\frac{dx}{dt} = k_1\left(C_{0,CV^+} - x\right)\left(C_{0,OH^-} - x\right)$$
$$\int_0^T k_1 dt = \int_0^X \frac{dx}{\left(C_{0,CV^+} - x\right)\left(C_{0,OH^-} - x\right)}$$
$$= \frac{1}{C_{0,OH^-} - C_{0,CV^+}}\left(\int_0^X \frac{dx}{C_{0,CV^+} - x} - \int_0^X \frac{dx}{C_{0,OH^-} - x}\right)$$
$$\left(C_{0,OH^-} - C_{0,CV^+}\right)k_1 T = \int_0^X \frac{dx}{C_{0,CV^+} - x} - \int_0^X \frac{dx}{C_{0,OH^-} - x}$$
$$= \ln\left(C_{0,OH^-} - x\right)\Big|_0^X - \ln\left(C_{0,CV^+} - x\right)\Big|_0^X = \ln\frac{C_{0,CV^+}}{C_{0,OH^-}}\frac{C_{0,OH^-} - X}{C_{0,CV^+} - X}$$
$$e^{\left(C_{0,OH^-} - C_{0,CV^+}\right)k_1 T} = \frac{C_{0,CV^+}}{C_{0,OH^-}}\frac{C_{0,OH^-} - X}{C_{0,CV^+} - X}$$

$$\left(C_{0,\mathrm{CV}^+}-X\right)\frac{C_{0,\mathrm{OH}^-}}{C_{0,\mathrm{CV}^+}}e^{\left(C_{0,\mathrm{OH}^-}-C_{0,\mathrm{CV}^+}\right)k_1T}=C_{0,\mathrm{OH}^-}-X$$

$$C_{0,\mathrm{OH}^-}\left(e^{\left(C_{0,\mathrm{OH}^-}-C_{0,\mathrm{CV}^+}\right)k_1T}-1\right)=X\left(\frac{C_{0,\mathrm{OH}^-}}{C_{0,\mathrm{CV}^+}}e^{\left(C_{0,\mathrm{OH}^-}-C_{0,\mathrm{CV}^+}\right)k_1T}-1\right) \tag{12.18}$$

$$X=C_{0,\mathrm{CV}^+}\frac{C_{0,\mathrm{OH}^-}\left(e^{\left(C_{0,\mathrm{OH}^-}-C_{0,\mathrm{CV}^+}\right)k_1T}-1\right)}{C_{0,\mathrm{OH}^-}e^{\left(C_{0,\mathrm{OH}^-}-C_{0,\mathrm{CV}^+}\right)k_1T}-C_{0,\mathrm{CV}^+}}$$

Since X = [CVC], everything else falls into place.

Why All the Asides in This Book?

Too much of science is presented as a set of established facts. There are plenty of facts that are quite solidly established. What I hope you're seeing here is how one particular scientist thinks about the world. Sometimes, the answers just flow out smoothly. And sometimes, a researcher goes along blissfully until hitting a wall. Research is often a matter of hitting walls, then inventing a way to avoid the wall entirely. But how can this be communicated if the crashes aren't part of the conversation? When space probes work or aircraft make millions of trips without crashing, it's the result of untold person years of science, mathematics, engineering, human factors psychology research, and failure after failure after failure before systems finally work reasonably well. I don't hide from the head scratching and detailed calculations. I revel in it.

12.1 Phase Transitions and the Renormalization Group

Now comes an absurdly huge leap, a discontinuity in the logic and mathematics. Instead of looking at individual molecules that largely act on their own so that their behavior can be explained by a handful of probabilities to describe each step into the future, we are going to look at large collections of molecules, atoms, or electron spins, and see how they behave as a function of temperature. We are addressing collective behavior: phase transitions. Such transitions for weakly interacting particles involve liquids vaporizing into gases. Somewhat stronger interactions involve solids becoming liquids. Even stronger interactions involve the magnetization of solids, where nuclear spins produce comparatively large magnetic fields (spinning electrons also generate magnetic fields, but their phase transitions lead to superconductivity, and that's a topic I'm going to avoid). Magnetization is so complicated that it has to be treated with the same sort of mathematics that describes high energy particle physics: renormalization group theory. So let's explain the problem and then its solution. Fair warning: this is an area where reading the cited literature is necessary if you really want to understand what's going on.

Suppose you have two magnets. You put them on a surface and let go of them. What happens? Either the north pole of one magnet sticks to the south pole of the other magnet or the two magnets end up with their pair of poles attracted to each other, NS and SN. Either way, it takes energy to pry them apart. If we add heat (i.e., random motion) to the magnets, there will be some "give" to the polar attraction. At some sufficiently high energy, the magnets can pull far enough apart that friction with air or external surfaces keep the magnets from moving back towards each other. Thus, heating the system potentially can disassemble a set of magnets (at sufficiently high temperature, absent an external field, an iron magnet melts and demagnetizes). As we saw when discussing potential wells, the effect of temperature results in a change in a distribution function as $e^{-E/kT}$. If all the energy went into prying apart just two of the magnets, instead of one big magnet, there would be two smaller magnets which could be parallel aligned or anti-parallel aligned. Heat the system more, and there might be enough energy to pry the system apart into four sub-magnets, and they could be two small magnets and one large one or four medium-sized ones. Given enough energy, the whole magnetized domain falls apart and becomes a set of independent magnets. When does that happen? When the energy per volume of a single spin exceeds the binding energy between adjacent spins.

But now behavior gets complicated. Magnetic interactions fall off with distance the same as gravitational or electric fields. That means that while adjacent spins interact strongly, more distant spins are affected as well. Further, external fields can be imposed, so that the local behavior has a global component. If the sum of the influence of many aligned magnets at a distance overwhelms lower spin effects close by, the magnets can't easily be separated. Thus, we have a non-localized problem. We need to consider not just interactions of adjacent magnets, but magnets throughout a large volume of matter. When would the magnets decouple? They would when interactions at all distances are sufficiently weak compared to thermal energy that migration and reorientation are more probable then simply aligning the magnets. This requires that we look at spin-spin correlations at multiple distances, and that's hard. If we have a Markov model, we could look at each pairing, noting that a weak interaction has a small probability of aligning a spin, while a strong interaction would have a high probability. In one dimension, Ising solved the problem in 1924; in two dimensions, Onsager solved it in 1944 (Brush, 1967). Perturbation theory, often used in looking at weakly interacting systems that behave understandably if they aren't interacting with their neighbors, is not helpful here. What's needed is a method for looking at interactions that cover many scales and yet doesn't have such an explosion of parameters that the required calculations would take an infinite amount of time.

That's where the renormalization group comes in (Goldenfeld, 1992). We know from experiment that at a phase transition, properties such as density, magnetization, and vapor pressure scale as $(T - T_c)^p$ or $((T - T_c)/T_c)^p$, where T is the temperature, T_c the critical temperature where the phase transition occurs, and p is the critical exponent. In order to calculate what occurs, we already noted that we have to take interactions at various distances into account, but the overall behavior cannot depend on how we do the calculation — it can only depend on the chemistry and physics in the material under question and the gross size of the material. Specifically, it cannot depend on whether we integrate behaviors over a small distance or a large distance; any superimposed scale choice may be necessary for computation but cannot appear in the answer. "Renormalization" refers to performing a multiple scale computation where the scale employed may be present in mid-process but disappears from the answer. It will turn out that far from T_c, fluctuations and noise are small, but close to T_c, fluctuations can be quite important. This makes sense; when water is close to boiling, the forces keeping water from vaporizing are, relatively, less constraining than when we are far from boiling and the vapor pressure is either so low that the water is a liquid or solid or so high that the water acts nearly like an ideal gas. Near-condensation (just above boiling) or near-vaporization (just below boiling) features significant fluctuations.

How does this work? We set up calculations so that at large distances we average over system behavior, but at short distances, we calculate in terms of wavenumber $k = 1/\lambda$. At intermediate scales, the two calculations will match. At large scales, k will be irrelevant, and at small scales, only k will be relevant. We thus extrapolate to $L = \infty$ and $k = 0$, matching the expressions at middle scales. The fluctuations are dominated by k, the global behavior by L. "But where do we make the switch — isn't that arbitrary?" And that's the key insight — the switch in descriptions cannot be material in the physics, because the physics doesn't distinguish how calculations are done, it just is. Thus, the scaling at middle distances is chosen so that where the switching occurs is irrelevant.

Yet another way to describe phase transitions and critical behavior is via correlation length, ξ. A perfect crystal would have all its molecules perfectly aligned, and ξ is the length of the crystal parallel to one of its axes. For a gas, where particles are nominally independent, ξ is the mean distance between molecules. Since energy depends on the separation of particles and ξ describes how well-aligned the particles are, we have a linkage between ξ and the system energy (either L, the Lagrangian or H, the Hamiltonian. L = kinetic energy minus potential energy, while H is kinetic energy plus potential energy. Alas, H for enthalpy, H for Hamiltonian, and **H** for magnetic induction can only be distinguished by context.).

To measure ξ, we need a ruler; we compute H or L over a unit length or volume of the ruler, then average the behavior across all the measured distances or volumes in the system. If the ruler characteristic size is ℓ, then we measure ξ as $\xi(\ell)$.

How is H influenced by ℓ? That depends on the dimensions of the system, d. For a line, $d = 1$, for a surface, $d = 2$, and for a volume $d = 3$. For a rough surface $2 < d < 3$. For a porous solid, $2 < d < 3$. I could present a whole chapter on porosity and fractals, but I won't. What I will say is: the way that ℓ influences the calculation and the size of ξ have to precisely counterbalance so that the choice of ruler does not change the behavior of the system which, lacking declarative knowledge, must behave independent of the ruler. We thus look at $\ell^d\xi(\ell)$, write the Hamiltonian in terms of the coherence length and ruler size, then take limits near phase changes, i.e., where ξ goes to 0 (vaporization) or ∞ (condensation/solidification). Goldenfeld (*op. cit.*) covers the details in about 100 pages; Wilson required several dense articles in the *Physical Review* (Wilson, 1971a, 1971b, 1983). The energy of the system is written in the same terms all the way through the phase transition, but the correlation length goes to 0 or ∞ and the macroscopic characteristics change drastically.

How does this relate to humans who aren't doing physics calculations? Think of the many scales that matter to us daily. Chemical reactions involve behavior at a nanometer scale. Cells work on a micrometer scale. Organs function on a millimeter or centimeter scale. We ourselves range from 0.5 meter (typical newborn) to 2.7 meters (Robert Wadlow, 8 feet 11″, the tallest person reliably measured in the U.S.). Families, clans, tribes, cities, nations, and the entire human race scale up to covering the earth's 150×10^6 km^2 of dry land with 8 billion people or 53 people/km^2 = 18,750 m^2/person, about 4.6 acres per capita. Scientific description covers all of these scales (and larger ones as well — astronomical data stretches over billions of light years). Integrating over chemical events leads to biochemistry. Integrating over biochemistry leads to cellular biology. Integrative cellular biology is physiology and organismal biology. Integrating over organisms gives us ecology, sociology, and culture. Thus, we need to have multiscale ways to explain the physical world. We go into this in detail in Chapter 16. Here, however, we focus on the idea that continuous phenomena can be broken up into Markovian steps, and Markovian steps can be integrated over multiple scales to reassemble a continuum view of existence. Local and global scales are coupled; sequential events and continuous models can refer to the same phenomena.

It is far from intuitive how large-scale, multi-particle or multi-person phenomena emerge from small-scale behavior. All of what humans do is consistent with molecular behavior, but there are nearly infinite numbers of human behaviors that fail to violate the rules describing biochemistry. It appears that any time we go through a renormalization or phase transition, we lose the ability of smaller-scale phenomena to predict larger-scale behavior, even though the rules of the smaller-scale behavior still apply. And yet, there are hints that couplings across scale do influence behavior. The gut microbiome is made up of bacteria, fungi, viruses, and archaea. Which microorganisms live in our gut is affected by what we eat. Evidently, metabolism by these non-human organisms gives rise to chemical species that influence gut health, organ function, and even thought. Thus, there is trans-species coupling; whether it is symbiotic or parasitic is in the eyes of the beholder. Eating a moldy piece of bread may inoculate the gut with a species that, decades later, exacerbates an infection, or defends against it. Whether diet fads work as advertised or not, they certainly adjust conditions in the gut and thus, indirectly, influence metabolism. Since people's genetics vary, so will response to diet, to inoculation by various species, to association with various organisms, and so on. Markov descriptions are apt for looking at the behavior of small numbers of interacting microorganisms, while the systemic effects take place past a renormalization where all the gut organisms, skin and lung organisms, environmental interactions, and social interactions play off against the thousands of cells in any part of the organism. The physical descriptions and mathematics give us tools, but complexity and noise make definitive extrapolations from current conditions difficult.

The last three chapters of this book, in some sense, are a post-phase-transition view of the world, given the underlying thought processes revealed in the earlier chapters. There aren't as many equations or calculations written out, but the same sorts of calculation, concerns for information localization and processing, and quantitative vetting of qualitative ideas are at play. But before we get there, there are a few additional physical, chemical, and mathematical ideas we need to discuss.

13

Neural Networks

How do living beings (not just humans) learn? They make large numbers of measurements, detect patterns in the results, store information about the patterns, and then add that remembered pattern to data coming in from fresh measurements to structure the response to the new data. Whether the information is hard coded into sensory proteins in an organism's external membrane (as in bacteria) or adaptive via specialized cells (neurons) or a combination, the computational mechanism is called a neural network. Such networks can be mimicked on digital computers, and are often the basis for artificial intelligence. Let's explain the mechanics of these networks, then see how they can be generalized in software and in nature. Such explanation demystifies how biological computational and communications systems function.

Recall the structure of neurons, as shown in Figure 13.1. Dendrites sense the environment, including the behavior of other nearby neurons. The cell body sums the stimulations sensed by the dendrites, communicates that sum down the axon to the axon tip. A synapse forms when the tip of an axon connects to the dendrite of an adjacent neuron.

The basis for a neuron firing, or sending a potential spike into the surrounding tissue, is that its dendrites receive sufficient

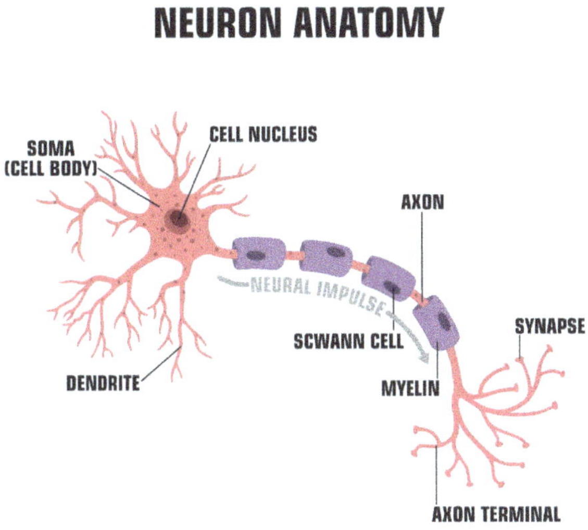

Figure 13.1. Sketch of a neuron.

stimulation for a burst of ions and small- or medium-sized molecular neurotransmitting chemicals to be emitted at its axon tips. Within the neural system, axon tips and dendrites nearly touch at a synapse; synapses also link terminal neurons to excitable muscle fibers, resulting in muscle contraction. In some ways, neuron firing is analogous to gently squeezing a trigger of a gun. At some pressure point, the trigger trips, a firing pin hits a primer, and the firearm discharges. Similarly, once the potential inside a neuron is high enough, a synapse discharges into the intrasynaptic space. Once a discharge occurs, the cell is passive for some time before the trigger is again responsive and there is an adequate supply of ions and neurotransmitting chemicals to allow a follow-up firing. The classic model for a neuron is the Hodgkin-Huxley model, proposed in 1952. However, the essential features need not involve chemical species. Mathematical mimicking of neuron firing requires a function that has one output level when inputs are below some threshold, then a pulsed output when the input threshold is exceeded. Such a function is the hyperbolic tangent:

$$f(t) = \frac{e^{kt} - e^{-kt}}{e^{kt} + e^{-kt}} = \frac{1 - e^{-2kt}}{1 + e^{-2kt}} \tag{13.1}$$

At $t = -\infty$, $f(t) = -1$. At $t = +\infty$, $f(t) = +1$. And at $t = 0$, $f(t) = 0$. The function triggers at $t = 0$. The scaling factor k determines how steeply the function rises near $t = 0$. It is easy to shift the moment of firing by offsetting t to some other time t_0 by replacing t with $t - t_0$. Instead of going from -1 to $+1$, the function can be offset to go from 0 to A by adding 1 to $f(t)$, then multiplying the whole modified function by $A/2$.

$$g(t) = \frac{A}{2}\left(\frac{1-e^{-2k(t-t_0)}}{1+e^{-2k(t-t_0)}}+1\right) \tag{13.2}$$

This formulation looks like a way to cause a step change in behavior at t_0. To get a pulse, just differentiate:

$$g'(t) = \frac{2Ake^{-2k(t-t_0)}}{\left(1+e^{-2k(t-t_0)}\right)^2} \tag{13.3}$$

Now instead of thinking of t as time, think of it as stimulus. If t_0 starts out as $+\infty$, learning consists of lowering t_0 so that triggering of either a step change or a pulse happens more easily. The slope of the response is made by adjusting k, and the amplitude by adjusting A. Figure 13.2 is a plot of g and g' functions for a particular set of (A, k) values, (1,1), setting $t_0 = 0$ for convenience.

Portions of the function look nearly linear. Other portions look nearly quadratic. Combinations of these functions can be used to approximate linear or quadratic behavior just by adjusting three parameters (if we want to tinker with the offset, i.e., the value of the function at $t = -\infty$, we could add a fourth parameter). We see that we can use these functions to do a lot of the work of responding appropriately to stimulation. But must we use humans to tune the parameters? What if nature (or a computer program) combined a large number of hyperbolic tangent functions (and their derivatives) and used the output of some of those functions to adjust the parameters controlling other examples of similar functions? We might build an automaton that could respond to stimuli.

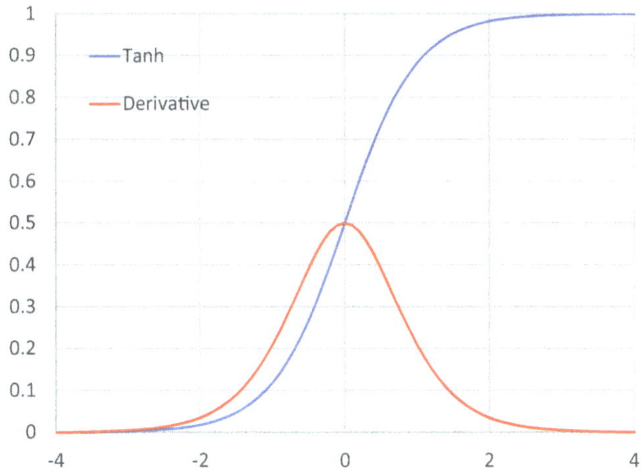

Figure 13.2. Offset hyperbolic tangent and its derivative.

13.1 Perceptrons and Their Uses, With a Side of Immunoassay

And that's exactly what we do in designing a numerical neural network. We use the output of one or more hyperbolic tangent functions to control others, either by adjusting parameter values or by firing pulses. We train the networks by using their output to drive their inputs so that they can "learn" to "recognize" input patterns. Just as with real neurons, we don't just have a single input leading to a single output. We have multiple inputs, which we combine as a weighted sum.

$$V_{out} = g\left(\sum_i w_i V_i, A, k, t_0\right) \tag{13.4}$$

where A, k and t_0 are parameters as shown in equation (13.3), w_i are the relative weights of the various inputs $-1 < w_i < 1$, and V_i are the inputs from either the outside world or other nodes of the neural net. The weighted sum is substituted for t in equation (13.3). The output of a node can be used as input to other nodes, either to go into a weighted sum or to serve as a parameter, i.e., a weight or a

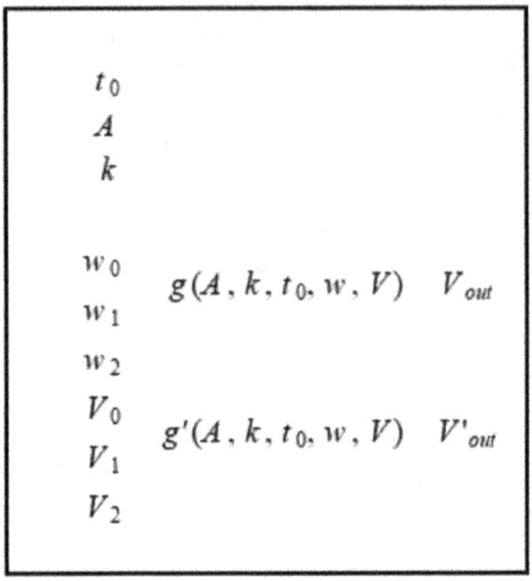

Figure 13.3. A single artificial neuron. A neural network may be assembled from large numbers of such neurons interconnected.

constant A, k, or t_0. A single neural network computational block may be drawn as in Figure 13.3.

While most of the papers I've seen about neural networks don't talk about the integral of input functions, there's no reason integrals couldn't be computed in an artificial neuron. Integrating equation (13.2),

$$\int_{-\infty}^{T} g(t)dt = \frac{A}{2}\int_{-\infty}^{T} \frac{\sinh(k(t+t_0))dt}{\cosh(k(t+t_0))} + \int_{-\infty}^{T} dt = \frac{A}{2k}\left(\int_{-\infty}^{\cosh(k(T-t_0))} \frac{du}{u} + t\Big|_{-\infty}^{T}\right)$$

$$= \frac{A}{2k}(\ln(u)+t)\Big|_{-\infty}^{T} = \frac{A}{2k}\left(\ln\left(\cosh\left(k(T-t_0)\right)\right)+T\right)$$

$$\int_{0}^{T} g(t)dt = \frac{A}{2k}\left(\ln\left(\frac{\cosh(k(T-t_0))}{\cosh(-kt_0)}\right)+T\right) \tag{13.5}$$

The divergence in the final expression at $t = -\infty$ disappears because the negative infinity from the second term is compensated by a positive infinity from the first term.

We now have a building block for a wide variety of computations. We just have to wire enough of these artificial neurons together, put data into the inputs of an input layer, choose the factors A, k, and t_0 for each set of inputs, and then judge how well the outputs give us an answer that seems sensible. Our first guess is likely to be wildly erroneous. So we change the parameters and try again. We keep changing parameter values and connections until the output we get and the output we want (for known examples) matches. This is analogous to how actual neurons appear to learn — positive reinforcement locks in connections between synapses, while negative reinforcement breaks connections, and the more useful a pattern of firing or responding is, the stronger the neural linkage.

Figure 13.4 is a situation with only six neurons. First we simply put them adjacent to each other, with no connecting wiring.

A weakness of Figure 13.4 is that there are only four outputs from each layer while there are nine inputs for each neuron in each layer. We can arbitrarily set any input for which we don't have a feed-forward path from an earlier layer (we can call the connection to the outside world at the left: Layer 0, the Input Layer: Layer 1, the Hidden Layer: Layer 2, and the Output Layer: Layer 3). Each neuron can be either analog, using actual potentials, or digital, using numbers instead of potentials. Living nerves are typically viewed as analog, and models are typically configured to be digital, but if the number of neurotransmitting molecules is small or the number of dendrites and synapses is small, living cells can be thought of as digital. Further, operational amplifiers and assorted electrical components such as capacitors, resistors, inductors, and diodes can be used to make an analog circuit mimicking a neuron.

The earliest neural networks had hardwired links between layers. This meant that the main "learning" that happened was accomplished by varying the weights in summing the output of one layer into the inputs of the next. In these cases, $A = 1$, k is ½, and t_0 is 1, so that a zero input gives close to a 0 output, and a high input gives something close to 1 as an output. Lowering k gives a lower, more analog-like (smooth variation) response, while increasing it gives a more digital-like (stepwise) response.

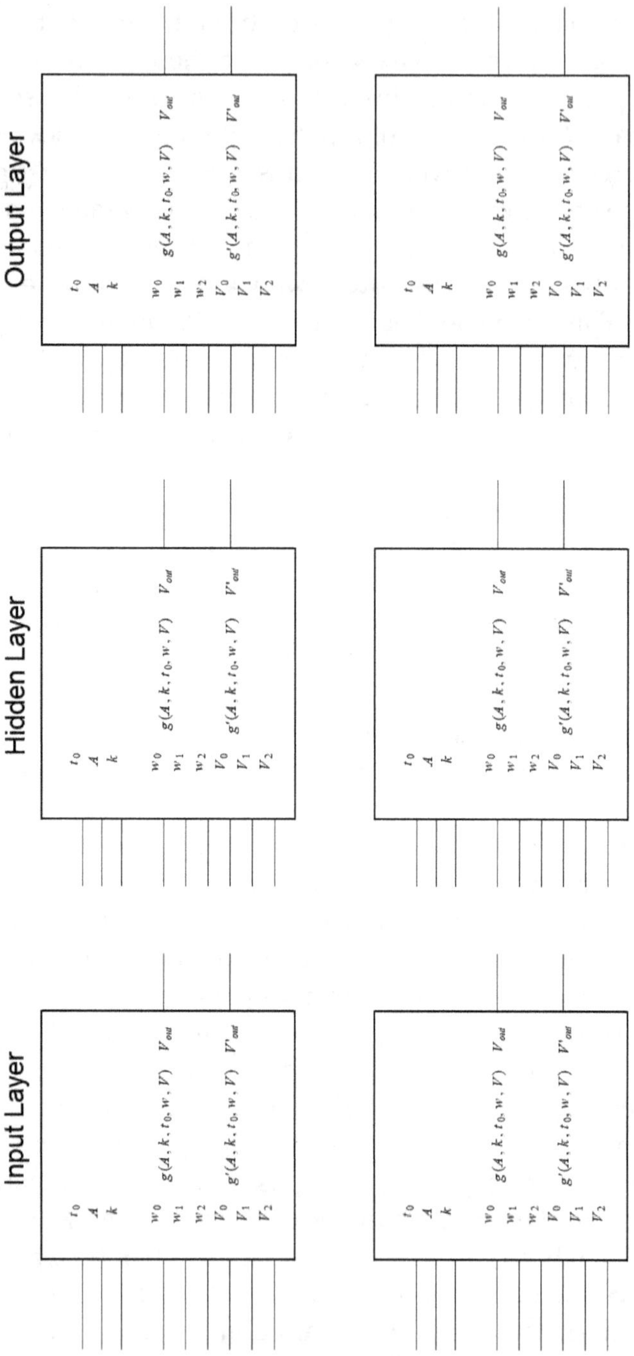

Figure 13.4. A set of six neurons, arranged in layers, but not yet connected.

However, just as real neurons connect differently as they learn, so artificial neural networks can be reprogrammed for changed connectivity. Learning can be viewed as a sort of evolution, an insight explored by Gerald Edelman in his book *Neural Darwinism* (Edelman, 1987). Neurons can be added (or removed), as can connections between successive neuron layers, and then response optimized for a given connectivity. Because we don't know initially what connectivity or coupling strengths we desire, the secret to making neural networks work is to make many, many guesses, look at which guesses give the best response, i.e., are most predictive of an expected result, and then keep the best while scrapping most of the rest.

We then augment the kept networks by adding connections not previously tried and varying coupling strengths over a range of values, and again keeping most of the best results and getting rid of most of the worst. Why not get rid of all of the worst results? Because sometimes the absolutely best answer occurs for connectivities not anywhere near those for almost-good results. Suppose you're trying to get a neural network to figure out the optimum path to take to deliver packages in a city with lots of one-way streets and cul-de-sacs. One early optimum might be starting at the northwest corner and snaking through town to the southeast corner. Another might start at town center and circle outward. But the road grid might actually have an optimum for starting in the northwest corner, heading straight east, dropping packages on the right side of the boulevard, following by a westward track, again alternating, until most of the town was covered, followed by two random drop points that aren't otherwise on efficient routes. Hitting this somewhat odd optimum requires that a suboptimal approximate solution be available for final optimization. We look at this example in more detail in the next chapter.

A completely arbitrary connection of the artificial neurons in Figure 13.4 is shown in Figure 13.5.

Three inputs are combined, using weighted, default values for the parameters, and one of the output neurons isn't even wired into the network. Input J goes into both Input Layer neurons, while

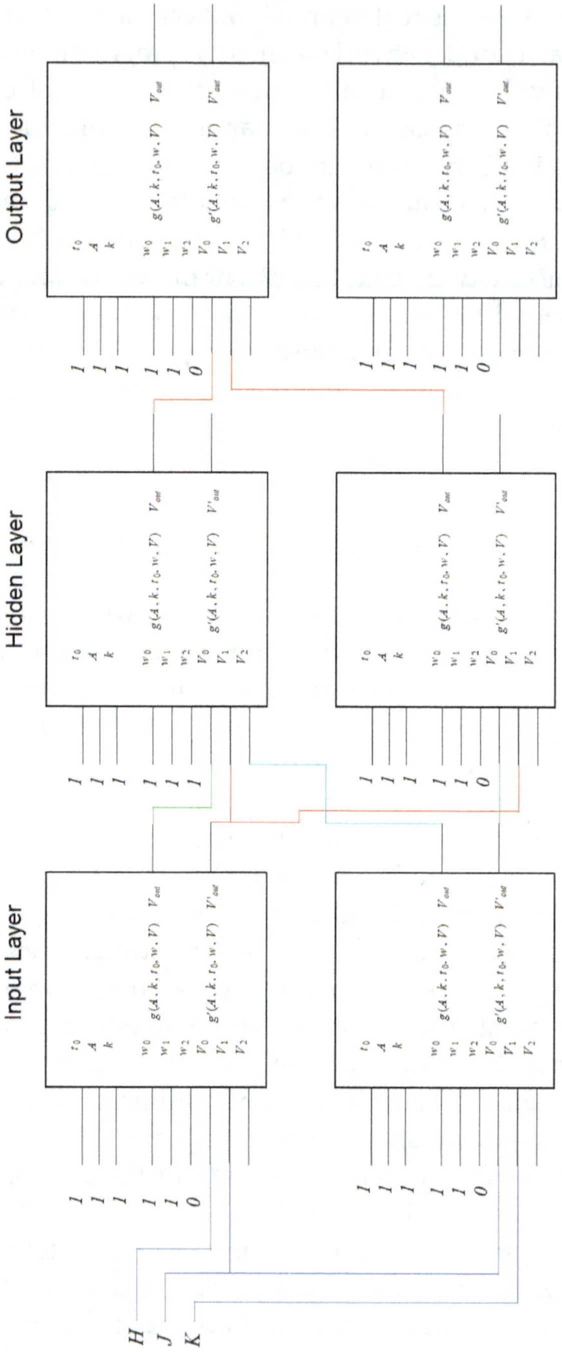

Figure 13.5. Some connections for the neural components in Figure 13.4.

inputs H and K only go into one of each of the neurons. Weight w_2 for each neuron except the lower one in the hidden layer is set to 0 since there's no connection for V_2 wired there, and we don't want random signals at V_2 to add noise to the output. The input is live for the lower, hidden layer neuron input V_2.

> Random advice: unless an input to an integrated circuit is specifically designed to be disconnected, figure out what it should be connected to and connect it. Otherwise, the open pin is an antenna, and you'll receive noise through it.

Why would anyone want to wire a neural network the way it's wired in Figure 13.5? I have not the foggiest notion. But let's devise a network that will serve a useful purpose. Suppose there is a fluorimeter, used to measure the amount of some antibody. You want to decide if a person has been exposed to a virus, and if the amount of antibody is high enough, they probably have. We might use an immunoassay to detect the antibody. So let's describe fluorescent immunoassay, show a neural network that would do what we want, and then show how the network could be trained to perform the desired diagnostic starting without "knowing" the immunoassay's behavior.

In immunoassay, the analyst looks for the presence of an antibody (to show that an organism has responded to some insult) or the absence of that antibody (to show that the organism hasn't been infected). The amount of antibody, a particular variety of protein, is typically tiny, and the amount of other proteins, especially albumin, is typically huge. That means we need to find a needle in a haystack. How do we do that? We can synthesize or grow the antigen (to which the antibody will stick), and we can make an artificial antibody (a monoclonal antibody) that is modified to include a fluorophore, a compound that will emit light if excited by light of another, shorter wavelength than the fluorophore's fluorescence wavelength (there are other approaches as well, but we are trying to describe an example for use with neural networks, not write a treatise on immunoassay). Here are the reactions involved:

$$\mathrm{Ag} + \mathrm{Ab} \underset{k_{r1}}{\overset{k_{f1}}{\rightleftharpoons}} \mathrm{AgAb}$$
$$\mathrm{Ag}+\mathrm{Ab}^* \underset{k_{r2}}{\overset{k_{f2}}{\rightleftharpoons}} \mathrm{AgAb}^* \tag{13.6}$$
$$\mathrm{Ag} + \mathrm{X} \underset{k_{r3}}{\overset{k_{f3}}{\rightleftharpoons}} \mathrm{AgX}$$

The k's are rate constants for forward and reverse reactions. "Ag" is the antigen. (Some readers may look at the symbols and think, "Hey, I thought Ag was the chemical symbol for silver!" It is, just not in this case!) "Ab" is the antibody we're looking for. "Ab*" is the fluorophore-labeled antibody. X is any other substance that can stick to the antigen; it's the "haystack". If the large amount of protein in blood serum sticks to the antigen, we will be blind to the antibody we're looking for. The experimenter supplies Ag and Ab*; the analyte Ab comes from a blood serum sample (i.e., blood with all the cells spun down in a centrifuge to remove them from the sample). We let everything develop to equilibrium.

Since we start out with a known amount of antigen (perhaps a virus bound to a membrane, perhaps a bacterial protein bound to a membrane or a glass slide), $[\mathrm{Ag}_0]$,

$$[\mathrm{Ag}_0] = [\mathrm{Ag}] + [\mathrm{AgAb}] + [\mathrm{AgAb}^*] + [\mathrm{AgX}] \tag{13.7}$$

Since we're at equilibrium and equilibrium constants can be obtained from the rate constants in equation (13.6),

$$\frac{k_{f1}}{k_{r1}} = \frac{[\mathrm{AgAb}]}{[\mathrm{Ag}][\mathrm{Ab}]} \qquad \frac{k_{f2}}{k_{r2}} = \frac{[\mathrm{AgAb}^*]}{[\mathrm{Ag}][\mathrm{Ab}^*]} \qquad \frac{k_{f3}}{k_{r3}} = \frac{[\mathrm{AgX}]}{[\mathrm{Ag}][\mathrm{X}]}$$
$$[\mathrm{Ag}_0] = [\mathrm{Ag}] + [\mathrm{AgAb}] + [\mathrm{AgAb}^*] + [\mathrm{AgX}] \tag{13.8}$$
$$= [\mathrm{Ag}]\left(1 + \frac{k_{f1}}{k_{r1}}[\mathrm{Ab}] + \frac{k_{f2}}{k_{r2}}[\mathrm{Ab}^*] + \frac{k_{f3}}{k_{r3}}[\mathrm{X}]\right)$$

How much fluorescence do we now see? It's proportional to [AgAb*]. If we ignore fluorescence in the absence of AgAb* (inadvisable in practice, but again we're trying to describe neural networks, not discuss immunoassay nuances), then the fluorescence intensity F is proportional to [AgAb*].

$$F = K[\text{AgAb}^*] \tag{13.9}$$

Now for the trick: if we use blood serum that lacks the antibody (i.e., blood from an uninfected individual or an animal that isn't susceptible to the infection in question or synthetic blood serum that is antibody free), then we get some maximum value for fluorescence intensity. If we have unlabeled antibody present, then we can measure the relative amount of fluorescence, F'.

$$F' = \frac{F([\text{Ab}])}{F([\text{Ab}]=0)} \tag{13.10}$$

Important real-world caveat: if X does bind antigen, and the level of X differs between samples and standards, the system response is a lot less predictable than shown here.

In the absence of analyte antibody, $[\text{Ab}] = 0$, $[\text{Ab}^*] > 0$, and $F' = 1$. What if $[\text{Ab}] > 0$? If $[\text{X}] = 0$ or k_{f3} is so small that no AgX forms, then we can plot F' as a function of the amount of analyte. We can choose several ways to do it, three of which are shown in Figure 13.6.

The blue lines show the function traced out by F' or its inverse. The red lines show what happens when 1% intensity noise is present. Noise in the optical signal makes a linear working curve useless. Inset B looks promising, especially in light of the hyperbolic tangent function in Figure 13.2. How can we map tanh onto [Ab*]/([Ab] + [Ab*])? From equation (13.2), $t_0 = 1$, the ordinate is (at least roughly) $1 - F'$, $A = 1$, and the only fitting parameter is k. Using *Excel*'s Solver, the optimum k is 0.6688, and the fitted tanh function compared to $1 - F'$ is shown in Figure 13.7 Inset A.

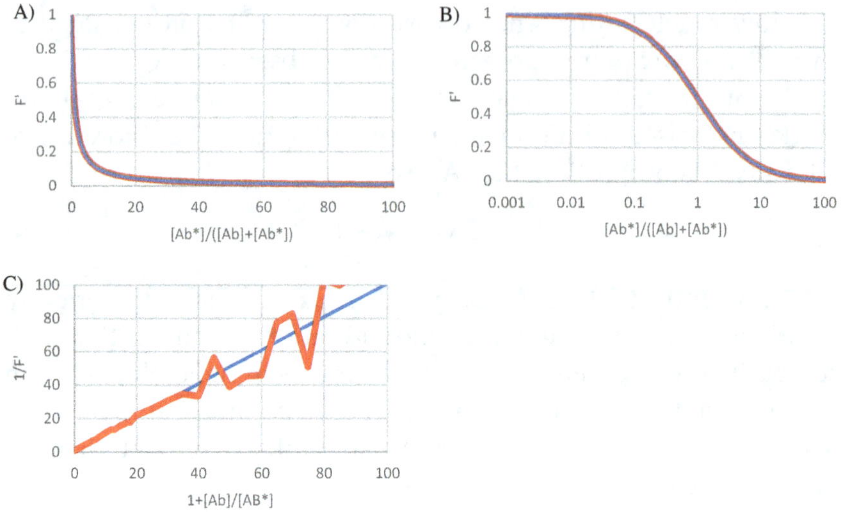

Figure 13.6. Immunoassay, unaffected by non-specific binding (Ag + X). A) F' as a function of [Ab], linear scale. B) F' as a function of [Ab], logarithmic scale. C) Linearized response ($1/F'$).

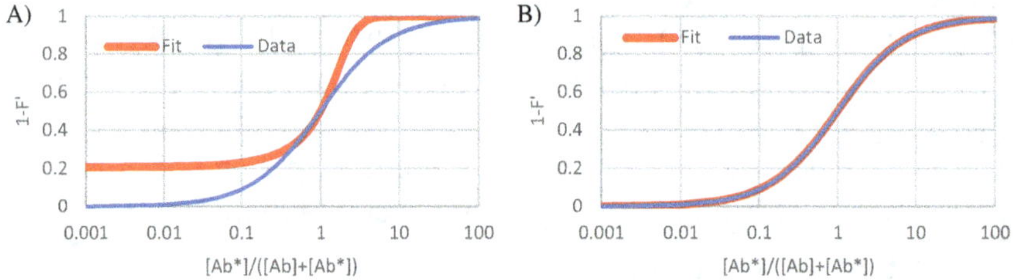

Figure 13.7. Fitting hyperbolic tangent function to immunoassay data. A) Simple fitting with tanh. B) Fitting with ln([Ab*]/([Ab] + [Ab*])).

The fit is terrible! The cause of the misfitting is clear — at low values of sensed antibody, $1 - F'$ goes to 0 but tanh as written in equation (13.2) does not. But let's get creative. Instead of having the argument in equation (13.2), use $(t - t_0)$, let's substitute $\ln t$, with $t = [Ab^*]/([Ab] + [Ab^*])$. Now when we fit, we get Figure 13.7 Inset B, the fitted k is 0.5 to nearly four significant figures, and we have what we need to wire up the neural network.

Now let's program the neural net. The input is light intensity, the output we want is [Ab]. To keep the number of neurons small and the connectivity easily visible, I'm going to cheat yet again. We'll run the control experiment (all Ab*, no Ab) manually and set the output of one neuron to a value corresponding to [Ab*]. In a real experiment, the neural network would have to discover how to do this on its own.

We then need to bring in an experimental fluorescence signal. The intermediate values we need are:

[Ab] + [Ab*]
[Ab*]/([Ab] + [Ab*])
ln([Ab*]/([Ab] + [Ab*]))
tanh(ln([Ab*]/([Ab] + [Ab*])))
1 – F' = 1 – observed value/reference value

> It happens that tanh(ln(x)) = $(x^2 - 1)/(x^2 + 1)$. Interesting.

Whatever value of [Ab] makes the last two intermediates equal is the measured [Ab].

First, how do we do addition? From Figure 13.2, if t is between –0.5 and +0.5, the tanh function is close to linear. If we take two inputs, scale them with equal, small weights and use a small value of k so that the linear region runs over a large range of x, we can do addition with a single artificial neuron. By using a small, negative weight for one input, we can do subtraction.

Multiplication and division make use of exponentials and logarithms.

$$x \times y = e^{\ln x + \ln y}$$
$$x / y = e^{\ln x - \ln y} \tag{13.11}$$

Since we already know how to add, we only need to figure out how to do exponentials and logs. Exponentials are easy — for $t \ll t_0$, tanh rises exponentially. We just need a high t_0, an appropriate A, and a small k. How do we find a logarithm? It's hard to think of an algorithm, and we can't run the artificial neuron backwards. But what we can do is to take the output of a neuron, compute its exponential, feed that input to a second artificial neuron, take the output of the second artificial neuron, and compare it to the input to the first neuron. If they're both the same, then the output of the first neuron must be the logarithm of the input. That is:

$$V_{out,1} = V_{in,2} = y = \ln V_{out,2}$$
$$V_{out,2} = V_{in,1} = e^{y} \tag{13.12}$$

Whatever values of A, w, t_0, and k make equation (3.12) consistent is what we desire. So we feed an unknown potential to one of the V_2 inputs, feed back the V_2 output to a logarithm circuit, take the output of the log circuit, and then set the controls on neuron 1 so that the output of 1 and input to 2 match. Let's draw it (Figure 13.8).

The top row, output layer, computes the difference between $V_{in,2}$ and $V_{out,1}$ (with a large A, $t_0 = 0$, and a small k to keep operations linear). The only way that the output of the top row, output layer, can be 0 is if $V_{out,2} = \ln(V_{in,2})$. There are many A, t, k, and w values not shown. They can be computed by feeding various of these potentials to the neurons in the second row (and perhaps additional neurons if need be). That's the key to neural networks — what they lack in efficiency or functionality is compensated by having a lot of them and juggling the parameter values until everything works. We've shown a set of analog artificial neurons. The digital equivalent can also be created. Look up "neuromorphic systems" and Carver Mead for the details.

If you remember Calculus I, you might say, "isn't calculating a logarithm easy? Just use a Taylor series!" General formulas can be found at http://www.math.com/tables/expansion/log.htm. The Taylor series for natural logarithm, expanded about $x = 1$, which is useful for $0 < x \leq 2$, is

$$\ln(x) = \sum_{n=1}^{\infty} \frac{(-1)^{n-1}(x-1)^n}{n} \tag{13.13}$$

For x close to 1 so that $(x - 1)^n$ falls off rapidly, we only need a few terms, but for x close to 0 or 2, convergence is slow and we need a lot of terms. Nevertheless, if we write the series in nested form:

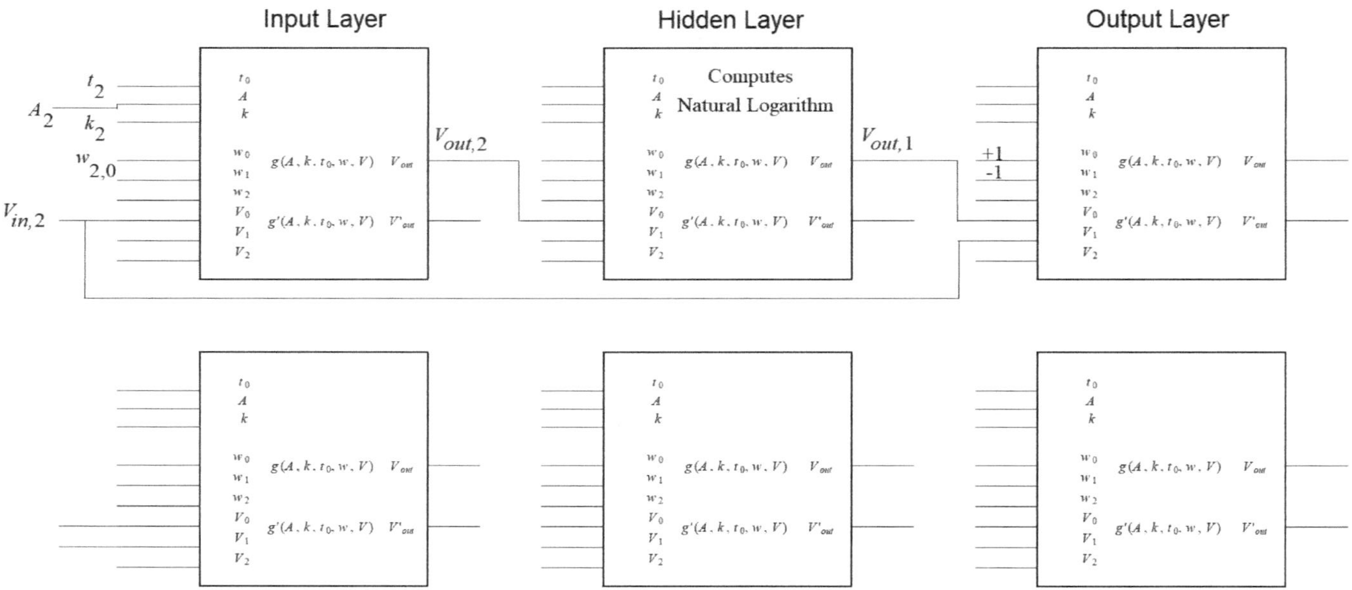

Figure 13.8. A small neural network to compute $\ln(V_{in})$. Only partial wiring is shown.

$$\begin{aligned}\ln(x) &\sim x-1-\frac{(x-1)^2}{2}+\frac{(x-1)^3}{3}-\frac{(x-1)^4}{4}+\cdots \\ &=(x-1)\left(1-\frac{x-1}{2}\left(1-2\frac{x-1}{3}\left(1-3\frac{x-1}{4}(1-\cdots)\right)\right)\right)\end{aligned} \tag{13.14}$$

We can recast the ln calculation as a large number of multiply-and-add operations, with each nested parenthesis requiring one extra neuron. Just as in biology, we can throw extra neurons at the problem without having to innovate structure.

Now we have all the tools we need to make a neural net to analyze immunoassay data (Figure 13.9). If we need some operation other than a single neuron doing a single tanh operation, we'll draw a block that contains multiple neurons doing whatever operation we need. If multiple neurons are needed, we'll label a single neuron as doing the operation, since a number of embedded neurons can in fact carry out the function, and all neurons or networks of neurons have the same input and output ports. There are

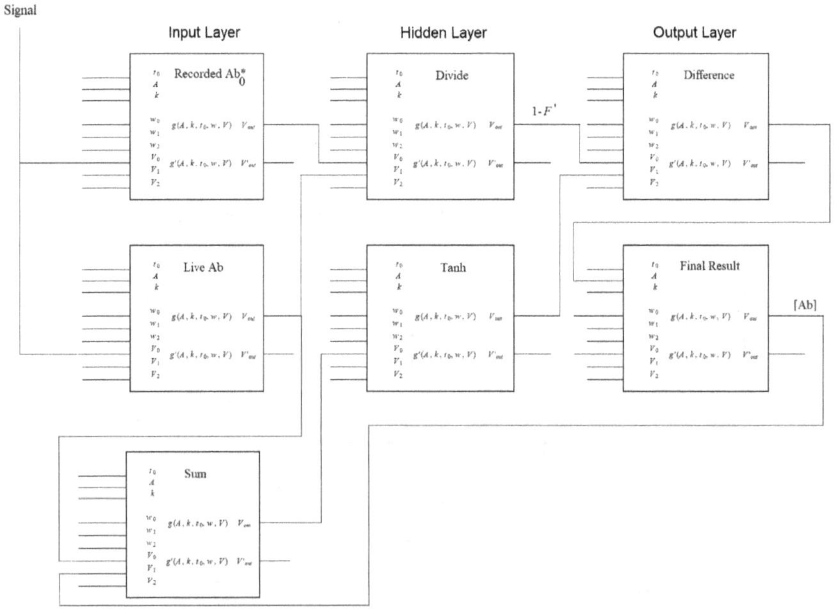

Figure 13.9. Neural net to calculate antibody concentration from immunoassay.

many ways for neurons to generate a useful result, just as there are many ways for brain-equipped species to accomplish useful tasks. "Whatever works, do it!"

12.2 Skeptical View of Neural Networks

We have a network that will do the desired computation, but there's a lot missing. What are the gains and weights? Do we have all the connections we need? This is where the assets and liabilities of neural networks emerge. We neither know the answers to the questions just posed, nor do we need to have a theory for how to get the answers. We just throw random values into the system and see what behavior results. For, say, 2^{16} examples, we might find that 2^6 of them are better than the other $2^{16} - 2^6$. So we keep those 2^6 and modify those each in 2^{10} additional ways (different values for A, w_k, etc., and maybe even breaking some connections and adding others). We keep this up until the outputs agree with our preconceived notions of what the outputs should look like within some error margin. This is one of the strategies known as "artificial intelligence"; do a random walk among parameters until something works, then see if new data, running through the optimized network, give expected values. If humans judge the quality of the output, it's "supervised learning"; if the machine trains itself, it's "unsupervised learning." There are whole journals devoted to strategies to avoid over-constraining or under-constraining the search for the best connectivity, parameter setting, and weighting. In some respects, "artificial intelligence" is rapid-fire artificial stupidity, with poor fits thrown out so that the best fits can be improved upon. Yet, isn't that what biological neural networks do? Individuals start out flailing, discover what actions are rewarding, and gradually discontinue unproductive activities. Failure to discontinue unproductive effort is often described as pathological (addiction, self-flagellation, repetitively failed relationships), although many other descriptions might be used (sub-optimal resource allocation, trapped in a potential well, confined to an attractor, failure to launch).

Perhaps Figure 13.9 is incomplete. We could add one more neuron and use the output [Ab] to feed V_0 of this extra neuron. We could then set the other parameters so that if [Ab] exceeded some threshold, V'_{out} would fire for the extra neuron. This arrangement would then give an output pulse any time the unknown antibody level was high enough to indicate that the specimen being observed had been infected sufficiently to generate a high level of antibody. Once there's a digital pulse indicating that an event happened, it is easy to count how many such events occurred, to convey to a user that the event occurred, and so on. All the calculations are hidden. All the details of learning and programming the network are hidden. The pulse says, "this patient is (or has been) sick!" The neural network acts as if it is doing a diagnosis. It is actually carrying out an algorithm which humans use to perform a diagnosis without a human intervening between sample collection and obtaining a result. The validity of the result is only as good as the network algorithm.

Would I actually use a neural network to compute results from immunoassay? If the system were well behaved, no. But if it weren't? Possibly yes. What a neural network allows is arbitrary weighting of input data where the human doesn't have a good idea of what is going on. The network can be trained (as explained shortly), and may spot patterns in the data that humans miss. The parameters and connections are juggled until the output, under a range of conditions, gives acceptable answers. It's just like mastery learning in the classroom — students keep working at a task until they are acceptably proficient. What's acceptably proficient? Answers within 10% on 95% of the samples? Answers within 20% for 99% of the samples? That's up to the humans to decide.

Where neural networks come into their own is in pattern recognition. Suppose you have a camera. Is the camera looking at the letter A? There are many ways to determine if an image contains an A, but one is to look at the light and dark pixels and when the right pixels are dark, that's an A. An A or an A won't have exactly the same pixels darkened, but it's close. Meanwhile, a or a or a look quite different, so recognizing uppercase A is different from recognizing lowercase (though, in character recognition, we might have one circuit to recognize each, and then add an "or" function to combine recognition in cases where capitalization doesn't matter).

Wouldn't it be nice if there were better ways to optimize the functioning of neural nets than just randomly making connections and setting parameters? One way is to follow the procedure we used in partially wiring the immunoassay example — by having a physical model, some of the connections can be hardwired or preset, avoiding the need to optimize. But how can we develop models for complicated situations? Whether we call the process chemometrics or applied statistics, it comes down to identifying parts of the problem that look familiar, using well-understood tools to solve those parts of the problem, and then turning the random parameter/connection algorithm loose on what's left. Common ways to find useful parameters include principal component analysis (and the related parameter setting algorithm, principal component regression) (Jolliffe, 2002) and linear or nonlinear regression. John Koza and co-workers have even devised programs to write programs that generate logic trees, modify connections, and set parameters in the same way that genetic mutations are described: replication, mutation, suppression, and amplification (Koza *et al.*, 2005). His work is a descendent of the work of John Holland and others on the "genetic algorithm".

If we can write explicit models, neural networks are frequently inefficient approaches to problem solution. But where we don't have simple models, they may be the only way to build machine-directed control or learning.

Just as we don't fully understand how neuronal networks and brains generate thoughts and consciousness, artificial neural networks often provide useful output just because they work, not because we can explain what they're doing. This causes angst to many people (of whom I am one), and with good reason. What if having a neural net give the right output is a fluke, dependent on having looked at quite specific instances of data, such that any minor change to the data would provide a wildly different answer? After all, if we have three non-coincident data points, we can always draw a circle going through those points. However, that doesn't prove that a circle describes the process giving rise to the points! Using all the data to build a model is overfitting a system. Thus, training of neural networks has something in common with all good science: never use all the data to reach a model of what is happening. Use much of the data to define a model, then use the additional data to check if the model is consistent with data not used for devising that model. Just because a model works for one data set does not prove it will work for any other set. Skepticism and a willingness to adapt when predictions are poor is a mark of good science, regardless of how patterns are spotted.

Everyone reading this book has within them a biological neural (or neuronal) network. The connectivity and strength of nerve synapses were the biological inspiration for artificial neurons. Is there any more to thinking than just lots of neural structure firing in a network? Roger Penrose would attribute consciousness to quantum phenomena. Edelman would say structure plus evolution of connections are all that is needed to explain thinking. Various religions and philosophies would take issue with these two views. I was greatly impressed by Edelman's approach, but I have no independent insight to contribute. What do you think?

14

Qualitative, Quantitative, Triage

We started this book considering measurement. After describing various aspects of measurement, we proceeded to use those measurements to build models and an understanding of the world. Once we have useful models, how do we apply them? One way is to use the information qualitatively, quantitatively, or for triage. Let's define these terms:

Qualitative: listing or naming what objects or components are part of a greater whole.

Quantitative: With foreknowledge of the constituents of an object, assigning numbers to how much of each constituent (or, at least, those constituents of interest, or of which we aware) is present.

Triage: Deciding among approaches for obtaining knowledge of a situation. This includes the possibility that we decide not to seek further knowledge.

When analytical chemistry was developing, it was often divided between qualitative and quantitative analysis. Later, instrumental analysis was added, and instruments were used for both qualitative and quantitative analysis. Triage was usually not associated with chemistry — it was used by medical personnel to decide which patients stood a good enough chance of survival to be worth receiving further attention.

Let's give an example. You see a white powder. What is it (mostly)? Sodium chloride? Sodium cyanide? Glucose? Sucrose? Sodium bicarbonate (baking soda)? Cocaine? Assuming that all other substances that are present at low levels are contaminants, figuring out which of this list (or any of the thousands of other possibilities) is the powdery substance is a qualitative question. One way to figure out which is which is to measure the amount of sodium in the powder. If the amount is tiny, then we know the substance isn't sodium chloride, sodium cyanide, or sodium bicarbonate. Thus, by quantitatively determining the amount of sodium, we assist in qualitative measurement. Would you try to do qualitative analysis by tasting the powder? I wouldn't recommend it. Neither sodium cyanide nor cocaine should be imbibed. If someone has diabetes, the glucose and sucrose could pose a problem. But if we're sure that the substance isn't hazardous to humans (or particular humans), then taste might be a quick way to distinguish the sugars from salt or baking soda. Deciding whether the substance is safe to taste is a matter of triage.

But now let's combine the various topics we've discussed already. If we make a measurement, it has random and determinate errors. When we say that a measurement is quantitative, we typically mean that the numbers we report are sufficiently precise that we have confidence the numbers are meaningful. If we say that the amount of sodium in a white powder is roughly 40% of the weight, which of the compounds are we referring to? We can rule out anything that doesn't have sodium as a major constituent. But that leaves four choices. Four? Only sodium chloride, sodium cyanide, and sodium bicarbonate have significant amounts of sodium.

Table 14.1. Percent composition of three sodium-containing compounds. Atomic weight of sodium is 22.990 g/mol.

Compound	Formula	Formula Weight (g/mol)	Percentage of Sodium
Sodium chloride	$NaCl$	58.44	39.3
Sodium cyanide	$NaCN$	49.007	46.9
Sodium bicarbonate	$NaHCO_3$	84.007	27.4

The fourth choice here (and always!) is: or perhaps something else, not in the list, that we didn't anticipate. Let's see what percent, by weight, sodium is of each of the compounds we think are candidates (Table 14.1).

Sodium chloride comes closest to 40% sodium, but remember, all measurements have uncertainty. If the amount of sodium is 40 ± 1%, there's little doubt that the compound is indeed sodium chloride. But what if it's 40 ± 20%? Then statistically, we can't distinguish any of the compounds from each other, based solely on measured sodium content. We are using a quantitative measurement to make a qualitative decision, and only with sufficient precision and accuracy can we determine, with any statistical certainty, the compound's identity. Thus, quantitative measurements are needed for qualitative analysis, but it's even more complicated. Suppose the amount of sodium is 40 ± 5%? We can readily eliminate the possibility that the compound is sodium bicarbonate because the amount of sodium in that compound is more than 3 standard deviations away from the measured amount. But sodium cyanide? It's less than 1.2 standard deviations away from the measurement, so there is a better than 30% chance that we're looking at the cyanide compound. We have triaged bicarbonate out of the picture, but we are left with ambiguity as to whether the white powder is safe to taste, much less what it actually is.

In other words, quantitative measurement is needed for both qualitative and triage measurements, but the precision required is sometimes less stringent than for performing true quantitative analysis. Let's explore this further. Suppose we looked at a transparent glass bottle and saw a white liquid inside. What are we observing? As noted in *HMS Pinafore* by W. S. Gilbert, "Things are seldom what they seem. Skim milk masquerades as cream." Anyone on a low-fat diet knows this difference matters. I am told there's a subtle color difference between skim and whole milk; I can't see it. I even have trouble distinguishing the difference in the viscosity of cream and milk. How can the two be distinguished? "Everyone knows cream has fat, whereas skim milk has a lot less." How do we detect fat? In fact, what is fat?

Fat is composed of esters of fatty acids. A fatty acid is a chemical compound with formula $CH_3(CH_2)_nCOOH$, with n sufficiently large (typically in the teens). Some fatty acids lose some of their hydrogens to become monounsaturated acids $CH_3(CH_2)_m$ $CH{=}CH(CH_2)_kCOOH$ or polyunsaturated acids (two or more $CH{=}CH$ groups). Esters substitute some other chemical species for the terminal H. Glycerol esters are common, as are phosphate esters. An example with both ester types is:

$$\begin{array}{l} CH_3(CH_2)_{16}COOCH_2 \\ \qquad\qquad\qquad\quad | \\ CH_3(CH_2)_{16}COOCHCH_3(CH_2)_{16}COOPO_3^{2-} \\ \qquad\qquad\qquad\quad | \\ CH_3(CH_2)_{16}COOCH_2 \end{array}$$

What distinguishes these compounds? The $–CH_2COO–$ moiety. This is different from proteins that contain –CHRCON– (where R is a side chain, different for each amino acid). How can we detect the identifying functional group? There are essentially three choices: mass spectrometry, Raman spectrometry, and infrared absorption spectrometry. Mass spectrometry can often identify functional groups, but can also be misled because what it actually measures is the ratio of mass to charge of molecular fragments. Both Raman and infrared spectrometries measure molecules' vibrations. Raman requires a bright, narrow frequency range light source (typically a laser, though atomic emission from mercury was used in the early days), while infrared works with broadband light sources (or, in special circumstances, synchrotron storage rings or infrared LEDs). Infrared, in turn, is divided into near-infrared, mid-infrared, and far-infrared regions, covering 650–2200 nm, 2.2–25 μm, and 15 μm – 1 mm, respectively (yes, mid- and far-infrared overlap). Raman signals typically generate data with energies corresponding to far- and mid-infrared vibrations.

The ester functional group characteristically has an energy of about 1735–1750 cm^{-1}, corresponding to a wavelength of ~5.71–5.76 μm. The problem with using infrared absorption at this wavelength is that water also absorbs infrared light, so while there are ways to mitigate the influence of water, it is more convenient to find ways to look at aqueous systems some other way. Just as musical instruments generate not only pure tones but also overtones, so do molecular vibrations. If you hit middle C on a piano, the other C's in higher octaves also vibrate. Analogously, molecular vibrations have overtones, and while they aren't quite as in-tune as octaves on pianos, they're approximately at two times, three times, and so on the fundamental frequency of the vibration. The second overtone of the ester vibration is at ~3470–3600 cm^{-1}, corresponding to 2.85 μm. This is just past the low energy edge of the near infrared. Fortunately, infrared spectra can be complicated, since every chemical bond can participate in vibration (though not every vibration can be seen by absorption — let's not get side-tracked talking about quantum mechanical selection rules). The upshot is that within the near infrared region, there are spectral features indicative of carbonyl groups including fats. There are features that correspond to alkanes (CH_2 chains). In fact, there are so many overtones and combination features that, to the human eye, the data look rather bland, more like the rolling topography of Iowa, Nebraska and Kansas than the mountains of Colorado or Utah. Nevertheless, the near-infrared absorption (or NIR, as it's often abbreviated) is commonly used to assay foodstuffs for protein, carbohydrate, water, and fat. In order to answer the question, "is this low-fat milk?" one has to assay the amount of fat, relative to protein, carbohydrate, and water. This is an area where artificial neural networks and other statistical means for detecting patterns in poorly resolved data really shine. It's also a good example of how a qualitative question must be answered using quantitative data. And if we have several unlabeled bottles, sorting those bottles into low-fat and high-fat milk (or cream) is a matter of triage based on qualitative classification based on quantitative data.

14.1 The Danger of Uncritical Quantitation

This goes even deeper. As soon as we think we have a technique for characterizing samples, nefarious exploiters start to figure out how to leverage our methods to low-ball their costs while avoiding triggering any alerts that they are offering substandard product. An infamous example occurred in 2008, when powdered milk (baby formula) was adulterated with melamine. Let's look at what happened.

Among the nutrients found in milk is protein. Under many circumstances, no one really cares what the protein source is so long as it contains a broad enough range of amino acids. In turn, amino acids contain an amide nitrogen and, in some of the amino acids (examples: lysine, arginine, asparagine, glutamine, tryptophan, and histidine), additional nitrogens in the side chains. Because different proteins have different amino acid sequences, a proxy for the amount of protein in food is nitrogen, since the nitrogen in nucleic acids is also nutritious and many vitamins also contain nitrogen. In order to assay all the various forms of nitrogen, the approach typically employed is a Kjeldahl titration.

There are assorted variations of the Kjeldahl method, but the essence is:

1. Weigh out a known amount of sample (or take a known volume of a fluid containing the specimen).
2. In a suitable flask, add sulfuric acid and perhaps a catalyst such as copper (II) sulfate, and add some Na_2SO_4 or K_2SO_4 to increase the ionic strength and raise the boiling point of the acid. Hot sulfuric acid converts most of the carbon in organic compounds to CO_2, and it liberates the nitrogen as ammonia which, in acid, becomes ammonium ion, NH_4^+. Organic sulfur is oxidized to SO_2 which may dissolve as sulfurous acid, H_2SO_3, and phosphorous is oxidized to phosphoric acid, H_3PO_4. Biological metals such as iron, calcium, magnesium, and sodium either

dissolve as sulfates or precipitate. This hot digestion destroys the original sample, turning it into the small molecules and ions listed.

3. The acid solution is cooled and the outlet of the flask is connected to a burette that can be used to add NaOH to the sulfuric acid/sample mixture. The outlet also is connected to a condenser, the outlet of which is placed below the surface of a standard weak acid solution, commonly boric acid, H_3BO_3. Also prepared is a standard solution of a strong acid, most commonly hydrochloric acid, HCl. Why all the solutions? So we can precisely measure the amount of NH_4^+ released by the sulfuric acid, and thus how much nitrogen was in the original specimen. Before we describe the details, let's look at the acid-base chemistry involved.

Once we no longer need the digestion H_2SO_4 to be a reactant, we can neutralize it with NaOH in two steps:

$$H_2SO_4 + NaOH \rightarrow NaHSO_4 + H_2O$$
$$NaHSO_4 + NaOH \rightarrow Na_2SO_4 + H_2O$$

We don't do this quickly because the solution would get quite hot, but adding a drop at a time of NaOH solution eventually neutralizes all the sulfuric acid and the solution becomes basic due to excess NaOH. What happens to the ammonium ion? Ammonium ion is a weak acid. It can lose a hydrogen ion:

$$NH_4^+ \leftrightarrows NH_3 + H^+ \qquad pK_a = 9.25 \tag{14.1}$$

What this means is that we can adjust the relative amount of ammonium ion (which is non-volatile) and ammonia (which we know is volatile — just smell any ammonia-based window cleaner) by changing the amount of acid:

$$\frac{[NH_3][H^+]}{[NH_4^+]} = K_{a,NH_3} = 10^{-9.25} = 5.6\times10^{-10} \tag{14.2}$$

If $[H^+]$ is large (say, 0.1 molar) and the combined amount of ammonia and ammonium ion is similarly ~ 0.1 M, than the amount of ammonia, the volatile, smelly form of the species, is less than 1 nM, quite tiny. If the amount of hydrogen ion is small, say 10^{-12} M as would be the case in 0.01 M NaOH, then the amount of ammonia would be about 560 times greater than the amount of ammonium, and almost all the ammonia/ammonium would be in the volatile, gaseous form. Thus, by adjusting the acidity or pH, we can either keep the ammonium dissolved or boil out the ammonia.

While HCl is a stable molecule in a water-free system, and the gas-phase molecule HCl is strongly bound as a diatomic molecule, in water it's a strong acid and falls apart into H^+ and Cl^-. Sulfuric acid? Anhydrous sulfuric acid holds together, but when water is added it becomes H^+ and HSO_4^-. The ionization of the second proton doesn't happen quite as easily; the pK_a of HSO_4^- is about 1.92, still quite strong but observable in aqueous solution. What about boric acid? It has three acidic protons with pK_a 9.24, 12.4, and 13.3. In other words, its most acidic proton is almost exactly as easy to dissociate as the proton on ammonium.

Suppose we dissolve boric acid in water at a concentration of 0.1 M. So that we don't get too far afield, I won't go through all the calculations here; suffice to say that the pH of the solution will be roughly 5.1, i.e., the concentrations of the four species derived from boric acid will be $[H_3BO_3] = 0.1$ M, $[H_2BO_3^-] = 5.6$ μM, $[HBO_3^{2-}] = 3.5$ pM, and $[BO_3^{3-}] = 22$ zeptomolar. Almost everything is the undissociated boric acid. If we start adding base (for example, ammonia), the pH increases as we form $H_2BO_3^-$. If we were to add acid, the pH would drop. If we want to find out how much base we added to the boric acid, we could titrate the acid with HCl, and when the pH dropped to 5.1, the amount of standard acid we added would exactly match the amount of unknown base that had pulled the pH higher than 5.1.

So back to the Kjeldahl procedure.

4. Slowly add NaOH to the sulfuric acid digestion solution. As the pH rises, ammonium turns to NH_3 and distills out of the

acid solution. After we've added enough NaOH that the solution becomes basic, we even heat the sulfuric acid solution to drive all the ammonia out. The ammonia is cooled as it passes through the condenser, and then dissolves in the boric acid solution, which we have carefully prepared to have known volume and known concentration, so we know how many moles of boric acid are present.

5. Now we titrate the boric acid solution with standardized HCl. The number of moles of HCl that it takes to drive the borate solution to pH 5.1 equals the number of moles of ammonia that have been added to the borate, which in turn is the number of moles of nitrogen in the original organic sample. Since we know how many moles of nitrogen were present, we multiply by 14 grams/mole to get the number of grams of nitrogen in the sample, we know the weight of the sample, and we thus know the amount of nitrogen in the sample.

It's easy to say, "Drive the borate solution to pH 5.1," but how do we do that? We can use glass electrodes as discussed in Chapter 9. If we calibrate such electrodes, we can measure pH as we add HCl, plot pH as a function of added HCl volume, and interpolate that graph to find at what volume we hit the desired pH. By doing so, we can see if there are any unexpected pH jumps that would indicate that somehow there's something reacting other than ammonia and H_3BO_3. Alternatively, we could find an indicator, a dye that changes color, at or near pH 5.1. Looking at the list of pH indicators on Wikipedia (https://en.wikipedia.org/wiki/PH_indicator) or in David Harvey's free online analytical chemistry textbook (http://dpuadweb.depauw.edu/harvey_web/eTextProject/AC2.1Files/AnalChem2.1.pdf), possible indicators are listed in Table 14.2.

Why bother using Tashiro's indicator when Methyl Red is the compound changing color just as in the case of using only Methyl Red? Because a green/violet transition is easier to see than a red/yellow transition. Further, at close to the equivalence point, the grey color is distinctive.

Table 14.2. Acid-base indicators useful for Kjeldahl nitrogen titrimetric determination.

Indicator	Acidic transition	Basic transition	Acid color	Basic color
Methyl Red	4.4	6.2	Red	Yellow
Bromocresol Green	3.8	5.4	Yellow	Blue
Tashiro's indicator*	4.4	6.2	Violet	Green

*Grey at pH 5.2, so equivalence point has unique color. Indicator is a mixture of Methylene Blue and Methyl Red.

Until the melamine disaster, this worked well to assure people that the amount of protein was as-labeled. The chemistry was accepted worldwide, the method had been largely automated where labor costs were high, but could equally well be carried out manually where labor costs were low.

Which would you pay more for — baby formula that is low in protein or high in protein? The latter. Which is more expensive, chalk dust or milk? The latter. If you wanted to cheat the world and make fake milk, what would you do? Make the calcium portion of milk out of chalk dust (calcium carbonate) that won't dissolve, and then find a cheap source of nitrogen to fool the Kjeldahl titration. And that's exactly what these bad actors did. Melamine has the following structure:

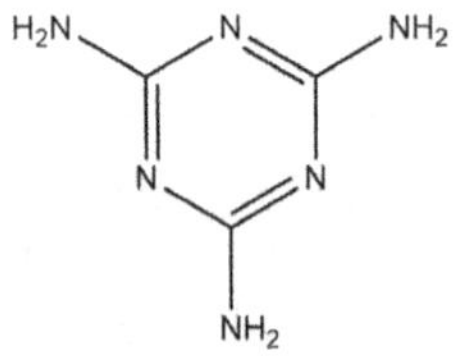

You don't have to understand chemical structure notation to see that there's a lot of nitrogen present. The atomic formula is $C_3N_6H_6$. Two-thirds of the weight of the molecule is nitrogen. As far as the Kjeldahl procedure is concerned, that's nitrogen that counts as if it were protein. But what does melamine do to humans? PubMed, the U.S. Government's publicly available trove of medical information, pops up an article, https://pubmed.ncbi.nlm.nih.gov/20195812/, by Carl G. Skinner, Jerry D. Thomas, and John D. Osterloh that specifically addresses the question. In humans, but not in some laboratory animals, melamine precipitates as kidney stones. Trust me — you do not want kidney stones ever; they are incredibly painful (alas, I speak from experience). And in infants? The kidney stones can be fatal.

So here we have a case of a widely used chemical known not to be generally toxic but that, used in the wrong circumstances, kills babies. But the standard way to measure quality of infant formula missed it! We have a triage failure. We have a qualitative analysis failure. But quantitatively, the Kjeldahl titration got the answer right! Parents asking a quantitative question, "Is there enough protein in this formula?" turned out to be assuming that a related question, "Is there enough nitrogen in this formula?" gave a useful answer. What could have been done to prevent this problem (aside from not trying to cheat the customer)?

Is there a way to identify melamine? There are many. Infrared absorption or Raman scattering spectra for vibrational transitions more likely due to melamine than other molecules may be indicative. From https://www.sciencedirect.com/science/article/abs/pii/S0963996913006054, there's an infrared transition at 7200 cm^{-1} (1.39 μm) and a Raman transition at 682 cm^{-1} that are characteristic. However, since spectra can be crowded and thus make it difficult to see small amounts of contaminants in complicated mixtures, these may not be the best way to search for melamine in formula. Calibration for quantification is tricky (for reasons that would demand yet another aside). Mass spectrometry might work, but getting good quantitative results would be challenging, and the low molecular weight of melamine means that many other molecules would give characteristic peaks at or near the mass of melamine. Again, it could work, but cost and sample preparation complexity make this approach less than ideal. I would probably use liquid chromatography. One procedure that looks reasonable is published by Agilent, one of the large analytical instrumentation companies. If curious, see https://www.agilent.com/cs/library/slidepresentation/Public/Melamine_in_Milk.pdf. While there are a lot of acronyms to wade through, the data show that melamine can be cleanly identified both qualitatively and quantitatively. But it will also be clear that the analysis takes a long time and a lot of human effort. If this technique were routinely performed, the baby formula would be safe, but likely too expensive for many consumers. Yes, when available, breast milk avoids the problem entirely, but that's not the only approach to infant feeding that people employ.

What have we learned? Sometimes, quantitative measurements fail because of qualitative changes in the system under study. Almost always, qualitative measurements depend on quantitative characterization of samples, although the precision required may be somewhat relaxed from what is needed for high-precision measurements. Deciding if a specimen is problematic can often be decided by quantitative measurements, but in other cases qualitative measurements reveal complexity that quantitation alone cannot reveal.

But now we think of Chapter 7. We cannot learn everything we might wish to know in finite time. If we characterize the system one way, we'll miss some of what we could learn if we measured it a different way. Each measurement takes time, people, insight, and often equipment. The less unexpected the circumstances, the more likely that routine, low-cost measurements will give us the desired information. But now we see one path to criminal behavior: if we understand what consumers routinely want and how quality control labs routinely determine that they're getting what they want, all the criminal has to do is devise an inexpensive way to successfully pass the usual screening procedures. The unsuspecting victim will be convinced that everything is working just fine, and will give their resources to the criminal because the criminal has figured out how to make a situation look ordinary when it isn't. What's an infant worth if a little melamine can harvest some income for the purveyor?

14.2 Decisions, Decisions, Decisions

John Boyd, a U.S. Air Force Colonel, described how decisions are made in terms of a series of actions: Observe, Orient, Decide, and Act, the OODA loop. As we see the world, we observe it until something catches our attention. We then orient to figure out what options we have in dealing with what we observed. From those options, we decide what to do, and then we act. Following the action, we go back to observing and repeat the loop. Thus, when people decided to measure the quality of infant formula, they observed that children grow best if they have enough calcium and enough protein. Because milk automatically has calcium in it, assaying for protein in formula powder became a proxy for formula quality. So each batch was acted upon in light of the decision to use the Kjeldahl method. As long as everyone played by the rules, the system worked. When melamine was used to cheat the system, there was a need for additional observation and orientation, which was missing until some number of infants were injured or dead. The problem was not in the assay, nor in the quantitative numbers the assay produced; it was in the qualitative problem with which the quantitative measurement was ill-equipped to deal. However, a latent party to the proceedings now saw an opening: the lawyers. Who's to blame for the injured and dead infants? Certainly the people who added melamine to the formula were primarily at fault. But what about those who characterized the formula? Would the lab technician who did the Kjeldahl procedure be liable? Would the supervising scientist who oversaw the technician be liable? How about the company that sold the formula but didn't think to look for legerdemain with their product?

Some of those who worry about change believe humanity should follow the "precautionary principle." That is, when something new comes along, it should not be used until it can be proven definitively that the new procedure, chemical, or invention will cause no harm. From what we have seen, "no harm" is an impossible bar to reach. Anything that causes great harm will of course be readily detected and should not be used. However, to know that something has no negative attributes requires an infinite number of measurements; the precautionary principle, taken literally, would grind all changes in society to a halt. I'm a proponent of cost/benefit analysis. When the benefit of something new outweighs the cost imposed by the innovation, go for it. The counterargument is that something that looks good in the short run may prove terrible in the long run (see, e.g., how insects became resistant to the indiscriminately used DDT, while harming other species, even though in early use and even now with careful limits to use, the substance can dramatically reduce insect infestations.). The world is not static, and to function in a complex, dynamical system requires perpetual adaptation. Internal combustion engines, invented in the late 19th century, were a tremendous advance in human mobility. The vast amount of CO_2 they put into the atmosphere is now widely recognized as harmful, necessitating a change in where humanity gets its energy from combustion to non-combustion sources. Yet, the technologies that will replace combustion were not available in 1870, nor was the understanding of atmospheric chemistry advanced enough to fully foresee the influence of human-derived CO_2. We should have the modesty to try to advance the wellbeing of our species, while being alert to changes necessitated by new information as it becomes available.

Questions like these, at the boundary between science and law, or science and commerce, or science and society in general, are critically important. Every answer has the potential to reward the wrong players for the wrong reason if sufficient context is missing, and every lawyer, politician, and debater knows that framing the question to benefit a particular party is a large part of success of any claim. This is because framing an issue sets the terms of discussion, and such terms create bandwidth issues. If I sue a lab technician, turning the law away from that technician to focus on someone else takes significant time, money, and education of a judge or jury. It takes longer to change the terms of discussion than to provide information within a predetermined framework. Operating a repetitive, quantitative method is economical, reliable, and, when appropriate, serves everyone's interest. But when someone changes the terms of engagement via illicit activity, or by legitimate activity that is inadequately communicated, costs skyrocket and benefits vanish (or, conversely, costs implode and benefits soar, depending on the uncommunicated change).

Thus, while quality control is often thought of as quantitatively verifying expected performance, triage of unusual circumstances via qualitative observation is necessary to avoid being surprised, and this consumes bandwidth. The qualitative observations, in turn, require quantitative measurement of parameters not usually measured during routine quality control. The lowest cost, most reliable performance occurs when no one is undermining the expected, yet change that allows for possible improvement or possible disaster occurs as new information is generated outside the usual system dynamics. This leads us to the work of mathematician Kurt Gödel, corollaries of his theorems, and the limits of rational knowledge.

15

Doug Hofstadter Got It Right: The Gödel Theorem

A subroutine is a part of a computer program that performs some independent operation and can be invoked at any time. The main subroutine invoked in a brick and mortar library is either "borrow a book" or "read a book," although "stare at the ceiling," "sleep at the desk," or "peruse a website" are other such operations. I highly recommend executing a particular subroutine at this moment: find a library, borrow a copy of, and read Douglas Hofstadter's classic essay, *Gödel, Escher, Bach, an Eternal Golden Braid* (Hofstadter, 1979). The current chapter, far less elegantly, but more concisely, covers the same ground. If you prefer greater rigor, websurf to https://plato.stanford.edu/entries/goedel-incompleteness/.

Statistical analysis, calculus, topology, and linear algebra are fairly recent additions to the tools humans have for describing phenomena. English expatriates had already replaced Dutch settlers on Manhattan Island before Newton or Leibniz worked out the essentials of calculus. That's only 350 years prior to the writing of this book. If there are precedents to calculus outside of Northwestern European cultures, I'm unaware of them. What we recognize as modern chemistry post-dates the ceding of hegemony in Canada to England from France, about 250 years. The displacement of the earth from the center of everything to orbiting the sun (and thence later demotion to just another dust speck in the vastness of the universe) is considerably older: while Aristarchus deduced that the sun was the center of astronomical motion, Western civilization didn't generally accept this view until the work of Copernicus in the early 1500s, after Europeans stumbled into the American continents. But that's still only half a millennium. The STEM disciplines (science, technology, engineering, and mathematics) had precedents going back to antiquity, but the disciplines as we currently understand and use them are recent. If it weren't for the printing press and the ability to accumulate, store, and transmit knowledge more economically and resiliently than was feasible with manual transcription and oral tradition, modern thinking and accomplishment would be severely limited.

Once calculus was available, physics and mathematics developed at breathtaking speed. By the turn of the 20th century, there were only a few observations that didn't fit into a neat, deterministic, mechanical view of the world. Why did atoms emit line radiation? How could we quantitatively model the behavior of turbulent fluids? How far away were the stars, and how did they generate light? Could mathematics be proven to be a true, internally consistent, universally logical mode of expression?

Here we are, 1.2 centuries later. Turbulence is still a problem. Everything else has been dealt with. The last topic, however, is enough to give some people heartburn. By the end of this chapter, I hope you'll feel intellectually queasy too. The attempt to show that a part of mathematics, number theory, can prove its own internal consistency, as proposed by David Hilbert, was spectacularly shown to be impossible by Kurt Gödel in 1931 (Raatikainen, 2018). But, arguably, Gödel's result has additional implications.

Hilbert was looking for a proof that mathematics was internally consistent, that from a limited set of axioms, all mathematical truths could be derived, and that the validity of any mathematical statement written in a grammatically correct form (i.e., using the rules laid down by the axioms) could be decided algorithmically. Hilbert did not discuss non-mathematical truth. As we shall see, whether mathematics can address truth outside some formal realm is an interesting and hugely important problem. We can turn the issue around and ask: is there any aspect of tangible reality that cannot be usefully expressed in formal mathematical terms? We'll defer discussion, but the question lurks.

15.1 Formal Systems Have Limitations

Gödel showed that Hilbert's hopes could not be realized. The incompleteness theorems are transcribed from the Stanford reference above.

> "Gödel's First Incompleteness Theorem: Any consistent formal system *F* within which a certain amount of elementary arithmetic can be carried out is incomplete; i.e., there are statements of the language of *F* which can neither be proved nor disproved in *F*.
>
> Gödel's Second Incompleteness Theorem: For any consistent system *F* within which a certain amount of elementary arithmetic can be carried out, the consistency of *F* cannot be proved in *F* itself."

Let's explain them. Please be aware that discussion of Gödel's Theorems are replete with commentators saying, "no, it isn't thus-and-thus explanation, it's this other explanation." To get the flavor of such doctrinal debate, see https://www.quora.com/What-are-your-thoughts-on-characterizing-G%C3%B6dels-incompleteness-theorem-as-meaning-that-there-are-true-statements-which-are-unprovable/answer/Alan-Bustany.

A formal system is one in which reasoning is defined by axiomatic rules. An example of such a rule from Euclidean plane geometry is: the definition of parallel lines in a plane is that the lines never intersect. We can thus prove whether two lines are parallel by determining if they intersect. It's completely unambiguous. Note, however, that the only portion of the universe under consideration must be a plane. If instead the system is the surface of a cylinder, only lines with equal inclination to the axis of the cylinder can be parallel. There can be any number of non-intersecting

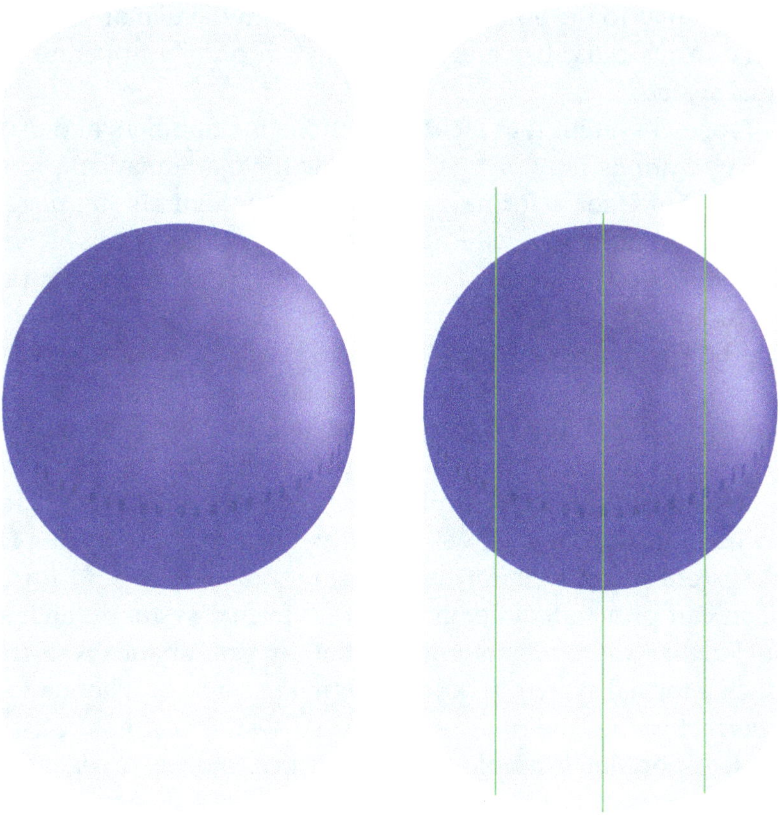

Figure 15.1. A cylinder tangent to a sphere. The green lines are parallel to the cylinder axis and tangent to the sphere. If projected onto the sphere, they will all intersect at the poles of the sphere.

ellipses or circles, but these are closed two-dimensional constructs, not lines. As shown in Figure 15.1, on a sphere, there are no parallel lines in the sense described in a plane. While a sphere tangent to a cylinder can be constructed and we can identify an infinite number of parallel lines on the cylinder that contact the sphere of identical radius at a single point each, trying to transfer those lines to the sphere results in having the lines project into circles. Two points on each circle are universal intersections at the poles (or, if the lines aren't parallel to the cylinder axis, at pseudopoles rotated with respect to the sphere's polar axis). So are line segments perpendicular to the equator parallel lines? In the planar sense, no. All the terms must be carefully defined in order to operate in a formal system.

A formal system that lacks definitions for numbers and arithmetic operations may or may not allow for mathematical proofs. Gödel's choice for a formal system is one where all language is converted to numbers. All English language symbols can be written in ASCII code, where A = 65, a = 97, 1 = 50, and so on (just Google an ASCII table for the full list). Thus, this entire book could be written as one long integer. The mathematical sentence 2 + 2 = 4, translated to ASCII, and written as 3-digit decimal numbers, is 051075051109054. A proof that 2 + 2 = 4 can also be expressed as an integer; so can a proof that the concepts expressed by the English words "two plus two" equals 2 + 2. What Gödel showed is that there is no way to prove the assumptions in a formal system using that formal system, and therefore no formal system can prove all statements in that formal system which are true. Further, there are statements that are grammatically correct in such a formal system whose truth (in the sense of whether they are correct within the rules of the formal system) cannot be ascertained. A popular example of this inability to draw a conclusion concerning truth within a formal system is the Russell Paradox (named for Bertrand Russell). Take a piece of paper. On each side of the paper, write:

The statement on the other side of this paper is true.

Now determine if the statements are true. Either both are true, or both are false. There is no ambiguity. The simplest situation is that they are both true. However, if the statement on the front of the paper is false (i.e., it asserts, incorrectly, that the statement on the back is true), then the statement on the back is also false (because it asserts that the statement on the front of the paper is true, which is wrong).

Now change the game. On both sides of a piece of paper, write:

The statement on the other side of this paper is false.

If the statement on the front correctly asserts that the statement on the back is false, then the statement on the back claiming that the statement on the front is false is in fact false. Similarly, if the statement on the front asserting that the statement on the back is false is itself false, then the statement on the back must in fact be true, which is internally consistent. So while in these first two instances the statement on the front of the paper can be either true or false, either way we get an internally consistent evaluation of the truth of the statements.

But now comes the real fun. On the front, write the statement as it was:

> The statement on the other side of this paper is true.

but on the back, state:

> The statement on the other side of this paper is false.

If the statement on the front is taken as true, then the second statement must also be true. But we already said the statement on the front is true, and we have a contradiction. So the statement on the front cannot be true. If we thus say the statement on the front is false, the statement on the back is now true, which again is a contradiction. We have thus shown that the two statements are contradictory and cannot both be true or both be false. We have shown that the two sentences, while following the rules of English grammar, are inconsistent. This is Gödel inconsistency — two perfectly reasonable sentences, juxtaposed, make the truth of the sentences indeterminate.

Here's the mind-boggling consequence: all written languages can be mapped to integers (that's the basis of the Unicode character set, now commonly used in computers). Proofs of logical consistency are carried out in formal systems, and those formal systems have blind spots and inconsistencies. Specifically: all human languages that are capable of expressing arithmetic (and that's a lot of languages. I'm not sure it's all of them, but it's certainly most of the common ones.) are Gödel inconsistent and incomplete.

Now let's connect the limitations of formal logic to the problem of bandwidth. Alan Turing picked up where Gödel left off and asked: supposed that some problem can be described in a way that there is a formal logic proof of the relationship. How long might such a proof take? In some cases, an algorithm can be specified that is compact, sequential, and takes a fixed number of steps no matter what values the parameters of the problem assume. An example is solving a quadratic equation. For an equation

$$ax^2 + bx + c = 0 \tag{15.1}$$

for a, b, and c any complex number except $a = 0$, it can be shown that

$$x = \frac{-b \pm \sqrt{b^2 - 4ac}}{2a} \qquad \left(x + \frac{b}{2a}\right)^2 = \frac{b^2}{4a^2} - \frac{c}{a} \tag{15.2}$$

while if $a = 0$ then, if $b \neq 0$,

$$x = -\frac{c}{b} \tag{15.3}$$

You probably saw the derivation from equation (15.1) to (15.2) in high school, and it likely looked daunting at the time. Is it still? Here it is (in all cases, if there's division, we assume the denominator does not equal 0):

$x^2 + \frac{b}{a}x + \frac{c}{a} = 0$ Recall that $(x + d)^2 = x^2 + 2xd + d^2$.

Thus $\left(x + \frac{b}{2a}\right)^2 = x^2 + \frac{b}{a}x + \frac{b^2}{4a^2}$

$$x^2 + \frac{b}{a}x + \frac{c}{a} = x^2 + \frac{b}{a}x + \frac{b^2}{4a^2} - \frac{b^2}{4a^2} + \frac{c}{a} = \left(x + \frac{b}{2a}\right)^2 - \frac{b^2}{4a^2} + \frac{c}{a} = 0$$

(Continued)

(*Continued*)

$$\left(x+\frac{b}{2a}\right)^2=\frac{b^2}{4a^2}-\frac{c}{a}$$ Take square root of both sides.

$$x+\frac{b}{2a}=\pm\sqrt{\frac{b^2}{4a^2}-\frac{c}{a}}=\pm\sqrt{\frac{b^2}{4a^2}-\frac{ac}{a^2}}=\pm\frac{1}{2a}\sqrt{b^2-4ac}.$$

Equation (15.2) follows.

Otherwise, if both a and b are 0, either $c = 0$ or the equation is inconsistent. There are other ways to solve such equations. An inefficient one might be: start guessing values for x. When you get close, start guessing small increments from your first guess. Keep going until you have a value for x that gives $ax^2 + bx + c$ close enough to 0 that you don't want to work at it anymore. That's a huge waste of time, but if you don't know how to solve quadratic equations in closed form, equation (15.2), it's a way that could work. There's also an iterative approach, successive approximations again, as previously described in Chapter 5, where we rearrange the original equation to

$$x=\pm\sqrt{-\frac{bx+c}{a}} \tag{15.4}$$

We make an initial guess of x, call it x_0. We then iterate:

$$\begin{aligned} x_{1+}&=\sqrt{-\frac{bx_0+c}{a}} & x_{2+}&=\sqrt{-\frac{bx_{1+}+c}{a}} \\ x_{1-}&=-\sqrt{-\frac{bx_0+c}{a}} & x_{2-}&=-\sqrt{-\frac{bx_{1-}+c}{a}} \end{aligned} \tag{15.5}$$

and so on until $x_{k\pm} - x_{k-1\pm} <$ some desired precision. This algorithm doesn't always converge, and even if it does, it may take a long time. Nevertheless, there's a way to truncate the calculation in a finite number of steps.

But what about other problems? Is there always a shortcut to an answer, or a way to solve the problem better than trying every possible answer? Let's give an example. It's the traveling salesperson problem.

15.2 Simple Problems Can Take Forever to Solve

As we first asked in Chapter 13, suppose you are to visit three locations on a rectilinear grid and you want to minimize the total distance you travel (why waste fuel or footsteps?). What are the paths you can take, starting at, and returning to, location 0? They're listed in the leftmost column of Table 15.1, and the cases are drawn in Figure 15.2.

That's it. We've fully enumerated the possibilities. 03210 is the same as 01230, but backwards. Notice that, aside from a degeneracy (equivalent paths) for Case A, only one of the visitation orders is optimal, depending only on the angles between rays 12, 23, and 31. In all cases, the distance from 0 to 1 is 1, from 1 to 2 is 2, and from 2 to 3 is 3.

If there are one-way streets, the paths are no longer reversible, and all six visitation orders are, at least in some cases, different. Is there a way to be sure that the route has been minimized without testing every one of these routes? The answer is no. While there are algorithms to achieve a short route by partitioning the problem and solving smaller subnetworks, the full optimization requires that every possibility be explored. This is known as an *np*-complete

Table 15.1 Distances for each case in Figure 15.2.

Visitation Order	Case A	Case B	Case C
01230	12	$6+\sqrt{20}\sim 10.47$	$6+\sqrt{2}\sim 7.41$
01320	12	$4+\sqrt{13}+\sqrt{5}\sim 9.84$	$5+\sqrt{5}\sim 7.24$
03120	15	$2\left(1+\sqrt{5}\right)+\sqrt{13}\sim 10.08$	$3+\sqrt{2}+\sqrt{5}\sim 6.65$
02130	= 03120		
02310	= 01320		
03210	= 01230		

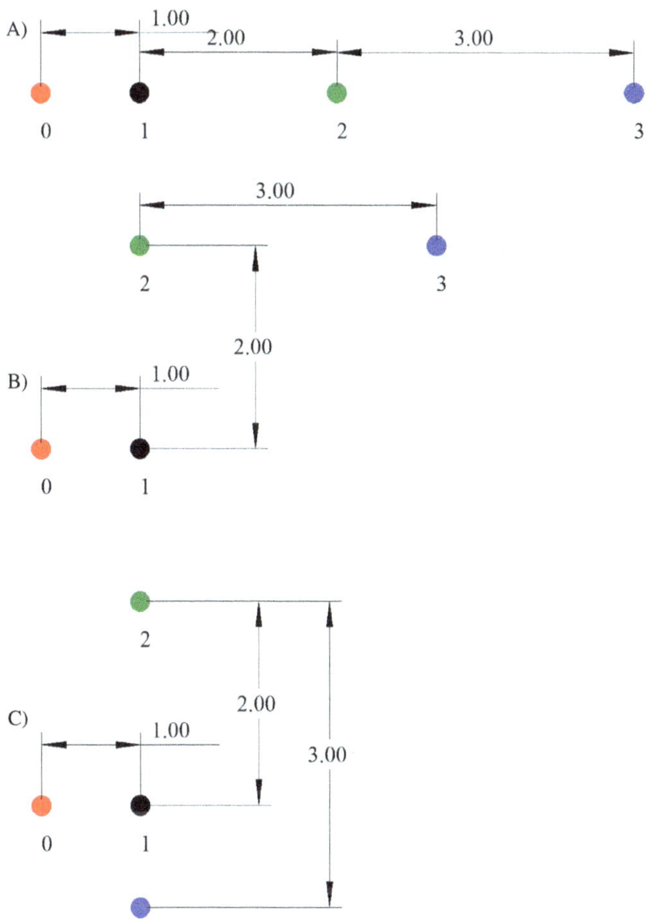

Figure 15.2. The Traveling Salesperson Problem. We choose the distance from 0 to 1 to be one unit, the distance from point 1 to point 2 to be 2 units, and the distance from point 2 to point 3 to be 3 units. Note that the order of visitation that minimizes total travel distance depends on the angle between the paths leading from one point to another. Distances are tabulated in Table 15.1 and assume all paths are bidirectional.

problem. For more than a handful of places to go, the computing time explodes as the number of stops (other than the origin, to which the traveler returns) increases as $n!$ where n is the number of stops and the factorial function ! is

$$n! = n(n-1)(n-2) \ldots 2*1 \quad (15.6)$$

For $n = 10$, $n!$ is over 3.6 million. For $n = 20$, it's over 2×10^{18}. Now imagine you're a delivery service and have 100 packages to deliver. 100! is about 10^{158}. If we figured out the efficiency of one route every microsecond, testing all the possibilities would require 10^{152} seconds or 10^{144} years. Are we there yet?

Since bandwidth deals with the rate of information transfer, we see that there are easily conceived, practical problems that cannot be exhaustively solved. We also see that there are problems that are just as easy to describe that are simply solved. When we are first introduced to mathematics, for many if not most people, all problems look difficult and time consuming to solve. Yet, we now see that some problems are excruciatingly time consuming, even if solvable in principle, while other problems aren't solvable at all, and we can get to such a conclusion rapidly. Complexity is sometimes in the eye of the beholder and sometimes is fundamental. Encrypting data is an area where we protect privacy by making calculations so time consuming that we expect no one will have the ability to get past our obfuscation unless they have the decryption key. However, when those who wish us harm sometimes figure out how a seemingly impossible problem can be rapidly solved (other than by just trying untold trillions of guesses), such insightful shortcuts can be our undoing (unless we can stand back and be awed by the ingenuity of the cypher cracker).

15.3 Getting Outside Our Potential Well

How can such seemingly intractable problems yield to rapid solution? Often, the problem yields to perspective outside the original formal system in which the problem was originally defined. Figuring out why the planets appear in the sky where they do was a difficult problem until humanity changed its perspective from feeling the earth was the center of all existence to deciding that planets orbited the sun. Kepler figured out that orbits were elliptical, Newton derived that this meant that gravity followed the inverse square law for interbody force, and then all the refinements of the next 1.5

centuries fell rapidly into place. Perturbations in the orbits of the planets led to the discovery of Neptune, precise prediction of eclipses, and identification of the problem of Mercury's precession. Changing perspective to assuming there were no fixed reference systems, but that the laws of physics should be independent of which moving reference frame an observer occupied, led to Special and General Relativity. Devising formal systems with alternative assumptions may thus allow for simple solution of formerly complicated problems. Such redefinition requires imagination, coupled to rigor.

As new concepts arise, they immediately face a problem: how can the inventor of a new idea convey that idea to others? Language has to be developed to compactly, and clearly, convey what is meant. Sometimes, the language invention is simple. There are languages, such as German, that make development of new or compound words straightforward. There are others, such as mathematics, that make symbolic communication so meaning-intensive that learning the language and culture is difficult for those not already steeped in the existing language. For English speakers, hearing "there exists a member of set *A*, *x*, that is not a member of set *B*" probably communicates more clearly than the mathematical equivalent, "$\exists(x \in A) \wedge (x \notin B)$". For a significant fraction of humanity, the latter expression might as well be Cuneiform. The English sentence has 64 characters (including spaces). The mathematical sentence has 20 characters (including spaces), and so is more efficient in communicating — but only to people who know the code. But language, in general, compresses information. Whether I write the English word "table," the German word "tisch" or the Vietnamese word "bán," most people who speak only one of these languages will be baffled by the single word in the other language but will envision a flat surfaced piece of furniture, supported on three, four, or perhaps more legs, from just one or two syllables. If you tried to convey the idea of a table to someone with whom you had no language in common, how could you do it without having a table available for demonstration purposes? Trees, sawmills, planing, sanding, joining, finishing, leveling, and some uses of the table are encapsulated in one word. We see that compressing hierarchies of concepts into simple expressions is a way to accelerate not only communication but also thinking and problem solving. We may utilize a concept that cannot be proven, either in the Euclidean plane geometry sense or in the Gödel formal system sense.

We use language to transmit culture. We use language to communicate with our fellow creatures, human and otherwise. And language is inconsistent and incomplete. We cannot use it to prove its own underlying assumptions; we can only use it within the limits that those assumptions impose.

Literate humans with adequate eyesight who have been exposed to the Roman alphabet, upon seeing the shape

W

recognize that shape as the English letter "double you", the German letter "vay", the French "doo-bluh-vay" and so on (in each case transliterated for the English reader, with apologies to others for the fracturing of their language). The sound corresponding to that shape is "wuh" in English, "ve" in German, and other sounds in other tongues. It's a matter of social convention. It did not exist in Latin. A linguist could describe its evolution, but there is no extrinsic reason for that sound and that shape to be linked with each other. The number of sides to a piece of paper is independent of the character we use to express the concept. It is not, however, independent of the shape of the piece of paper. A piece of paper may have only one side, as in a Möbius strip.

A good way to get into an argument with a scientist is to say that science is a sub-culture, or chemistry is a sub-subculture, or someone like your friendly author is a member of a tiny sub-sub-subculture of analytical chemists who use a lot of math. Some would say, "No, scientists are just people." Others would say, "Scientists are people who are part of their national culture, or their religious culture, or both, but a particular scientific subdiscipline isn't itself a culture." My take is that science is a set of cultures. Mathematicians are quite different from naturalists. I only had to sit in an organic chemistry seminar for a few minutes to discover that at least some organic chemists are quite different from analytical chemists, and not just because of the topics they find interesting. They think differently. Most scientists I know think the grade school version of the Scientific Method is hopelessly naïve. You may recall it:

- Identify a problem
- State a hypothesis
- Devise a means to test the hypothesis
- Carry out the experiment/calculation/simulation
- Compare the results to the hypothesis, thus demonstrating whether the hypothesis was correct.

Sorry, world, that's not how it works. Once a problem is well understood, the multiple hypotheses that were necessary to reach a solution to the problem can be stated. The experiments and calculations are explicable. But to have everything nice and crisp and linear from the start? Not a chance on anything that's truly new. Science is far more chaotic and nonlinear, and proceeds more like:

- See something in the lab. Say, "that's funny."
- See if the observation can be repeated.
- Go to the library (tangible or online) to see what other people know about what was just seen, hoping you are using terminology sufficiently similar to what others have used so that you don't miss relevant papers.
- Decide who has time to play with what was seen within the available budget in time, equipment, and people.
- Ask colleagues if they can make sense of it.
- Develop multiple hypotheses so that we aren't deluded that the first idea is an explanation (or the only explanation).
- Do several experiments or calculations to show that the problem is real, results are attainable, results are interesting and significant, and that further work is justified.
- Write an initial paper.
- Write a research proposal to fund the work.
- Keep doing the work, writing papers, generating and testing hypotheses, until the system is well enough understood that further work seems unlikely to be significant.

Science in practice is not a formal system. There's a lot of random walking involved. That means that the assumptions may be different in different subfields. While scientists strive for broad consistency across disciplines, and mathematics links many fields, in fact various subfields may be incomprehensible to practitioners of other fields. One of the reasons there is so little in this book on fashionable areas of artificial intelligence or quantum computing is that I had to choose between learning about these fields or writing the book. There's another bandwidth limitation — to allow some information to go out, I couldn't be focused on bringing other information in.

Is there, then, a better definition of science than the stereotypical scientific method? I think so. As a formal system, science assumes:

1. The universe, everything in the universe, and all activity in the universe, has perceptible structure. In short, within a scientific culture, the world makes sense.
2. At least some people under some circumstances can identify the orderly structure of the universe and its substructures.
3. All knowledge is tentative.

In the absence of the first assumption, there's really nothing for science to study. If we're trying to develop a coherent picture of existence and build the ability to predict, but nothing is coherent, repeatable, or predictable, what's the point? "Stuff happens" may be a way to look at the world, but it's not a scientific view. Science assumes there is structure to be found, then goes looking for it. The second assumption says humans can learn about the world in a structured way.[1] Even if we stumble into ideas or areas of interest, we eventually end up with logic explaining what we found. Science is a human activity, and we humans have proven remarkably adept at improving our structural understanding of the world

[1]There may be multiple ways to understand the world. Science, while useful, is only one of them.

in the last half millennium. The third assumption is humility. Newtonian gravity describes the universe to a degree, but the model is incomplete. Einstein's Theory of General Relativity has Newtonian gravitation as a low speed, low mass limit, but explains some aspects of space, time, and motion that Newton missed (in part because he didn't know what questions to ask). But then Gödel rears his head. Because the internal logic of language and understanding approximates or is a formal system, somewhere there will be contradictions, or problems we can't solve, or problems that cannot be expressed in a way that science can answer.

Suppose you have your doubts about science. You read the last paragraph and said, "AHA! Even the scientists know that they can't explain everything." But be careful. The flip side of Gödel is that *every* explanation humans have is expressed in words, language is a formal system with social conventions, and that means NO language and NO human system can be consistent and complete. Whatever we believe, whatever we advocate, will eventually run into inconsistencies or phenomena that cannot be explained. Science and mathematics, invoked through engineering and technology, have had profound impact on humanity and the world around us, much of it positive. That does not mean that it all has been positive. Military destructiveness, for example, has been greatly enhanced at the same time as diseases have been cured and lives extended. As Neil deGrasse Tyson has famously observed, the reason astrophysics has been so handsomely supported by the U.S. Federal Government isn't out of curiosity — it's because the tools required to do astrophysics are useful for projecting military and diplomatic power. It works the other way too; an accident involving mustard gas during the Second World War led to treatments for certain types of cancer.

A binary view of science is thus inappropriate. It is neither all powerful nor useless. I am more likely to trust it than many others because I have been steeped in science and technology all my life, and the self-critical nature of science well done assures me that honest scientists are more likely to solve problems and improve the human condition than many members of other professions. I don't "believe" in science, I trust honest scientists, but evaluate assertions in the broadest context I can find. Given that I cannot know every field, both due to the potential wells in which I reside and the limited rate at which information can be conveyed, in many instances I trust the scientific culture over others unless I see evidence of dishonest, contradictory, weakly reasoned, noisy, or biased work. My complaints about other approaches to solving humanity's problems are that they appear to be less objective, less reproducible, less disinterested, or more biased than science done well.

However, Gödel shattered the edifice, built up in the previous chapters. Science attempts to build useful, internally consistent models of the world, and thus to allow prediction of the future, interpretation of the past, and orderly existence in the present. Mathematics is the language of science, more general than the languages of any of the cultures that have contributed to its rise. Yet we now face a limitation: science is communicated with tools, both linguistic and mathematical (or, perhaps, with mathematics as one of the languages) which are provably incomplete and inconsistent. Further, the assumptions underlying a formal system cannot be proven within that system. We will explore the consequences of a scientific viewpoint in dealing with humanities problems, and with the limitations that science encounters, in the last few chapters of this book. In some cases, the principles of the first 14 chapters concisely explain complex events and conundrums. There are also cases where science can describe, but cannot solve, problems. Before we get to the specifics, let's figure out the spatiotemporal scales to consider.

16

Mental Zoom Lens

At a shallow level, this book has covered a significant amount of physics, chemistry, and mathematics, while touching on assorted other fields. Specialists in all of these fields can look at the explanations and defensibly note that while the exposition isn't exactly wrong, the coverage is shallow, the nuances are missing, with too few literature citations, and the choice of where to provide details is uneven.

Both the author and the reader have a finite attention span. The publisher has only so many resources to apply to copyediting, review, warehousing, and so on. Electronic book purveyors have only a finite number of hard disks. If we tried to cover everything at comprehensive depth, no one would have the patience to wade through it all, nor could they keep track of all that would have been written. Everyone has finite bandwidth.

We now confront a central problem that everyone faces: how do we choose between depth and breadth? How do we confront those parts of life where we know we are shallow, or communicate with those who lack the depth that we have? If we run into an expert in some field with whom we disagree, how do we know if the depth of the expert blinds them to our breadth, or know if our breadth means we can't possibly fathom what the expert's depth reveals? And is there a way we can have both breadth and depth, at least in some areas of endeavor?

A photographic zoom lens is a useful analogy in dealing with the problem. Many (though not all!) people have a three-dimensional view of existence, so using such widely available experience to discuss philosophical matters improves the likelihood that many people will be able to share insights. I, for one, have a distorted perception of tridimensionality. I was born wall-eyed, and even with surgery, I do not have simultaneous binocular vision. My two eyes do not work together; I read primarily with my left eye, while looking at distant objects with my right eye. That means that the way I see sculpture cannot possibly be the way the sculptor saw it. Autostereograms? They're just a blur.

To understand a zoom lens, we start by noting that the picture has a fixed size. In the days of film, a 35 mm camera had a ratio of width to height of 4:3 and a diagonal distance of 35 mm. In the modern, array detector world, a detector has a fixed number of pixels. My earliest digital camera had 1024 by 768 pixels (that same 4:3 ratio); my current mobile phone has 9248 by 6936 pixels. That's 9.03 times bigger in each direction, or 81 times bigger (roughly) in total pixel count.

How much more information do I get? That depends. The level of photographic detail depends not only on the number of pixels, but also on the engineering of the lens and how accurately the detector follows the lens's focal surface. Typically, blur occurs across multiple pixels. But let's suppose the image quality is independent of the focal length of the zoom lens.

Figure 16.1 is an example. Starting in the upper left, we see a large stone, some mulch, and purple leaves. Going down the first column, we add context; the rock is part of a set of plantings on the side of a hill. At the top of the second column, we see that there is a wooden wall in front of the plantings; there is thus a hint that there's a sidewalk behind the wall (where I placed my tripod when taking the first three images), but there is no information about the material of which the sidewalk is made, nor its width. In fact, without the first three pictures, there might not be a way to know that there's space

Figure 16.1. Reality filtering with a zoom lens. Magnification 6×, 2×, and 1× from each of three camera positions.

between the fence and the slope with the stone and flowers. Only in the middle photo in the second column is a body of water seen, and in the last picture, we finally see that the body of water has a dock, is adjacent to a building, and the sidewalk goes up the hill to the left. In the third column, we pull back farther (with the camera on the other side of the lake) and finally see a lovely evening at Crystal Lake Park in Urbana, Illinois, framed by trees and an azure sky. The rental boats are only clearly visible in the next-to-last frame. The stone in the center of the first image is present in every image, but does not catch the eye after the picture in the middle of the montage.

Given the ubiquity of zoom lenses and smartphones, what's the point? If we are trying to prevent erosion on the hillside, the most zoomed-in image is critically important. If we are looking for a placid evening scene, the last two pictures are most compelling. If we are deciding if we should bid on painting the Lake House (the building on the right), two of the middle images are most helpful.

But if we are managing Crystal Lake Park and its wetlands, we need information on all scales, zooming in not only on rocks and plants, but also on the condition of the Lake House, the population of amphibians in the lake, algae growth, nutrient and pollutant levels in the water that will discharge into the Salt Fork that flows into the Vermillion River and down the Wabash River to the Ohio, the Mississippi, and into the Gulf of Mexico. This is the nature of the universe and scientific understanding of it — information on many scales in space and time must all be observed, modeled, coordinated, and manipulated, while human attention can only deal with a narrow scale range at once. Details are prominent close up and invisible when zoomed out, yet the zoomed-out scene is a composite of all the zoomed-in details. Zooming out reduces visual bandwidth for detail and increases it for context, even though the number of pixels is constant. The most zoomed-out scene is a renormalized version of the sum of the details.

16.1 Zooming Between Scales

Accurate, non-misleading measurement depends on being able to repeatedly zoom with agility. My scientific training is in optical spectroscopy — the study of the interaction of light and matter. What skills go into an optical spectrometric measurement? As there are many different types of such measurements, let's get specific. Suppose I want to know how much magnesium is in the water coming out of the tap, an aspect of water hardness? I need to know about quantum mechanics, statistical mechanics, electrical plasmas, weighing, volume measurement, statistics, algebra, calculus, optics, diffraction, atomic theory, interferences in analytical measurements, flow control for gases and liquids, spray atomization, metallurgy, preparation of analytical standards, computing, analog electronics, digital electronics, interfacing analog signals to digital electronics, error propagation, vibration isolation, cleaning glassware, purchasing management, environmental regulations, regulating electrical power, professional ethics, and probably some other topics that aren't coming to mind at the moment. Within each area, I could drill down to narrower, more specific skills or parameters to control or monitor. And that's just for one element in one liquid (tap water). If any aspect of any of these items is inadequately dealt with, the quality of the answer I get will be degraded.

At this point, some of my analytical chemistry colleagues might chime in: "Why not use a magnesium-selective electrode instead? Why not do ion chromatography? Why not precipitate the magnesium as magnesium ammonium phosphate and assay the magnesium gravimetrically? Why not complex the magnesium with Xylidyl I or Xylidyl II and do spectrophotometry?" Each of these approaches requires a long list of contributing and subsidiary scientific and engineering aspects to be considered. Since one wrong bit in a computer memory could wreck any of these measurements, we find that we have to consider everything from the atomic scale to the electric power grid every time we want to measure anything. Is it any wonder that I work through arithmetic examples in detail in this book? The arithmetic matters. The units matter. The context matters. Everything matters all at once. But we can't think of all these details simultaneously; while brains have some parallel processing capability, it's not adequate to the task. So we use a mental zoom lens and dive into each of the aspects sequentially. But we don't consider anything in isolation. After we choose a particular computing algorithm, we zoom out to the big picture, look around for where that algorithm interacts with something else, then zoom in to see how a change in the algorithm influences how that other aspect of the problem should be treated. We do this over and over and over, until we have an internally consistent system that admits the possibility of precise enough and accurate enough measurement. Then we do some experiments. In many cases, we'll find we missed something. So we zoom in and out and over and around again, refining our approach.

This is the doctrine of experimental science: do everything as well as you can, given the temporal and financial constraints, and then question everything. Look for inconsistencies. Revel in glitches uncovered. When behavior appears to be consistent, report a result. Is that some great truth, applicable at all places and times? No. It's one measurement. With luck, other people will see where the approach could be improved — that's what peer review is for. The dogma is that we can learn from measurement, but what we've learned is gelatinous and is subject to change and improvement over time.

How can anyone do a full zoom on every parameter on every measurement? They can't. There's not enough bandwidth. Yet quantitative measurements of magnesium in water are made millions of times a day worldwide. This works because we parallelize optimization of each parameter. Engineers ensure that instruments are not disturbed by anticipated levels of vibration. Software is checked and debugged. Parameters for each of the steps in a measurement are optimized. But errors can still creep in. One specialist forgets to tell another specialist about some parameter. An interferent is missing from the calibration solutions that happens to show up in the sample. Measurement quality degrades.

How do we deal with such complications? After all, if we do a full research project on every sample, the fussing over the measurement will be excessive, the speed will be low, the cost exorbitant. One approach is to have generalists make measurements, while specialists design the components that go into those measurements. Another approach is for one person to learn all the technologies necessary to make a quality measurement, and have them review all the components and their interactions. Which approach is faster? Having many people working in parallel to bring all the components together. Which approach ensures that all the levels of component operation and interaction are confirmed to be appropriate? Neither. There isn't enough time in one lifetime to do everything that goes into modern technology. We are bandwidth limited. We can think faster than we can talk or type; we can think faster than we can read or hear. But breaking down a complicated activity into sub-activities that multiple people can pursue at once is far faster than training one person to do it all (though, as a graduate student, I was advised to master as many aspects of science, technology, and life as I could, to have both breadth and depth.).

Assuming that someone will take care of the fine points at each level of each component leads to fragility in large systems.

Let's take a specific situation. Modern computing relies heavily on the ability to create extremely pure, single crystal silicon, which is then sliced into wafers to be turned into integrated circuits. Who ensures the quality of the silicon? It's not the programmers. It's not the PC vendors. It may not even be the circuit fabricators. In 2020, the 10 largest manufacturers of polysilicon, worldwide, produced 589,000 metric tons, much of it used for solar cells. Polysilicon is processed in zone refining furnaces to produce single crystal silicon used to manufacture electronics. A handful of companies make such wafers, and while a significant number of workers must operate the electromechanical machinery, only a few people at each firm know all the ins and outs of parameter setting and optimization, why operational nuances are performed just so, and what happens if temperatures or feedstocks are slightly (or grossly) outside acceptable ranges. As we noted in Chapter 7, we don't know how many such experts there are, and it is unlikely that Intel, Taiwan Semiconductor, IBM, or other circuit fabricators are going to release such information. But we can surely say it is not a large fraction of the 8 billion people on the planet. We thus have a difficult problem. For civilization to continue developing with electronic support, it is essential that nuanced knowledge of how to grow ultrapure, crystalline silicon be transmitted from generation to generation, and that no firm be limited to only a single person who understands the process. On the other hand, if more than a handful of people at each firm try to be experts, there isn't enough workload to keep them employed, there aren't enough problems to solve to build up expertise, and the cost of keeping so many people on staff "just in case" is excessive. Early work on silicon refining was the subject of much academic research. But now? It is unlikely that any assistant professor would be hired if their proposed research was "maintaining a knowledge base on how to purify silicon just the way it's already being done." We depend on what used to be forefront technology, and from its near perfection we deny the next generation the opportunity to creatively fail while developing detailed understanding of how essential procedures are best performed.

16.2 Lost Information, Overwhelming Complexity

In my own field, I have significant worries about the survival of high-quality work on elemental analysis. Prior to the 18th century, while people knew of copper, lead, iron, and some other chemical elements, there was no systematic understanding of the differences between elements and compounds. By the late 19th century, elements were clearly defined and the use of atomic emission of light to identify elements was developing. Commercial atomic emission instruments appeared about 1920, and following World War II, the field prospered. In 1987, I determined that there was an average of one professor doing research in atomic emission spectroscopy in each U.S. state, there was about the same level of interest in each Canadian province, and there were stellar research programs in at least 12 other countries I can think of without checking the literature. In the U.S., at least nine companies sold instrumentation, and highly trained individuals easily found positions in industry, government, and university laboratories. Now? The youngest academic elemental analysis faculty I know are in their 40s, there are fewer than 10 active research groups other than those researching laser ablation to generate sample emission, and it is common for papers I review to be oblivious to half a century of careful, intensive work. I am contributing to a massive review article that is being spearheaded by George Chan, Gary Hieftje, and Nicolo Omenetto that is trying to preserve the accumulated knowledge. The lore, the details, the minutia that are at the deepest levels of the field, will likely be lost. It's a matter of bandwidth; we can't communicate everything because if we tried, nothing would be accomplished. But if we don't communicate at some level, a core technology without which metallurgy, environmental monitoring, industrial quality control, and maintenance of pharmaceutical purity are impossible. How tightly can we focus? How broadly should we educate? How do we ensure that people can zoom in and out to the appropriate level of detail when working on a problem?

Because the distribution of focus on the various aspects of solving a problem inherently requires multiple people to agree on an approach, social interaction, politics, and psychology become part of problem solving. In fact, the choice of problems worthy of being solved has a significant political component. Was the U.S. wise in investing in rocketry to send people to the moon in the 1960s? "Surely any nation that can send a man to the moon can … " led to any number of suggestions of ways to spend billions of dollars. But consider the nature of the moon shot: the goal was narrow, well defined, readily communicated, easily visualized, and dexterously dissected into sub-problems. The people working on defining rocket trajectories had little need to think of space medicine. The people working on space medicine didn't need to worry about engineering heat balance (though they did need to specify to the thermal engineers what range of temperatures were allowable). The people who paved the crawlway over which the rockets were moved from the Vehicle Assembly Building to the launch pad didn't need to think about lunar geology, much less design experiments to carry to the lunar surface. Compartmentalized tasks with well managed communications concerning subtasks led to the successful accomplishment of a single goal, "of landing a man on the moon and returning him safely to earth by the end of this decade." The outcome was defined digitally. Either someone went up, touched the lunar surface, and returned, or they didn't. What they did there, how they did it, and if there were any side effects weren't part of the goal. This contrasts with most other activities, where context, details, sequelae, and foregone competing opportunities intrude.

In zooming between perspective and details, there are always somewhat arbitrary limits. In Figure 16.1, I could conceivably have zoomed out to the "pale blue dot" image that Voyager 2 took of the solar system before turning its camera off in the 1980s, or use some type of microscopy to look at the crystallinity of the rock. I chose the range I did because I could take all the pictures in a single session with my cellcam. It's unlikely that anyone considers quantum electrodynamics or cosmology when solving the problem of what to have for a snack. But we do have to decide what scales to consider in choosing a scientific problem. If there are relevant scales within which information is missing, poor bandwidth at that scale may prevent optimal problem formulation. Let's examine this from several perspectives.

16.3 Endless Frontier?

In 1945, Vannevar Bush wrote an influential report, *Science: the Endless Frontier* (https://www.nsf.gov/about/history/vbush1945.htm). It advocated for the U.S. Government to support fundamental research as an underpinning to national defense, economic development, improved health care, and the general spiritual development of humanity. By the 1960s, with the space program ramping up, jet aircraft displacing reciprocating engine-powered craft,[1] organ transplants becoming feasible, and dozens of other developments, school children were given to believe that smart[2] people should go into science, with its endless opportunities, and that exploration *for its own sake* was an American value, traced back to the European explorers who "discovered the New World." It was a matter of faith that any research would improve humanity, as wise people (engineers, physicians, and enlightened politicians) would adopt the new discoveries to everyone's benefit. In 2022, such thinking is at best perceived as hopelessly naïve, and at worst as deceptive. The European explorers were not out just looking around to see what they could learn; they were in search of commerce with East Asia, preferably at the expense of competing fiefdoms. They did not discover a new world; they collided with a continent, its nearby islands, and millions of fellow humans of which and of whom they had previously been unaware.

I bought into the "scientific exploration is an unalloyed boon to humanity" viewpoint. What this meant was that my zoom lens stopped zooming out when it found an interesting problem that was apparently not yet solved. Early in graduate school, Prof. James Taylor started advising me that the significance of research

[1]In the 1960s, jets were presented as a faster way to fly. In 2021, jets, or turbofans, are valued for their reliability and efficiency.

[2]A reviewer took exception to the value judgment "smart." My recollection is that such judgment occurred.

was an important criterion in choosing a topic. He often repeated this advice, and I repeatedly missed his point. At the time, when the National Science Foundation considered whether to fund research proposals, the criteria (consistent with *Science: the Endless Frontier*) were: 1) research performance competence, 2) intrinsic merit of the research, 3) utility or relevance of the research, and 4) effect of the research on the infrastructure of science and engineering (with 1) and 2) of primary concern). To the considerable consternation of many scientists, the criteria were changed in 1997 to Intellectual Merit and Broader Impacts. Proposals evincing poor reasoning would not be funded in either case, but merging competence into merit devalued the academic genealogy of the proposer. No longer was an Ivy League degree or a Nobel prize on one's *Curriculum Vita* a *de jure* leg up in competing for funds. Relevance to societal needs and development of personnel beyond the students and professionals working on the project became of greater importance. Simple curiosity was no longer a sufficient reason to pursue a question.

By the late 20th century, as noted in Chapter 7, massive scientific productivity meant that much published work simply disappeared into the vastness of the scientific literature. In chemistry, an important index to the literature was *Chemical Abstracts*, started in 1907. It has long since gone online as *SciFinder*, but when it appeared as hard copy, anyone could judge the rate of chemical information expansion by measuring the number of linear feet of shelf space occupied by its volumes. In 2000, the halfway point on the shelf (personal observation) was about 1987. Half of all chemistry known to humanity had been published after I had received tenure. By 2011, over 250,000 citations were being added to the literature each year. As also noted at the beginning of Chapter 7, even when we can enumerate all members of a set to be encountered, actually encountering them takes time. To read all those papers would require internalizing 685 papers a day or one every two minutes (even if the dedicated reader never stopped to sleep, eat, talk, or do anything productive). For science as a whole, there are several million publications per year. Since no one person can read all those papers or, even in communication with others, absorb all that information, the fraction of total knowledge extracted from nature which any individual knows decreases every year. The fraction of what has ever been known that we can be aware of in detail also decreases.

Now we can see why just doing research based on curiosity may be entertaining but not an easily justified use of public funds. Have a question? Get a grant, find an answer, write a paper and ... the answer disappears into the ether. However, if the work is significant in solving a problem with identifiable impact, the answer may generate economic activity, health benefits, or other outcomes that more than justify the cost. To which the fans of Prof. Bush (of whom I am one) reply: if you don't generate lots of random ideas, how will you ever come up with anything truly original, something as revolutionary as transistors or electric motors or light bulbs or computers or RNA-based COVID-19 vaccines? To which, in turn, the counterargument is: study of solid state physics and development of computers was backed by Bell Laboratories to improve the reliability and cut the energy consumption of the telephone network. Electric motors came about as Faraday studied the interaction of electric and magnetic fields, an area widely of interest in the early 19th century. Many people besides Edison were looking for a practical electric light bulb; Edison just got there with a bright, practical bulb before others in the US, though after Swan in England (and designs by others later have displaced Edison's invention with more efficient fluorescent and LED sources. Edison's carbon fiber was replaced by tungsten filaments in the 1920s). Computers developed in response to military needs for rapid data processing, and then spread as opportunities for small, inexpensive machines became evident. Curiosity can be directed into useful paths.

At which point scholars in the humanities will say "curiosity is a social construct." Yes, many people in many cultures over uncounted generations have been curious, but the areas that excite curiosity in any era are in part due to the influences of surrounding culture. There were doubtless people who were curious whether people could fly in 1500, but interest in flying exploded in the 20th century when powered flight became practical. Interest in science dates at least to the time of the Greeks; interest in mathematics goes back as far as the beginnings of recordkeeping. Most of what we call modern mathematics came into existence within the last 350 years. What fields of endeavor have the deepest roots? Agriculture, engineering, biology, economics, politics, and theology. Science has accelerating development in all of these areas, with the influence on politics and theology more complicated than the other subjects. Science also influences and is influenced by literature, as any science-fiction fan can attest.

16.4 Information Renormalization

Different problems require solution on different scales. Radio transmission and reception occur in WiFi networks, AM and FM broadcasting, cellular phone networks, deep space communications, radio astronomy, Global Positioning System localization, and in some sense in any system where light moves from a source to a destination. We hardly think of our eyes as radio receivers, yet they sense well between 400 nm and 700 nm, corresponding to frequencies of 430 to 750 terahertz. Thus, each of the rods and cones on our retinas are radio antennas. When Leeuwenhoek and Galileo were developing microscopes and telescopes, they could not have known of the connection; it was Maxwell in 1865 who definitively connected light to electromagnetism. Chemists started using radio frequency absorption in the 1940s with the invention of electron and nuclear magnetic resonance spectrometry. Recasting thinking about probing atomic and molecular structure into the language of radio transmission and reception, with heterodyne detection, frequency combs, antennae, dynamic range expressed in decibels, and Fourier transformation, while consistent with ideas expressed earlier, did not become common until the 1970s. The change in perspective neither invalidates earlier work nor, necessarily, guarantees new insights. However, the spread of a common language for physicists, chemists, electrical engineers, and material scientists facilitates communication and teamwork. Similarly, familiarity of chemists with electrical engineering principles accelerated adoption of automated instrumentation. The mental zoom lens is accelerated when limited numbers of bytes (phonemes, gestures, patterns) synchronize the work of various people with deep knowledge in narrow areas.

Science has always sought to elucidate general explanations for specific phenomena; using common language helps connect the specific to the general and the particular to the big picture. What is blurry or noisy or unclear at one scale may be precise at another scale; as we saw in Chapter 12, going through a phase transition can give behavior consistent with a smaller scale but not explicitly predicted at that scale. Visible light can reveal details of objects down to roughly half-micrometer size. Radio waves can only reveal details down to centimeters or millimeters. X-rays, on the other hand, can elucidate structure at the single atom scale. We thus zoom not just conceptually, but also physically, choosing tools appropriate to the level of the problem. While this book was being written, science was at work on the COVID-19 pandemic. This required knowledge of structures as small as half-a-dozen atoms, and of structures as large as the entire human population, from tenths of a nanometer to thousands of kilometers. Times from picoseconds (the duration of chemical bond formation) to decades (the duration over which a novel pathogen may influence life) were relevant. And, of course, human activity both scientific and otherwise overlaid all that was occurring. Science is systematic, but is part of a complex system, such that some blurriness is inevitable on some scales even when there is clarity at other scales. Yet, those less familiar with the challenges of scale in science sometimes condemn one aspect of science when limitations occur on other scales in time, space, or energy, or when terminology that helped move knowledge forward in one decade has different meanings in another.

Uncharacteristically, our discussion of zooming has omitted equations. Let's remedy that oversight. We need a reference scale. For length, let that reference be L_0 (perhaps 1 meter, perhaps a furlong. As long as a unit is used consistently, the exact value won't matter.); for time let it be T_0 (1 second? 1 year?). The argument has been that the amount of information perceivable at scale L or T is largely independent of L or T. Information I then scales as:

$$I_{a,b}(L,T) = \frac{1}{\sqrt{ab}} I\left(\frac{L_0}{a}, \frac{T_0}{b}\right) \tag{16.1}$$

where $a = L_0/L$ and $b = T_0/T$. Information becomes infinite as a, $b \to 0$, i.e., as space or time become infinite. Similarly, as a or b become infinite, the information goes to 0. This formulation is known as a wavelet transform, Such scaling is used in the JPEG photo-compression standard. By truncating the ranges of a and b, we limit how much information we retain, with the tradeoff between image quality and file size selected as appropriate. Which do you want — lots of little files with slightly blurry pictures, or a few huge files with crisp details? Every time you take a selfie, there's bandwidth involved, and scaling too!

17

Theology and Religion

"Not everyone thinks like you." — *Alice Berkson*

In the language of differential equations, everyone comes into the world constrained by a set of initial conditions and boundary values. The initial conditions are genetics, gestational environment, parental attention, perinatal nutrition, and any sensory information that penetrates the womb. The boundary conditions are the typical confinement of humans to living on or near the earth's surface (astronauts excepted), limited lifespan, sensory bandwidth, and ..., well, the rest is the subject of this chapter!

Learning is the incorporation of incoming data with pre-existing structure. English speakers learn far more rapidly when hearing English than when hearing Pashtun because their ears are attuned to the signal represented by the English language compared to the noise represented by Pashtun speech. Of course, to a Pashtun speaker, the opposite would be true. Each language, or even dialect, forms a potential well as discussed in Chapter 10. Language and culture are linked, and past culture feeds current language. Thus, religion and language are highly correlated variables. Recall that Newton had a minister for a stepfather and that, in addition to being a principal founder of modern Western physics and mathematics, he also wrote on theology and alchemy. The interaction between Galileo and the Catholic Church is part of the catechism for those who worry about the denial of science by theologians, politicians, and others who don't start out enamored of empirical evidence over belief (or, as we discuss in the next chapter, authoritarian control).

In Judeo-Christian religions, the fundamental assumption is the first few words of Genesis: In the beginning, God … If one is a true believer, all else is viewed through that lens. No observation, no empirical data, no assertion can be in violation of that fundamental assumption. In contrast, the first assumption of science, as noted in Chapter 15, is: the world makes sense. If something doesn't make sense in the scientific world, the rationalization always available is, "We don't know enough yet to make sense of that particular observation, but give us time; we'll figure it out." Of course, there are people who have more diverse thinking and adopt some aspects of both religion and empiricism. But each time new information flows in, they have to incorporate it into their existing assumptions, decide that it fits better with one assumption than another, or live with cognitive dissonance. We also learned in Chapter 15 that essentially all symbolic systems are incomplete or inconsistent, so such dissonance is inevitable when using language to describe the world.

Everyone starts out in some potential well whose parameters are set by the world into which they are born. It's not just family that creates that world; history beyond immediate relatives had an influence. Imagine Mr. and Mrs. Squirrel in 1844. They and their parents had run through tree limbs, across fences, and along the ground, and then suddenly, in Mr. Morse's backyard, some thin metallic wires on poles appeared. The Squirrels most likely hesitated; what might happen if they set paw on these new, unfamiliar structures? Likely their offspring, being adventurous, hopped on the telegraph lines, skittered to the next poll, turned around and screeched the rodent equivalent of "Come on over! No problem!" Thereafter, running along wires became second nature; the potential well of standard squirrel behavior had been expanded slightly.

Humans have similarly transited numerous behavior changes over recorded history. My grandmother never learned to drive; my sister and I assumed from an early age that of course we would learn to drive when we were old enough. My mother had a mental block on using the "backspace" key on a computer keyboard to delete the character before the cursor; my daughters never knew a world free of display screens. Initial conditions evolve, generation after generation. Some people readily adapt; others prefer to be slow and cautious. Still others see all change as a threat to the one, true established order. Eratosthenes demonstrated that the world was round about 2600 years ago (whether anyone else had done so earlier). Yet there are still serious members of the Flat Earth Society.

The way technical (and biological) evolution is perceived may depend on theology. At one extreme, everything that happens is ascribed to "God's will". At the other extreme, random fluctuations are reinforced by interactions with other random fluctuations, and purpose is ascribed to actions and events only in retrospect. Why did I start writing this book? If I were sufficiently theocentric, I would say I got a message from God. But my outlook is not theocentric. I had accumulated a vocabulary, a numerical approach to problem solving, and had heard, as in the epigram of this chapter, that I didn't think like many other people. So I decided to write up what you are reading in the hope that either others with a similar approach wouldn't feel quite so misunderstood or that others might find the approach useful, pick it up, and develop the theme more extensively or rigorously. My purpose was developed in the context of the various activities I've done over the last seven decades. It's a response to what happened, not a motivator.

Darwinian evolution in specific and theories of evolution in general are based on the idea that random changes happen, and what happens next depends on what wasn't obliterated by what happened earlier. Markov processes are fundamentally Darwinian, since what occurs on step $n+1$ is purely a function of what was left over at the end of step n. There's no purpose, no direction, just iteration. After sufficient iterations, it becomes feasible to see what Markov chains terminated, and perhaps why. From this, lessons for future steps might be discernable. The opposite viewpoint extreme is to say that God directed each step of the process. Any scientist should pop up at this juncture and observe "or perhaps there are other explanations; just because you are contrasting two possibilities doesn't mean there aren't third, fourth, and more possibilities you're ignoring." I concur. But we can only discuss a limited amount of information at once, so I'm sticking with a God/physics dichotomy to maintain clarity and coherence at the expense of completeness.

17.1 Purpose in Prospect and Retrospect

Humans are comfortable with the idea of purpose. If you insist that I claim some purpose, I wrote this book to show how 21st century physics, mathematics, and chemistry can be used to explain social phenomena, to help other people clarify their thinking on the role of science in society, to make a little money on the side, and maybe to get a few of my Andy Warhol expected 15 minutes of fame. It is a simple extrapolation to say that everything we encounter has a purpose or was placed here with a purpose. Yet one of the primary cautions to the use of statistics is: interpolation is safer than extrapolation.

Many phenomena or events happen either without purpose or in contradiction to purpose. If I am rear-ended by a drunk driver, that certainly wasn't something that happened on purpose from my end, and the reason driving under the influence is illegal is that connecting purpose to action is impaired for those who consume excessive alcohol. What is the correlation coefficient between human action and human purposes? It is demonstrably <1 (imperfect correlation), and seemingly >-1 (at least some occurrences don't happen in opposition to our stated purposes), yet it seems doubtful that it is zero (no correlation). What is the correlation between God's will and human action? Science has no way to provide insight, as there is no way to independently measure God's will in advance of an event. Religion sometimes claims there is correlation, but such correlation is often detected *post facto* (by interpreting biblical verses) or predicted without a hard timeline so that a random event at a random time is declared to be consistent with a vague prediction. The mathematical or statistical rigor demanded of science is outside the assumptions or propositions governing (Western) religion, and the imprecision of religious prediction is out of accord with the requirement for falsifiability (stating assertions in a way that they may be proven wrong) of science. The two approaches not only cannot prove or disprove each other's assumptions and explanations, they use language in ways that make such comparisons impossible.

17.2 Conventional Approaches, Unconventional Expressions

Some 21st-century atheists are quite derogatory about religion and believers. Perhaps harshest was Christopher Hitchens, who had no use for any religiosity past or present. Less harsh are others who see religion as an attempt to understand reality, and that the God hypothesis was as good as any other for a starting place. The lack of quantitative rigor in making and interpreting predictions, to the latter anti-religionists, is taken as disproof of religion's viewpoints. It is not disproof. It is the use of one culture's norms to denigrate a different culture. Alternatively, it is dwelling in one potential minimum and casting aspersions on those inhabiting a different potential well. For a thorough discussion of the types of atheism found among American and British scientists, see the recently published *Varieties of Atheism in Science* by Elaine Howard Ecklund and David R. Johnson (Ecklund & Johnson, 2021). Professor Howard Ecklund is director of the Religion and Public Life Program at Rice University; if you desire scholarship instead of polemic on the interaction of religion and science, I commend you to look into her publications and program.

Casting aspersions on others' approaches is hardly limited to scientists. Part of the tension between Hindus and Muslims is the prohibition of killing (sacred) cows by Hindus in contrast to the willingness to eat appropriately slaughtered beef (Halal) by Muslims. Protestants and Catholics were at war with each other from Luther's time until the more conservative Protestant movements joined with Catholics to oppose therapeutic abortion. Tom Lehrer's *National Brotherhood Week*, verse 3, from the 1960s pointedly sums it up:

Oh, the Protestants hate the Catholics
And the Catholics hate the Protestants
The Hindus hate the Moslems
And everybody hates the Jews!

Getting people to change from one potential well to another, or changing their basic assumptions, we know from previous chapters is a matter of getting enough energy into the well to raise the temperature of the contents, and thus the probability that some of the contents will escape the well, of changing the parameters that define the well so that the contents spill out onto adjacent terrain, or of having information diffuse into the well. We can observe that information diffusion is unlikely to change people's assumptions. Scientists continue to maintain that much is sensible in the world, while believers continue to believe, in both cases mostly independent of whether some particular piece of information is consistent with their assumptions. The contradictions between quantum mechanics and general relativity are ignored on a day-to-day basis because both theories work so well in the domains to which they most directly apply. We can model molecular structure using only quantum electrodynamics and classical mechanics, making small relativistic corrections for the behavior of electrons near nuclei. We can model the overall structure of the cosmos using general relativity, with quantum mechanics only invoked to explain the atomic and molecular spectra used to interpret observed light flooding (or leaking) into our telescopes. Yet, to date, there is no unified field theory, and even if one is never promulgated, scientists will use what works in their theories, while religious dogmatists will simply say, "It's God's way," thus not needing to worry about whether the theories are consistent. Here is a place where my biases are in evidence. I have not discussed Bell inequalities, spooky action at a distance, or how some aspects of quantum theory contradict general relativity. My mental zoom lens hasn't taken in problems where these theories and observations are necessary to consider, and other than in this paragraph, they're ignored. That doesn't mean that they should be, it doesn't mean the perspectives I have given deny their relevance or that my viewpoints wouldn't be different if I focused on them. It means that when Gödel comes calling, these are inconsistencies with which I am willing to live. Samuel Beckett, meet Doug Hofstader![1]

At the very least, people dwell in their potential wells out of necessity. There is only so much language, so much interpretation, so much flexibility, and so much adaptability to which any individual can aspire. While I have known people who speak seven languages, they are rare. I know people who can explain multiple religions including details of their dogmas, but almost every believer chooses one sect (or one at a time) with which to intensively participate. Bandwidth is the core limitation to adapting a different religious perspective. In 24 hours per day, with people with whom we must interact in nearby geography, we need to follow certain limited trajectories to accomplish anything. As soon as we lock in on a specific language, dogma, or mode of functioning, we are locking out other languages, other dogmas, and other approaches to living. Because universal language and philosophy have not been achieved, the finite rate of adaptation ensures that it will never be achieved. By the time one idea is promulgated between two people, a different idea will be promulgated between others, and the non-uniformity is amplified. We can write down a set of Tower of Babel equations:

$$\begin{aligned}
&\frac{dL_i}{dt} = \left(p_i(t) - k_{1i}N_i^2(t)\right)L_i \\
&\frac{dN_i}{dt} = k_{2i}N_i(t) - \sum_{j\neq i} k_{3ij}N_iN_j \\
&\mathit{If}\; L_i(t) - L_i(t') > \varepsilon,\; \mathit{then}\; L_i(t) \to L_m,\; m \neq i
\end{aligned} \tag{17.1}$$

In this formulation, N_i is the number of people speaking language L_i, and p_i is the probability that there's a change in language i. For example, would an English speaker in 1865 know what radar is? The term hadn't been invented. By 1945, most Europeans, East

[1]Waiting for Godot, waiting for Gödel.

Asians, North Americans, Anzacs, and a fair fraction of the rest of humanity, knew the term. At the same time, anyone talking about "heavy metal" probably was thinking of gold, lead, or uranium, not music. Such additions don't lead to different languages, just to the evolution of individual tongues. However, if a culture is under siege ($k_{2i} < 0$), is assimilating into another culture (k_{3ij} large), or both, the language may disappear. The stress comes from the interaction of people in competing cultures (thus the N_iN_j term). If some speakers of a language become geographically or culturally distant from other speakers of the same language, differences in p_i result in different dialects and, if the differences are large enough (last line of equation (17.1)), a new language is spawned. The rate of language change depends on the number of speakers. Further, the more people within a culture interact with each other (large k_{1i}), the slower the language changes. There is a field of Quantitative Linguistics, whose literature was not consulted in intuiting equation (17.1). In fact, until I'd written the equation, it didn't even occur to me to ask if such a field existed.

17.3 Dichotomies

Let's explore some of dichotomies associated with religion and theology, see how physical explanations describe them, and make observations of how some religious distinctions appear odd to scientists while scientific thinking can appear odd to believers.

Science seeks truth but never reaches it; the best it claims is a useful understanding of and the ability to make predictions about the physical world. Who is an authority in science? Whoever makes the most sense. Thus, Linus Pauling was revered for his work on quantum chemistry, protein structure, and much else, but when he started pushing Vitamin C as a cure-all, the work was questioned (and found wanting by many). There is no parallel to God in science, i.e., an ultimate authority. Rather, scientists seek consistency in empirical evidence.

This contrasts with much of Western religion, where God is the ultimate authority, and any inconsistency is taken as human inability to fathom God, not a limitation of the Almighty. Having an ultimate authority suggests that there is an ultimate truth. Science makes no claim as to how many layers of understanding humans may eventually obtain, while Western religion puts a cap on the hierarchy. Such capping is a two-edged sword. If one believes that the hierarchy primarily sends information top to bottom, then God talks to religious authorities, who hand down rules to everyone else. On the other hand, even the highest human authorities are nominally subservient to a higher power. The divine appointment of kings enforced hierarchy; the only limitations on royal power were either the refusal of people to submit to authority or the fear by an emperor, king, pharaoh, or other potentate that God would not stand for certain types of behavior. There is a biblical story (in Numbers) where a populist (Korach) tried to flatten the hierarchy. The story ends with Korach's demise. Such a story reinforces hierarchy and obedience. It also supports claims by authoritarians that they are God's chosen and so should be obeyed. It is amusing to speculate if such a biblical populist would have tried to assume autocratic authority if the biblically dominant hierarchy had been displaced.

An interesting question at the juncture among ethics, hierarchy, and politics is whether laws (derived from holy writ or legislation) govern everyone, regardless of rank, or whether the top of the hierarchy can selectively opt out of the rule of law. Dictators frequently take the law into their own hands. Religious leaders, e.g., Popes, in principle are subject to religious law, but the scandals in various religious organizations (sexual abuse of minors in the Catholic church, enrichment of ministers in some Protestant ministries, absolutist rule by Ayatollahs, and the occasional Rabbi who murders his wife) show that some parts of the hierarchy are less than obedient to the rules. Similarly, scientists often pride themselves on using peer review and replication of results to prevent or at least filter errors before they propagate. Assorted scientific scandals show that the system is less than perfect. The interested reader might look up Jans Hendrik Schön, Leo Paquette, and Elizabeth Goodwin. Many scientists find perplexing the recent practice in the U.S. government that the President cannot be arrested under most circumstances, and cannot be investigated by those who report to him (or, perhaps someday, her), as if the President is the ultimate power in the country. Federal employees swear to uphold the Constitution, implicitly making rules the ultimate power. In science, there is no ultimate power — only attempts to consistently explain the world and then persuade others of the insights so gained.

This leads to another contrast. Religion thrives on stability and lays claim to ultimate, unchanging truths. Science, on the other hand, is always tentative, and conclusions may ultimately prove transient. Newtonian gravity was superseded by General Relativity, separate conservation of mass and conservation of energy were succeeded by conservation of both through the linking of rest mass with equivalent energy. "Junk DNA" is no longer considered junk. Intestinal flora aren't just waste; they heavily influence metabolism, mood, and diseases intestinal and non-intestinal alike. During the recent COVID-19 pandemic, the evolving understanding of the disease was seen by scientists as typical progress, while by some non-scientists as general incompetence, manipulative inconsistency, or dishonesty.

17.4 Ethical Evolution?

As scientific understanding and engineering prowess progress, should rules for human behavior change or evolve? Ethical adaptation over time is a friction point between belief and empiricism. Western religions set their ethical roots before modern science took root. As late as 1790, average life expectancy was 35 years, 10% of children died before age one, 1/3 of women died in childbirth or shortly thereafter, and such rules as "be fruitful and multiply" made sense so that the human population was stable. Abortion was unsafe for the mother, infections were untreatable except by draining abscesses, the only common anesthetic was alcohol, and, although microorganisms had been seen for 100 years, microbiology wasn't understood. Even into the 19th century, the mechanism of human sexual reproduction was not known (the events that correlated to starting a pregnancy were of course understood, but not exactly what happened between copulation and birth).

While behavioral changes resulted from lengthened lifespans, increasing population, advances in medicine, and reduced childbirth mortality, the arrival of chemical birth control in the mid-20th century triggered arguments that still persist. When does an embryo or fetus assume legal human status? Do people have souls, given by God, or are souls an invention of the ancient mind? Should women continue to be perceived primarily as nurturers of subsequent generations rather than independent actors who happen to bear children a few times, if at all, during a lifetime? Should societal roles be defined by biology? This is not the place to argue the specifics, but rather to point out that if someone does not feel technology should influence ethics (because ethics were specified by divine writ for all time), they may well have different answers than if that individual thinks ethics depend on changing constraints and boundary conditions. Indeed, "hot button issues" can often be viewed as tension between those in a potential well that says "Ethics should never change (or change slowly)" and those who say, "Now that we have technology X, everything changes!" In these situations, bandwidth is not what limits conflict resolution; it's the deep potential wells that inhibit people from giving credence to other views.

In my lifetime, the effect of modern medicine, birth control, and longevity on the role of women has been a prominent example. Famously, Phyllis Schlafly made a career of opposing women's rights, while acting in ways similar to those she opposed. The abortion debate comes down to those who feel fertilization makes a human with a soul vs. those who feel fertilization creates the potential for a human, but one whose development should be influenced by parental desires, population density, genetic specifics, economics, and likely other factors. This wouldn't be a problem if the warring factions would say, "We disagree — you do it your way, we'll do it ours."

Instead, some in traditional religious potential wells insist on forcing their views on American society, while those in more adaptive potential wells are equally, if oppositely, adamant. Some sects bar women from the ruling hierarchy, but others don't. Nevertheless, there are seemingly universal goals, though the way they are worded varies. Does any common philosophy or religion support the random abuse of women by men? Some religions call such behavior "sin," others "exploitation," others "abuse." Feminism concurs, as it advocates for women to have autonomy equivalent to men. But choose the wrong language (i.e., the wrong subculture) to describe allowable behavior, and the fury flies. If someone lavishes unwanted attention on another, almost everyone concurs that such attention is undesirable, but some would blame the individual illicitly advancing while others would blame the individual advanced upon, and still others would blame unseen (or unseeable) forces. As a scientist, I wonder why the society can't simply say, "No one should invade another's space unless by mutual agreement." But with different rationalizations for different "isms," such simplicity escapes us.

Similarly, following the destruction of 9/11/2001, some groups feared the small U.S. Islamic population would somehow impose Shariah (Muslim law) on the other 98% of the populace, while simultaneously advocating the imposition of some particularist version of Christian law (never mind that there are dozens of Christian sub-groups with subtly different views of what that law is, or that Jewish law or Halacha might be of interest to some, or that some citizens do not subscribe to Western religions). In these cases, people in one potential well fear being pulled into another potential well, and back-react by threatening to impose the same approach in reverse. Once again, the treatment of women highlights the baffling intensity of the arguments. Should women go cavorting, naked, down the streets? Catholic: no (and some advocate nuns should wear habits). Muslim: no (some wear burkas, some hijab). Jewish: no (modesty in dress is strongly advised, especially by the traditionally observant, to the point that male and female adults, not each other's spouses, are not to touch). Feminists: no (it's everyone's responsibility. Women should have control of their circumstances, but men should be trained to control themselves as well). Essentially, everyone needs to act responsibly, not bait others, and learn not to respond to unintentional cues. So what's the squabbling about? Power, control, and identity.

Given that complete uniformity cannot be obtained, even if we all dwelt in shallow potential wells (weak affiliation with a particular philosophy or sect), simply living with a variety of groups, each living internally according to their wishes, leaving room for others to do the same, but admitting that some areas require collaboration and compromise, seems sensible. The growing unwillingness to compromise or ignore other people's differing behavior is puzzling if someone thinks that there is an overall understandability to the world, and it collides with assertions concerning monotheism (with God having assorted names depending on sect and language).

17.5 Freedom

Astonishingly, some documents that consensus holds were written by people, not God, have achieved the status of holy writ, though interpretation of the various chapters and verses is as sectarian as the interpretation of any religious text. Religion and civil society both speak of "freedom". Who, other than a tyrant, could oppose freedom? Yet the word has radically different meanings to different people.

We can identify at least three types of freedom: freedom FROM, freedom OF, and freedom TO. Franklin Roosevelt spoke of freedom from hunger and freedom from fear. The First Amendment of the U.S. Constitution speaks of freedom of speech, freedom of the press, and freedom of religion. It further mentions freedom to assemble and petition. More generally, freedom to act on one's own insights rather than someone else's is exemplary of freedom TO. *Freedom from* blocks one group of people from imposing their will on others. *Freedom of* establishes classes of action that are sheltered from majority regulation. *Freedom to* protects individual autonomy.

Mathematically, freedom from means that whatever behavior is described is not a function of whatever the freedom is from.

$$Life = f(x, y, z, \ldots), \; want, fear \notin (x, y, z, \ldots) \qquad (17.2)$$

Freedom of gives a result on the left-hand side of the equation.

$$Speech, religion = f(life) \qquad (17.3)$$

Similarly, freedom to gives a left-hand side result.

$$Assembly = f(life) \tag{17.4}$$

Unfortunately, one person's autonomy is another person's sin. One culture's constitution is another culture's license to violate all that is good, just, and pure. Who could object to freedom from hunger? Those who fear that the right to food, clothing, shelter, or medical care will subsidize the lazy at the expense of the energetic, thus encouraging everyone to consume, no one to produce, and the collapse of society. One person's freedoms for all time are another person's straitjacket from previous generations, prevented from adjusting to changing times by others' intransigence. Many religions have holy persons who arbitrate among these competing visions; the civic religion of the U.S. delegates such debates to the Congress, the Executive, and the Courts. Privacy is freedom from oversight, yet that privacy is differentially valued across society. Few want the government recording their every move, but some want the government to surveil the streets for potential criminal activity. Others want surveillance to prevent private activity that they themselves find abhorrent. Nonbinary gender roles have been gradually, though not universally, accepted in recent years; this allows some freedom to associate (marry) under circumstances that were previously violently resisted (look up the fate of Alan Turing, one of the geniuses of the mid-20th century). While religion was an early source for ideas of freedom, the ways in which religion interacts with freedom is complicated, fraught, and hardly universal.

Might it be that the total freedom of the world is constant such that as one person or institution gains freedom, another loses? If so,

$$\begin{gathered}\sum_{i=1}^{8\times10^9} F_i = 0.5\times8\times10^9 \\ \prod_{i=1}^{8\times10^9} F_i = 0.5^{8\times10^9}\end{gathered} \tag{17.5}$$

where F_i is the freedom for an individual to do something. The resemblance to the assumptions of statistical mechanics, conservation of particle numbers and energy, with consequent maximization of entropy is intentional.

17.6 Conscience and Consciousness

The nature of life and of human life is a matter of interest and debate across much of human activity. We sense that we are conscious, but the nature of consciousness is poorly understood. Some flavors of religion say that consciousness is the spark of life from God, thus leaving the specifics in the spiritual realm and beyond understanding. Roger Penrose, a polymath who received the Nobel Prize in 2020 for modeling formation of black holes, has written that he believes some quantum effect is responsible for consciousness (*The Emperor's New Mind*). In contrast, some scientists take a view that consciousness is a phenomenon of feedback loops and neural networks (*Neural Darwinism*) or nonlinear dynamics. For science to claim understanding of consciousness, it is likely that artificial consciousness must be generated and demonstrated (i.e., that there be a way to measure a device being both conscious and unconscious in response to controlled stimulus or parameters). A quantitative theory and corresponding experiments explaining consciousness remain outside of my awareness.

If consciousness is only vaguely defined in physics or religion, the other extreme contrast between the two comes when the desires for physical measurement collide with the beliefs of a substantial group of people. Such is the case with the Mauna Kea volcano in Hawaii. To native Hawaiians, the mountain is holy and should not be defiled by commoners and outsiders. To astronomers, the clear, stable air and high altitude make the mountain one of the best places in the northern hemisphere to build large telescopes. While there are numerous telescopes currently on the mountain, there are assorted protests and demands that no more telescopes be built or that some (or even all) of the existing telescopes be removed. This is a case where only binary results are acceptable to some — either science triumphs (and the telescopes continue to function) or spirituality triumphs (the pristine mountain, free of humans above a certain level except for spiritual purposes). Both groups live within value systems/potential wells that in their purest form give little heed to the needs of the other culture. Hawaiian officials have attempted to find common ground and compromise. Some have been satisfied with compromises on the number, size, and placement of telescopes, but not all.

It is easiest to discuss the differences in perspective between groups as if they are binary. In fact, many people (myself included) derive some of their viewpoints from a religious or spiritual approach and other aspects of their views from an empirical approach. Purist thinking, everything from one approach and deprecation of all others, is a recipe for confrontation, dissention, and conflict. Seeking insight from other viewpoints, while time consuming because of the reduced potential well depth, greater uncertainty, and longer time needed to access, absorb, and synthesize additional information, may allow for less tension, less confrontation, and more of what the spiritual world advocates: peace, the calm interaction of people and cultures with each other. (Actually, some religions foresee their triumph at the expense of other approaches to life; their definition of peace is victory for their viewpoint, defeat for others.) Rather than do a mediocre job of discussing such balanced, complex thinking, may I again suggest you read Raima Larter's, *Spiritual Insights From The New Science: Complex Systems And Life* (Larter, 2021).

Besides belief, epistemology, and the appropriate role of individuality and rationality in life, religion emphasizes ethical behavior. We have already discussed how what is ethical to some may be reprehensible to others and vice versa. But let's stand back and ask a different question: given some statement of ethics, what is the correlation among religiosity, belief, and righteous, ethical living? Table 17.1 tabulates the possibilities.

Thus, no one aspect of religion or behavior is perfectly correlated with any other. Strong religiosity doesn't have a correlation coefficient of 1.00 with any other parameter in Table 17.1. Weak religiosity isn't anticorrelated with acceptable behavior. It's all a muddle, but the true believers of all faiths assert that proper living requires adhering to their beliefs and practices. Perhaps it is intuitively clear to large swaths of the American populace that purist

Table 17.1. Correlations among belief, religiosity, and ethics.

Religiosity	Belief	Ethical living	Possible classification
Yes	Yes	Yes	Saint
No	Yes	Yes	Good person despite lack of religious participation
Yes	No	Yes	Supports religious group and society as extension of demographic classification
No	No	Yes	Secular humanist
Yes	Yes	No	Besmirches religiosity
No	Yes	No	Trusts that belief will lead to reward in a subsequent life or after death
Yes	No	No	Goes through the motions without absorbing what religious dogma means or acting on ethics
No	No	No	Areligious criminal

religious claims are not supported by data; abandonment of denominational membership of late has been the fastest growing trend in U.S. religious affiliation in the 21st century.

Nevertheless, large fractions of humanity gain significant psychological and material benefit from membership in a chosen religious institution. My main objection to religious particularism is the tendency of some true believers to narrowly construe that their group is somehow especially good and all others unworthy. Once the viewpoint is, "Here's what we advocate, and why; what do you think?" the room created for diverse insights allows space for multiple religions, spirituality or the lack thereof, and yet no sectarian bloodbaths. Sectarian slaughter, whatever the rationalization, seems to me to be a universal evil.

I'll end this chapter with an anecdote (and, mind you, one of my favorite aphorisms is "the plural of anecdote is not data"). Many spiritual people claim to have contacts with the deceased, to get messages from God, and otherwise to interact with the unseen world. Science has no way to verify or nullify such claims; how would a control experiment be done? So here's what happened to me. In the winter and spring of 1979, I was a post-doctoral fellow at the National Institute for Standards and Technology in Gaitherburg, MD. I had accepted a position at the University of Iowa starting late in the year, after the post-doc ended. The University said I could put plans in to the Physics Machine Shop to get parts of my instrumentation built before I got there. The head machinist, Edmund G. Freund, had worked with James van Allen on Explorer I, the first U.S. earth satellite. What could be better? So I bought a drafting board (in these pre-CAD days), a roll of vellum, pencils, triangles, all the paraphernalia I might need. I got everything set up, and then stared at the paper. How could I get started? I drew a blank. Every other design project I'd ever done had been in collaboration with my graduate research advisor, Prof. John P. Walters, in Madison, Wisconsin. In those days, long-distance phone calls were expensive, video calls a distant dream, and I wouldn't send my first email for another year or two. "If only I could talk to John, he'd get me started," I thought. And then I started having a discussion with Prof. Walters — inside my head. I had internalized enough of how he approached research and engineering to be able to ping-pong questions and ideas with my thought processes and my model of his thought processes. Shortly, I got going, and made significant headway (though, about two weeks later, I hit a snag that meant I did have to phone him up). And then it hit me — one of the earliest thoughts I had that ended up in this book: if I could hold a conversation with someone who wasn't there, but whose mind I could model, couldn't conversations with non-present individuals, or God, actually be a product of the human mind modeling how another intelligence would function, and then converse with that modeled intelligence? Surely we know our own relatives well enough to do that, and so can "converse" with the dead. And perhaps the ancients, unhappy with the ruthless behavior of absolute autocrats, imagined what they'd like to have for an all-powerful ruler, out of which came the Buddha, the God of Genesis, the somewhat different God of Exodus, and the further revised God of the Gospels, the Talmud, the Koran, and the Book of Mormon. Now, when we argue about theology, we may start with one or more of these treatises, the effects of culture over the last many centuries (how many depending on which sect, which language, and geography), and how we want the world to work, and build backwards to the God under whom we'd like to serve. Such starting with the conclusion and working back to the data is anathema to science, but to a scientist it looks like a rational, if apocryphal, explanation for the evolution of religion. Years after this event, when I read Michael Shermer's *The Believing Brain*, I was ready to believe him. No one should consider an anecdote as more than a good story. But I at least had an experience that allowed me to say, "The people who say they have a connection to God or to their ancestors could experience what I experienced, yet interpret it the way they say they interpret it." Indeed, granting someone with whom you disagree the benefit of the doubt by asking, "What if we're both right?" is a path to holding one's own beliefs, letting others hold theirs, and yet lowering the barriers to information diffusion.

In the intervening four decades, religious fanaticism has brought ill repute to zealous belief. Fundamentalist Jews murdered Yitzhak Rabin. Fundamentalist Muslims brought down the World Trade Center and spread terror in numerous places, including at least France, Iraq, Syria, and Afghanistan. The disjunction between Christian biblical teaching and the actions of some Christian fundamentalists has been breathtaking; how could the vilification of Bill Clinton be so intense when related behavior of Donald Trump led to adulation among similar groups? Ill behavior by some members of a group should not, in my view, be generalized to indict the group as a whole, but the increasing tendency for thoughtful people to walk away from religion seems partially justified in light of what "true believers" do.

18

Politics, Business, and Law in Light of Mathematical Concepts

Suppose some legislature passed a law or an autocrat wrote a decree that everyone must float 100 feet off the ground without assistance of a balloon or other device. Could that law be obeyed? Human experience is an emphatic No. Even the most invasive, controlling politico is constrained from violating physical reality. They may not, however, be constrained from punishing others for not doing the impossible. The infamous Stalinist-Soviet agronomist, Trofim Lysenko, imposed agricultural policies at odds with accepted scientific views of biological mechanisms, and as a result starved millions to death (whether on purpose depends on one's politics). If, on the other hand, legislators or autocrats passed or wrote a law saying $\pi = 3.14$ (instead of transcendental 3.14159265…), what would happen? The mathematicians, of course, would explain that a transcendental number can't be turned into a decimal number of only three significant figures arbitrarily, although

3.14 is the closest approximation to π with only three digits. Others would suggest that using 22/7 or 355/113 would be preferable. Others might recommend more significant figures or fewer. The whole debacle would degenerate into the sorts of squabbles that shed more heat than light on many controversial matters.

18.1 Scientists as Politicians

The number of scientists and mathematicians who serve in political roles is small. Herbert Hoover was a mining engineer; Jimmy Carter was an engineer in the U.S. Navy's submarine corps. Otherwise, no U.S. president has been primarily trained in technology (though George Washington did do surveying, which was quite challenging in the late 18th century, and Jefferson was a polymath). International leaders who come to mind include Angela Merkel and Margaret Thatcher, both chemists. Miguel Diaz-Canel has some technical background.[1] In the U.S., Harrison Schmidt walked on the moon and then became a Senator, and several House members have been recognizable scientists. It was sufficiently unusual that Steven Chu was both a Nobel Laureate in Physics and Secretary of Energy to receive significant notice at the time of his appointment.

Why have scientists largely steered clear of politics? One suspects there are several parameters that correlate with this disjuncture. First, science and engineering are empirical fields. It doesn't matter how much anyone might wish to have room temperature superconductivity; unless someone can invent a material with the desired characteristics, we can't have it. In politics, a desired goal may be attainable through legislation, dishonesty, manipulation, or spending other people's money. This is not to imply that all

[1] A Cuban expatriate told me in 2014 that Diaz-Canel would be the next leader of Cuba and that he'd take a different tack than his predecessors because "he was an engineer." While he was awarded a Doctor of Science degree March 23, 2021, it is not clear to this non-Spanish speaker what review his doctoral thesis received, and it is suspicious that he did not receive the degree until after he became President of Cuba. As of July 25, 2021, the Wikipedia entry that says he got a Ph.D. is at odds with the March 23 announcement of his receipt of a D.Sc. (at least in the U.S., the two degrees are not the same).

scientists are honest. However, if the outcome of some dishonesty matters, it is likely that dishonesty will be found out, called out, and the perpetrator's career destroyed, impaired, or at least inconvenienced. And if the dishonesty is in an area to which few pay attention, then the reward for having cheated is, typically, limited. Corruption is so rife in politics that many scientists want nothing to do with it. In addition, personal destruction has often been a favored means of getting elected. Accusing one's opponent of nefarious deeds is routine in political advertising. Who needs that grief when there is literature to read, students to teach, problems to solve, calculations to perform, and inventions to invent?

Among my colleagues, I have known faculty who range all across the political spectrum. Libertarians? Progressives? Reactionaries? Members of assorted political parties? Yes to all. Some see their scientific work as impacting their political views, others not. Some are good at figuring out how political pressures may suggest research topics that are easier to fund than others, others do research independent of the political climate. In my experience, the correlation coefficient between scientific outlook and political views is low.

18.2 Law

Even the meaning of the word, "Law," is different between political and scientific thinking. In science, a law is a relationship that appears so consistent with observation, and so strongly embedded in theory, that everyone in a field to which that law relates assumes it is correct unless some new observation makes that law untenable. Conservation of momentum, conservation of energy, and conservation of mass were considered laws until Einstein derived a relationship between mass and energy. Now, while the separate conservation of mass and energy is an excellent approximation under most circumstances, it is the conservation of the two together that is regarded as a law.

Contrast this with the law that says no one should jaywalk. It is unsafe to jaywalk on a crowded freeway at rush hour, so the law is sensible, but who hasn't jaywalked at 2 AM after looking both ways before crossing the street? Legislation is an attempt to regulate behavior. Because some people like to regulate others, and many people do not like to be regulated, political law is often more controversial than the scientific variety. Nevertheless, when science questions existing physical law, the arguments can be intense. It has been observed (by Max Planck, among others) that the opponents of new science within the scientific community often are not convinced; they eventually die, thus removing them from the conversation. This was particularly true when relativity and quantum mechanics made their appearance.

18.3 Choices

Economists and businesspeople see science as a means to an end, while some scientists see science as an end in itself. From the time that Thomas Edison invented the industrial research laboratory, which in turn led to incandescent light bulbs, electric railways, phonographs, motion pictures, and the most common early electronic microphone, many businesspeople hopped on the bandwagon. They figured that if they turned ingenious people loose to invent things, the business would prosper, i.e., the benefit of giving free reign to the technologists would exceed the cost. This worked from about 1880 until about 1984. In the latter year, the breakup of American Telephone and Telegraph Company removed the monopoly cash flow that had sustained the organization whose research gave us transistors, communications satellites, dial telephones, some early cellular telephones, and just about everything to do with fiber optic communications except the fibers themselves (which were developed by Corning Glass).

When AT&T was splintered, it wasn't long before other major corporations resized their research operations to support their central mission and not much more. Pharmaceutical companies still had massive operations targeting new bioactive molecules, but duPont, Dow Chemical, ExxonMobil, and others downsized. They decided that curiosity-driven inquiry should be performed in universities, while they did development that yielded more immediate cash flow. The universities, in turn, were told to focus on problems with demonstrable benefits. The result is that in the 21st century, we are more likely to innovate details of existing paradigms than to invent new approaches to understanding. Fortunately, enough scientists have kept their burning curiosity alive that RNA-based vaccines were available when COVID-19 appeared. Such vaccines might have been available several years earlier had governments not defunded RNA vaccine research and testing after they were found unnecessary to block SARS, MERS, and Ebola.

A further reason that free-range research has been downsized in industry is that leadership has a mediocre track record in exploiting their own scientists' developments. Eastman Kodak was at the forefront of array detector photography. Because the early CCD and CID cameras couldn't equal the performance of Ektachrome and Kodachrome film, nor would they allow profit from continuous consumable demand, Kodak didn't aggressively work to displace film. The result? Kodak went bankrupt, while the typical cell phone camera now makes snapshots at least the equal of film cameras. The story of Xerox PARC inventing the graphical user interface, only to have Apple produce a commercially viable graphical PC, and then Microsoft exploit the idea with Windows, is well known. If information is freely and widely available, does an individual or organization wish to produce or consume that information? The answer of a corporate finance officer may not be the same as a product engineer, inventor, or scientist.

A vast amount of scientific literature is freely available, often by government mandate. Since the public paid for the research, shouldn't they be able to read it? That's an argument for open access publishing. Such availability makes it easy to learn from the sweat others expended how to build new technology. That is, technology has become a commodity. This drastically reduces the value of any individual research contribution. Inventing a light bulb when there were no economical competitors opened a vast market. Making a longer-life bulb when all existing bulbs were short-lived did the same. But when an invention improves efficiency by half a percent, or cuts production cost by 0.1%, is the benefit worth the cost? If the cost savings from a patent is less than the cost of a lawyer to pursue that patent, is it better to forego the patent and license access to it if someone else files, or to build a defensive wall? In many cases, using something as a trade secret with no paper trail "outside the fence" is more economical.

18.4 Overwhelmed

It's no different in publishing. When Guttenberg invented a practical movable-type system, there was an explosion in publishing. From 1452 until 1980 or thereabouts, presses became more efficient, typewriters were invented, as were linotypes and photoengraving, but producing and distributing information was efficient only from established presses. Striving for access to written material was as much a part of the Abraham Lincoln legend as the death of Nancy Hanks Lincoln. Even when books became widely available, each new book had the potential for significant impact on culture and learning. Then personal computers and electronic distribution of widely authored, poorly vetted information became possible. Today? The reader can search the web as fast as they could flip to this tome's bibliography to locate most citations. The essential point is that we are fabricating information (in the sense of bitstreams) at a rate exceeding any ability for one person to consume it, much less critically evaluate it or synthesize what we encounter into a coherent whole. It strains credulity to think that the rate will slacken.

Video and books are commodities. The chances are excellent that only a vanishingly small fraction of humanity will read this book, and that it will get lost in the libraries of the world as additional avalanches of words follow it. Prior to 1980, knowledge production and distribution choked on inaccessibility to existing

> One modern approach to teaching is "active learning," in which (to quote David Goldberg) the instructor is "a guide on the side, not a sage on the stage." This is deeply disconcerting to earlier generations of professors and teachers who revel in lecturing. Nevertheless, from the standpoint of bandwidth, it makes sense. Teachers can model thought processes, but the speaking/note-taking/report-back (on the test) that the information transferred is oblivious to what Google and its competitors have delivered.

(*Continued*)

(Continued)

> Any fact can be obtained faster by searching than it can be recalled. But to dig through the petabytes, exabytes, and more accessible through the web? That takes self-teaching skills, judgment as to whether proffered bytes are relevant or accurate, and integration of new information with that previously learned. These skills have to be experienced internally, not just heard or seen.
>
> Why did lecturing work well for prior generations? First, storytelling has transmitted information as long as there has been language. Second, prior to Guttenberg, oral transmission was the main economically feasible means of maintaining information. Third, when formal education became common, it was exploited by those who read widely before the majority of society took part. Especially in small classes, lectures evolve to discussions readily. In classes of several hundred? Not so much. Finally, if a class has read and internalized the material, or been exposed to it in daily living, before listening to a lecture, the lecture becomes active, as students compare what the instructor says to their preconceived notions, making every moment a silent argument.

information. Now it chokes on excessive availability. Consequently, information aggregators cluster into narrow potential wells with internally consistent information that may completely exclude areas of knowledge, not to mention alternative approaches to digesting particular fields. Perhaps humanity is approaching the point where information is in dynamic equilibrium — the rate at which information disappears and is produced are equal.

What happens when attempting to transfer information when the supply is immense? Prior to the invention of the printing press, most people obtained information at the speed of speech. Once books, newspapers, and periodicals became more common, information transferred at the speed of speech or reading, but the rate at which one could afford to obtain books limited the latter.

The establishment of public libraries, so that aggregated funds could support literacy for an entire community, further accelerated transmission and reception. Radio and network television increased the flow further, but now the rate of information transmission taxed the ability of anyone to keep up with everything. Because individual recording for later playback had not yet reached the market, if someone watched Walter Cronkite, they weren't watching Huntley and Brinkley on the competing network at the same time (or, if they were, there was competition for limited attention). If someone subscribed to *Time*, *Newsweek*, and *U.S. News and World Report*, a significant amount of time was consumed in reading these weekly periodicals, cutting down the time available to read books.

And then along came fiber optics and the World Wide Web. Bytes can now be transferred at rates beyond human ability to notice, much less absorb, them. We have reached the point where accelerated communications cannot increase the rate of learning by people (and even if automatons filter the bytestreams, eventually people have to be able to comprehend the digests). Free speech enhances communication if, as in the Lincoln Douglas Debates, people can consider all the information being produced, but if there are 100 simultaneous debates, most of the information is never apprehended by anyone. It is this supersaturation of bytes than can lead to people tuning out anything with which they disagree or they find irritating; they can always find a bytestream that reinforces what they already know. Each potential well becomes deeper over time. The only way to free up time to sample new bytestreams is to slow the streams down. But who controls the throttle? Whoever sets the rate of communication and limits the channels controls the society. The concept of free speech presumed that production and consumption of that speech would be approximately 1:1. With current technology, there is so much speech that all signal can be perceived as noise, drowning out substance and clarity with interference.

The meaning of "debate" has changed over time. Lincoln and Douglas met six times across the State of Illinois. Their speeches were transcribed by newspaper reporters, and while the exact wording was different in competing newspapers, the essential wording was similar. While each politician's argument was repeated six times, at least half-hour blocks of time were allocated for exposition. Agree or disagree, the logic had nuance. The Kennedy-Nixon debates in 1960 presaged what currently passes for debate: canned answers to moderator questions, where there is no penalty for going off-topic, no means of developing, much less attacking or defending, any argument, and the shallowest of discourse used to message true believers to get them motivated to go to the polls. What would happen if politicians were required to give half-hour position papers on particular topics, followed by 15-minute rebuttals from the competition, followed by critique by non-candidates of the accuracy or context of candidate statements? One fears that such intensive, critical discourse would be ignored as PACs spread soundbites, "gotchas", and misinformation, designed to steer supporters to the polls and opponent supporters to give up in disgust. Soundbites are the antithesis of deeply considered thought.

We can use the equations describing signals, noise, and interference to formalize these insights. Suppose each individual transmitting a signal produces S_i. Noise in that individual's transmissions (misspelled words, mispronounced words, gaffes, and so on) are labeled N_i. For a one-on-one conversation, the listener's or reader's comprehension C would be:

$$C = K\frac{S_i}{N_i} \tag{18.1}$$

K is a scaling factor integrating the familiarity the listener has with the language of the transmitter, the conformance of S_i to the potential wells of the listener, how alert the listener is, and so on. K is likely a function of S; this is a nonlinear problem.

Now add in all the parallel streams of information. The listener has some ability to tune in one stream in the presence of all the others. Call that a selectivity factor χ_i. Now

$$C = K\frac{\frac{\chi_i S_i}{N_i}}{\sum_{k=1}^{M}\frac{\chi_k S_k}{N_k}} \tag{18.2}$$

There is some $k = i$. If $M = 1$, then the multiplier of K is 1.0, and the rate of communications is controlled by K. Any other situation means C is reduced, and given enough terms in the denominator, the ratio goes to zero. Thus, communications is most effective if χ_i is large, all the other χ's are small, and K is large. The moment you choose the network you'll watch, you've chosen the message you'll receive, even if it's nonsense. Further, many channels work hard to ensure that you perceive the other channels as nonsense.

18.5 Dunning-Kruger and Information Flow

Many people think they know more than they do, or at least that they know a lot that others who try to assert control do not know. What are some manifestations of this Dunning-Kruger effect (Kruger & Dunning, 1999)? While this book was being written, people with no training in virology, epidemiology, physiology, or respiratory therapy were ignoring, opposing, or denigrating the advice of people with knowledge in all these areas. The trained individuals were struggling; COVID-19 was a novel disease that was causing vast misery and death, and those trained in the relevant medical and scientific fields were working to exhaustion to try to ameliorate the disease and save lives. Yet, individuals who had never studied the relevant areas grabbed significant attention with theories that could be easily disproved by experiment or experience. Once vaccines were available, many sought inoculation as fast as they could, but others, for political, religious, and contrarian reasons, refused (for many months) to be inoculated. As the experts expected, the virus continued to mutate, and eventually strains that were not stopped by the earliest vaccines evolved. Even if everyone were inoculated, continued viral evolution would be expected, but the behavior of tens of millions of people optimized the likelihood of developing resistant strains. Strains evolved randomly, but high viral load (in the uninoculated) spread mutant virii to the inoculated, where only those strains that weren't stopped by the vaccine could survive. The same thing occurs in many areas of endeavor.

Information flows through networks, the most obvious of which are an organism's neural network, wired telephone systems, or the fiber optics of the internet. In what direction does that information flow? For an authoritarian society, information starts with the head individual and is propagated out to the rest of the society. Back-diffusion of the consequences of the information is slow, filtered, and easy to ignore. Examples of such societies include the Former Soviet Union and the People's Republic of Korea (North Korea). Such a structure optimizes control and minimizes creativity or flexibility among non-elite members of society. The child's game, "Mother May I", illustrates the problem. Leader: "Take one step forward." Player: "Mother may I?" Leader: "Yes, you may." The player advances. If the player forgets to say the requisite phrase, "Mother may I?", or if they cannot accomplish the assigned task, they get sent back to the starting line. A skilled leader can always find commands to prevent players from advancing all the way to tagging the leader and becoming the new "Mother". This is totalitarianism in a nutshell.

In contrast, anarchy has information flowing through random networks with no organization. Random events by random people occur, but coordinated, directed action is impossible. For social creatures, whether ants, bees, porpoises, or people, some common language and organized activity are essential for survival (an assertion with which a committed anarchist would disagree).

Direct democracy integrates information across a society at a given moment (the moment when votes are cast), while representative democracy interposes an additional level of abstraction and data integration. Representatives can consider input not only from individuals, but also experts, adjusting the relative weighting among experts, voters, and campaign funders as seems fitting. The voters then filter candidates based on the sum of their prior behaviors; in effect,

$$P(C_n) = K\sum_i p_i e^{-kt_i} \tag{18.3}$$

where P is the preference score, C_n is candidate n, K is a normalization factor, p_i is the magnitude of preference (if greater than 0) or dislike (if less than zero) for a particular position of the candidate at a particular time, t_i is time since an event occurred, and k is the rate at which people forget (or forgive) what was done in the past. Thus, a potential voter need not totally agree with what any candidate espouses; whoever maximizes P with the most voters in a district gains or retains office. History suggests large values for p_i occur for incumbents, members of co-labeled groups (parties), candidates with large campaign budgets, and those who can induce large negative p_i's in people's thinking about candidates $C_{n'}$, $n' \neq n$. Such summing and averaging can reduce noise in setting policy. Information is blurred over time.

Adam Smith described information flow in a free market as an "invisible hand". The information flow cannot be mapped; only the consequences of flow are visible. In other words, the network is fractal and chaotic. Price, word-of-mouth, reviews, sales volume, and willingness of potential workers to be involved with some activity all communicate, partially, the value of some activity or product. Where the terminal information about something can be assayed by a purchaser, markets work extraordinarily well.

Where markets fail is where communications fail. If a cost related to a product does not show up in the price, that cost isn't communicated to anyone; it contributes to the tragedy of the commons (the decay of resources useful to the entire community because their maintenance and improvement are the passion and focus of no one). I love prime rib (rare, please). For 2/3 of a century, I ate it with great joy (never ketchup!). The clogging of my arteries? Not on the menu, not in the taste, not in the price, not in anything but the health community, who couldn't convince me that beef was a problem. The methane produced by the cows? Invisible to human eyes. Thus, the environmental impact was invisible. What limited my consumption, aside from the glare in the eyes of more enlightened people, was the higher price of good beef compared to chicken or vegetables. I lived long enough to write this book when the bill came due, and a clogged lateral artery descending was stented open by a surgeon (and let me tell you, what they and the support staff earned would buy them quite a few dinners!). Why not include the marginal cost of clogged arteries, greenhouse gases, and offense to the hundreds of millions of people who are vegetarian or at least believe that cows should not be killed in the price of beef? There's no way to set such prices because the impact is intangible, diffuse, remote, and comes due far removed from the point of expenditure. In other words, the costs fall outside the bandwidth of the transaction. Furthermore, including such costs (if quantifiable) inflate price, thus reducing demand, and anyone dependent on the product for livelihood will be opposed.

If we ignore externalities, i.e., those aspects of a transaction not within the bandwidth of the buyer or seller to see directly, the transaction will happen more frequently than if the externalities force their way into the potential transaction. Thus, regulation forces more information into a potential transaction than would otherwise be included. We might say

$$N = kBC(1-C)(1-R)(1+I) \tag{18.4}$$

where N is the number of transactions, k is a scaling constant, B is the benefit, C is the cost (on a scale of 0–1), and R is the regulatory burden (also on a scale of 0–1). I is any external incentive (government subsidy). R and I represent information imposed on a transaction that isn't local to the buyer or seller. Often, neither buyer nor seller desires regulation, as the number of transactions is restricted or the cost increases. Note that if cost is 0, no

> While conceptually useful, equation (18.4) cannot be taken literally. At the very least, terms such as $(1 - C)$ need to be modified to allow for more complicated feedback mechanisms, i.e., $(1 - \psi C)$ or $(1 - \psi_1 C - \psi_2 C^2)$.

transaction can occur, because there is no seller incentive. If cost is 1, there is no buyer. And what did we learn about logistic equations, where there are terms like $C(1 - C)$? They can go through bifurcations into chaos! Some might say that regulation can encourage a transaction (say, for putting solar panels on residences or moving to an electric vehicle), so perhaps equation (18.4) should have an $R(1 - R)$ term, leaving I to represent non-regulatory incentives.

In any case, buyers and sellers are influenced by R but may lack the perspective that went into R. Similarly, whoever set up the regulations cannot know what is in the mind of buyer or seller, since regulations, by definition, precede transactions. *All parties to a transaction are missing information.* Someone who has never been to a farm may not understand what regulating standing water implies to a landowner. Someone who has never lived in a high rise may not understand what it means to have hundreds of neighbors only a few feet away (and likely to ride in the same elevator often). Yet regulations are made by people with assigned jobs who may not have time to fully internalize the viewpoints of all affected parties. In fact, they may not even be aware of some of the affected parties, as we noted in Chapter 7. No, the regulator isn't brain-dead, nor are the parties to a transaction wrong to resent what the regulations are, nor are those who advocate for more regulation advocating for something undesirable. They simply lack the bandwidth to integrate the range of information that should be brought to bear to fully communicate costs and benefits in context. Living in a potential well that excludes information critical to alternative views only makes successful problem resolution less likely.

Environmental regulation is a perpetual source of angst, in part because of the information included in considering policy. Deoxygenation in the Gulf of Mexico adjacent to the mouth of the Mississippi River is in part due to runoff independent of humans, in part due to phosphates and nitrates from agricultural runoff, in part from detritus from non-farming activity, and all of the sources are delocalized over half the land area of the United States. The costs are localized to the detriment of marine life and fisheries, imposed by actions with no direct link to the Gulf Coast. When a

Midwestern farmer is told to limit fertilizer application (to minimize runoff), is the impact on that farmer's crop yield considered? Is the impact on waterfowl who graze on late fall stubble part of the discussion? Since the market for the grain may be half a world away, is the impact of total human population taken into account? Clearly this list of considerations is limited, but linking costs, benefits, and impacted individuals adds to contention.

18.6 Tunnel Vision

Failure to integrate information across a range of perspectives is easily seen in the handling of "hot-button" issues. What's your favorite? Guns? Race? Sex? Abortion? National origin? Surely the reader, or someone known to them, has a specific view on at least one of these issues. I'd like to suggest that every strongly held view on any of these (or other partisan) topics are examples of people trapped in potential wells where the only parametric change in recent times is for the wells to deepen and narrow, while a well-functioning society would have those wells shallow so that information could fluidly be exchanged between them. Someone being sure they are right while demonizing contrary approaches to a problem excludes information, prevents parametric change, and rigidifies problems rather than leading to solutions. How might such deep potential wells be made shallower? I have no realistic approach, but one unlikely approach is to suggest to all involved: what if, within the range of information considered, both sides are right? (That last sentence just aroused a back-reaction from some quarters that bemoan "both-sidesism" in discussing political views, particularly when they vehemently dislike one of those sides or perceive that the "information" proffered by that side is untrue. In separate potential wells, different statements will be perceived as true.) I give as an example how someone should view the Greek tragedy, *Oedipus Rex*. Oedipus was driven in part by a lust for power. But he did love his mother.

Of the many hot-button issues, the one that has the least connection to religion and therefore is most in the realm of politics and economics is firearms regulation. What everyone I have ever encountered agrees on is: suicide, murder, and other crimes perpetrated using firearms are undesirable. What this means is that I have never knowingly talked with a murderer, robber, kidnapper, criminal of some other ilk defending their turf, or someone intent on ending their life with a gun. Those not using firearms with intent to do harm sharply split between those who view firearms as essential to a properly functioning society and those with a decidedly opposite view. To avoid turning this paragraph into a discourse on firearms policy, I will look only at a tiny corner of this complicated subject (I once argued with someone that there isn't "a" gun culture, but at least 17 of them — that shows why I'm limiting the discussion, without tabulating specifics that doubtless are incomplete). As simple a question as "how many firearms were used illicitly" is difficult to answer. Finding answers to questions slanted towards one position or another, hosted by advocacy groups, is easy. But "how many firearms were used in crimes" reveals neither government nor private data. "How many firearms were used in murders?" "How many were used in suicides?" "How many were killed in Year X?" These have answers. But to determine the percentage of firearms used for non-benign purposes is not simple. At which point, advocates take over. Pro-gun groups claim most guns are used safely. Anti-gun groups note the number of murders, suicides, and other crimes assisted by firearms. Victims and their relatives accentuate the negative, while those who have been around firearms much of their lives commonly accentuate the positive. Anti-hunting groups and pro-hunting groups assume different positions; conservation groups may advocate for deer harvesting (to prevent overgrazing) while animal rights advocates say no violence should be employed (other than that perpetrated by non-human species). See the pattern? No one is looking at all the available data, nor does it seem anyone takes a comprehensive view of the statistics, especially since the U.S. Congress forbade certain types of research to be federally funded. So everyone cherry-picks data that support their preferred outcome — exactly what is expected in a deep potential well. True believers simply ignore questions that are central to the worldview of those in other wells. Someone living in a rural setting, who sees other people only occasionally, will have quite different perceptions from someone in a large city that sees an average of more than one firearm murder per day. If they presume that circumstances are identical everywhere and that one set of rules must apply as well, naturally each location will gravitate to an incompatible potential well.

One even finds different potential wells for how to view people with problems. "Blame the victim" vs. "Blame the cause or the perpetrator" applies to many of the hot button issues. Suppose an individual is identified as having an income below the Federal poverty line. Why are they there? Poor education? Lack of initiative? Profession no longer needed by society? Drugs? Bankrupted by medical bills and no longer able to work? Someone in their family absconded with their bank account? Laziness? Unemployment compensation? Lack of adequate societal investment in education? There's 10 possible reasons, and that's just what I could think of without having to slow down while typing. Without knowing the causes, how could anyone recommend what interaction to have with the impecunious individual? Yet, when poverty is discussed, intense camps for or against all sorts of proposed remedies form, each loudly proclaiming that this or that program, or this or that character flaw, is the cause or cure for the situation. Potential wells prevent information accumulation.

Correlation is a necessary feature of causation, but demonstration of correlation is not sufficient to prove causation, as we saw earlier. To a measurement scientist, one of the strangest aspects of human existence is a behavior dating to antiquity: why is the ability to kill someone from a different group thought to correlate with any plausible problem solving? Rome defeated Carthage, the Romans succumbed to the Barbarians, for 130 years European Protestants battled European Catholics, and so on. Killing ability may correlate with some technical advances, with commitment to a cause, or simply with population. But how does it correlate with justice? Approximately 600,000 citizens, 2% of the population, were killed in the U.S. Civil War/War Between the States/War of Northern Aggression/Southern Rebellion. How was any of this slaughter related to the issues that caused the war, variously defended by interested groups as the maintenance or abolition of slavery, the dominance or subservience of states vs. the Federal government, of governance mainly by landowners vs. the population as a whole? In the first half of 2022, the Russian invasion of Ukraine rekindled concern about how to deal with military strength vs. economic desires and political viewpoints. Those siding with Ukraine could claim that whoever shoots first is wrong. Those focused on balance of power could claim that tricentric spheres of influence have been common in recent centuries (in the 18th century: Britain/France/Spain, in the 20th century: US/Soviet Union/China, and of course Orwell's fictional Oceania, Eastasia, and Eurasia). Where does the pain of disrupted communities, destroyed cities, and starving populations fit into this? An unrelated potential well. Of what concern is the collapse of distant countries to a hegemon?

Maintaining a potential well with a particular viewpoint can become an end in itself. The occupants actively exclude consideration of the justification for their chosen parameters and selected information, and thus use violence not to solve problems or look for coherent approaches to living, but simply to maintain a power structure, belief system, or other limited objective. Because of the intentional limiting of access to unapproved information, only external force can change the well's parameters. One of the main tools used by autocrats to control the population is locking down information to create a potential well with parameters favorable to the autocrat. Parochialism can most easily flourish when information flow is controlled. This may not limit the total number of bytes transmitted, but it certainly limits the content of those bytes.

18.7 Too Much, Too Little

I haven't had the time to read it, but in 2011, Harvey Silverglate published *Three Felonies a Day: How the Feds Target the Innocent* (Silverglate & Dershowitz, 2011). While Silverglate worries in part about the vagueness of laws, he also notes that the number of laws has exploded to the point that no one can know them all. How can you follow a law of which you're unaware? We know that we can't take in all the information in the world even if we want to, and I, for one, usually don't have time before a trip to sit down and read the law code for any state or country I'm about to visit. I may read a tour book, hope they hit the highlights, and then just try to be courteous. The only time I nearly got arrested using this approach was when I jaywalked in Jerusalem (not only is jaywalking illegal there, but the law is enforced). Here, the limits of bandwidth are a two-edged sword. There are so many laws that many won't be enforced because no one has time to chase down violators, or violation of some minor law may provide a handle to arrest anyone as a matter of convenience. Such capricious and arbitrary use of law breeds contempt for law and legislatures alike. So why are laws created faster than they are erased? Every law has information and an advocacy group supporting use of that information for societal betterment, as perceived by the advocates. Reading each law, in isolation, may show what is worthwhile. But the sum of all the rules yields an overdetermined, inconsistent, incomprehensible system. Those who feel we should scrap the system and start over may have many motives, but one may well be to clear out an excess of constraints that are unknowable if someone is to accomplish anything during a single lifetime.

Despite all the rules, there are still areas where society suffers for lack of policy or so many conflicting views between groups in their individual potential wells that problems fester. We can think of each camp as sitting in their own potential well, while a compromise solution is desirable by the average citizen. Unfortunately, that solution does not sit in a well — it sits at an unstable fixed point. Suppose the problem you want to solve is that some 3-year-old is going to bed hungry. "Deliver healthy fruits, vegetables, and proteins to all the hungry children!" says one group. "Give their parents/guardians jobs!" says another. "If the parents couldn't support their kids, they shouldn't have had them in the first place!" says a third. "Put 'em up for adoption!" says a fourth. "It's a cruel world; not my problem!" says a fifth. "If they ever do have a full stomach, they'll appreciate it all the more!" says a sixth. "Have 'em join a church; the congregation will look out for its own!" says a seventh. "We need better communal childcare!" says an eighth. "Let 'em starve!" says a ninth. My guess is that you, the reader, could add to this list. Some of the proposed solutions are possibly to your liking; some probably aren't. What is common to all of them is: if one-ninth of people subscribe to each possible solution, no one can agree to anything and the child remains hungry. Yet, within each group, there is a smug assurance that if only everyone adopted their viewpoint, the problem would be solved. Welcome to a society that values moral certitude over practicality.

When policies are set, they are often critiqued for imperfections rather than evaluated on their merits. That is, if a policy has a benefit, the opponents of the policy ignore those benefits, find examples of slip-ups, missteps, loopholes, or misapplication, and then vilify the policy for its failures. Given the complexity of civilization, all (or effectively all) policies will have problems. Thus, honestly attacking a policy requires that alternatives be proposed and critiqued. For a decade, the Affordable Care Act was attacked by those who disliked taxpayer support of health care for non-veterans of limited means. "We'll replace it with something better!" was the claim, but the proposed alternative was never disclosed. Could there be alternative policies that had different assets and liabilities? Of course. But to criticize, indeed vilify, a policy without proposing a tangible alternative, including costs, is simply a way to seek power without justification. It is rare to see policies debated on the substance, admitting predictable limitations. It is small wonder that many citizens are disgusted with politics that appears to have degenerated to power grabbing and meanness in the democracies, little different in result from power grabbing in autocracies. At least in a diffuse, bureaucratic state with many levels of government, enough people are working at cross purposes that enterprising individuals can find some locus where problems can be solved because solving such problems feeds the power base of that corner of the body politic.

From 1932 to 1968 in the U.S., while there was certainly as much political disquiet as in any other period, a coalition managed enough compromise to survive the Depression, gain Western hegemony during World War II, build a consumer economy thereafter, police much of the world (not always successfully), and attack problems of poverty and inequality. But as in any system as nonlinear as Society, the forces solving problems during that period set up reactions that have played out since. From my perspective, the Grand Bifurcation occurred in 1968. The Left, dissatisfied with advances against segregation, bias, and poverty, and vehemently opposed to U.S. actions in Vietnam, overreached. Ever since, The Right has been fueled by being against what The Left was for. Politics is a Markov process; we can't turn the clock back. Excursions travel along the strange attractor of policy. We have long periods near a fixed point, then a jump to some far reach of policy space, followed by gradual return to near a fixed point, often not the same one. At one time, the most advanced societies on earth were in China, Mesopotamia, India, and Central America. About 2000 years ago, Mediterranean civilization (Greece and Rome) would be added to the list. What was going in in Africa at that time? I don't know — Western history to which I've been exposed seems oblivious to Africa outside of Egypt until the era of European exploration began following the Black Death of 1348–1351. "So go look it up!" That would delay finishing this book — I don't have the bandwidth! In order to do *something*, I am knowingly not doing *something else*. This is inevitable in politics and economics. Remember that during the next electoral campaign. Of course current office holders haven't done everything. Of course they made decisions with too little information. But did they attempt to gain information and act with good judgment within the bounds of the information to which they had access? No one's perfect, because no one has complete information and they're starting in a particular potential well.

18.8 Money as Information

Money is a means of time-shifting information. For workers and retirees, money indicates that at some time in the past, something of value was produced, so that equity requires that something of similar nominal value be delivered to the bearer. For the young consumer, money indicates that someone else produced something. Loans enable consumption before production (and require the lender to trust that future production will allow repayment). Such simplistic description uses tools developed prior to electronic communications to describe modern practice. The end of the gold standard and floating currencies means that money is worth whatever a society, at a given moment, thinks it's worth. With value exchanged largely as bytes in the 21st century, it is far from clear what a dollar, yuan, or euro represents; let us hope they each represent more than a Reichsmark in the fall of 1923. When the economy or unemployment are a problem (when aren't they?), advocates push one-sided solutions. Keynesians typically worry about inadequate demand. Supply-side economists typically worry about inadequate incentives to generate sufficient supply. Dynamical systems scientists (or which I immodestly consider myself to be an example) worry about whether supply and demand are converging to a stable fixed point or whether they are diverging to chaos. A dream world would be a steady state where everyone's needs and a fair fraction of their desires, i.e., demand, is adequately met by supply at full employment. But this steady state is unstable, leading to exponential rises in prices (a wage price spiral), recessions (collapse in employment and demand, leading to reduced production). In the spirit of Chapter 11, with D = demand, S = supply, L = labor (all normalized between 0 and 1), and O = optimism, constrained to be positive (so O_D is the populace's optimism about the future, O_S is producer's optimism, and O_L is labor's optimism), we may surmise

$$
\begin{aligned}
O_{D,n+1} &= k_1\left(L_n + S_n\right)\\
O_{S,n+1} &= k_2\left(L_n + S_n - k_7 D_n\right)\\
O_{L,n+1} &= k_3\left(S_n + D_n - k_8 L_n\right)\\
D_{n+1} &= k_4 D_n O_{D,n} O_{S,n} O_{L,n}\left(1 - D_n\right)\\
S_{n+1} &= k_5 S_n O_{S,n}\left(1 - S_n\right)\left(1 - L_n\right)\\
L_{n+1} &= k_6 L_n O_{L,n}\left(1 - L_n\right)\left(1 - D_n\right)
\end{aligned}
\tag{18.5}
$$

We see the coupling among the three variables, the nonlinearity, and the potential for chaos. The steady state occurs for all the *O*s = 1 and all the *k*s small enough that the steady state *D*, *S*, and *L* values are between 0.25 and 0.66. If any of *D*, *S*, or *L* have no steady state value above 0.25, the system collapses to (0, 0, 0). And if the steady states are ever above 0.66, the system goes through period doubling to chaos. Obviously, the real world is even more complicated, but the point is that chaos is the normal state expected for economic behavior. Contrast this with blaming or crediting individual politicians or policies for everything from stock market behavior to the price of gasoline, and in real time rather than with a time/phase delay between policy implementation and an outcome! Political campaigning and understanding of induction time between policy changes and response are at odds.

We now narrow our focus to see how the sum of the prior insights influence how we perceive science and how we should view individual autonomy of scientists and others as communications bandwidth has saturated and potential wells have deepened.

19

Research and Freedom in Light of Mathematical Concepts

When I started writing this book, I thought that Chapter 7 would be the central concept that permeated the book and guided the commentary in these last few chapters. To my discouragement, Chapter 10 came to dominate my thinking. Yes, there are limits on how rapidly information can be produced, transmitted, and absorbed, but the need to have a point of reference to efficiently process information makes potential wells inevitable and, alas, dominant in how many people approach the world. Research, honestly pursued, tries to break out of potential wells, out of the constraints left to us at time t_{n-1}, adding insight at time t_n so that the world is more livable at times $t > t_n$. As with every other concept we have encountered, there are multiple views of what research is, how to select the topics, how to constrain its pursuit, and how to employ the results. We will explore some of the ideas I have encountered and then draw some wider conclusions, both about research, the physical sciences approach to understanding the human condition, and perceptions of human activity and constraints as a result.

In the beginning, people instinctively looked for patterns, but because they lacked refined instruments, the concepts of controlled experiments, and mathematics, they typically saw inexplicable behavior which they attributed to gods, fate, or the unknowable. Various cultures had engineering and scientific insights (most famously in the West, driven by a few generations of Romans and Greeks, while mathematics was developed in the Arab world). However, at least in Europe, religion was the dominant mode of explaining the world from the Fall of Rome. Following the catastrophe of the Black Death, a few people started wondering if there wasn't something better to explain life. Francis Bacon dreamed up the controlled experiment. Nicolai Copernicus hypothesized that the earth, Venus, and Mercury orbited the sun, though thinking that all the other heavenly bodies orbited the earth. Then instruments appeared — the microscope and the telescope. To explain what was seen, calculus was invented. By the time of the American Revolution, modern concepts of chemistry and classical physics flourished. By the end of the American Civil War, James Clerk Maxwell was in the process of unifying the laws of electricity and magnetism; indeed it was in 1865 that he unified optics with electromagnetism when noting that his predicted electrical waves would travel at the speed of light. 22 years later, Hertz observed the waves. Also in the 19th century, the germ theory of disease appeared, and microscopic examination of sperm and eggs demonstrated how mammalian reproduction worked. Up to the end of the 19th century, science was a small-budget, modest-impact activity, often self-funded, often carried out as a hobby out of curiosity by well-to-do polymaths. Darwin's voyage on the Beagle was what we would now call a gap year (though it took him five years to make it back to England). The enterprise was small enough that everyone in a field knew everyone else. The literature was small enough that a handful of journals kept everyone up to date. There was no general, timely index to the chemistry literature until

W. A. Noyes founded *Chemical Abstracts* in 1907. The concept of radio didn't arise until after Hertz's 1887 experiment, and the first trans-Atlantic Morse code transmission didn't occur until 1900. While the 19th century was massively influenced by engineering, the development of electric lights, electric motors, affordable iron and steel, anesthesia, and aseptic surgery, much of what happened was, in effect, tinkering and invention. In fact, "Yankee ingenuity" is, in large measure, what happens when people have inclination and time to fool around with improving processes and devices with which they're familiar.

19.1 Big Science Appears

Science as an economic enterprise derives from Edison's invention of the industrial research laboratory, about 1875. Science, as known to much of the world, may be traceable to the 1300s, but our attitudes are based on events that have happened in the last 1.5 centuries. Compared to all of human development, this is a startlingly short period of time, barely eight generations. Since each generation approached life based on the initial conditions left by their predecessors, it is little wonder that many people have not yet migrated to scientific ways of thinking. A few still long for the world prior to 1865. More idealize the late 19th or early 20th centuries as optimal periods, although any number of colonized or suppressed peoples have a distinctly less rosy view of the period. 1896 was a great year for Roentgen; he discovered X-rays. African Americans remember it as the year of Plessy v Ferguson, the Supreme Court decision that cemented "separate, but equal" treatment between races. Why was scientific research purely curiosity driven through the 19th century? Because it was largely a hobby, of little economic consequence. Thermodynamics may have been an exception to this characterization. Carnot's work on heat engines was of critical economic importance because of the dominance of steam engines for transportation.

There is no single date when science became Big Science. It wasn't in 1900 when Planck stumbled into inventing quantum mechanics. It wasn't Einstein's miraculous year of 1905 when he devised explanations for the photoelectric effect, developed special relativity, explained Brownian motion, and derived the equivalence of mass and energy. It wasn't 1913 when Bohr first explained the discrete nature of atomic structure. It might have been during the First World War, when mass extraction of ammonia from air by the Haber process kept Germany in the war when external supplies of "fixed nitrogen" were cut off, or when the vacuum tube amplifier, invented in 1907, was used in wartime radios and sonar. Perhaps it was in response to the Spanish flu pandemic near the end of the war. It might have been a consequence of the rapid development of aviation. Whatever it was, by the early 1920s, it was recognized that science and technology development, health, economic vitality, and national power were intimately linked. Nevertheless, the image persisted of Pasteur, Curie, Einstein, and the other "Great Men" (sorry Marie — it would be decades before gender exclusivity cracked in North America, and opportunities for women weren't all that equal anywhere else either) dreaming up important results off the tops of their heads. Quantum mechanics was developed by fewer than 100 Europeans and visitors to their institutes, all communicating intensively with each other. As the great industrial labs needed trained workers, universities produced ever more scientists, engineers, and technicians. Chemical instrumentation gradually improved; Arnold Beckman's pH meter of 1928 is often cited as the beginning of the end of purely wet chemical measurements, although elemental analysis using sparks began in 1865 and other spectroscopic measurements were being performed throughout the late 19th century.

As already noted, at the end of World War II, Presidential Science Adviser Vannevar Bush published *Science: the Endless Frontier*. I didn't actually read it until after I retired as a university professor, so what it said is not what mattered to me. It's what I thought it said that guided me and others that I knew in developing attitudes towards scientific research. (At this point, the enlightened reader will say: you mean you spent your entire career not understanding what you were doing or why? You trusted parents, teachers, journalists, and government propaganda? You were a Dunning Kruger example of thinking you knew what you were doing when you didn't? Yup. Guilty as charged!) The essential message was that the U.S. Government recognized that through radar, aviation, The Bomb, antibiotics, proximity fuses, and other technological developments based on fundamental science, the U.S. won the war (news to the 20 million Soviet citizens, 50 million Chinese, and numerous other people who died in droves; fewer than 1 million U.S. citizens were killed). And thus, going forward, the U.S. government would heavily subsidize individuals doing science just to learn interesting things so as to continue to advance The Greatest Country on Earth. Smart kids were encouraged to go into science; summer science programs proliferated. I chose research that looked interesting, not for its impact but for its intellectual challenge. Big problems. Lots of math. By the time I got my B.Sc., I had almost no training in the humanities or social sciences, but nearly enough chemistry courses for a Master's degree and was one course short of a mathematics minor.

19.2 Challenges to a Potential Well Dweller

Graduate school was more of the same. I figured my job was to make great discoveries that others would find in the library and apply to whatever problems they had. I presumed professional scientists spent a large fraction of their time just reading and learning, not doing. My research advisor posted a couple of quotes from a book by Garrett Hardin, of whose credentials and reputation I was unaware. I will repost them here, but I will give them context because you, unlike me half a century ago, need to understand them in context. Incidentally, other than the section I'm about to quote, I didn't read Hardin's book until after retirement either.

Hardin was a Professor of Human Ecology at the University of California at Santa Barbara. It was he who coined the term "the

> "There was a time when hereditary wealth, coupled with a tolerance of eccentricity, created the necessary conditions [for creativity]. In the more recent past, freedom from workaday cares and responsibilities has been more often furnished by an academic position. Scientists occupying university posts produced

(*Continued*)

so much pioneering research precisely because they weren't paid to do it. For, as the Nobel Laureate, J. J. Thomson, remarked:

> ... if you pay a man a salary for doing research, he and you will want to have something to point to at the end of the year to show that the money has not been wasted. In promising work of the highest class, however, results do not come in this regular fashion, in fact years may pass without any tangible results being obtained, and the position of the paid worker would be very embarrassing and he would naturally take to work on a lower, or at any rate a different, plane where he could be sure of getting year by year tangible results which would justify his salary. The position is this: you want this kind of research, but if you pay a man to do it, it will drive him to research of a different kind. The only thing to do is to pay him for doing something else and give him enough leisure to do research for the love of it.

As it became generally realized that an important fraction of the world's research in pure science was done by academic men, administrators defined research as part of the job, and made productivity in research a criterion for advancement. The consequences of this meddling have been about what one would expect. There is now a tendency to choose projects that are pretty sure to give quick results and to avoid questions on tabooed subjects. ... As research has become more expensive, the academic man has had to develop a talent for begging. ... The successful beggar often gives more attention to the committee than to the scientific problem. ... Orthodoxy is encouraged ..."

tragedy of the commons" for the destruction wrought when the cost to others and to the natural world is not considered by individuals making decisions. The book containing the nearby boxed quote was *Nature and Man's Fate,* in which he makes the case that humans should not stop considering the implications of their actions at the end of a project, job, or life. We should always ask, "Then, what?" The Second Law of Thermodynamics ensures that there will always be waste, but we can anticipate what sorts of wastes various paths will generate, and can anticipate at least some of the long-term consequences of our choices. In these days of Greta Thunberg and others focusing on the implications of modern industrial society and hydrocarbon-based environmental changes, it is hard to remember that modern environmentalism dates only to Rachel Carson's *Silent Spring* in 1962, and that people conquering nature was a common theme of the 19th and early 20th century. Hardin internalized that anticipating blowback from ill-considered actions and adjusting actions accordingly was critical in living a just life.

The last chapter of *Nature and Man's Fate* is entitled "In Praise of Waste," by which he meant that evolution tries many paths, but only the successful changes under a particular set of conditions survive multiple generations. Thus, many mutations and many failures, wasted changes, are desirable for whatever comes out of generation N to be optimized. He is pessimistic that any particular path will be optimal, so that many paths should be tried. This is the same argument we used in describing how neural networks are optimized. On pp. 344–345, he makes the case for unfettered science as quoted in the nearby box (I quote the sexist language, as that was what was written. The sentiments that matter are gender-independent).

What is missing from Hardin's argument, from Bush's perspective, from my youthful assumptions, and from science policy based on each of our perspectives, is the impact of information avalanche and potential well formation. Doing what we find interesting without concern for broader impact on society is a hobby. Some people find body building to be entertaining. Some prefer painting or crocheting or skeet shooting. Using their own resources and their own time, each can be relatively harmless. But who is aware of all the paintings in the world? Or in a particular country? Or even in a particular city block? We lack the bandwidth to see them all.

Who gets paid to shoot moving targets? Perhaps a few of the best shooters in a given sport, plus professionals who support, protect, and defend society. So who pays scientists? Those who want society's problems identified, understood, and solved. Studying viruses consumes vast amounts of money because people do not wish to be ill, do not wish to die young, and do not want to be incapacitated. Studying plant viruses was in vogue in the last half of the 20th century because such viruses could be safely grown and contained. In agriculture, they are still studied, but the health research establishment typically wants studies of communicable diseases and virally induced cancers to focus on mammalian or human viruses. Even if tobacco could be protected from tobacco mosaic virus (TMV), that wouldn't necessarily protect humans from anything, though developing laboratory or diagnostic techniques may justify additional work on TMV. Besides, what's the point of writing a paper that no one will read? Hardin, Bush, and I would argue, "well, maybe someday someone WILL read the paper and WILL care." The counterargument is: consuming resources to study something prevents study of something else, either by consuming the time of the researcher, the resources of the institutions, or the funds of the taxpayers or foundation donors who are supporting the inquiry. Overall, the research enterprise must produce at least as much as it consumes, lest it be an overall detriment to humanity.

How can we ensure a positive outcome? We can't. The correlation coefficient between research attempted and useful results obtained is less than 1.0. Experience suggests the correlation coefficient is significantly greater than zero. What are the implications of various project selection strategies?

- Fund whatever interests the researcher. This is a gamble in several respects: are the people being funded sufficiently creative, productive, and insightful, or are they just playing around? If we think about motion on an attractor, are they orbiting a focus, spiraling into a fixed point, or are they going to leap to a new, important region of phase space, the way Maxwell, Feynman, several people at Bell Labs, or Edison changed the world? Combine funding individuals with tenure, and one wonders whether the freedom to explore will lead to dynamic innovation or whether stagnation and over-refinement of a narrow range of topics will result. While I can think of some scientists who have had significant impact in a variety of fields during their career, I also know of some who, in effect, wrote a handful of papers many times over, each time refining the same basic ideas. There is nothing inherently wrong with great depth or with great breadth, but a hands-off administrative approach enables both extremes.

- Fund compelling proposals for their intellectual merit, regardless of short-term impact. On the one hand, this builds the store of human knowledge. On the other hand, if there are so many papers to search on a topic that no one can find (or even takes the time to find) what has already been found, of what good is it? If those studying problems budget significant time to learn what others have devised as solutions, this approach is defensible. If researchers don't mine the literature, this approach puts ideas into "write-only memory". Electronic literature mining may make this approach plausible, but given the difficulty of indexing, the evolution of terminology, and the range of languages chosen by researchers, it is easy to argue that this approach is inefficient.
- Fund targeted, compelling proposals for their short-term impact. For research funded by U.S. Government agencies, this is the most common approach in the early 21st century and has been common since 1969 when the Nixon administration turned to a focus on "research applied to national needs" (RANN). It presumes that the ability to write, think clearly, produce useful results, administer grant funds, and convince review committees of the importance and likely success of a project is highly correlated with ingenuity, ability to hire and collaborate with other talented people, and with society's actual (as opposed to perceived) needs. It also assumes that as "hot" areas change, researchers can respond rapidly enough

and insightfully enough to answer radically new questions. It disadvantages anyone who is poor at selling or highlights problems instead of solutions, is attracted to difficult questions of vague importance even if answered, or is more interested in exciting questions than potentially useful, but dull, opportunities.

- Fund random proposals. Given the many possible screening strategies, we throw our hands in the air, give up on selectivity, and send funds to random qualified people. I have mused about doing a controlled experiment along these lines. In some area of science or technology, write a Request for Proposals (RFP). Review them all. Rank them all in the normal way, but ignore those rankings and fund a randomly selected subset of the proposals. 20 years later, evaluate the impact of the funded work. Compare impact to that for a similar RFP where standard hierarchical, judgmental sieving of proposals is carried out. Hypothesis for those who doubt the efficacy of review committees: the randomly selected proposals will result in as much impact as the carefully reviewed proposals. If reviewer bias or low correlation between "grantsmanship" and creativity are important, the randomly chosen proposals will do just fine!
- Fund specific institutions or specific researchers. This is approximately what happens in parts of the world where governments fund central research laboratories, so that competitive funding need not be pursued. Experience suggests that outstanding work can be expected, but adaptation to new problems is slow.
- For additional thoughts on funding approaches, see Braben (2004) and Meyers (2007).

19.3 Other Potential Wells Appear

Of course, another issue is that what is worthwhile to one person may be viewed as catastrophic to someone else. For many years, the exploratory voyage led by Christopher Columbus was presented to U.S. school children as a great advance for civilization.

The Native American population has a distinctly different perspective. The neutron bomb (kills people, leaves infrastructure intact) might be a great development for scavengers and looters, but for citizens? Not so much.

Regardless of how projects or people are chosen, all research takes place in a particular society at a particular time. Everyone involved starts from particular cultural roots, working in one or a handful of languages, having been exposed to specific technologies, dwelling in a specific potential well with information flow constrained in specific ways. Thus, from the researcher's viewpoint, they believe they choose from a wide range of research topics, but from a global perspective the projects are contextually confined. From my perspective, I have been free to choose research projects throughout my half century in science. Internally, my viewpoint was: I have freedom of inquiry. To someone outside my potential well, what might my choices have looked like? To find out, you be the person outside my potential well, and I'll list some of the things I and my co-workers did.

- Only research projects with low budgets were possible in high school. I was interested in aviation, astronomy, and biochemistry. Because the structure of DNA and the beginnings of molecular genetics were hot topics, and a lot more accessible than anything to do with rocketry, playing with DNA purification made a good science project.
- Only research projects of interest to faculty at my chosen university with openings for undergraduates in their research groups were possible when I was an undergrad. Of the available groups, I chose the one with the most comfortable topic and group culture. Were kinetics methods of analysis as critical to civilization as alternatives in solvated electron chemistry, X-ray crystal structure, electrochemistry, or molecular synthesis? Good questions.
- A suggestion by one of my lab mates (plus coordination with the research interests of my then-girlfriend) directed my choice of graduate schools. Talk about a Markov process! A seminar

given at my undergraduate school by my future graduate advisor led to the main experimental work I pursued in my graduate thesis. Yes, I was free to choose that work or the work of any of the other faculty in Madison, Wisconsin, but peer standards and enthusiasm, plus my own penchant for liking big, expensive instrumentation projects rather than wet chemistry, drove my decision. In retrospect, there were at least two other groups where I would have fitted at least as well. Moreover, in retrospect I would probably have been better advised to become an engineer or computer programmer than a scientist. There were bifurcation points where that could have happened. They didn't.

- Once a graduate research topic is chosen, changing fields is challenging (though some eminent people have done so successfully, perhaps even succeeding because of their multidisciplinary background). I stayed within spectroscopy. My post-doctoral training stretched my graduate training rather than jumping me to an unrelated field.
- Throughout my career, I could choose any area that I thought interesting to pursue. However, the need to fund the work and attract students meant the interests of reviewers and potential co-workers were at least as important as any insights I imagined. The dedication of this book reflects that a handful of seminars by Dwight Nicholson cemented my interest in nonlinear dynamics. One article by Lars Olsen gave me the specifics of my focus on peroxidases (Olsen, 1983). The peroxidase work led to development of sensors; an undergraduate friend who had taken up research in auditory biochemistry coupled to my sister's deafness led to our effort in probing free radicals in the inner ear. Our levitated drop work was inspired by one visit to Eugene Trinh's lab, which in turn happened because of a collaborator with whom I was visiting the Jet Propulsion Laboratory happened to know him, and we had a little time on our hands for an impromptu visit. The last ten years of my research group's efforts came out of a random visit to a random lab.

- Finally, my post-retirement obsession with stacked, mutually rotated diffraction gratings and their application to low-budget spectrometers was fallout from an international exchange program organized by others. I was the fourth University of Illinois faculty member to participate, with the initiating circumstances for a student lab set up through a comedy of errors involving incorrect ordering or part delivery, and conflicting rules between the airlines and the Transportation Safety Administration. A student with a love of photography for a hobby acted inventively, but didn't fully understand what she'd created until several years later. Every step was a response to local stimulus and random events. I felt I did the best teaching of my career; since no one was supervising me (they just trusted me to teach well), I had a free hand that paid off spectacularly.

My impression is that freedom means being allowed to ignore information not resident in my potential well. The less information I need to consider, the freer I feel. The fewer perspectives I consider, the more rapidly I can act. I thus project that others feel and function similarly. Notice that "free" and "wise" may not be the same.

Thus, within the scope of what I encountered (i.e., within my potential well), I absorbed information voraciously and chose among the options available with the data accumulated at the point of decision. At no time did I have information from a future time, from a remote continent, from a language other than English, French, Spanish, Yiddish, Hebrew, German, Greek, Vietnamese, or Latin (and, from that list, over 99% of the time I was limited to English, German, Hebrew, and Latin), or from a culture other than Central Pennsylvania Scots Irish, Analytical Chemistry and Spectroscopy, North American Judaism, or Midwestern Academia (rest assured that anyone who has known me and was left off this list will loudly reprimand me after publication!). My wife's anthropological background, perspective that I gained from talking to dozens of librarians, and my children's interest in fiction all pushed me out of my native potential well into seeing how others perceived where I was coming from.

19.4 A Disquieting Conclusion

Stephen Colbert captured this microscopic worldview that perceives itself to be global with his initial WØRD definition in 2005: "Truthiness" (Colbert, 2005). In our own minds, we are all acting rationally and our worldview seems "truthy". How in the world could anyone not see things as we do? In fact, they can't because they're working in their own silos, responding to the information that penetrates those silos and isn't rejected because it isn't understandable (e.g., Chinese to me — I don't know the pictographs, calculus to those who never learned about derivatives or integrals, or scientific thinking to those locked in to some other doctrinal belief) or is so alien to everything else in the silo (e.g., devil worship, when I don't think there is such a thing as a devil, much less one to be paid homage). Free inquiry is the perception that, within our environment, we can ask any sensible question and act on the answer as our preconceived notions allow. We are, however, forever trapped in not knowing many of the questions or their answers because we either cannot access context that would lead to the questions, cannot conceive of the answers, cannot understand others' answers, or already have answers so at odds with others that our entire worldview would collapse if we changed our minds. Apostates and religious believers are examples of those so at odds that they share no common language or perspective. The "might makes right" of would-be conquerors is orthogonal to the nearly universal Golden Rule of ethics.

We now see the unnerving conclusion of this book. Can we express societal issues using physical principles? Yes. Can we put those principles in the form of equations? Yes. Can measurement help us understand, control, and improve the world? Sometimes. Does this show you something of how my brain and the brains of some other people function? Yes. Does that change anyone's opinion of what society's problems are or how to solve them? Unlikely, but possible. Writing this book in first person has emphasized that the way that scientific discourse is often worded conceals a critical piece of information. Science is not outside of the physical world, observing it, but embedded in that world, trying to describe it from inside the system. Gödel showed that we would never have all the answers because we could never prove our assumptions nor ensure consistency and completeness. Shannon showed that we could never acquire even a fraction of the perspective we would need to discover global solutions to our problems because the communications channels are too slow. We exist in active voice, but for centuries science was communicated in passive voice. See what I just did? Passive voice (at least in English) sounds authoritative, unimpeachable, and universal. First person brings with it subjectivity, personal weaknesses, and character (and not the kind of character associated with group theory, and the group is a mathematical group, not your bridge club!). Now if only there was an equation for that…

Appendix 1

Laser Pointer/Drinking Glass Colorimeter

(Or: Now That I Wrote This Book, I Can Finish My Ph.D. Thesis)

Light beams are attenuated by scattering and absorption. Presumably, the concentration of scatterers is small enough that only single scattering occurs. Also, scattering and absorbance are independent (but see work by Thomas G. Mayerhöfer and Jürgen Popp: Mayerhöfer *et al.*, 2016; Mayerhöfer, Höfer, *et al.*, 2019; Mayerhöfer, Pipa, *et al.*, 2019; Mayerhöfer & Popp, 2019a, 2019b).

$$I_{laser}(y) = I_{0,laser} 10^{-y(\sigma_{scat} + \varepsilon C)} \quad \text{(A.1.1)}$$

Here, y is the distance the laser beam propagates in the solution/suspension. We observe the signal in the x direction. The light is scattered, passes through a distance $x(y)$, and then we photograph it. The setup is shown in Figure A.1.1(a). The first inset shows a sketch of how the components were arranged using items

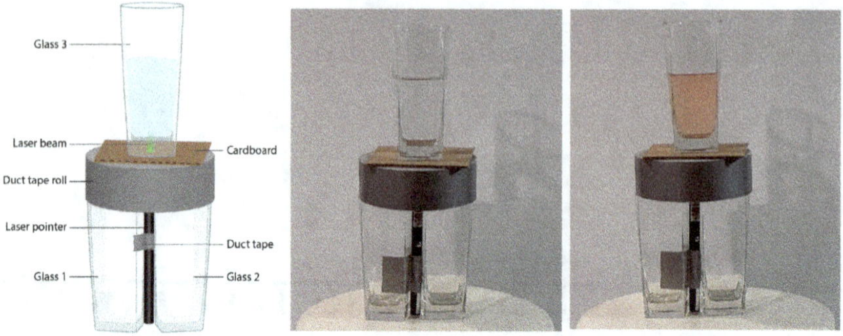

Figure A.1.1. Beer's Law Demonstration Apparatus made from commonly available components (plus a green laser pointer). (a) Sketch of components. (b) The setup, shown with water plus a few drops of milk, for the blank or I_0 measurement. (c) The same setup, with some Red Dye #40 added.

commonly found in American homes: square-ish glasses (to avoid distortion from the edges of round glasses acting as a lens), cardboard, and duct tape. As a light source, I used a laser pointer with a wavelength of 532 nm, a wavelength at which the common food coloring, Red Dye #40, Allura Red, absorbs.[1] If I were doing the experiment with a red laser pointer at 633 nm, I'd choose either blue food coloring, Blue #1, Brilliant Blue, or the common dye Methylene Blue. I had a white poster board as a backdrop, the ability to totally darken the room, and the camera mounted on a tripod. I used manual focusing since the usual cues used by autofocusers were missing in the darkened room, and flash had to be avoided. The laser beam is invisible from the side unless there are scatterers added to the solution. A few drops of skim milk work nicely. Water plus milk looks clear to the typical human, but there are enough protein globules floating in the water to reveal the laser beam easily.

The amount of light scattered depends on polarization, which we ignore because the relative position of camera and laser are

[1]CAUTION. Any laser can blind you. Be careful that neither the beam nor a reflection of it gets anywhere near anyone's eyes.

fixed. The amount seen by the camera depends on the angular dependence of scattering (scales as cos θ, but θ is small) and vignetting function of the camera (for the central part of the observed field, this too is close to 1.00). Overall, then

$$I(y) = I_{0,laser} 10^{-y(\sigma_{scat}+\varepsilon C)} \sigma_{scat} k_{optics} 10^{-x(y)(\sigma_{scat}+\varepsilon C)} \quad \text{(A.1.2)}$$

If the laser beam is perpendicular to the camera and the distance to the sides of the glass, $x(y)$, is constant,

$$I(y) = I_{0,laser} 10^{-y(\sigma_{scat}+\varepsilon C)} \sigma_{scat} k_{optics} 10^{-x(\sigma_{scat}+\varepsilon C)} \quad \text{(A.1.3)}$$

Lumping together what we can't measure into a single lead constant,

$$I(y) = I_0 10^{-(x+y)(\sigma_{scat}+\varepsilon C)} \quad \text{(A.1.4)}$$

We have data for $C = 0$ and $C \neq 0$. That means that we can't measure I_0 independently. We can, however, measure εC and σ. While the peak absorbance of Red Dye #40 is at 504 nm, the laser is at 532 nm, where from https://assets.thermofisher.com/TFS-Assets/MSD/Scientific-Resources/FL53099-food-dyes-beers-law-qc-lesson-plan.pdf, the absorbance is about 5/6 of peak. http://www.fao.org/3/br639e/br639e.pdf gives the absorptivity as 54 L/g cm. Since molecular weight is 496.43 g/mol, the estimated molar absorptivity is 2.68×10^4 L mol^{-1} cm^{-1} at peak, or 2.23×10^4 L mol^{-1} cm^{-1} at 532 nm.

If we plot $I(y)$, we get:

$$\log_{10} I(y) = \log_{10} I_0 - x(\sigma + \varepsilon C) - y(\sigma + \varepsilon C) \quad \text{(A.1.5)}$$

If x is independent of y, we can compare the slope with and without sample present and estimate C. Further, if we then assume I_0 is the same in both cases, we can estimate x. Since we know that $x \sim 2$ cm, we can get an approximate measurement of whether the assumptions are reasonable.

All of this assumes we can measure intensity linearly. Is this feasible with common digital cameras, either standalone or in tablets, computers, or smartphones? It is well-documented that the pre-processing typically done to generate JPG files badly distorts intensity measurements. Exposures are set for optimum use of the detector's dynamic range. The raw data are adjusted so that selfies have the correct colors as perceived by humans. Since data are collected with silicon photocells overcoated with colored filters, this takes some adjusting. https://en.wikipedia.org/wiki/Color_balance gives readily accessible insight.

I used a Nikon D50 digital camera to obtain illustrative data for showing Beer's Law. I set the camera for *f*/11 and varied exposure from 1/10th second to 1/200th second. Nikon highly compresses raw data into .NEF files. NEF is proprietary; data reduction requires a pixel-by-pixel readout of the data. The camera generates 12-bit data, so a .BMP file is inappropriate (BMPs have only 8 bits of intensity per color), JPG (also 8 bits per color, but 24 bits per pixel) is lossy, so TIFF is a convenient format. I did not want to spend the time to write my own NEF-to-TIFF file converter. I didn't see how to get freeware such as GIMP to just report the raw data, so I used a free online service to do the conversion: https://convertio.co/nef-tiff/. Output of pixel intensity was RGB, 16 bits per color. I thought I was in good shape. Looking at individual images, the brightness corresponded to exposure, the intensity fell off from where the laser beam entered the water glass at the bottom, and the fall-off was faster for milk + Red Dye #40 than for milk alone. (I didn't precisely measure the amount of Red Dye #40 — I just added enough to make the solution pink.) Qualitatively, everything looks great! A superficial review of the data said this is a clean demonstration. Then I looked more closely. This turned out to be a demonstration that:

1) Superficially well-behaved data may turn out not to be well-behaved upon close examination.
2) The TIFF converter did not report absolute, raw data. It used white balance information embedded in the NEF file and, as a result, gave nonlinear exposure/output results.

3) For low dynamic range situations, TIFF (and, presumably, JPG) can appear to be well-behaved when, over a wider range of exposures, they aren't.
4) Inter-camera, inter-algorithm, and inter-instrument calibration transfer, complicated even for a single instrument design, are hugely complicated by the embedded pre-processing of modern cameras (Burggraaff *et al.*, 2019; Pitula *et al.*, 2021).

First, let's look at pictures of the laser beam passing through the solution. Figure A.1.2 shows the case for an exposure of 1/20th second, chosen as neither the longest nor shortest exposure, and visually likely to be most appealing when printed in hardcopy. Each image is rendered twice. In the left hand, linear image, the eight most significant bits of the TIFF image are shown. In the right image, the logarithm of intensity is displayed, scaled so that the brightest pixel in the image has a numerical value of 255 in the green.

$$N_{pixel,g} = \text{round}\left(\frac{255}{\ln\left(I_{\max}\right)}\ln\left(I_{pixel,g}\right)\right) \tag{A.1.6}$$

The laser enters at the bottom, is attenuated as it ascends through the liquid column, then shows a bright spot as it exits the liquid. The bright spot is due to reflection as the beam moves from water, with a refractive index of 1.334 at 532 nm, to air with a refractive index so close to 1 that we'll call it 1.000. Reflection at normal incidence from such discontinuities can be shown, from Maxwell's laws, to be:

$$R = \left(\frac{n_{water} - n_{air}}{n_{water} + n_{air}}\right)^2 = \left(\frac{1.334 - 1}{1.334 + 1}\right)^2 = \left(\frac{0.334}{2.334}\right)^2 = 0.0205 \tag{A.1.7}$$

2% reflected does not sound like much, but with a 5 mW laser, that's 100 μW, a huge amount of light. When looking at the data, anything near the laser entry point or exit point should be ignored.

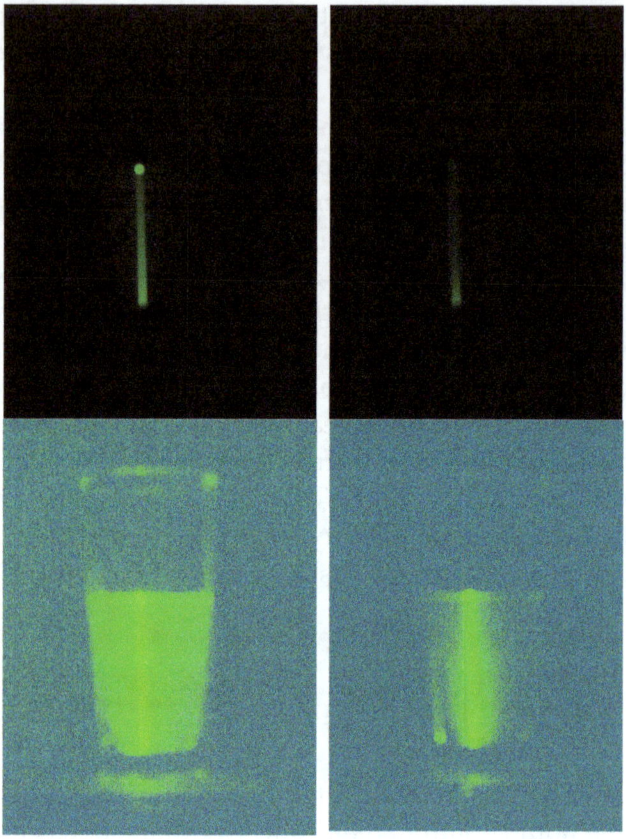

Figure A.1.2. 50 ms exposure of water plus a few drops of milk (left) and the same with some Red Dye #40 added (right). Top: BMP of the original image. Bottom: Logarithmic rendering of the same image.

Separately measured, y was easy to calibrate: 1,000 pixels correspond to 6 ¾″ or 17.1 cm (based on measuring images and the glass).

It's easy to see that as the laser beam goes up through the water, the beam is attenuated. Furthermore, it falls off faster when Red Dye #40 is present (the amount of milk acting as scatterer is essentially unchanged; to the extent it has changed, it's from dilution by adding the Red Dye #40 solution). To keep measurement noise down, we'll average across 8 pixels (the laser beam width is about 18 pixels near the entry point of the beam in the absence of red dye). Figure A.1.3 shows the numerical data.

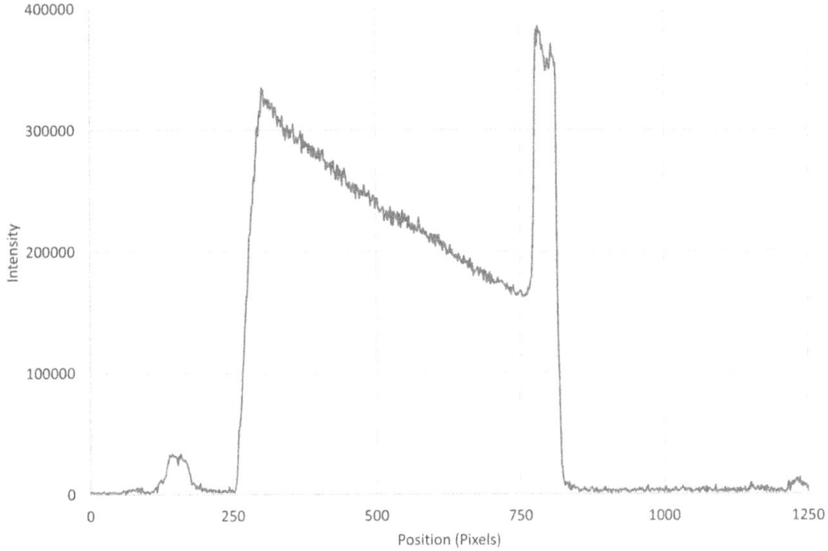

(a)

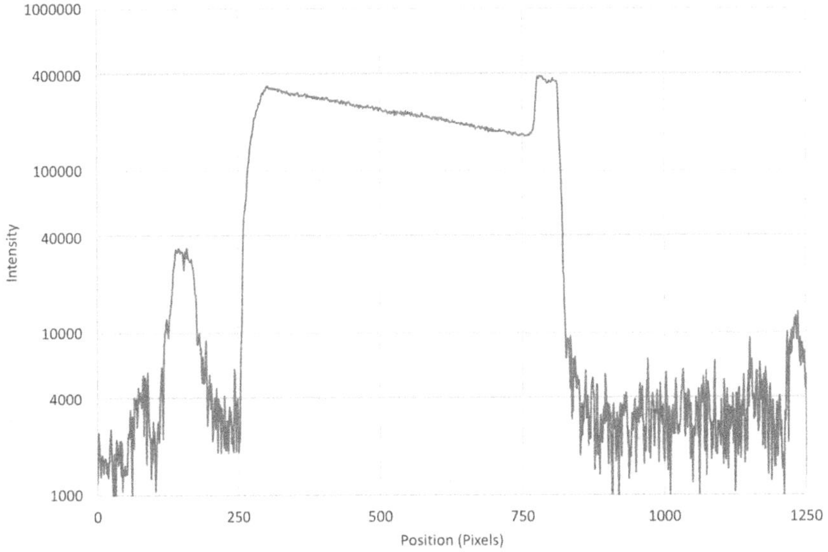

(b)

Figure A.1.3. Numerical data from scattering-only laser colorimetry/turbidimetry, 50 ms exposure. (a) Linear plot (laser enters at left). (b) Same data as (a), display with logarithmic scaling. (c) Same as (a) and (b), looking only at region where scattering occurs.

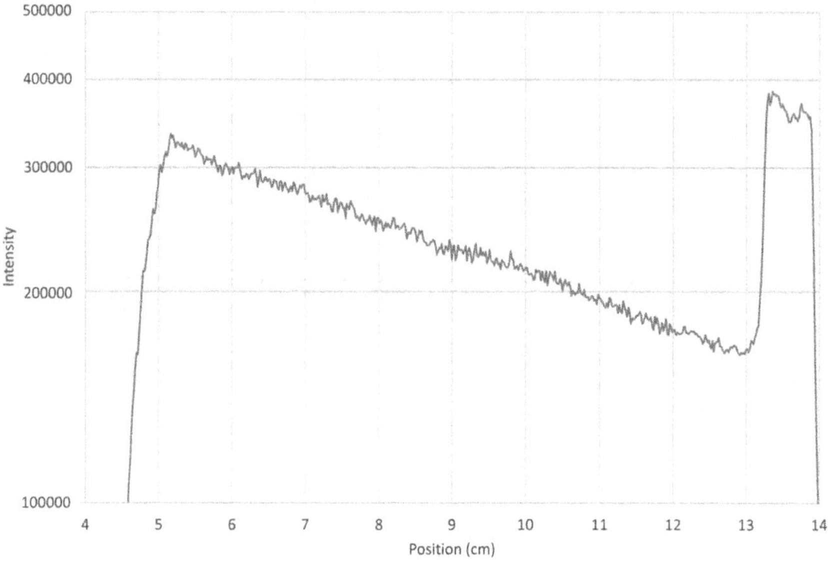

(c)

Figure A.1.3. (*Continued*)

Inset A.1.3(a) shows the raw data, with the laser entering at the left. As the laser emerges from the bottom of the glass, there is a significant amount of scattering. As the laser ascends through the water in the glass, intensity decreases. In inset A.1.3(a), that decrease has some curvature to it (at the meniscus, the bright spot gives a jump in intensity). We saw in earlier equations that log(intensity) should fall linearly with distance, so we replot the data on a log scale in inset A.1.3(b). Now the linear portion is so compressed and the fluctuations at low intensity (where the laser beam is passing through glass or air) are so prominent that we really can't see what we're looking for. Thus, in inset A.1.3 (c), I made two changes: I changed the ordinate scale to only show the part of the data where the laser is going through water, and I changed the abscissa so that the units are centimeters, not pixels. It looks great! It looks just like the equations! Everything seems to work!

Except it doesn't. If the data accurately report the decay in light intensity, then the data should show nearly the same decay

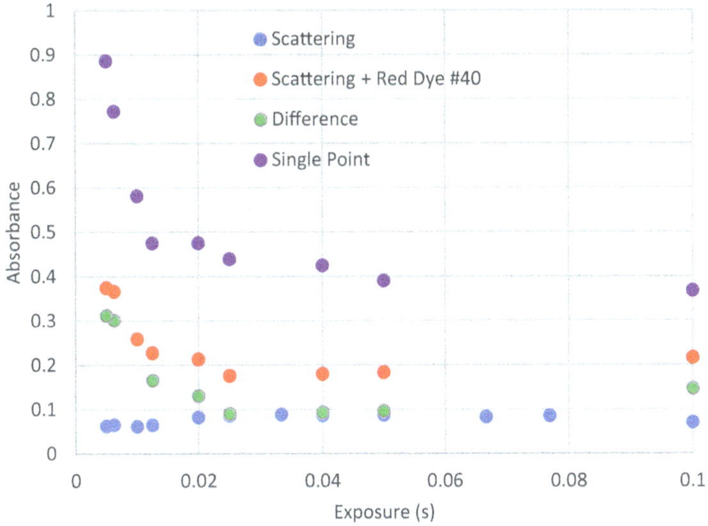

Figure A.1.4. Slope of logarithmic intensity decay as a function of exposure.

behavior, regardless of exposure time. At too long an exposure, the camera will saturate; at too short an exposure, the decay will be noisy and fade into the baseline before reaching the top of the liquid. But in between, the decay constant should be just that — constant. If we look at the slope of log(signal) vs. distance (cm), we get Figure A.1.4 (I haven't yet discussed the "single point" data — stay tuned). For exposures between 20 and 77 ms ($1/13^{th}$ to $1/50^{th}$ s), the slope for scattering only is 0.089 ± 0.002 cm^{-1}. Precision of 1 part in 40 is quite consistent. However, longer and shorter exposures have lower slopes. But what about when Red Dye #40 is added? $1/20^{th}$ to $1/40^{th}$ s (25 to 50 ms) have slopes of 0.180 ± 0.004 cm^{-1}, while all the rest have higher slopes. The difference between these two slopes should give the absorbance of the dye. The 25, 40, and 50 ms exposures have a difference of 0.09 absorbance cm^{-1}. Everything else is higher (though at longer exposures, not by much). Why would short exposures give nonlinear results? There's still plenty of signal. Let's see if more data provide enlightenment.

If, instead of looking along the length of the laser path through the solution, we cut transversely across the beam (think of cutting a carrot so you can see the yellowish center and more orange outer layer, or of cutting an onion so you can see the rings), we get data as shown in Figure A.1.5. The bright laser beam is clearly in the center of the graph (I truncated data on the left and right extremes of the image to ensure centering). But what happens outside the beam? There's light coming out! Where did that come from? The light scattered from inside the beam is rescattered outside the beam (but still inside the glass; the scattering protein globules are uniformly distributed in the solution). What form does the scattering intensity take? Let's make two assumptions:

1) All the light that is scattered outside the beam comes from re-scattering the light that was scattered inside the laser beam. Where else would it come from? So the excitatory light all comes through the edge of the laser beam at a radius r_0.
2) Scattering is proportional to local light intensity, which falls off because of additional scattering and because of the cylindrical symmetry of the beam.

That means that for $r_0 < r < r_{max}$,

$$I = I_{r_0} \sigma \frac{r_0}{r} \tag{A.1.8}$$

The falloff is asymmetrical between left and right sides, but that may well be because the laser beam is not centered in the glass, and I wasn't careful to square up the flat glass side of the container to be perpendicular to the observation direction.

If we look only at the maximum intensity in the center of the laser beam in the cross-sectional view, we have an additional way to measure absorbance — it's the logarithm of the signal absent the dye and the signal in the presence of the dye. That's the "single point" data in Figure A.1.4, and it is most obviously not constant as a function of exposure. While the glass was moved between no-dye and

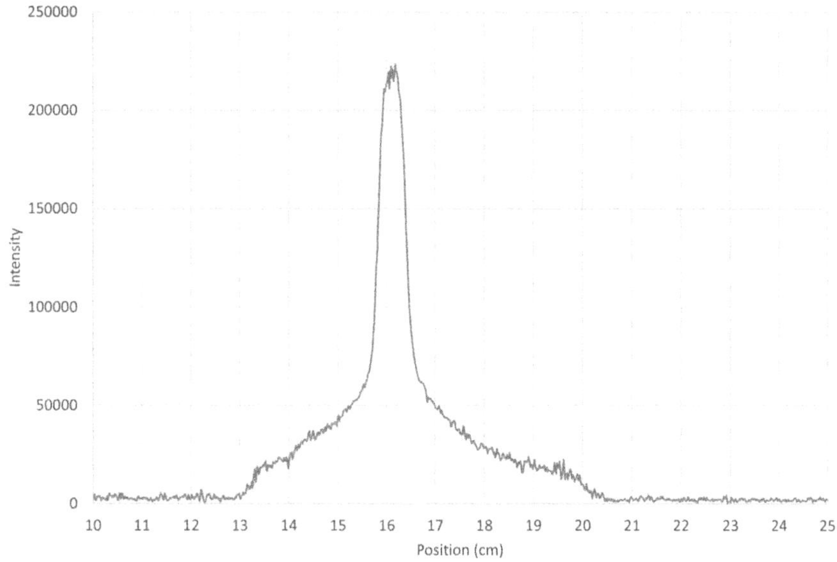

(a)

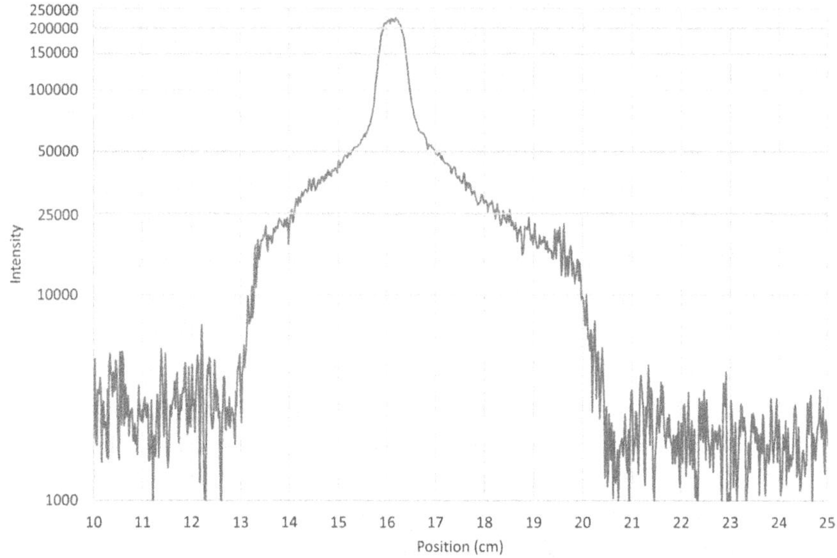

(b)

Figure A.1.5. A transverse view of the laser beam being scattered. Exposure 50 ms. (a) Linear axes. (b) Logarithmic intensity axis. Cross-section centered 270 pixels or 4.6 cm (1.8″) from the entry point of the laser through the bottom of the glass.

with-dye measurements, neither the camera nor the glass nor the laser moved perceptibly between measurements at different exposures. We thus see that the measurement is not independent of exposure, and somewhere, one or more assumptions are inaccurate.

The main problem is that we are not looking directly at raw pixel data. Nikon claims the data are raw, but embedded in the compressed raw data file is information on the differences between how the camera perceives color (RGB) and how humans perceive color. Combining data from multiple pixels, human-perceived colors are interpolated. Thus, while combining 4 or 9 or 16 pixels to get accurate colors, the image is slightly blurred. Additionally, some intensity counts are transferred from one pixel to another. If we select a pixel that detects nearly pure green (and how purely it detects that color vs. blue or red is another, somewhat lengthy discussion), a human perception-optimized pixel will have a mix of red, green, and blue counts. The exact rebalancing depends on what illumination source was used; an incandescent bulb has more red and less blue than sunshine, and sunshine has, relatively speaking, a lot less blue than a white LED bulb. The camera guesses what light source was used (or has a user-defined setting to clue it in) to set the "white balance."

One of the reasons I chose a green laser for the demonstration is that, regardless of white balance, regardless of intensity, the distortion of the rebalancing algorithm will be identical for all pixels. All the light is at 532 nm, so all the signal is generated at, effectively, a single wavelength (actually, for the purists, over a narrow range of wavelengths). But that turns out not to be sufficient to prevent distortion.

Because I did not write my own algorithm to convert the compressed NEF file to a 16-bit uncompressed TIFF file that I could load into software I could write, I had to use the online TIFF converter noted above. And that converter looked not only at white balance, but at another aspect of human light perception: our response is nonlinear. While solid state detectors don't have perfectly linear response, the response is a lot closer to linear than the human eye. Thus, embedded in the NEF is information on how to intentionally make the signal response pleasingly nonlinear for the humans who will look at the pictures. But we aren't taking pictures, we're trying to take spectrometric data. We require linear response. How do we learn just how distorted the reported intensity is?

The method is derived from how photographic film and plates were calibrated back in the early days of photographic photometry. I learned of this method as a Hurter and Driffield (H&D) Curve (http://self.gutenberg.org/articles/Hurter—Driffield_curve). A detector is exposed to a constant intensity source for a short amount of time, and then for times 2, 4, 8, 16, ... times the original time. We thus know how much light, relative to the minimum exposure (exposure = intensity times time) each datum represents. If the system were linear and the lowest signal had a value S_0, the longer exposures would have signals of $2S_0$, $4S_0$, etc. But they don't. At low exposures, the signal increases more slowly than linearly. At medium exposures, it increases roughly linearly. And at high exposures, the signal saturates (and at exorbitant exposures, the photographic system may oversaturate or "solarize," and the signal may actually drop off!). Doing a full explanation of how I made an H&D curve for the Nikon D50 is another long explanation which I will spare the reader. Suffice to say, Figure A.1.6 shows the H&D curve, not from the data shown here, but from an experiment I had done several years before.

The nonlinearity is obvious. *This is why raw data must be directly accessed, bypassing all pre-processing, if anyone hopes to do smartphone, webcam, or tablet computer spectrometry!*

I thought that would be the end of the story. But then I looked at Figure A.1.5 and equation (A.1.8) and my blood ran cold. What would happen if instead of the kluged setup I used here, I took a fish tank, carefully aligned a laser pointing horizontally, and carefully aligned a camera with linear response looking down at that tank through the water/air free surface? I could get a cleaner version of the current data, and I would know the radial distribution of scattered light intensity. If I added a fluorophore to the tank in addition to the scattering protein/fat globules, I could have a system with known spatially distributed, cylindrically symmetrical optical properties that scattered, absorbed, and emitted light. This is a problem that occurs in atomic and plasma spectroscopy; data

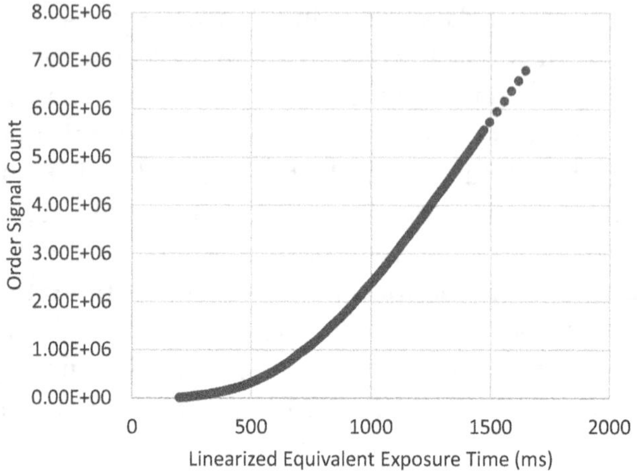

Figure A.1.6. Response of Nikon D-50 to 532 nm light as a function of exposure. 1 = lowest exposure detected in a multi-order diffraction experiment.

reduction is handled by an algorithm called an Abel inversion (Mork & Scheeline, 1987; Scheeline & Walters, 1976). For a purely emitting, cylindrical source (think lightning that isn't a zigzag, but rather a straight line), the problem of viewing the system side-on and figuring out the radial structure of the emission has long since been solved. If $J(r)$ is the emissivity as a function of radius and $I(x)$ is the intensity seen along a line cutting perpendicular to the cylinder's axis, we can think of the problem as figuring out how the cross-section of an onion looks by staring at the onion from the side.

$$\begin{aligned} I(x) &= \int_{-\infty}^{\infty} \frac{J(r)\,dr}{\sqrt{r^2 - x^2}} = 2\int_{x}^{\infty} \frac{J(r)\,dr}{\sqrt{r^2 - x^2}};\ r \geq x \\ J(r) &= -\frac{1}{\pi}\int_{x}^{\infty} \frac{dI(x)}{dx} \frac{dx}{\sqrt{x^2 - r^2}};\ x \geq r \end{aligned} \tag{A.1.9}$$

Alternatively, if we look at a set of equally space positions $x_0, x_1, \ldots, x_n$ with $I(x_n) = 0$ and $x_{k+1} - x_k = \Delta x$, and similarly we look at concentric rings of emission with $\Delta r = \Delta x$, the problem can be revised to a matrix multiplication problem:

$$\begin{aligned} \mathbf{I} &= \mathbf{A}\mathbf{J} \\ \mathbf{J} &= \mathbf{A}^{-1}\mathbf{I} \end{aligned} \tag{A.1.10}$$

with **I** and **J** column vectors, and **A** and its inverse square upper diagonal matrices.

Here $x = 0$ corresponds to the place where $r = 0$, and the smallest r observable for a given x is $r = x$. Two chapters of my Ph.D. thesis were on the Abel inversion (Scheeline, 1978); these chapters were also published as a journal article and a book chapter. The book chapter had the theory of what to do for an emitting/absorbing cylindrical system, that is, a system where some light is absorbed and some emitted in each concentric ring of the cylinder. I didn't get a journal article out of that portion of the work because I couldn't figure out how to do an experiment to demonstrate the emission/absorption theory. One of my graduate students later did some additional computational work, but he also didn't do related experiments. *Figure A.5 is a preliminary demonstration of how to do the experiment!* There are, of course, details and subtleties to consider, but it is conceivable that my last research article (to be written after this book is published) will be based on what you've seen here, and it will close the loop on the theory I worked out in the middle of my second year of graduate school. As my graduate advisor, John Walters, used to say, "You learn what you teach (and not much more)." By trying to show you how you could visualize Beer's Law and simultaneously showing you the problems of using snapshot cameras to do science, I stumbled onto how to do an experiment only 45 years after I could have!

Appendix 2

Human Relationships as an Iterated Map

In Chapters 5 and 11, we described iterated maps as a way of looking at patterns in successive, constrained events. Personal interactions are successive events. We meet people, and then either get closer to them or move on without further interaction. We become friends and then either bond for decades or eventually have a falling out. How might that look, plotted as an iterated map on the "Friendship" interval? Because friendship is a qualitative concept, there may well be a literature along these lines. Yaneer Bar Yam and others at the New England Complex Systems Institute have long had an interest in nonlinearity in society (https://necsi.edu/research). There's a psychology interest group at the Society for Chaos Theory in Psychology & Life Sciences (https://www.societyforchaostheory.org/home/). While these organizations have recently been focused on the dynamics of the COVID-19 pandemic, they have also looked at economics, biodiversity, health care, and other dynamical systems that incorporate feedback including team building, which is closely related to my speculations here. Others with similar interests are often published or cited in such journals as *Physical Review E*, *Chaos*, *Complexity*, *Complex Systems*, and the weekly blog *Complexity Digest* (http://comdig.unam.mx), founded by Gottfried Meyer-Kress, a colleague at the University of Illinois in the early 1990s, and continued by his successors at Universidad Nacional Autonoma de Mexico.

We look at two models here. The first assumes that friendship follows a cubic relationship, i.e.,

$$\begin{aligned} F_{n+1} &= \sqrt[3]{a + bF_n + cF_n^2 + dF_n^3} \\ F_n &= k_3\left(F_{n+1}\left(F_{n+1} - k_1\right)\left(F_{n+1} + k_1\right) + k_2\right) \end{aligned} \tag{A.2.1}$$

The second form is computationally economical, while the first shows the thought behind the shape of the function. With $k_1 = 4$, $k_2 = 70$, and $k_3 = 0.1$, we see Figure A.2.1.

There are three regions of the relationship between F_{n+1} and F_n. On the lowest branch (blue curve), successive interactions lead people towards warmer interactions. Eventually, at a sufficiently high friendliness, the lower branch folds back, and the relationship jumps along the blue arrow to the upper branch of the curve, the yellow "best friend forever" branch. If friendliness decreases sufficiently, the relationship falls off the upper branch and crashes

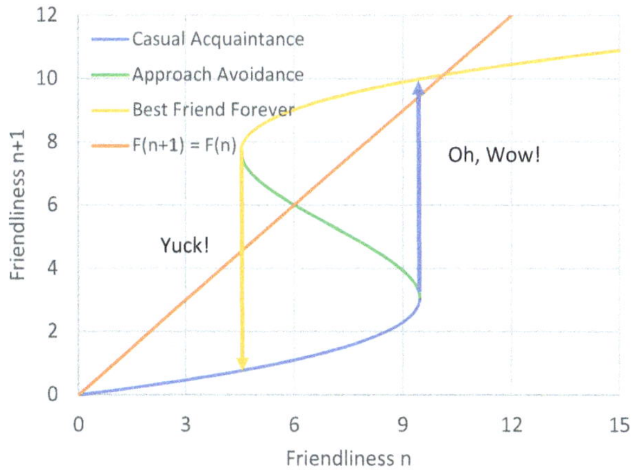

Figure A.2.1. Friendship as a nonlinear, iterated map.

along the yellow arrow back to the lower branch. Both the top and bottom branches have stable fixed points — 0 (unfriended) and the point where the yellow branch intersects, $F_{n+1} = F_n$. The intermediate branch that doubles back between the upper and lower branches also has a fixed point, but that fixed point is unstable, as any infinitesimal movement from that branch's fixed point leads to an outward spiral until either the upper or lower branch is reached. Where the green and orange plot lines cross, i.e., a relationship that is close, but not too close, there needs to be some exogenous control or feedback to stabilize the fixed point. Lacking such additional feedback, the relationship will, sooner or later, diverge to the upper or lower branches.

Not all relationships are so simplistic. What happens if we allow for a "friend, but not BFF" relationship to be stable? Then we need a pentic equation. Choosing subscripts so that it's clear what is added while leaving as much as possible the same as in equation (A.2.1):

$$\begin{aligned} F_{n+1} &= \sqrt[3]{a + bF_n + cF_n^2 + dF_n^3 + eF_n^4 + fF_n^5} \\ F_n &= k_3\left(F_{n+1}\left(F_{n+1} - k_1\right)\left(F_{n+1} + k_1\right)\left(F_{n+1} - k_4\right)\left(F_{n+1} + k_4\right) + k_2\right) \end{aligned} \quad \text{(A.2.2)}$$

Now, leaving $k_1 = 4$, but setting $k_2 = 1{,}000$, $k_3 = 0.007$, and $k_4 = 5.5$, we get Figure A.2.2:

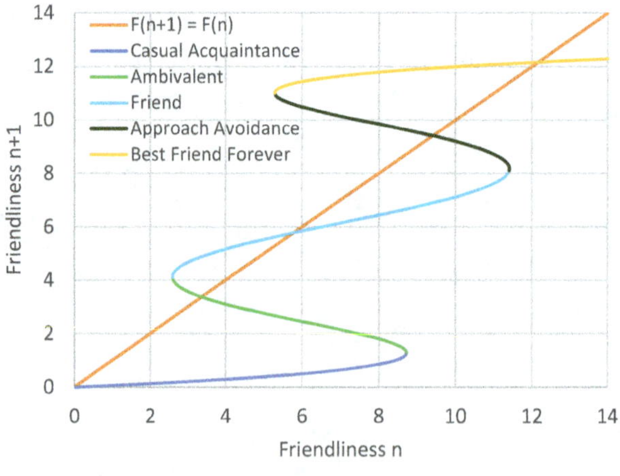

Figure A.2.2. Friendship as a nonlinear iterated map, with increased nuance.

Clearly, the various k values can be adjusted to stretch or distort the iterative map. The point is that a smooth manifold can be used to mimic the discontinuous jumps most people have seen in how close they feel to other people. Resemblance to the dynamics of dating, marriage, and divorce is suggestive.

If the parameters are adjusted so that the relationship curve is less nonlinear, it may be feasible to have relationship closeness closer to linear or smoothly changing in intensity, meandering back and forth as may happen for acquaintances. If the curve never doubles back on itself, the relationship could evolve monotonically, something like the progression of students from one grade to another (with a small jump in maturity between school years, but a big change in relationships between the students and each class's teacher). A way to spend a pleasant afternoon with a spreadsheet is to adjust parameters in the equations, look at the plots, and then look for parallels in your own experience with relationships that evolved in particular ways.

Appendix 3

Calculus in Five Pages

Much of the discussion in this book uses calculus. Let's condense a year's calculus course into five pages. Start with an automobile. The odometer says how far the car has gone — it sums up distance. The speedometer measures how fast the car is going at any time — the speed. The accelerator and brake adjust the rate at which speed changes — acceleration (deceleration is just acceleration with a negative sign).

If distance is D, speed is S, and elapsed time is T, and if the speed is constant, then

$$D = ST \tag{A.3.1}$$

Speed says how rapidly distance changes — in a given time, the faster you go, the farther you get. In calculus terminology, speed is the *derivative* of distance and written:

$$S = \frac{dD}{dt} \tag{A.3.2}$$

Of course, speed may not be constant. If we go at a speed S_1 for a time interval t_1 and a speed S_2 for a time interval t_2, with $T = t_1 + t_2$, then

$$D = S_1 t_1 + S_2 t_2 \tag{A.3.3}$$

Why stop at two intervals? We could sum up the distances over N intervals each with speed S_k and time interval t_k (so $k = 1, 2, 3, \ldots,$ up to N; k is a way to identify a specific interval in an ordered list):

$$D = \sum_{k=1}^{N} S_k t_k \tag{A.3.4}$$

We feel most comfortable when the speed changes gradually. What happens if we only have tiny fractions of a second over which we assume S_k is constant? Then each t_k is small but the total time interval is fixed at T. For each t_k infinitesimally small, but the sum of all the t_k's still = T, we write "the *integral* from 0 to T of speed = distance" or

$$D(T) = \int_0^T S(t)\,dt \tag{A.3.5}$$

Now speed can vary with time any way at all, but we still can figure out how far we go in time T.

This is the essential utility of calculus. We can figure out how far things extend if we know the rate of change, or we can figure out the rate of change if we know the function value at two instants barely separated in time or position. But why stop at single derivatives or single integrals? Acceleration is the derivative of speed. Thus, if A is acceleration,

$$\begin{aligned} A &= \frac{dS}{dt} = \frac{d^2D}{dt^2} \\ D(T) &= \int_0^T S(t)\,dt = \iint_T A(t)\,dt \end{aligned} \tag{A.3.6}$$

There are some functions that are easy to integrate or differentiate (but due to space, we won't list them here). There are others that are hard or impossible to integrate or differentiate using a formula. For many (but not all) of those, we use numerical methods to integrate or differentiate. Analogous to equation (A.3.4), we can sum up the values of the function over a large number of small intervals; that's the Euler integral approximation:

$$D_{Euler}(T) = \sum_{k=1}^{N} S(t_k)\Delta t; \quad \Delta t = t_{k+1} - t_k \tag{A.3.7}$$

There are more complicated, and more accurate, formulas, but this is the simplest method to use, especially if you're using a calculator rather than a computer. Want to differentiate instead of integrate? Then

$$S = \lim_{\Delta t \to 0}\left(\frac{D(t+\Delta t) - D(t)}{\Delta t}\right) \tag{A.3.8}$$

The smaller Δt is the more accurately we compute S (in principle), but at some point the finite number of digits in any calculation keeps us from shrinking Δt without getting absurd results. Let's do this for a simple case: suppose acceleration is increasing at a constant rate so that $A = A_0T$. If $A_0 = 1$ m s^{-3}, then at 1 s, the acceleration is 1 m s^{-2}. From the previous equations (plus the formula list we're omitting to keep this to five pages!), it works out that $S = A_0T^2/2$ and $D = A_0T^3/6$. So we already know that S(1 s) = 1 m s^{-1}. Now apply equation (A.3.8) with various values for Δt near $t = 1$ s (Table A.3.1). Assume we can only represent seven digits for any number (just so this blows up easily; the same thing will happen for higher precision, but for smaller values of Δt).

If dt is too big (> 0.01 s in this case), the value for S is way off. When dt is sufficiently small, the value is exactly right. But what happens when dt is too small? At 1×10^{-7} s, the two values for D are the same to seven significant figures, so their difference is zero and the numerical estimate of S is 0. Numerical analysis focuses on dealing with round-off and truncation errors while efficiently computing estimates for derivatives and integrals (and other functions).

Table A.3.1. Derivative as a limit in equation (A.3.8).

Δt	**D(1 s)**	**D(1 s + Δt)**	**S (equation (A.3.8), seven digits)**
1 s	1/6 m = 0.1666666 m	1.3333333 m	1.166667 m s^{-1}
0.1 s	1/6 m	0.2218333 m	0.551666 m s^{-1}
0.01 s	1/6 m	0.1717168 m	0.505010 m s^{-1}
0.001 s	1/6 m	0.1671672 m	0.500500 m s^{-1}
0.0001 s	1/6 m	0.1667167 m	0.500000 m s^{-1}
0.00001 s	1/6 m	0.1666717 m	0.500000 m s^{-1}
1×10^{-6} s	1/6 m	0.1666672 m	0.500000 m s^{-1}
1×10^{-7} s	1/6 m	0.1666667 m	0.000000 m s^{-1}

The Fundamental Theorem of Calculus is: the derivative of the integral is the function itself, i.e.,

$$f(t) = \frac{d}{dt}\int f(t)\,dt \tag{A.3.9}$$

We can thus turn integral problems into derivative problems and vice versa depending on what's easiest for analyzing a situation.

There's more to calculus than computing derivatives and integrals. There are many situations where it is easiest to state a problem in terms of derivatives or integrals, but one wants an answer as either numbers or graphics. In these cases, we solve differential equations or integral equations. For example, a mass m (kg) oscillating on a spring of length z (m) and spring constant k (kg m s^{-2}) that has frictional losses L (kg m s^{-1}) can be described by:

$$m\frac{d^2z}{dt^2} + L\frac{dz}{dt} + kz = 0 \tag{A.3.10}$$

"That equation doesn't tell me anything." How about the equivalent algebraic equation that expresses $z(t)$ in terms of the initial position of the mass, $z(0)$ — $z_{equilibrium}$ and the initial speed, $dz(0)/dt$?

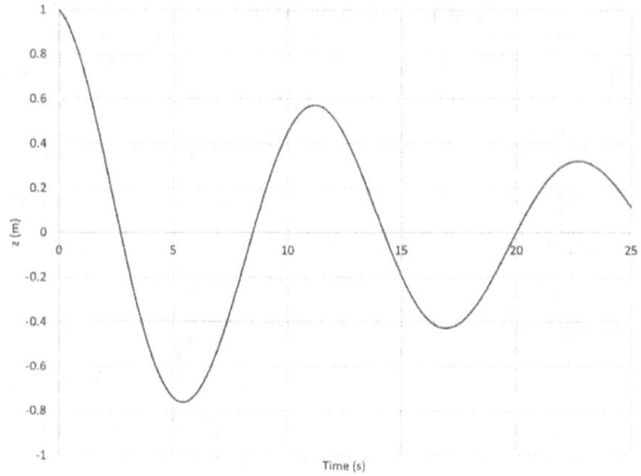

Figure A.3.1. Damped harmonic oscillator.

$$
\begin{aligned}
&z(t) - z_{equilibrium} = Ae^{-bt}\cos(\omega t + \phi) \\
&\omega_0 = \sqrt{\frac{k}{m}} \\
&b = \frac{L}{2m} \\
&\omega = \sqrt{\frac{k}{m} - \frac{L^2}{4m^2}} = \sqrt{\omega_0^2 - b^2} \\
&\phi = \tan^{-1}\left(\frac{1}{\omega}\left(\frac{L}{2m} + \frac{\frac{dz(0)}{dt}}{z(0)}\right)\right) \\
&A = \left(z(0) - z_{equilibrium}\right) / \cos\phi
\end{aligned}
\tag{A.3.11}
$$

Or, graphically, Figure A.3.1.

And the rest is details (lots of important details, but details nevertheless).

Notes and Literature Citations

Anderson, N. G. (1970). Basic Principles of Fast Analyzers. *Am. J. Clin. Path.*, *53*(5), 778–785.

Baird, D. (2004). *Thing Knowledge: A Philosophy of Scientific Instruments*. University of California Press.

Bass, T. A. (1999). Black Box. *New Yorker*, *75*(April 26 & May 3), 114–129.

Bass, T. A. (2000). *The Predictors*. Henry Holt and Co.

Beach, S. F., Hepworth, J. D., Mason, D., & Swarbrick, E. A. (1999). A Kinetic Study of the Hydrolysis of Crystal Violet and Some Terminal and Bridged Analogues. *Dyes Pigments*, *42*(1), 71–77.

Belchamber, R. M., & Horlick, G. (1982). Noise-power Spectra of Optical and Acoustic Emission Signals from an Inductively Coupled Plasma. *Spectrochim. Acta B*, *37*(1), 17–27.

Braben, D. W. (2004). *Pioneering Research: A Risk Worth Taking*. John Wiley and Sons.

Brush, S. G. (1967). History of the Lenz-Ising Model. *Rev. Mod. Phys.*, *39*(1), 883–895.

Burggraaff, O., Schmidt, N., Zamorano, J., Pauly, K., Pascual, S., Tapia, C., Spyrakos, E., & Snik, F. (2019). Standardized Spectral and Radiometric Calibration of Consumer Cameras. *Opt. Express*, *27*(14), 19075–19101.

Cain, J. M., & Powers, Z. R. (2020). *Developing an Analytical Technique for PFAS in Water using SPE and NMR*. https://digitalcommons.wpi.edu/mqp-all/7337.

Canales, J. (2011). *A Tenth of a Second: A History*. University of Chicago Press.

Cardona, L., Jiménez, J., & Vanegas, N. (2015). Nuclear Quadrupole Resonance for Explosive Detection. *Ingeniare. Revista Chilena de Ingenier*, *23*(3), 458–473.

Chainani, E. T., Choi, W.-C., Ngo, K. T., & Scheeline, A. (2014). Mixing in Colliding, Ultrasonically Levitated Drops. *Anal. Chem.*, *86*(4), 2229–2237.

Chaplin, V., Bhat, N., Briggs, M. S., & Connaughton, V. (2013). Analytical Modeling of Pulse-pileup Distortion Using the True Pulse Shape; Applications to Fermi-GBM. *Nucl. Instrum. Meth. Phys. Res. A*, *717*, 21–36.

Colbert, S. T. (2005). *Truthiness*. Comedy Central. https://www.cc.com/video/u39l6v/the-colbert-report-intro-10-18-05.

e Ham Radio ~ Ham Tools. (2010). http://www.radioing.com/hamradio/antcalc.html.

Ecklund, E. H., & Johnson, D. R. (2021). *Varieties of Atheism in Science*. Oxford University Press.

Edelman, G. M. (1987). *Neural Darwinism*. Basic Books.

Feigenbaum, M. J. (1980). Universal Behavior in Nonlinear Systems. *Los Alamos Science*, *1*(1), 4–27.

Feigenbaum, M. J. (1983). Universal Behavior in Nonlinear Systems. *Physica D*, *7*, 16–39.

Fitch, A. (1998). Lead Analysis: Past and Present. *Crit. Rev. Anal. Chem.*, *28*(3), 267–345.

Goldenfeld, N. (1992). *Lectures on Phase Transitions and the Renormalization Group*. Addison-Wesley.

Gradshteyn, I. S., & Ryzhik, I. M. (1980). *Table of Integrals, Series, and Products*. Academic Press.

Hardas, B. R., & Scheeline, A. (1984). Stability and Chaos in a Voltage-Thresholded High-Voltage Spark Source. *Anal. Chem.*, *56*, 169–175.

Harvey, D. (2009). *Analytical Chemistry 2.0: An Electronic Textbook for Introductory Courses in Analytical Chemistry*. http://fs6.depauw.edu:50080/~harvey/eText Project/AnalyticalChemistry2.0.html.

Hill, R., Masui, K. W., & Scott, D. (2018). The Spectrum of the Universe. *Appl. Spectrosc.*, *72*(5), 663–688.

Hofstadter, D. (1979). *Gödel, Escher, Bach: An Eternal Golden Braid*. Basic Books.

Huff, D., & Geis, I. (1993). *How to Lie With Statistics*. W. W. Norton and Co.

Irvin, J. A., & Quickenden, T. I. (1983). Linear Least Squares Treatment When There Are Errors in Both x and y. *J. Chem. Educ., 60*, 711–712.

Jackson, J. D. (1975). *Classical Electrodynamics*. John Wiley and Sons.

Jolliffe, I. T. (2002). *Principal Component Analysis, Second Edition*. Springer.

Khan, H., Ahmed, M. J., & Bhanger, M. I. (2006). A Simple Spectrophotometric Method for the Determination of Trace Level Lead in Biological Samples in the Presence of Aqueous Micellar Solutions. *J. Spectrosc., 20*, 285–297.

Koch, K., McLean, J., Segev, R., Freed, M. A., Berry, J., Balasubramanian, V., & Sterling, P. (2006). What the Eye Tells the Brain. *Curr. Biol., 16*(14), 1428–1434.

Koza, J. R., Keane, M. A., Streeter, M. J., Mydlowec, W., Yu, J., & Lanza, G. (2005). *Genetic Programming IV: Routine Human-Competitive Machine Intelligence*. Springer.

Kruger, J., & Dunning, D. (1999). Unskilled and Unaware of It: How Difficulties in Recognizing One's Own Incompetence Lead to Inflated Self-Assessments. *J. Personality Social Psych., 77*(6), 1121–1134.

Larter, R. M. (2021). *Spiritual Insights From The New Science: Complex Systems And Life*. World Scientific.

Lorenz, E. N. (1963). Deterministic Nonperiodic Flow. *J. Atmos. Sci., 20*, 130–141.

Lu, Y., Yao, D., & Chen, C. (2013). 2-Hydrazinoquinoline as a Derivatization Agent for LC-MS-Based Metabolomic Investigation of Diabetic Ketoacidosis. *Metabolites, 3*, 993–1010.

Lundell, G. E. F. (1933). The Chemical Analysis of Things as They Are. *Ind. Eng. Chem. Anal. Ed., 5*(4), 221–225.

Mallamace, F., Corsaro, C., Mallamace, D., Vasi, S., Vasi, C., Baglioni, P., Buldyrev, S. V., Chen, S.-H., & Stanley, H. E. (2016). Energy Landscape in Protein Folding And Unfolding. *Proc. Nat. Acad. Sci., 113*(12), 3159–3163.

Mandelbrot, B. B. (1982). *The Fractal Geometry of Nature, Second Edition*. Times Books.

Marino, R. A., Wade, D., & Klainer, S. M. (1977). *An NQR Study of TNT Characteristics*. https://apps.dtic.mil/sti/pdfs/ADA046729.pdf.

Marquardt, D. W. (1963). An Algorithm for Least-squares Estimation of Nonlinear Parameters. *J. Soc. Ind. Appl. Math., 11*, 431–441.

May, R. M. (1976). Simple Mathematical Models with very Complicated Dynamics. *Nature, 261*(5560), 459–467.

Mayerhöfer, T. G., Mutschke, H., & Popp, J. (2016). Employing Theories Far beyond Their Limits — The Case of the (Boguer-) Beer–Lambert Law. *ChemPhysChem, 17*(13), 1948–1955.

Mayerhöfer, T. G., Höfer, S., & Popp, J. (2019). Deviations from Beer's Law on the Microscale-Nonadditivity of Absorption Cross Sections. *Phys. Chem. Chem. Phys., 21*(19), 9793–9801.

Mayerhöfer, T. G., Pipa, A. V., & Popp, J. (2019). Beer's Law-Why Integrated Absorbance Depends Linearly on Concentration. *ChemPhysChem, 20*(21), 2748–2753.

Mayerhöfer, T. G., & Popp, J. (2019a). Beer's Law Derived From Electromagnetic Theory. *Spectrochim. Acta A, 215*, 345–347.

Mayerhöfer, T. G., & Popp, J. (2019b). Quantitative Evaluation of Infrared Absorbance Spectra — Lorentz Profile versus Lorentz Oscillator. *ChemPhysChem, 20*(1), 31–36.

Meyers, M. A. (2007). *Happy Accidents: Serendipity in Modern Medical Breakthroughs*. Arcade Publishing.

Mork, B. J., & Scheeline, A. (1987). Determination of Arbitrary Concomitant Absorption and Emission Distributions in Spark Discharges Using the Abel Inversion. *Spectrochim. Acta B, 42B*, 1063–1076.

Ng, R. C. L., & Horlick, G. (1981). Practical Aspects of Fourier Transform and Correlation Based Processing of Spectrochemical Data. *Spectrochim. Acta B, 36B*(6), 529–542.

Olsen, L. F. (1983). An Enzyme with a Strange Attractor. *Phys. Lett., 94A*, 454–457.

Onuchic, J. N., Luthey-Schulten, Z., & Wolynes, P. G. (1997). Theory of Protein Folding: the Energy Landscape Perspective. *Annu. Rev. Phys. Chem., 48*, 545–600.

Pirsig, R. M. (1974). *Zen and the Art of Motorcycle Maintenance*. William Morrow and Co.

Pitula, E., Koba, M., & Seitana, M. (2021). Which Smartphone for a Smartphone-based Spectrometer? *Opt. Laser Technol., 140*, 107067.

Porumbu, D., & Necşoi, D. V. (2013). Relationship between Parental Involvement/Attitude and Children's School Achievements. *Proc. Soc. Behav. Sci., 76*, 706–710.

Potter, M. C., Wyble, B., Habmann, C. E., & McCort, C. S. (2014). Detecting Meaning in RSVP at 13 ms per Picture. *Attention, Perception, Psychophys., 76*, 270–279.

Press, W. H., Flannery, B. R., Teukolsky, S. A., & Vetterling, W. T. (1992). *Numerical Recipes in Pascal: The Art of Scientific Computing*. Cambridge University Press.

Raatikainen, P. (2018). *Gödel's Incompleteness Theorems*. The Stanford Encyclopedia of Philosophy (Fall 2018 Edition). https://plato.stanford.edu/archives/fall2018/entries/goedel-incompleteness/.

Rössler, O. E. (1976). Chaotic Behavior in Simple Reaction Systems. *Zeitschrift Für Naturforschung A*, *31*(3–4), 259–264.

Rothman, L. D., Crouch, S. R., & Ingle, J. D. (1975). Theoretical and Experimental Investigation of Factors Affecting Precision in Molecular Absorption Spectrophotometry. *Anal. Chem.*, *47*, 1226–1233.

Sauter, A. D. I., & Sauter, A. D. Jr. (2018). Droplet Injection Using Induction. A 1000x Sample Input Rate Increase Compared to Sprays? *66th ASMS Conference on Mass Spectrometry*, TP376. http://www.nanoliter.com/asms2018finalposter2.pdf.

Sauter, A. D. Jr. (2016). *Induction Based Fluidic (IBF) and Hybrid Devices for the Movement, Treatment, Measurement, Introduction and Manufacturing of Liquid/s and Other Matter* (Patent No. 9,327,298).

Savitsky, A., & Golay, M. J. E. (1964). Smoothing and Differentiation of Data by Simplified Least Squares Procedures. *Anal. Chem.*, *36*, 1627–1639.

Scheeline, A. (1978). Techniques for Observation and Control of High Voltage Spark Discharge. *Ph.D. Thesis*. University of Wisconsin-Madison.

Scheeline, A. (2017). Focal Point: How to Design a Spectrometer. *Appl. Spectrosc.*, *71*(10), 2237–2252.

Scheeline, A., Olson, D. L., Williksen, E. P., Horras, G. A., Klein, M. L., & Larter, R. (1997). The Peroxidase-Oxidase Oscillator and its Constituent Chemistries. *Chem. Rev.*, *97*, 739–756.

Scheeline, A., & Walters, J. P. (1976). Considerations for Implementing Spacially-Resolved Spectrometry Using the Abel Inversion. *Anal. Chem.*, *48*, 1519–1530.

Schey, H. M. (2004). *Div, Grad, Curl, and All That: An Informal Text on Vector Calculus, Fourth Edition*. W. W. Norton and Co.

Shannon, C. E. (1948). A Mathematical Theory of Communications. *Bell Sys. Tech. J.*, *27*, 379–423, 623–656.

Silverglate, H., & Dershowitz, A. (2011). *Three Felonies a Day: How the Feds Target the Innocent*. Encounter Books.

Tellinghuisen, J. B. (2018). Least-squares Analysis of Data with Uncertainty in y and x. Algorithms in Excel and KaleidaGraph. *J. Chem. Educ., 95,* 970–977.

Tellinghuisen, J. B. (2020). Least Squares Methods for Treating Problems with Uncertainty in x and y. *Anal. Chem., 92*(16), 10863–10871.

Turgeon, J. C., & LaMer, V. K. (1952). The Kinetics of the Formation of the Carbinol of Crystal Violet. *J. Am. Chem. Soc., 74,* 5988–5995.

U. S. Department of Commerce. (2016). *United States Frequency Allocations.* https://www.visualcapitalist.com/wp-content/uploads/2018/07/us-frequency-allocations.jpg.

Wilson, K. G. (1971a). Renormalization Group and Critical Phenomena. I. Renormalization Group and the Kadanoff Scaling Picture. *Phys. Rev. B,* 4(9), 3174–3183.

Wilson, K. G. (1971b). Renormalization Group and Critical Phenomena. II. Phase-Space Cell Analysis of Critical Behavior. *Phys. Rev. B,* 4(9), 3184–3205.

Wilson, K. G. (1983). The Renormalization Group and Critical Phenomena. *Rev. Mod. Phys., 55*(3), 583–600.

Winfree, A. T. (1984). The Prehistory of the Belousov-Zhabotinsky Oscillator. *J. Chem. Educ., 61,* 661–663.

Winfree, A. T. (2001). *The Geometry of Biological Time, Second Edition.* Springer.

Wolfram, S. (2002). *A New Kind of Science.* Wolfram Media.

Wolfram, S. (2020). *A Project to Find the Fundamental Theory of Physics.* Wolfram Media.

Index

www.ingramcontent.com/pod-product-compliance
Lightning Source LLC
Chambersburg PA
CBHW050525300426
44113CB00012B/1955
9789811238543